SONGS SHE WROTE

SONGS SHE WROTE

Forty Hits by Pioneering Women of Popular Music

Michael G. Garber

ROWMAN & LITTLEFIELD
Lanham • Boulder • New York • London

Published by Rowman & Littlefield
An imprint of The Rowman & Littlefield Publishing Group, Inc.
4501 Forbes Boulevard, Suite 200, Lanham, Maryland 20706
www.rowman.com

86-90 Paul Street, London EC2A 4NE

British Library Cataloguing in Publication Information available

Library of Congress Cataloging-in-Publication Data
Names: Garber, Michael G., author.
Title: Songs she wrote : forty hits by pioneering women of popular music / Michael G. Garber.
Description: Lanham : Rowman & Littlefield, 2025. | Includes bibliographical references and index.
Identifiers: LCCN 2024030563 (print) | LCCN 2024030564 (ebook) | ISBN 9781538158654 (cloth) | ISBN 9781538158661 (ebook)
Subjects: LCSH: Popular music—United States—20th century—History and criticism. | Women lyricists—United States. | Women composers—United States.
Classification: LCC ML82 .G27 2025 (print) | LCC ML82 (ebook) | DDC 782.42164092/52—dc23/eng/20240705
LC record available at https://lccn.loc.gov/2024030563
LC ebook record available at https://lccn.loc.gov/2024030564

♾️™ The paper used in this publication meets the minimum requirements of American National Standard for Information Sciences—Permanence of Paper for Printed Library Materials, ANSI/NISO Z39.48-1992.

This book is dedicated to

my mentor, John Diamond, MD, champion of women composers;

my wife, Sue Carpenter, PhD, partner in all our life endeavors;

my mother, Amey Acheson Geier Garber, who wrote us a lullaby;

and the thousands of women of Tin Pan Alley I could not mention.

Also by Michael G. Garber

My Melancholy Baby: The First Ballads of the Great American Songbook, 1902–1913

CONTENTS

ACKNOWLEDGMENTS

In addition to my dedicatees, my gratitude to: my sisters, Katherine Cook Garber Dilao, Amey Develin Garber Lesnick, and Elizabeth Acheson Garber (who shared with me her subscription to *Ms.* magazine); Bud Coleman and the University of Colorado, Boulder; Henry Bial, Paul Laird, and the University of Kansas; Mille Taylor, Inga Biden, and the University of Winchester; Robert Gordon and Goldsmiths, University of London; Valencia Wallace and the State University of New York, Purchase College; Kathy Iglesias, the Lewisboro Public Library, and the Westchester Library System; Janet McKinney, Gillian Mahoney, and the Library of Congress; Andrea, of the Permissions and Reproductions Services, New York Public Library; Miles Kreuger and the Institute of the American Musical; George Calderaro, Robert Lamont, Jerry Felix, Magda Katz, Lynne Funk, and the Tin Pan Alley American Popular Music Project; Peter Mintun; Peter C. Muir; Ivan Hunter; Erika Hunter; Susan Burghardt Diamond; Patricia Williams; Susan D. West; Georgia Pike Rowney; Molly Ruggles; Mark Walter; Korey Rothman; Keith A. Dames; Sandra Penny; Tricia Leach; Steve Ross; Karin Mango; Olaf Jubin; Micahel Allwood; Anne Allwood; Ashley Diamond; Jill Bloomfield; Kelly Bloomfield; Darcy Hilton; Tara Hilton: Ayanna Nicole Thomas; Kate Newington; Andrea Werner; Barbara Singer; Gloria Gribin and Jesse Gribin (family of Doris Tauber);

David Osser (family of Edna Osser); Lynette Gould (family of Irene Higginbotham); Doren Voeth (family of Joan Whitney); Marsha De Sylva Strickhouser (family of Sylvia Dee); June Silver (family of Carolyn Leigh); Holly Foster Wells (family of Peggy Lee); Simon Wallace; Will Friedwald; Charlie Cochran; Janie Bradford; Michael Tan; and Rowman & Littlefield.

FOREWORD

While I reflect on the little-known history of women songwriters, I proudly stand in the distinctive class of women songwriters at Motown Records. To name a few, Valerie Simpson, Gloria Jones, Dee Dee McNeil, Sylvia Moy, Sandra Green, Marilyn McLoud, Lula Hardaway, Syretta Wright, Pam Sawyer, Lena Mann, Vicki Basemore, and Pam Moffett were all contributors to "The Sound of Young America" as is evident by label credits. Long before our footprints were laid, the history of recorded music was hummed, sung, memorized, and familiarized . . . without a clue that the songs were crafted by the countless women whose creativity was overshadowed by their male counterparts, or their credits simply eliminated from the recording. Therefore, one is not aware of the countless tunesmiths of yesterday that penned their favorite song, that is, "Willow Weep for Me" composer Ann Ronell, "I'll Never Smile Again" composer Ruth Lowe, "The Way You Look Tonight" lyricist Dorothy Fields, "How High the Moon" lyricist Nancy Hamilton, and so many more.

With the passing of time women have demanded more and more credit for their contributions to the world of songwriting and producing, claiming their creative input as they seemingly compose from the soul, setting the tone for lyrical imagination. As an example, the weeping, heartrending emotions of "Distant Lover" co-written by Motown secretary, Sandra Green, who is missing her lover who is far away in the armed forces.

Michael Garber has raised the curtain on female songwriters and thrust them into the spotlight of deserved recognition. As I continued to read his manuscript, I was in awe to discover that a lot of my favorite songs are penned by women who were not identified by label credit, or otherwise. On occasion when women were given their rightful credits on a recording, for unknown reasons, they were not given recognition or PR equal to their male counterparts. Furthermore, the reader is taken as far back as the early 1920s where songwriters usually composed in small, smoke-filled back rooms with only a piano and unmentionable language coming from men who shared the notion that the writers' room was no place for a lady. To add insult to a woman's "place" as a songwriter, Garber unveils the indifference female songwriters encountered in seeking compensation for their contribution to a song. Convinced to accept a small flat fee or offers of pennies on the dollar extended by publishers, these early female writers forged beyond the industry barriers, emerged into prominence, and eventually won a fair share of name recognition, and royalties. The reader will welcome a few gems in this writing as Garber gives us a little history on performance rights organizations, ASCAP and BMI, as well as songwriter benefits of "A" side, "B" side records . . . which the young people of today know nothing about. The "B" side got a free financial ride from the success of the "A" side.

The research that Garber has put into this book will be music history to some and a refresher course to others, while it's all news to me. The author takes one back to the early 1900s. He brings back to life the songs that you sang forever but had no idea that a female was the creator or co-creator. For years our creativity has been diminished or hidden. But now, we're coming out! Be reminded of the current female songwriters, Miley Cyrus, Taylor Swift, Billie Eilish, Meghan Trainor, and many more who have advanced to the frontlines as we are now marching to the song of Helen Reddy, "I Am Woman" . . . hear me roar!

—Janie Bradford

As a singer, composer, and lyricist who regularly performs and records original music as well as Great American Songbook gems, I have throughout my life admired the female songwriters of Tin Pan Alley—Dorothy Fields, Bernice Petkere, Carolyn Leigh, and so many others. However, when searching for available research about the lives of these women and the art they produced, I have often come up short. There simply has not been enough reliable research conducted about the many female contributors to the Great American Songbook canon—until now. Through this book Michael Garber takes a step toward filling this void in the literature and determines to give these important songwriters more of the honor, credit, and remembrance they rightly deserve.

From the prolific pens of Dorothy Fields and Fran Landesman to the few but mighty offerings of Annie Ross and Billie Holiday, Garber puts forward a volume that celebrates the relatively unsung female contemporaries of the male titans that readily come to mind when considering Tin Pan Alley and The Great American Songbook. The works of Gershwin, Arlen, Berlin, Mercer, Van Heusen, and Kern need no advocacy—their names have been etched in history for their outstanding and noteworthy works of art. But their fellow songwriters, Higginbotham, Ross, Landesman, Leigh, and Dee require considerably more effort to bring into the spotlight to the degree that they deserve since the momentum of women's careers was frequently curtailed and their perceived importance diminished by the male-dominated culture of the first half of the twentieth century (and beyond).

In many cases, women were not even credited for the songs they wrote. If a woman collaborated on a song with a man, often the woman's role in the creative process was minimized to the extent that most or even full writing credit was given to the male collaborator. Before 1950 a woman, if married, was commonly viewed exclusively as a helpmate to her husband—a homemaker, wife, and/or mother. With her career accomplishments ever in the shadow of her familial role, the female songsmith was bound to be undervalued and overlooked by society and even by leaders in the music industry. Her talent and hard work were most often assumed to be supporting a hobby rather than a serious career.

Due to the domestic responsibilities of raising a family and maintaining a home, a woman's career was typically much shorter than a man's (if she wanted marriage and family), leaving the female songwriter far less time to create a substantial legacy of music. Time has not been kind toward the remembrance of many of these women or of their stories, and Garber's book begins to rectify that wrong.

Garber offers newly unearthed biographical information about the women whose names have been tied to many of the greatest songs of Tin Pan Alley. These enlightening stories help the reader to better know the challenges women faced in the music industry, the lives they lived, their writing styles, and heaps of information about both the familiar and less well-known songs they penned. Garber's emphasis on forty great songs and the women who wrote them sheds new light on important people who created or cocreated some of the most treasured music of the past century.

This book belongs in the library of every modern singer, instrumentalist, producer, lyricist, and composer—regardless of gender. Knowing from whence we came as artists, creatives, songwriters, and musicians, including who paved the roads upon which we walk daily, assists us in discovering our own distinct niches and facilitates our musical growth and creative maturation. Until we acknowledge and begin to understand those from previous generations who gave us the songs that spawned the music we work with today, we remain incomplete, ignorant artists. We owe a tremendous debt to those who established our profession and directly or indirectly enabled us to relish the work and art in which we participate, whether we pursue it as a career or for mere enjoyment.

Younger generations who intentionally explore the songs and writers of a bygone era will be inevitably enriched by doing so. The act of honoring past "sheroes" elevates social awareness about female pioneers in the music business as well as the women unjustly lost to history. Spotlighting these female creatives who were indispensable to the development of American song exercises a compassion that lifts us outside of ourselves and cultivates appreciation for those who have gone before us, encouraging artists to better care for our culture and our world.

—Dr. Tish Oney

PREFACE

The Grammy Awards broadcast in 2024 felt like a lively party in celebration of women's accomplishments in popular music. Miley Cyrus proclaimed, "Watching women win and rule the music industry makes me proud."[1] Celine Dion and Joni Mitchell (her first performance at the Grammys) got standing ovations. Monét emerged as a star performer in her own right after years in the background as a producer and songwriter. Taylor Swift made history by winning a fourth award for Album of the Year. She seized the opportunity to bring Lana Del Rey up to the podium with her, announcing, "So many female artists would not be where they are and would not have the inspiration they have if it weren't for the work she's done."[2] The following book could almost take its title from Swift—*The Work She's Done*—because it is through the labor of their female predecessors that Mitchell, Dion, Del Rey, Monét, Cyrus, Swift, and their peers have been able to flourish.

The spirit of uplift bubbling up from the 2024 Grammys signals a good time to raise a toast to women songwriters of the past. Just as Swift was inspired by Del Rey, so in turn Del Rey was inspired by Frank Sinatra, and female songwriters placed him on the map. In 1940, Sinatra became a star singing Ruth Lowe's "I'll Never Smile Again." In 1954, he regained stardom by singing Carolyn Leigh's "Young at Heart." And he maintained his status with compositions by the likes of Dolores Vicki Silvers, who supplied words and music for Sinatra's highest-charting hit of the fifties, "Learnin' the Blues." If women "win and rule the music industry" in the 2020s, it is due to the work and creativity of their foremothers like Lowe, Leigh, and Silvers.

The top quality of records, broadcasts, and live performances by Sinatra and peers like Nat King Cole, Ella Fitzgerald, and Peggy Lee helped result in their repertoire being labeled "the Great American Songbook." All of these singers drew from the labor of female songwriters—indeed, Fitzgerald and Lee were themselves songwriters. Yet studies of this central genre of the mid-twentieth century have traditionally focused on music and lyrics by men. My goal is to return the stories of women to the narrative. If, as Taylor Swift says, Lana Del Rey can be called a "legacy artist," so these women are "legacy songwriters" of high stature.

I write as a man who came of age in the 1970s, in an upbringing saturated by second wave feminism. I was reared not just on Cole Porter, Harold Arlen, and Rodgers and Hammerstein but also on *Ms.* magazine, which at that time had a children's section. Fascinated, I listened over and over to my LP of *Free to Be You and Me* with its songs by Mary Rodgers, Carol Hall, and Shelley Miller. In my youth, my mother and three older sisters all occasionally created lyrics and music—and, since then, so have my wife and women friends with whom I sometimes collaborated.

Apart from my ingrained feminism, my reason for writing this book is that I love songs. I can never know the world from behind a woman's eyes. But about songs I can speak deeply, for I am a lifelong song appreciator.

The writers focused on in this book are only some of the many women who strove in the popular song business of the early to middle twentieth century. The limit of forty songs was set to keep the book within practical bounds. Most of these works are among the famous standards and, therefore, are often represented in tributes to women songwriters of the era. The final selection had to be balanced as a group, chronologically and among styles and subgenres. Within those parameters, when I could focus on two women collaborating, I did.

"Women's history is women's right," proclaimed Gerda Lerner, one founder of the women's history discipline.[3] I hope this history of female songwriters of the Great American Songbook contributes to the furtherance of women's rights.

A NOTE ON SONG POPULARITY

By creating hits and enduring songs, women influenced the popular song market. I list hits and standards for fourteen of these female songwriters. Fans of this repertoire might be surprised by some of the items on my lists. I have used every resource I reasonably could to construct these credits and have been very careful. Edward Foote Gardner and Joel Whitburn both created charts ranking hit songs; they are standard sources. Also, though, I have been able to expand on that data, thanks to the ProQuest databases available to me through universities that supported my work. I looked at materials from the period revealing live performances, live radio broadcasts, jukebox play, and sheet music sales. Gardner and Whitburn mainly trace national popularity, but I pay attention to regional and international (particularly British) success too. I also looked at information drawn from discographies (including SecondHandSongs.com) and YouTube postings, et cetera.

Getting a song placed on the flip side of a hit single was profitable because royalties were paid to the writers of both the A-side and the B-side. The money was nice, but it did not necessarily make the B-side count as a hit. Still, for some years *Cash Box* surveyed regional success; in many instances they documented notable disc sales and play on jukeboxes and radio for B-sides that were not credited with success in *Billboard*. This situation probably held true throughout the period I study; therefore, sometimes I credit the B-side of hit recording as also a success. Also, I often base this on a music artist, at the top of their fame, using the song in their performance and broadcast repertoire. For instance, Mabel Wayne's "A Cabana in Havana" was the flip side of Glenn Miller's hit "My Prayer," at a time when the band was in a long stretch of peak popularity. Crucially, radio transcriptions reveal the band's singer, Marion Hutton, purveying "Cabana" over the airwaves in a period when the band was broadcasting up to three times a week. Another important factor occurred when a particular singer kept using a song for years and became especially identified with it. Examples include Pearl Bailey with Doris Fisher's "Tired" and Beulah Bryant with Irene Higginbotham's "Fat Mama Blues."

I've come to have great respect for songs that achieved popularity. I also respect works that endure. John Diamond, MD, psychiatrist and proponent of the healing power of music, outlined through his research that hits had a special quality (to oversimplify, they contain a desire to be in sync with the society of their time); and enduring songs have a separate virtue (the creators expressed a deeper, more honest inner truth). Of course, many songs were both hits and enduring standards and thus can boast both of these positive aspects.

Despite the efforts of many songwriters, promoters, performers, and publishers, numerous worthy songs never became hits or standards. Women songwriters were among those who created quality songs that did not get a proper chance. There might be factors of prejudice, bad luck, a surplus of songs out on the marketplace, or a song coming along too late—or too early. That is why the longer essays in this book feature lists of "neglected gems" that deserve a hearing. Today, audiences can listen to most of these songs online and discover how talented these women were.

I

WOMEN IN THE WORLD
OF TIN PAN ALLEY

This book celebrates women who wrote popular songs in the early twenti-eth century. These female composers and lyricists deserved greater oppor-tunities and fame and to be more highly valued. Generations later, the same could be said for many of their sisters in songwriting in the early decades of the twenty-first century. Hopefully, looking at the past will inspire change in the future. To do this, we must travel in our minds back to what was, in effect, a different world.

It was a world where music publishers were the center of American popular music. Above all, these firms hungered to sell copies of sheet music. Across the nation there were millions of households with pianos and ukuleles. The amateur musicians eagerly bought the printed musical scores for the latest hit songs.

Most of these popular compositions were issued by the big publishing houses. The majority were in New York, like Remick's, Haviland, Harms, Mills, Witmark, Stern, Feist, and Shapiro, Bernstein. From 1900 to 1940, these businesses moved in stages up Broadway, from 14th Street to 49th Street. Some publishers had their main headquarters in Chicago, like the firms of the brothers Harold and Will Rossiter (who were bitter rivals), Consolidated, and M.M. Cole.

Around 1903, the popular song industry centered on 28th Street and Broadway in Manhattan. Because these publishers had people demonstrat-ing songs for performers all day long on tinny-sounding pianos, and because the songs were considered like tin pans, cheaply made items that would not last long, the popular song industry came to be called Tin Pan Alley. Time has shown that some of these compositions were not made of tin but of long-lasting titanium.

From one viewpoint, it was a period of tremendous continuity in Tin Pan Alley. For instance, quintessential Alley songwriter Irving Berlin produced hit songs from 1909 to 1957, spanning almost two historical generations. Nevertheless, trends and technology underwent a minor shift every three years and a major shift every ten years. Thus, from another viewpoint, there was nearly constant change: from the 1910s, with waltzes, ragtime, and early blues heard almost exclusively live, in vaudeville, dance halls, and cabaret; to the 1950s, with amplified urban rhythm-and-blues, the spread of country-western, and the blend of those two into rock-and-roll, heard almost exclusively in recordings, on Top Forty radio, in movies, and on television.

By 1960, the Tin Pan Alley era had ended. The home piano faded in importance, and with it died the sheet music industry. Tin Pan Alley mutated into something else—the "Brill Building sound," exemplified by younger songwriters who flocked to the vicinity of 49th Street and Broadway, crafting hits for rock-and-roll singers.

While the machinery of Tin Pan Alley was still running, women made it tick. If you were a performer walking into the office of a music publisher in 1912, the first person to greet you at the front desk would probably be a woman, like the young Ms. Stern at the office of her father Joseph W. Stern. At Haviland's, in a piano cubicle, May Zimmer would play and sing you a new song, hoping to convince you to perform it. If you wanted a free copy of a number at Leo Feist's, May Flannigan of the professional department would dispense it along with one of her trademark witticisms. If you had made up a song but could not write down music, Reta Comer at the small office of Jeff Branen would create a lead sheet with the basic melody and chords, in between her duties as a typist and pianist. At the office of F. A. Mills, if you were a bandleader, Mamie Coyle could help you out with stock orchestrations of their song catalog. If Remick's owed you money, or if you owed them for sending you cash to get a train home after closing out of town, cashier May Tierney would help you out. Women were bustling around busily throughout Tin Pan Alley. Up in a tiny office of the third floor of the Regal Building, in the smalltime firm of Frank Clark, Flo Jacobson had even advanced to professional manager, the boss of the whole outfit—the only woman of the early decades to attain that status. Thirty-five years later, by the late 1940s, several women were co-owners of some of the smaller Tin Pan Alley publishing houses.

Sometimes the publishers paid the songwriters a fair royalty on profits. But at other times the writers would get a flat fee and sign over all their rights to the piece. The writers might get no credit and as little as five dollars for what would turn into a valuable copyright. It is not surprising that, once a writer found success, their first step often was to set up as their own publisher. Many men and several women did this, usually to go out of business swiftly.

The publishers were the ones who did the grunt work to get songs known throughout the nation. They would buy dozens, even hundreds, of tunes to get one hit. The expenses were never ending. In return, the publishers got the bulk of the profits when a song did make a lot of money. These companies accumulated tremendous power over the songwriters.

Women were there for every twist and turn in the history of popular music. Dolly Morse could proudly claim to be a charter member of the American Society of Composers, Authors and Publishers (ASCAP). She was witness to ASCAP winning the right to be paid for the use of music in theaters, restaurants, hotels, and bars. Later the organization fought long and hard and won the right to earn fees from radio and television too.

Dolly Morse lived to witness landmark events. In the late 1920s, Hollywood converted to sound movies and purchased most of the Tin Pan Alley firms. In 1941, ASCAP banned its music from radio—the networks revolted against the high fees of ASCAP and in retaliation started Broadcast Music Incorporated (BMI). In 1943 and 1948, the musicians' union banned recordings by its members. Nevertheless, the union's nightmare came true: by 1949, radio was no longer dominated by live broadcasts. Now radio disc jockeys were kings, making recordings popular through airplay. Women had to grapple with all these developments.

One woman who rose to a position of power was Miriam Stern, the executive director of the Songwriters Guild of America (SGA). This organization was formed in 1931 to establish a standard contract that made sure publishers gave writers a fair share of royalties. From 1947 to 1969, Stern took charge of SGA. She was an expert on copyrights and contracts who also implemented a major plan to help with the collection of royalties. Despite Stern's example of leadership, for many decades it was impossible for women to get elected to board positions in ASCAP, BMI, or the SGA.[1]

How many of the era's songwriters were women? We can never know precisely, but women probably represented about 4 to 10 percent of pop songwriters, from one in twenty-five to one in ten. When the receptionists, song demonstrators, clerks, and managers had all gone home, the female

Figure 1.1   The only woman in the room in 1912: amid twenty-three men, one woman. At bottom center, composer Grace LeBoy with her lyricist (and, from 1915, husband) Gus Kahn. (*Billboard*, December 14, 1912, 45. Public domain.)

lyricist or composer might be left as the only woman in the offices during an intensive all-night work session. This book is a start at making them visible.

The glory period of the Great American Songbook lies in the twenty-plus years starting about 1924. The form and range of styles for these songs became very standardized. Songs were written in a conventional form,

Figure 1.2 The only woman in the room in 1944: amid eleven men, one woman.
Composer-lyricist Joan Whitney squats at the front right at a National Press Club get-together.
Second from the left squats her bespectacled writing partner (and, from 1950, husband) Alex
Kramer. (Photo courtesy of Doren Voeth.)

usually with very clear sections. The tunesmiths mostly wrote refrains in
the form of ABAC (like "Take Me Out to the Ball Game") or AABA (like
"When You Wish Upon a Star"). That fact became an important part of the
creative lives of many women songwriters who collaborated with others.
For instance, a woman might write the main strain, and a man the middle
section, or vice versa. Before the refrains, they would put an introductory
section called the verse. Come radio, the bands began to drop the verses;
soon, the writers sometimes stopped bothering to write them.

Earlier and later in the period, the lyricists might be content with
off-rhymes, such as an assonance (like pairing *alone* with *home*) or an
augmented rhyme (like *down* and *around*). But in the heart of the era,
lyricists tried to use exact rhymes (like *alone* and *phone*, or *down* and
town), particularly in songs with serious emotions. All these intricate
details combined to create magic. Female songwriters were among those
who perfected these techniques of Tin Pan Alley. These women were also
sometimes innovative, helping to popularize content, forms, and styles that
set new trends.

To get the public to buy sheet music, the publishers had to get people to hear songs. Song demonstrators in stores were often women. The best of them got jobs at the publisher's offices, singing and playing piano to demonstrate the ditties for performers. Bernice Petkere ("Close Your Eyes"), Doris Tauber ("Them There Eyes"), and many other women were among the best song demonstrators of Tin Pan Alley. Publishers, their employees, and songwriters themselves went out into every dance hall, restaurant, nightclub, movie house, and theater to try to get performances of their songs. These were called "plugs," and those who won a plug were songpluggers—usually men, for they could more safely roam the city at night.

The songpluggers scrambled to keep up with all the new ways to get tunes heard by audiences, from tent shows and vaudeville to Broadway musicals, records, radio, movie musicals, world's fairs, and television. The classical singers, jazz singers, organ grinders, dance bands—the list of possible performers was endless. They plugged works of all kinds: songs sad, cheerful, silly, or philosophic; galvanizing fast rhythm numbers; charming medium-tempo soft-shoe tunes; or, most prized of all, slow love ballads.

HOW THEY COLLABORATED

Most of the songs focused on in this book are collaborations, usually of women with men but also occasionally with other women. One complicated aspect of the Great American Songbook is the wide range of ways in which people collaborated; and one frustration is that it is often hard to know whom to credit with writing a great song. The frequent mysteries and confusion over authorship are also an indication of one of the glories of the Tin Pan Alley genre, because it shows how similar to folk music it was. The problem for women and other people who could easily be taken advantage of—Blacks, Latinos, youngsters, immigrants, obscure musicians, the desperately poor, or the naïve—is that they might easily lose out on the money and fame that could come from writing a famous song.

People were often not credited for what they wrote. Even if the credit was accurate, the materials the writers used were often borrowed from earlier sources like classical music and folk songs. The current study examines famous songs, but often the women credited are obscure and untraceable.

Frequently, writers briefly used pseudonyms or created lifelong professional names. The reasons for such concealments were many: simplification, passing whims, family snobbery, violating a contract (to a publisher) or an affiliation (like to ASCAP or BMI), independence from a famous relative, and other reasons. People with Jewish ancestry found a welcome on Tin Pan Alley (there were few US industries where they were allowed to thrive). To become part of the mainstream, an aspiring songwriter like Israel Baline was content to Anglicize his name to Irving Berlin; and Jacob Gershwine happy to become George Gershwin. Women often did the same.

Sometimes the publishers reckoned female customers would be attracted to a song written by a woman. For instance, Robert A. King used many pseudonyms, including feminine ones. (Because he was so prolific, he over-flooded the market with sheet music bearing his name.) It was as "Mary Earl" that he published his most enduring credit, "Beautiful Ohio" (1918), now a state anthem.

It could work the other way. In 1906, Alfreda Stanberg brought her first songs to the Haviland firm, and the manager Theodore Morse insisted "a song by a woman would not sell."[2] So they credited the lyric to "Alfred Scott." Two years later, Stanberg married Morse but still disguised her identity under the gender-neutral moniker "D. A. Esrom" ("Morse" spelled backward). She used her truer professional name, "Dolly Morse," for her later song, "Siboney," discussed in a later chapter.

Most songs were written by two people: a composer wrote the music, and a lyricist wrote the words. Sometimes (one in six) a single person would create the song alone. Other times (also one in six) all creators would equally share a credit of "music and lyrics by." Usually, lyricists got one-third of the profits, and composers got two-thirds. (Composers received more because of the many instrumental performances of songs.)

The process of writing a song could start with a melody, or a lyric, or most often a title. The creation could be hashed out by two people in the room together, batting ideas back and forth; or the collaborators might work separately. They might never meet. All approaches were used.

The method of collaboration was seldom reported. Anecdotes abound, but they are often too colorful to believe and sometimes can be proven to be straight-out lies. The origin of "I Won't Dance" is one of the more believable and well-documented stories and reveals how complicated the process of writing a hit song could be.

The tale begins in early 1934 with two Americans in London. Composer Jerome Kern and lyricist-playwright Oscar Hammerstein II were writing a show for London's West End, *Three Sisters*. One of the sisters was played by another American, Adele Dixon, who was doing a wonderful job. Shortly before opening, Kern and Hammerstein decided Dixon needed another featured number. Overnight, Kern came up with the melody for "I Won't

Dance," and Hammerstein wrote lyrics for a verse, refrain, and special chorus material. The show only had a brief run, and the song did not get any recordings.

Kern seems to have next handed the piece to another of his partners, lyricist Otto Harbach, with the idea of changing the lyric for the post-Broadway tour of their stage musical *Roberta*. Harbach used much of Hammerstein's version in rewriting it under the title "Armful of Flame." But that lyric was never performed. When the Hollywood studio RKO made *Roberta* into a movie in 1935, the film's star Fred Astaire requested the company buy the rights for "I Won't Dance."

At RKO, lyricist Dorothy Fields and her composing partner Jimmy McHugh were under a joint contract as a team. "I Won't Dance" was handed to Fields to tailor to Astaire's needs. At that point, she had never met Kern but nevertheless rewrote the words to fit the movie characters and situation; and because of the terms of their contract McHugh got cocredit. The result was a big hit and an enduring standard. In the end, 20 percent of the lyric was by Hammerstein, 5 percent by Harbach, and 75 percent by Fields—and, almost certainly, 0 percent by McHugh. All four were given credit for the final lyric. (This was rare. Unlike in the early twenty-first century, back then it was unusual for more than two, or at the most three, people to get credited for a song.) Posterity has given all the praise for the result to Dorothy Fields, whose version is superior to the earlier drafts but is substantially based on Hammerstein's original. It is very possible that a number of the songs written about in the following chapters have as many complications of authorship as "I Won't Dance" but less evidence to reveal the machinations behind the scene.

HOW THEY WORKED WITH MEN

The lives and careers of male songwriters are often narrated with little or no mention of the women in their lives. With their female counterparts, their relation to men is often one of the main facts we know. Thus, the cowriters, fathers, brothers, lovers, husbands, and sons of these women songwriters might seem to take on a disproportionate role in the chapters that follow. If so, it is a symptom of the patriarchal society in which these women flourished against all odds.

It was a world in which there was an ideal etiquette about how a man should behave in the presence of a woman. Of course, few if any lived up to that protocol in every moment of their lives. Nevertheless, it was common for people to adhere to many points in this code of behavior. In this universe, a man and woman in each other's presence must not use profanity, blasphemy, or even vulgar language. Neither could spit, belch, fart, get drunk, tell bawdy jokes, or talk about menstruation, pregnancy, childbirth, sex, or infidelity, or even lounge in a lazy posture.

In her presence, the man had always to put on his jacket, button his collar, and tighten his tie. He should avoid appearing with stubble on his face. When she walked in the room, he must rise and remain standing until she sat down. When she sat down at a table, he would pull her chair out, hold it, and help adjust it for her comfort. When walking together, he must open and hold the door, offer to carry her packages or give his arm for support, and be sure to walk on the outside of the sidewalk (to protect her from mud splashing on her legs from passing traffic).

All of these rules might change in certain contexts, such as the beach or a picnic. But in most indoor situations, including the workplace, people tended to keep to them. Of course, at the office a male boss would not stand whenever his female employee entered the room; and when to stick to this code of behavior and when to bend it or break it could be a delicate matter. People might easily make mistakes that would offend or repel others. Each successful collaboration would have to set its own rules, usually in ways that were tacit and only half-conscious.

Grace Henry managed to carve out a career as a lyricist in the late 1920s, writing songs like "Or What Have You" for the sophisticated revue *The Little Show*. She told journalist Rosalind Shaffer that "there were several things that made it almost impossible for a woman to have a career as a songwriter. Life was too tough for a woman. The hours were unheard of, work lasted all night sometimes and collaboration with other folks"—that is, men—"made complicated situations for a woman." One can imagine Henry beset by complexities from trying to find a woman's restroom in the building, dodging sexual harassment, and placating the jealousy of her boyfriend or the male tunesmith's girlfriend.[3]

Shaffer continues, "Hard boiled managers . . . were another thing hard for a woman to face." Even a male like J. Fred Coots ("Santa Claus Is Coming to Town"), mentor of Dorothy Fields, confessed it was tough. Songwriting was "a cold blooded and heartless racket." Speaking for himself and others, "many a night, hungry and miserable . . . you've cried yourself to slumberland, hoping you'd never wake up the next morning." From the perspective of his successful later years, Coots writes about it jokingly but nevertheless clearly implies that he considered suicide, "ready to take the easy way out of despair."[4]

Among the "real songwriters," the "guys and gals who do it the hard way," Coots counted composer Mabel Wayne ("It Happened in Monterey"). Near the end of her life, Wayne remembered that in the 1920s "it was practically impossible for a woman to get her foot in a music publisher's door." The reason: "prejudice." Jack Robbins was one of the most powerful men in Tin Pan Alley, in charge of sheet music for all the great MGM movie musicals, but he would not hire a female. He stated: "Women are too emotional. They become so discouraged if they turn out a flop that they can't lift a pencil any more. They're not dependable." Others might have been a tad more open-minded, but not by much: "Publishers gladly consider the work of the women but state quite frankly that the song is obliged to be superior in every way to the work of the men." Tin Pan Alley bragged that acceptance was based on merit; nevertheless, gender-based (and race-based) double standards often still applied.[5]

In 1928, speaking on the condition of anonymity, one woman offered a clear picture: "The songwriting business is an informal but clanny fraternity. The members sit around Lindy's" (the famed Broadway deli) "and exchange tips." Or the lugs would attend a theater producer's rowdy gathering. While "we girl songwriters are sitting at home . . . plugging away at a tune which we hope and pray we can sell" to that same producer, he "has already given the job to a songwriter who is, at that very moment, drinking his brandy and trying to steal his girl." Other reports make it clear that even in the men's room wheeler-dealers would be promoting their songs or grabbing at a better contract.[6]

Admittedly, composer Kay Swift ("Can't We Be Friends") had memories of a different color: "We never had the feeling we weren't equal. I don't remember ever losing chances because I was a woman, not at all." But Swift was part of the *crème de la crème* of New York City society, artistic and financial. She carried with her the heft of that status. Even so, in the 1930s a female journalist noted that Swift had "two Broadway hits . . . yet she can't stick her . . . nose into the movie industry." Despite her advantages and talent, Swift's pop music career was nipped in the bud.[7]

The world of jazz held the same limitations and more. Many enduring hit songs emerged from those who worked in the dance bands or smaller combos, but these groups mostly excluded women. When a male bandleader wanted to hire saxophonist Peggy Gilbert, the men protested: "We don't want a girl around. We can't talk the way we wanna talk, and we can't do things we want to do"—presumably curse, gamble, spit, drink, tell bawdy jokes, urinate by the roadside, and so forth. In the early 1940s, trumpeter Billie Rogers did succeed in being hired to tour with the Woody Herman big band; but she was ostracized until the men realized she could be trusted to keep their secret if they were unfaithful to their wives.[8]

Overall, women were encouraged to be passive. A woman born in 1920 tells this story. In the late 1930s she fell in love and began to phone the man and arrange dates. Her older sister told her taking the romantic or sexual initiative was "not ladylike." She must stop. So the relationship faded away, leaving the woman with a lifelong niggling regret. This vignette of the past highlights how remarkable was the social initiative taken by ambitious women songwriters—and how remarkable were some of the female protagonists of their lyrics who were romantically or sexually assertive. Clearly, such boundaries could make it uncomfortable for women and men to work together.

Mabel Wayne spoke from experience: "Men are always jealous of women in the same field."[9] There often was from men tremendous scorn, condescension, and prejudice against women as workers and artists. Male pride was easily bruised by the superior, or even the equal, abilities of a female. To these obstacles were added society's array of prejudices based on race, religion, age, ethnicity, regionalism, class, looks, and sexuality.

Transporting ourselves in imagination back into that world brings some understanding of why many women shunned professional life and why men did not always welcome women behind the scenes in the world of show business. It took an unusual female, an unusual male, or an unusual situation for women and men to work together comfortably, to be able to relax and not feel constrained. Perhaps the miracle is they did it so often.

We cannot travel back in time and enforce gender justice to make the career rewards of these women equal to those of the men around them. But we can give these women an equal chance today, through our respectful attention to their songs. Let their voices be heard.

2

THE TWENTIES

The 1920s—a decade of women voting, Prohibition, the Harlem Renaissance, tough times for farmers, high times for Wall Street; it also witnessed the spread of a couple handfuls of the most enduring American songs written by women. The jazzy instrumentalists and intimate singers of speakeasies were broadcast nationally on radio and effloresced on phono recordings, especially after the advent in 1925 of electronic recording and the microphone. It was the Jazz Age, the Golden Age of the American Operetta, the glory years of the classic blues and down-home blues, the crystallization in the heartland of country-western music—and, on Broadway and Tin Pan Alley, of the style of the Great American Songbook.

In the 1920s, the earnest Suffragette was followed by the playful flapper, and examples of the independent New Woman filled places in all subcultures—polite society, celebrity circles, and artistic bohemia among them. Some of these New Women spent time as songwriters in the popular song marketplace. Admittedly, in the early 1920s, women rarely were able to flourish and sustain a songwriting career in Tin Pan Alley. Many older female composers and lyricists saw their hits dwindle. Composer-lyricist Carrie Jacobs-Bond, an independent publisher of her own works, wrote songs at the turn of the century that sold sheet music in the millions and became standards for decades, like "I Love You Truly" (1906). She kept on creating into the 1940s, but her later works never again found that level of sales. Zelda Sears and Rida Johnson Young were popular lyricists for

Broadway, but they were also playwrights and mostly found success in the 1920s as dramatists. Anita Owen was a composer, lyricist, and publisher, but her biggest hits were earlier, "Sweet Bunch of Daisies" (1894) and "Daisies Won't Tell" (1908), and after 1920 her publication rate dropped abruptly. The zestful output of lyricist Junie McCree, such as "Put Your Arms Around Me, Honey" (1910), ended in 1918 with her death.

Nevertheless, many women forged on. As had McCree, some caught the era's exciting vernacular energy. Veteran lyricist Blanche Merrill heralded the Jazz Age with "Jazz Baby" (1919) and "Melodious Jazz" (1920), but after 1925 she vanished from Tin Pan Alley. Muriel Pollock was an accomplished pianist of jazzy pop for decades; and she kept up a steady string of song compositions with major Tin Pan Alley publishers, without ever having a breakthrough hit.

Composer-lyricist Lily Strickland straddled the worlds of classical music, popular song, and folk music ethnography. Her gently swinging standard "Mah Lindy Lou" (1921), highly praised by Alec Wilder, overlaps all three areas: highbrow, pop, and folk. Lyricist Annelu Burns produced a semi-high-class ballad lyric that endured for decades: "I'll Forget You" (1921), with its devastating final lines "I'll try to forget you / In vain," foreshadowing the bittersweet irony that would characterize the 1930s. Burns frequently collaborated with the prolific composer Madelyn Sheppard; and, in 1925, the two briefly formed a publishing company. Strickland, Burns, and Sheppard represent the strand of white Southerners who moved away to make their mark on the national scene. As will be shown later, there was a strand of Southern Black women who made an even stronger long-range impact on American popular music.

"SUGAR BLUES" (1919/1923)
Lucy Fletcher, lyricist

Sometimes celebrating women songwriters of Tin Pan Alley is like writing a mystery rather than a history. Thus is the case with "Sugar Blues" and, as will be discussed later, "Mexicali Rose." In both instances, it is the male composer who sustained a career in the public eye and had the opportunity to go on record. Meanwhile the female lyricists swiftly eluded the eye of the media, even while a single example of their work lived on.

African American Clarence Williams composed "Sugar Blues." From small town Louisiana, he gravitated to New Orleans, then to a flourishing career in Chicago and New York. Although he was an impressively able composer, lyricist, singer, pianist, multi-instrumentalist, and bandleader, his real genius was as an organizer and entrepreneur. Critic Martin Williams (no relation) asserts that "he was a superb promoter of the songs he published; around that talent all his other talents centered." He is lyricist for the great "West End Blues" and wrote words and music for the enduring "Gulf Coast Blues." He is listed as a co-composer on many publications, and judging by his own anecdotes and his reputation among his peers, for many of these he may have contributed only slight tweaking. In that light, "Sugar Blues," a rare melody for which he took sole credit, might be judged as his peak composition. He later declared it "the most consistent seller in his catalogue."[1]

Clarence Williams told this story about the creation of "Sugar Blues," as relayed in news articles of the 1930s and 1940s and later interviews of his widow, singer Eva Taylor: "A colored lady by the name of Lucy Fletcher, who had never written a song before, brought this idea to Mr. Williams and said that she had several children" (five, according to Taylor) "and that her husband was sick. She asked Mr. Williams if he would set the words to music, as she had to do something to help her family along. Mr. Williams told her that under those conditions he would consider it and charge her a set fee." This was a standard practice for smaller music publishers, charging amateurs a fee to set their lyrics to music. "So when the price went through," meaning presumably when Fletcher delivered the money, "Mr. Williams wrote the music and published the song."[2]

Decades later, when World War II loomed, Williams elaborated on a purported World War I rationing context for the "Sugar Blues" lyric. During 1918, he explained, "there was a shortage on sugar. At that time you were only allowed two lumps of teaspoons of sugar in your coffee or tea, in restaurants, and this inspired" Fletcher and Williams "to write this sensational song hit."[3]

The story continues: "Miss Fletcher" (she is not called "Mrs.," thereby creating some ambiguity about her marital status) "sold quite a few copies and made a good bit of money on 'Sugar Blues' and the song was then forgotten." The wording vaguely hints that at first Fletcher herself promoted the song, perhaps peddling sheet music to local music stores or performing and selling it at neighborhood soirées. This retrospective history is suspicious in several aspects, including its romantic pathos and claims about the amateur status of Fletcher.

There are two bits of evidence from the actual period. First, the copyright office received the registration for the song on December 9, 1919. This date is perhaps almost as long as two years after the 1918 date Williams later claimed. If the voluntary food rationing of that wartime era was still going on, it must have been at its tail end. This mismatch of timing casts suspicion on his story. Second, on February 28, 1920, the *Chicago Defender* began to run a series of ads by the Chicago publishing house run by Clarence Williams with Armond J. Piron, which listed the tune among others.

Williams continued his fable: "Two years" went by, and one day Williams was demonstrating tunes for the singer Sara Martin, and "then she spied the title of 'Sugar Blues' on the counter. . . . The minute she heard it she said, 'That's what I want.' Miss Martin put the song in her vaudeville act." On August 10, 1922, Leona Williams (also no relation) recorded the piece for the major label Columbia. On August 30, 1922, Clarence Williams copyrighted the piece for a second time; he was now in New York running his own publishing operation without Piron. On October 8, 1922, Sara Martin scheduled "Sugar Blues" for her first recording session, with Williams himself filling in at the last minute on piano. "The record sold into the thousands," with the result of "fame and fortune" for Martin and turning Williams into "a record star."[4] At the end of January 1923, Williams copyrighted the composition a third time. (But why?) A slew of 1923 waxings followed, establishing the song as a standard. Williams never said whether Lucy Fletcher profited by this revival and the subsequent decades of record and sheet music sales.

Of the many women named Lucy Fletcher during this era, some are mentioned in the African American press. A prominent figure in nursing is almost certainly not the lyricist, for Nurse Fletcher was successfully employed in New York at about the time the song was copyrighted in Chicago. Two other candidates flit through the social pages of the Baltimore-based *Afro-American* and, later, the *Chicago Defender*, but in neither case is there any hint that this is the collaborator on "Sugar Blues."

Fletcher's words for "Sugar Blues" became part of popular culture and are sensed implicitly even in the work's many instrumental renditions.[5] Blues historian Peter C. Muir analyzes the tune as being built on top of a version of the standard twelve-bar blues harmonies but stretched out to twenty measures. If Williams was truthful in reporting that Fletcher wrote her novelty lyric first, then her stanzas supplied the structure for Williams's chorus melody, and she can be credited with its interesting ABA′CC′ form.[6]

Fletcher wrote (as usual) two sets of lyrics for the introductory verses and also (more unusually, but not uniquely) two alternate lyrics for the B-section of the refrain. Her lyric is sometimes about sweet food, sometimes about a sweet lover, and sometimes about a sweet song called "Sugar Blues." Her equivocation sets the mood, which is that of lighthearted mischievousness.

At the juncture of the final two sections, Fletcher and Williams throw in a parenthetical phrase, "More sugar," which is comical and thoroughly addictive. Yet the song can also be genuinely plaintive, lamenting unsatisfied appetites for either loving or cuisine.

In the second lyric for the B-section, Fletcher is witty and playful as she paraphrases the first line of a couplet from the naughty children's folk song, "I like coffee, I like tea / I like the boys, and they like me."

I love my coffee, I love my tea,
But the doggone cream turned sour on me.

"Sugar Blues" became inextricably entwined with the reputation of white trumpeter-bandleader Claude McCoy. His recording supplied the original theme music for *Make Believe Ballroom*, New York City's first radio disc jockey program. McCoy infused "Sugar Blues" with brash wah-wah effects and growls that became a strong part of the performance tradition surrounding the tune. In contrast, the youthful Ella Fitzgerald mined the song's more childlike qualities in her 1940 big band recording. The least clichéd versions turn up intermittently: certainly right at the start, with the vocals by Williams and Martin; and thereafter, with certain instrumental renditions such as the one by Count Basie. The composition is versatile and has been done as a boogie-woogie, a mambo, and a novelty scat solo accompanied by dog howls, but most often is heard from Dixieland and New Orleans revival bands.

Fletcher's title has become a staple phrase in the fields of nutrition, dental care, and the study of diabetes. This is especially true since William Dufty's classic 1975 *Sugar Blues*, a best-selling book about the environmental and nutritional dangers of the overconsumption of refined cane sugar. Ironically, when Clarence Williams died in 1965, it was partly from diabetes. Posterity knows his fate, but unfortunately not that of the lyricist on one of his most famous songs, Lucy Fletcher.

"MEXICALI ROSE" (1922/1923)
Helen Stone, lyricist

Clarence Williams always gave credit for the "Sugar Blues" lyrics to Lucy Fletcher, but unfortunately the composer of "Mexicali Rose," Jack Tenney, was not as consistent. Between the contradictory stories purveyed by him and by journalists, the historical record concerning the song and its lyricist is permanently muddled. Tenney later became a lawyer, then a California politician, rising to the state senate. He reportedly swung around his politics, from left to right, as wildly as he did his tales about the origin of "Mexicali Rose."

Mexicali and Calexico sit on two sides of the border, as essentially one city straddling Mexico and California. After alcohol was illegalized in the United States in 1919, everybody was very happy to go and spend money for booze in Mexicali. Nightlife there thrived. Tenney lived in Calexico but led a band in Mexicali at the Imperial Cabaret. According to some reports it was a jazz trio, in others a seven-piece orchestra; perhaps the trio was a subunit of the orchestra.

On a Saturday night, October 7, 1922, the Imperial Jazz Band Trio for the first time performed a new composition, "Mexicali Rose." On Tuesday, the "arrangement" was claimed by the band's drummer-saxophonist Frank Mack, but by Wednesday the *Calexico Chronicle* clarified that "the music was written by Jack B. Tenney and the words by Helen Stone." This "new song hit . . . proved so popular that its authors plan to copyright . . . and place it on the market."[7]

In later years, Tenney reported on the creation of the song twice, in versions that contradict each other and these early reports, but both times he is very specific that he only created the chorus of the song. Five months went by, during which time Stone or Tenney contacted Walter A. Quincke, a publisher-songwriter in Los Angeles. On March 10, 1923, the copyright office received from Quincke the registration form for the song, and on that date in Mexicali the Imperial Music store, presumably an annex to the cabaret, began to sell copies. The sheet music featured a Spanish translation by Manuel Sanchez de Lara and, as well, an introductory verse (perhaps by Quincke) with the usual two sets of lyrics that were still a requirement for most pop songs.

Another month went by, and peripatetic entertainer Billy Jones rolled into Calexico-Mexicali. He boasted that he was winning applause with "Mexicali Rose" along the west coast and was now going to head east, intending to make the song (and the town) famous nationwide. As part of this report, a tidbit about the lyricist was offered to the public: at the Imperial, "Jack Tenney, the pianist set to music the words, written by Helen Stone, a singer in the cabaret at the time but now in San Francisco." In September 1923, Lewis James recorded the song, verse and chorus, for Okeh Records, a firm that was a pioneer in the fields of blues and country music. Throughout the 1920s further recordings followed at scattered intervals.[8]

By 1930 the "immense popularity" of "Mexicali Rose" had done more than "any publicity campaign" could possibly do to "advertise Mexicali." As a result, Hollywood made the first of two movies titled *Mexicali Rose*, with Barbara Stanwyck in the title role. In connection with the movie's release, Tenney now told journalists that he "wrote the melody of the chorus and used it instrumentally for several weeks. . . . The title was suggested by some one, evolving from the many 'Rose' songs and it seemed to be a good idea." Tenney thought of "Rose of No Man's Land" (1918) and "Rose of Washington Square" (1919), and, therefore, "we saw no reason why Mexicali should not have a 'Rose' as well." There was no real-life woman named "Rose," Tenney proclaimed; it was just a song convention. This saga credits the lyrics, beyond perhaps the title, to Stone, who supposedly "wrote the words the night before the manuscript was mailed to the publishers." This claim about the timing is probably not true, because the song was first performed a good five months before it was copyrighted and printed.

Jump to 1968, when Tenney relayed an almost completely different story. Now he spun the tale of a real-life Rose, a comic figure who ran a boarding house in a nearby town. While on her monthly spree to Mexicali, "sentimentally inebriated" on a "rainy evening," she was crying morosely until her friends took her home. Inspired, the band's saxophonist Jack Haislop suggested "Mexicali Rose" as the title of Tenney's recently composed instrumental waltz, and the phrase fit the first notes. Tenney further claimed, "Because Rose had been crying, I tried the next line 'stop crying.'" Referring to an Irving Berlin hit of the summer of 1922, "Some Sunny Day," Tenney continued, "The bad weather and the title of a current popular song suggested the next line 'I'll come back to you some sunny day.'"[9]

Tenney goes on to further erase any credit to Stone for the lyrics: "Helen Stone, a singer, liked the song so much that she put up the money for the first publication. I gave her a half interest in it and put her name on the number as the writer of the lyrics. It was a very fine investment as we are still drawing royalties." This all sounds plausible. But then how to account for Tenney's 1930 interview, which states Stone did write the lyric and there was no woman named Rose? Perhaps politeness to the two women motivated his earlier claims. Yet in light of the documented timing of the song's introduction and copyright registration, with Stone credited for the lyrics many months before the publication date, it seems more likely that the elderly Tenney was simply inventing a self-aggrandizing, colorful after-dinner story.

In 1935, the rights for "Mexicali Rose" were bought by M.M. Cole, a Chicago firm that specialized in country-western songs. In November that year, Bob Wills gave the ditty a jaunty western-swing duple meter rendition. The following month Gene Autry, the singing star of western movies and music, recorded it. The tune got a boost a few years later when Bing Crosby "happened to include the song in his recollection bit" on his high-rating weekly radio show.[10] Soon bandleaders were getting requests, and sheet music sales stirred. Crosby's disc of 1938 was a national hit (and particularly big on jukeboxes in New Orleans). In 1939, Gene Autry sang it in yet another movie titled after the song, and the star's single was reissued that year, and in 1940, and in 1946, and, as the decades rolled along, eventually on LP, CD, and into the twenty-first century.

What happened to Helen Stone? From 1931 to 1933 there was a singer named Helen Stone on the radio in Los Angeles, but nothing specific links her to "Mexicali Rose." There was also a Jim Stone who owned a business in Mexicali, and his sister Helen was known to visit him before she died in 1932 from a freak accident in the San Francisco Bay Area. (On the golf course, she walked behind her escort at just the wrong moment of his backswing, and the club hit her on the temple. When she regained consciousness, she seemed fine, but then she died later that evening.) Again, nothing beyond her visits to Mexicali hint at any link to "Mexicali Rose." "Helen Stone" is another name like "Lucy Fletcher" that is shared by many women, and perhaps the lyricist's fate is now untraceable.

Both of Tenney's accounts, despite their disparities, emphasize that "Mexicali Rose" drew on Tin Pan Alley conventions—songs about "Rose" and "Some Sunny Day"—an impression borne out by an examination of the piece. The refrain melody is a slow waltz in ABA´C form. The singer pleads with his beloved not to cry, comforting her with assurances of his affection, as in the last two stanzas:

Dry those big, brown eyes, and smile, dear.
Banish all those tears and please don't sigh,

Kiss me once again, and hold me.
Mexicali Rose, goodbye.

Overall, the piece is unashamedly sentimental and, for 1922, just slightly old-fashioned.

Stone creates a string of perfect rhymes to end each stanza: *day/away*; *sigh/goodbye*. She also features a pattern of imperfect rhymes, assonances, in the first three sections: *crying/pining/smile dear*. Through alliteration and the repeated long *i* and *e* sounds that create distant rhymes and assonances (*dry/eyes/sigh/goodbye*; *I'll/while/smile*; *year/dear/tears*), Stone creates a highly satisfying flow of sound and sense.

Tenney's tune and Stone's stanzas live on. True, they never found a place in the repertoires of Sinatra, Fitzgerald, and their ilk. Nevertheless, the song has been essayed by many easy listening maestros, done in Spanish, and in English performed by a wide range of singers from groups like the Mills Brothers, Andrews Sisters, and Lennon Sisters, to British crooner Vera Lynn and Italian American crooner Al Martino, movie star Clint Eastwood, folk singer Burl Ives, Scottish country yodeler Karl Denver, and, perhaps most surprisingly, frequently by a hard-rocking Jerry Lee Lewis. Most of all, the piece became a foundational ballad in the subfield of soft-country love ballads. This status has been boosted by the recordings of country-western greats such as Jim Reeves, Rex Allen, and Slim Whitman. Alongside the many reissues of Bing Crosby and Gene Autry's classic tracks, the renditions by these artists and many others mean that "Mexicali Rose" holds its own, carrying lyricist Helen Stone's name forward into the future.

"DOWN HEARTED BLUES" (1922)
Lovie Austin (1887–1975), composer
Alberta Hunter (1895–1984), lyricist

In the early 1920s two women from Tennessee crossed paths in Chicago and cocreated one of the most performed blues, "Down Hearted Blues." They remained friendly through the decades and recorded an album together in 1961. Nevertheless, some of the same uncertainties of authorship arise for their collaboration as for "Sugar Blues" and "Mexicali Rose."

Pianist Lovie Austin was one of the great jazz performers—although, as too often for women, not given quite the recognition she deserved. Starting in 1918, she had the savvy to copyright many of her works, including instrumental pieces, song tunes, and lyrics. She also kept busy notating and arranging for other musicians, creating the manuscripts her colleagues sent to the copyright office. Altogether, her name appears on over eighty-five registrations. From the 1910s to the 1940s, she made her career in Chicago, working with other greats of Black show business as a bandleader, arranger, accompanist, vaudevillian, and theater music director. When her style became outdated, she did World War II factory defense work and then became a dance studio pianist.

Alberta Hunter had, if anything, an even more illustrious career. In the United States she specialized in blues, often naughty, sung in intimate cabaret settings. In this way, many saloon singers developed their first songwriting skills. "The customers wouldn't stay downstairs," where her colleagues were singing rhythm songs and ballads. "They'd go upstairs to hear us sing the blues. That's where I would stand and make up verses and sing as I go along." One of these Prohibition-era Chicago nightspots was closed because of a mafia-related murder. In another, Hunter's accompanist was shot dead in the middle of a performance. Nevertheless, she flourished there as well as in musicals and vaudeville—including mainstream vaudeville, with mostly white patrons.

Later, in England, Hunter blossomed as a musical theater actor (in the 1928 London production of *Show Boat*) and mellifluous band singer of pop songs. Her cosmopolitan edge increased as she toured Egypt, the Middle East, and Russia, picking up new languages along the way. This experience must have served her well during World War II when she entertained the troops, including future president General Dwight D. Eisenhower.

Amid all this Hunter intermittently pursued songwriting, from the 1920s "Chirpin' the Blues" through the 1950s with the religious "I Want to Thank You, Lord," and then again in the 1970s when, after decades as a nurse, her singing career miraculously revived. Thanks to a famed gig at the Cookery in New York, Hunter became again the toast of the town (and the media) and the talk of the music business. Her sexual orientation also became more clearly perceived by some of the public during these last years, and during the new age of gay rights she became something of an icon of lesbian feminism.

Back in the age of classic blues, in April 1922, Lovie Austin sent in the first copyright for "Down Hearted Blues," with music credited to Austin and lyrics to Hunter. About this time, the singer upgraded from the Black Swan label to Paramount, with her first session in July including "Down Hearted Blues." That same month a new registration was filed in both the women's names, still with music credited to Austin and words to Hunter. Yet more than half a century later, Hunter denied Austin any share in the tune's creation.

Hunter told this story about "Down Hearted Blues": "I used to take one finger and just hit down on the piano . . . until I'd get the one I wanted. That's how I got 'Down Hearted Blues.'" The singer recounted how Austin put the song to paper, notating and arranging, and urged her to copyright it. In gratitude, Hunter gave the pianist cocredit, for Austin was a "good, honest woman, because somebody else might have stolen the whole thing from me."[11] It might well have happened that way; however, Hunter did not tell this story until Austin was dead and could not disagree. The copyright catalogs suggest another situation. For one thing, on the same day as the recopyrighting of "Down Hearted Blues," the office also received copyrights for (1) a song by Austin and lyricist Nathaniel Foster, registered to them both, and (2) a song written by Hunter, solo, registered to her but with an arrangement by Austin. The suggestion is strong that Austin was mailing in all three items and being scrupulously careful and precise when assigning both the registration owners and writing credits.

Though Hunter's 1922 disc helped launch her career at a major record label, it was in 1923 that the number soared into national popularity. As Hunter recounted in a 1982 live performance, her ditty was picked up by a rival: "The world's greatest blues singer, that awful Bessie Smith" (here Hunter gets the laugh she aimed for) "was asked to record for Columbia. She requested this particular song for her first recording. . . . And I'm still collecting royalties." The royalties came courtesy of Lovie Austin's expertise with copyright and, seemingly, negotiating a fair deal with the big Tin Pan Alley firm Jack Mills. Thanks to Hunter, Austin, Smith, and Mills, "Down Hearted Blues" has taken on a status as the quintessential classic blues. This is the type denigrated by some as "vaudeville blues," but such pieces played an important role in the incorporation of blues into the spectrum of Tin Pan Alley styles.

"Down Hearted Blues" has flourished ever since. It enjoyed a raft of recordings around the turn from the 1930s to the 1940s. Hunter is captured on record revisiting the song in 1939, 1961, 1977, and filmed in live performances in 1981 and 1982. In the later twentieth century, "Down Hearted Blues" became *de rigeur* for any singer paying tribute to Bessie Smith (Linda Hopkins on stage, Queen Latifah on screen, and so forth). In addition, it seems every female singer appearing with a band with any pretensions to the labels of Dixieland, trad jazz, or New Orleans revival has to feature it.

Hunter and Austin precede their blues refrains with a typical Tin Pan Alley verse. This verse is almost always used (although one of the few exceptions is Hunter herself on her 1939 disc) and gives a distinct identity to what otherwise might feel like a generic set of blues stanzas. This introduction is such a distinctly separate part of the number that, taken together with Hunter's claim that she alone wrote the song, the possibility arises that Austin wrote the verse, while Hunter wrote the blues sections that follow.

For "Down Hearted Blues," Hunter wrote a set of six blues stanzas that are loosely related to each other. In performance, she knits together the lyrics through sheer force of personality. Her various performances are all quite distinct, each time selecting a different sequence of four or five units, omitting one or two, and after her comeback sometimes stitching in a couple of new options. The majority of singers follow her in shuffling the verses around, occasionally adding to them, sometimes in very creative ways; some others borrow the selection and sequence of the revered rendition by Bessie Smith.

Smith mostly follows the same sequence as Hunter's recording, dropping only the first of Hunter's blues stanzas. Yet Smith conjures up a compelling emotional trajectory that is unique and magical. The singer starts out dejected:

Trouble, trouble, I've had it all my days.

With the third stanza, however, Smith transitions into a fresh mood:

The day you quit me, honey, it's coming home to you!

She ends transformed with self-assertive confidence:

I've got the world in a jug, the stopper's in my hand.

In her interpretation of Hunter's stanzas, Smith offers a fitting example of the fluid possibilities of the blues to express and empower the female voice.

"SERENADE," FROM *THE STUDENT PRINCE* (1924)
Dorothy Donnelly (1876–1928), lyricist

Lyricist Dorothy Donnelly was born for the theater. Her mother and father were actors, then they became managers of one of the fanciest theaters in Manhattan; and her brother was also an actor, producer, and theater manager. Although the family was Roman Catholic—a group still much discriminated against—her connections were somewhat elite: a second brother was a New York judge and state senator, and her uncle was a dean at the American Academy of Dramatic Arts. Born in New York City, she also died there, of pneumonia in the first week of 1928, age fifty-one. Her last writing success, *My Maryland*, with its hit song "Silver Moon," was still running on Broadway.[12]

Donnelly herself became one of the glorious women stars of the first decades of the twentieth century, acclaimed for many roles including as the title character of George Bernard Shaw's *Candida*. In 1916, about when she would have been outgrowing leading lady parts, she dropped around the office of author's agent Mary Kirkpatrick and found her struggling to adapt a

Figure 2.1   Dorothy Donnelly, during her years as a starring theater actor. (Frederick Bushnell, J. Willis Sayre Collection of Theatrical Photographs, University of Washington Special Collections, via Wikimedia Commons. Public domain.)

comedy for American audiences. Donnelly began to issue forth such good suggestions that Kirkpatrick convinced the producer to hire her friend as a writer for what became *Flora Bella*. This led Donnelly to her career as a playwright and, in the 1920s, lyricist.

Her biggest venture writing and directing was *Poppy*, a 1923 musical comedy that consolidated the stardom of W. C. Fields. Nevertheless, Donnelly truly made her mark in the somewhat more highbrow subgenre of operetta that was entering into its own Golden Age in the United States from about 1910, marked particularly by the flourishing of composers Rudolf Friml and Sigmund Romberg. They were both adult immigrants from Central Europe and steeped in the grand traditions of Viennese operetta. To make the genre American, however, Yankee playwrights and lyricists had to adapt European sources and then learn to create their own models. In the 1920s, Donnelly rose to the forefront of these efforts.

She formed part of a team: the Shubert brothers, producers and theater chain owners, instigated the projects; Sigmund Romberg composed the music; and Donnelly adapted the materials. They triumphed together with *Blossom Time* (1921) and then *The Student Prince* (1924), helping to mark the peak years of American operetta. The latter is based on the German drama *Alt Heidelberg* and centers on Prince Karl, coming of age as the product of a cold, stifling court environment. His kindly tutor arranges for him to study incognito at Heidelberg University. There he finds relaxed, warmhearted, fun comradeship with his classmates and first love with his inn's waitress, Kathie. After an idyllic spring, Karl unexpectedly inherits the throne, thus losing both camaraderie and true love.

Donnelly and Romberg created a top score. Over the decades, "Serenade," with which Karl, supported by his fellow students, woos Kathie in song, proved the most popular. The other highlights run almost neck and neck with that piece in their appeal and enduring success: "Deep in My Heart, Dear," a waltz ballad that was the biggest hit at the time; a quintessential male chorus, "Drinking Song" ("Drink, drink, drink / To eyes that are bright as stars when they're shining on me"); and Kathie's saucy, jubilant number with the students, "Come, Boys." In two lyrics, Donnelly conjures a bittersweet view of life that cuts deep. In "Golden Days," the tutor reminisces about his youth when, unlike during his mature years, he "laughed with a gaiety that had no sting"—a line that can send shivers down the spine. In "Just We Two," sung at a ball by the secondary couple, who are equally ill-fated, the waltz tune is "singing of love's sweet pain," foreshadowing their eventually separation.

Cursed with a generic title that has been used countless times, "Serenade" nevertheless for forty years became the prime example of the clichéd moonlit pleading to the beloved to appear at the window. It was purveyed by every big-voiced tenor and baritone in an era when the classically trained vocal style was still part of popular culture. The tune was rarely jazzed up, but, during a little mini-revival in 1953, Nelson Riddle, Billy May, LeRoy Holmes, and Ralph Flanagan proved it could be swung as an instrumental. Donnelly's words, however, sing best with an operatic vocal style. Her images are the standard ones attached to romantic love:

Overhead, the moon is beaming,
White as blossoms on the bough.
Nothing is heard
But the song of a bird
Filling all the air with dreaming.

These fit nicely into the world of genteel refinement. Meanwhile the music hints at unruly passions that burst forth in the second half. Romberg's flowing melody, in ABCA′ form, builds up to a midpoint climax, and again at this conclusion:

Could my heart but still its beating!
Only you can tell it how,
Beloved.
From your window, give me greeting.
Oh, hear my eternal vow!

Full-throated singers can savor the open vowel of the first syllable, "Overhead," which is echoed later with "Only" and at the end line, "Oh, hear."

There follows an interlude, equally fine. During it, the hero soars above the supporting male chorus in a swooning counterpoint, as in this excerpt:

Chorus: Visions flowing, around me throng.
Karl: My soul, my hope, my life, my dear,
Your heart must tell you that I am near.
Lean from above, while I pour out my love.

Through refrain and interlude, Donnelly achieves variety in the timing of rhymes; some come close together, others farther apart. The higher-pitched second refrain ending intensifies the message, concluding, "*I swear my eternal vow!*" The words and music build to an intensity befitting the ardor of operetta. This represents the most European-influenced boundary of the Great American Songbook.

Mario Lanza recorded one of the most famous renditions of "Serenade" when he supplied the vocals for the 1954 movie version of *The Student*

Prince. Unfortunately, only Donnelly's first two refrain stanzas remained intact; Paul Francis Webster created substitutes for the rest to match the cinematic staging. Millions still listen to Donnelly and Romberg's rapturous work as sung by movie stars like Nelson Eddy or Gordon McRae; and, from Richard Tauber to Placido Domingo, a who's who of famous opera singers continue to "Serenade" listeners with Donnelly's lyrics.

"I KNOW THAT YOU KNOW" (1926)
Anne Caldwell (1867–1936), lyricist

Composer Vincent Youmans had a knack for building songs out of almost nothing, just one or two insistently repeated melodic ideas, which he then spiced up with interesting harmonies underneath. They were murderously difficult to set with lyrics. (As with most of his generation of Broadway composers, Youmans almost always composed the music first and then handed it to the lyricist, except for certain plot-specific or comedy numbers.) Even Oscar Hammerstein II was defeated, with posterity ignoring his collaborations with Youmans such as "Toodle-oo" and "The One Girl." All the more credit, then, to those lyricists who managed to create an enduring lyric to Youmans's mesmerizing musical pinwheels. Anne Caldwell was one of them.

Caldwell is the doyenne of the Great American Songbook, the eldest of the anthologized wits who made popular music sparkle with fun in the early twentieth century. She was one of the most prolific and prescient of musical comedy playwrights and lyricists of the 1910s and 1920s, yet at the start of the twenty-first century her biographical details remain sketchy. Reportedly, during her childhood in the Boston area of Massachusetts, she got started as a lyricist by improvising words as her mother played operatic music on the piano. Her early theater career was as a performer. When she broke her leg while on tour, she grabbed the opportunity to pursue writing magazine articles and lyrics. Her early marriage, in 1885, ended in widowhood (her first husband was killed in a gas explosion in 1897), leaving her as the single mother of an eleven-year-old daughter. In the summer of 1904, she married James O'Dea, six years her senior, a lyricist and occasional composer. They collaborated as playwrights and songsmiths, slowly infiltrating the world of big-time Broadway theater. They finally won a major success in 1914 with the hit *Chin Chin*. Sadly, before it could open on Broadway, O'Dea died of pneumonia, leaving Caldwell this time in sole support of a teenage foster son whom she later adopted. Caldwell's solo writing career hit its stride from 1917 onward, writing and cowriting the lyrics and usually the scripts for a series of musical comedies with music by Ivan Caryll, Raymond Hubbell, and, most famously, Jerome Kern.

Many of Caldwell's earlier lyrics can still delight with their frothy, saucy stance, but others now seem stilted or trite. It was when Caldwell partnered with Kern that she most fully tuned into the era's development of a new slangy style, producing lyrics that forecast the accomplishments of her younger colleagues like Lorenz Hart. Caldwell and Kern numbers of the early 1920s, such as "Once in Blue Moon," "Raggedy Ann," and "The Left-All-Alone-Again Blues," are still treasured as musical theater and cabaret gems. Nevertheless, "I Know That You Know" remains Caldwell's best-known lyric. It is from her only collaboration with Youmans, the short-lived flop *Oh, Please*, which premiered on New Year's Eve, 1926.

Most often done as a fast-tempo jazz instrumental, nevertheless "I Know That You Know" has enjoyed vocals by some of the best, notably Nat King Cole (twice) and Doris Day (on both film and disc).[13] Although "Tea for Two" is Youmans's most famous song, "I Know That You Know" is perhaps his most quintessential tune. The sweet verse (done only occasionally) is in AABA form, and the famous refrain is ABA′C. The nugget of the melody is a series of "short-LONG-short" three-note units. This Caldwell sets with "that-YOU-know / that-I'LL-go" and so on, through twelve measures. Remarkably, Caldwell adds to the tremendous rhythmic momentum, including through the unusual technique of never repeating the opening title phrase:

I know
That you know
That I'll go
Where you go.
I choose you,
Won't lose you.

Finally, at the end of the B-section, Youmans throws in idea number two: an ascending scale followed by a series of lively jumping intervals. To these asymmetrical phrases, Caldwell fits a brief impassioned cry:

I wish you knew how much I long to
Hold you
In my
Arms!

Figure 2.2   Anne Caldwell, 1922, looking right up to date. (Genthe photograph collection, Library of Congress, Prints and Photographs Division. Public domain.)

These lines mark the point where Caldwell shifts the focus of the lyric. From general statements, the protagonist now more clearly describes the situation of an innocent nocturnal tryst:

This time
Is my time.

'Twill soon be
Goodbye time.
Then in the starlight,
Hold me tight.
With one more little kiss say nighty-night!

Youmans ends with another upward run, which Caldwell mates with an almost baby-talking, love-talking plea. It is a daring, almost flippant way to end the declaration of love, rocketing and disappearing like a meteor.

The fit between words and music fails at the penultimate line: Caldwell sets it as "hold ME tight," an awkward emphasis. Almost all singers rewrite the rhythm to make the words flow more naturally: "HOLD me tight." Except for that line, it is hard to imagine anyone finding a better match for the thoroughly American driving force of Youmans's tune. The style here is suspended between the refined aura of Donnelly's "Serenade" and the colloquial groove of "Sugar Blues" and "Down Hearted Blues." Caldwell and her younger colleagues achieved this point of balance, marking the advent of the core mode of the Great American Songbook.

After *Oh, Please*, Caldwell succeeded with several further Broadway musicals. Then she moved to Hollywood to work on a few screenplays and write some lyrics before her death in 1936 but did not create any further hit songs. Yet few of her generation managed to capture so well the youthful energy of the Jazz Age as she did with "I Know That You Know."

"BACK-WATER BLUES" (1927)
Bessie Smith (1892–1937), composer-lyricist

"The best blues singer in the whole world, barring none," so Bessie Smith was called by her peers in the 1920s.[14] Her career touring theaters, in vaudeville, or with her own forty-person troupe, a brief spot on Broadway, and especially a thriving recording career from 1923 through 1931, spread her fame across the nation. Smith was called the Empress of the Blues, the ruler among royalty.

Born in Tennessee, Smith and her six siblings were orphaned when Bessie was about eight. The performing career of older brother Clarence inspired her own efforts, starting with street performing and, by 1909, in vaudeville. By 1911, she had won star billing, taking "the house by storm." By 1913, the newly crystallized blues genre was spreading throughout Southern Black vaudeville, and Smith was in the vanguard, setting "the house crazy" singing "The Blues (But I'm Too Blamed Mean to Cry)." Gene Jones describes her contralto voice "as rich and powerful as a church organ, as pliant as a cello," and her Black contemporaries wrote about her "profoundly affecting . . . soulfulness," "that peculiar strain and quality" in her voice "that only is known to our people, and which makes for what is now called blues singing. . . . You must have that feeling, and Bessie Smith has got it." Even latter-day fans of the male guitar-playing, down-home blues musicians—fans who snobbishly dismiss women who only sang and did not play the blues—usually make an exception for Bessie Smith.[15]

In 1926, as New Year's Eve approached, Smith was in her home state heading by train to Nashville as the rains poured down, and the countryside began to flood. The flood proved to be a record breaker. The troupe was picked up by boats that conveyed them through the swamped streets to the undertaker parlor next to the theater, where they were given housing during the emergency. The other refugees begged Smith to stay and sing "The Back-Water Blues," but she did not know a song by that name. Once she got back to her home in Philadelphia, however, she wrote one.

On February 17, 1927, Smith went into the recording studio and recorded her seven-stanza "Back-Water Blues," accompanied on piano by James P. Johnson. A month later, on March 16, the copyright office received Smith's deposit copy, as an unpublished work. The recording was released on March 20, revealing Smith at her peak, her voice relaxed and rich as homemade bread dripping with butter.

In April, the previous season's floods in Nashville and elsewhere in the nation's central river system proved to be merely the opening act for the Great Mississippi Flood of 1927, the worst in US history. The deluge covered twenty-seven thousand square miles in up to thirty feet of water. Smith's piece seemed clairvoyant, and her disc (along with at least eighteen blues along the same lines by other singers), was snapped up by those who lived through those hard times.

David Evans reports, of "Back-Water Blues," that "it is probably Bessie Smith's most enduring and most covered song, which automatically makes it one of the best known of all blues songs, in a league with classics like 'St. Louis Blues.'"[16] James P. Johnson supplied one of the most powerful accompaniments of the era—stormy, evocative, swinging, keeping the momentum going, not fast but inexorable. (Johnson made a 1939 disc, accompanying Ruby Smith, niece of Bessie, and the label lists the pianist as sole composer, but the copyright registration and anecdotal evidence would belie his authorship.)

Figure 2.3 Bessie Smith, songwriter and Empress of the Blues, in the 1930s.
(Library of Congress, Prints & Photographs Division, Carl Van Vechten Collection.)

"Back-Water Blues" is a quintessential blues. Unlike "Sugar Blues," this piece uses the classic twelve-bar length; and unlike "Down Hearted Blues," there is no Tin Pan Alley–type verse to dilute the form. Each stanza is in pristine AAB structure, with the traditional form: each line has a half-break in the middle and a two-bar gap in the vocal part at the end. The melody arches up in the first half, in a passionate opening gesture; and its slow descent, as if in sober seriousness at the disastrous events, spans the second half of the line. The first stanza illustrates:

When it rained five days, [half-break] and the skies turned dark as night, [gap]
When it rained five days, [half-break] and the skies turned dark as night, [gap]
Then trouble taking place, [half-break] in the lowlands at night. [gap]

One of the most vivid images comes with the fifth stanza:

Then I went and stood, upon some high old lonesome hill. (*repeat*)
Then I looked down on the house, where I used to live.

Smith creates a fascinating dynamic between the large and the small, the objective and the subjective—the panoramic landscape and the poignant loss of one small home. Smith, in her recording, then varies the pattern, stretching out the word "blues": "That's why the bluuuues, done cause me to pack my things and go." In the end, the singer expresses a catatonic despair that defeats words, as she moans, "Mmmm, I can't move no more." The description of the flood, the devastation, is literally elemental. It also implies a poignant societal situation: the houses roosting in the vulnerable lowlands, the poverty, the thousands affected.

"Back-Water Blues" was championed by Dinah Washington, a Queen of the Blues who also excelled at jazz and pop, and a line of younger jazz singers after her. Among the jazz subgenres, Dixieland, Chicago jazz, and even avant-garde jazz has employed it.[17] Primarily, it has found a place in blues repertoires—big band blues, down-home blues, folk blues, acoustic blues, electronic blues, rhythm-and-blues, and blues rock—glam rock, progressive rock, and Krautrock. The increased worldwide experience of flooding due to climate change makes it likely that Bessie Smith's "Back-Water Blues" will continue to speak to audiences well into the twenty-first century.

"STRUTTIN' WITH SOME BARBECUE" (1927/1955)
Lil Hardin Armstrong (1898–1971), composer

Lil Hardin Armstrong was the pianist and often the composer and bandleader on some of the most revered 1920s jazz recordings. She went on to expand even further in a series of 1930s records for the Decca label, swinging with authority, revealing herself to be a fine singer and pop song-smith. Yet writers—even her own biographers—tend to focus more on her role as the wife of trumpeter Louis Armstrong, who is seen by many as the central figure in jazz history. Her most recorded composition is "Struttin' with Some Barbecue." Its history illustrates how hard it is to disentangle her reputation from that of her ex-husband.

Lil Hardin was raised by her mother and grandmother, first in Tennessee, then in Chicago. These strictly religious women scorned popular music as "vulgar" and tried at each step to limit the young pianist's journey into jazz. Eventually, Mrs. Hardin permitted young Lillian to buy sheet music for "Alexander's Ragtime Band," but when she found her daughter had a copy of "St. Louis Blues," she beat her with a broomstick. In her maturity Armstrong would say, "I was born to swing, that's all. Call it what you want, blues, swing, jazz, it caught hold of me way back in Memphis and it looks like it won't ever let go."[18]

Armstrong's talent was such that she was in demand by jazz bands even before she reached legal adulthood at twenty-one. Her long-standing job in Chicago with Joe Oliver led to her first recording dates. For two years, starting when Louis Armstrong joined the band in 1922, Lil and Louis slowly courted, then married in 1924. His extramarital relations started within a year, and yet the bond was close and they cohabitated to 1931, not divorcing until 1938. Meanwhile, she managed, promoted, goaded, flattered, pushed, and pulled him into being a famous soloist and bandleader. Among the many historic recording dates on which they collaborated was December 9, 1927, one in a long series released under the studio group name Louis Armstrong and His Hot Five. They waxed "Struttin' with Some Barbecue" by Lil, and it was the third-from-last recording Lil and Louis made together. Years later she reported she "didn't know it was going to be important," because at that time "you wouldn't even bother to write the songs you were going to play until you got to the studio." In the African American slang of the time, "barbecue" was a beautiful girlfriend, with whom a fellow might well be expected to strut proudly.

Consolidated Music, of Chicago, sent in a copyright registration for Lil's title, as an instrumental piece, in early July 1928. In 1938, Louis rerecorded the piece with his large band of the time, and he featured it on radio during this era. In 1947, he shifted from his long-standing big band setting to a small-group Dixieland ensemble. "Barbecue" became one of his most performed staples from then on.

The timing was right. A revival of ragtime and early jazz style and repertoire had been spearheaded in California in the early 1940s, and by a decade later had become a major vogue. Lil Armstrong's "Struttin' with Some Barbecue" rose back into prominence with it.[19] A number of instrumentals from the early jazz era were set with new words: from "Twelfth Street Rag" by Andy Razaf (1942) to "At the Jazz Band Ball" by Johnny Mercer (1960). In 1955, Don Raye put words to Lil Armstrong's tune, and "Struttin' with Some Barbecue" as a vocal composition was introduced as a duet by Gary Crosby and Louis Armstrong on a single. By that time, the slangy reference to parading with one's sweetheart was outdated. Instead, as often when a lyricist sets a famous melody, Raye's version is self-referential; it celebrates not just eating spare ribs but also the joys of hearing Dixieland jazz. The lyric rolls along happily. True, there are some touches that singers clearly feel the need to improve, but at least Raye created a useful scaffold for these performers' own variations.

It is odd that it took nearly thirty years for "Struttin' with Some Barbecue" to be published with lyrics, for Lil Armstrong's melody seems to beg for words. The form is that of a typical Tin Pan Alley piece, ABA'C. The first seven notes perfectly fit the title words. The tune is strong, singable, and memorable. The main strain is particularly wonderful: a jubilant, triumphant flourish of five ascending notes and then the repetition of the top note. Helped by a wonderful break at the end of the B-section, the momentum throughout is unstoppable—strutting, indeed. The listener can feel the sense of being a champion, which is exactly the image that Lil wanted to promote for her Louis.

Lil Armstrong renewed the copyright in 1955, but in 1958 there arose a dispute about to which Tin Pan Alley firm she had assigned the rights. Both International Music (the firm of Louis's manager Joe Glaser) and Leeds Music claimed that Lil had given them the tune, which, as *Variety* reported, "has been credited to both Louis Armstrong and his former wife, Lil Hardin, singly and together. . . . In a large number of recordings made on the song, both received credit at one time or another." In the case of the Gary Crosby–Louis Armstrong duet that premiered Raye's new lyric, the label credits authorship to "Louis Armstrong." The work fit Armstrong so well that he had taken it over. Nevertheless, slowly, over the next fifty years, the world has learned to acknowledge Lil Hardin Armstrong for her brilliance in composing this signature rhythm tune.[20]

Although "Struttin' with Some Barbecue" is Lil Armstrong's most recorded melody, about twenty of her other 1920s instrumentals and blues have become standards in the revival of early jazz style. Her 1930s Decca discs include neglected gems: the almost-protest song "(I'm on a) Sit-Down Strike for Rhythm" (1937), torch numbers "Bluer Than Blue" (1937) and "My Secret Flame" (1940), et cetera. Two tunes found enduring success. "Brown Gal" (1936), with lyrics by famed entertainer-lyricist Avon Long, became Lil's theme song. It got transformed into "Brown Boy" and then

"Bad Boy," a 1957 hit for the Jive Bombers that is a rock-and-roll standard. "Just for a Thrill" (1936), with a lyric credited at various times to Armstrong, Long, or Don Raye, became a 1960 hit for Ray Charles. With this revival, he made it into a standard.

Louis Armstrong died on July 6, 1971. Less than two months later, on August 27, Lil Armstrong was in Chicago performing at a memorial concert for her ex-husband. She was playing "St. Louis Blues," the song her mother had beat her for liking, when she had a heart attack. The jazz great died right there on the piano bench, swinging to the last possible instant.

3

"CAN'T WE BE FRIENDS" (1929)

Kay Swift (1897–1993), composer

In October 1987, in the middle of her ninetieth year, Kay Swift finally had a concert devoted entirely to her own compositions. The 449-seat Merkin Concert Hall, near Lincoln Center in New York City, was packed with celebrities, fans, friends, family, and colleagues. Ann Ronell ("Willow Weep for Me") was on the planning committee. The program focused on Swift's popular songs but also included samples of her chamber music and ballet scores. The composer, dressed in a chic, red, carefully tailored evening gown, played two of her most recent piano pieces. Then Burton Lane ("Ol' Devil Moon") awarded her a citation from ASCAP for her fifty-six years of membership. The evening was a belated celebration of the accomplishments of Swift's music-loving, hardworking career.

BIOGRAPHY

Katherine "Kay" Faulkner Swift led a colorful life that is well documented. She is the subject of one scholarly biography, a large chunk of her grand-daughter's family memoir, major passages in the autobiography of her first husband, and she plays a role in various other show business biographies. Her mother and father (a poor but prominent music critic) relished playing through opera scores on the family piano. By the age of six, Swift was already composing music "of form and coherence" and memorizing the music dramas of Wagner. Later, she studied composition with Percy Goetschius, the grandfather of future songsmith Marjorie Goetschius ("I Dream of You"), at the school now known as Julliard. She then married into a family that had helped found that conservatory, the Warburgs. Her husband, James "Jimmy" Paul Warburg, quickly blossomed in his family business of international banking, eventually influencing economic policies nationally and around the globe. A typical afternoon at the Warburg home might include the playing of Mozart trios with Swift at the piano and Albert Einstein on violin.[1]

Swift went on to have a famous lover in composer George Gershwin—an affair that led to her divorce from Warburg. After Gershwin's death in 1937, Swift had several other lovers and two more husbands: a tall, hefty rancher from Oregon; and then a charming show biz underachiever. Professionally, during these decades, she published a well-received autobiographical novel (based on her life with the rancher), wrote radio scripts, scored two successful Broadway productions, and composed one seminal Balanchine ballet, special occasion shows, theatrical incidental pieces, and a smattering of chamber works. Overall Swift wrote music and/or lyrics for over a hundred popular songs of which eighteen were published and four became hits.

Gershwin was a galvanizing force in Swift's life. He first came to her parties in 1925, and by mid-1926 they were good chums. He convinced her to change her moniker from Katherine to the nickname Kay. By then Gershwin was already successfully straddling the worlds of concert music (with his widely loved 1924 *Rhapsody in Blue*) and pop music (with his many Broadway scores). Swift taught him to master horseback riding, and Gershwin taught her to embrace the jazzy songs of Tin Pan Alley. Together they poured over the *crème de la crème*, such as Irving Berlin's freewheeling rhythm song "At the Devil's Ball" (1912) and Hoagy Carmichael's folksy, aria-like "Washboard Blues" (1926).

Swift joined the musicians union, became a Broadway rehearsal pianist, and began churning out pop melodies, haunting Tin Pan Alley publishers to no avail. Her husband, Jimmy, took up the challenge of being her lyricist. The banker was already a published poet with a yen for a writing career. Collaborating with Kay was also Jimmy's strategy to stay at the center of her new interests even while her romance with Gershwin deepened and intensified. Kay and Jimmy finally placed two songs in a short-lived Broadway musical in the fall of 1928. For these pop song efforts, Warburg took on the pseudonym Paul James, by reversing his first and middle names.

Figure 3.1   Kay Swift, composer, with her lyricist (and then-husband) Paul James, 1930. (Vandamm Theatrical Photographs, Bill Rose Theatre Collection, New York Public Library.)

Swift and James hit the peak of their songwriting careers as the 1920s turned into the 1930s. They got "Can't We Be Friends" placed in a 1929 revue, *The Little Show*. That success was swiftly followed by a full Broadway score in 1930, *Fine and Dandy*, featuring eight published numbers. The popular ballad in the musical comedy was "Can This Be Love." The rousing title song was an even bigger hit that also became an enduring standard, still used in the early twenty-first century as a curtain-raising instrumental for variety shows. "Fine and Dandy" runs neck and neck as a standard with "Can't We Be Friends," but the latter is the more emotionally complex song.

"CAN'T WE BE FRIENDS"

Early in 1929, Swift was striving to get songs published or placed in shows. Her friend, singer Libby Holman, had been rising in Broadway show business with painful slowness but was now cast in a new revue, *The Little Show*. The production would start a new trend, away from lavish spectacle and toward wit and sophistication. In her singing and image, Holman captured a sensuality that managed to be at once exotic, brooding, and cheerful. Her deep voice and jazzy, idiosyncratic phrasing, embellished with a subtle gulping effect, were considered quirky and cutting edge. When Swift played the singer a new melody, Holman was eager to include it in the upcoming revue.

To his wife's easily moving, evocative melody, James set one verse stanza and two refrains of lyrics—probably his finest effort. The protagonist of "Can't We Be Friends" is caught at the moment when she realizes her love affair is about to end, not with a bang but a whimper. Her sweetheart is going to ask that they be just friends. In this lyric, James skillfully mixes deflation with anger and defiance: "Never again!" the singer exclaims. The protagonist is sad and resigned yet also nonchalant: "Why should I care?" A wry, self-mocking attitude is expressed in slangy expressions like "What a bust!" James consolidates a new modern attitude toward the breakup of a romance. It is therefore intensely ironic that he severed from his own wife, the composer of his song, in one of the famous divorces of Tin Pan Alley history.

Journalist Josephine M. Bennett described how Holman "stopped the show with her flaming, sensuous singing." On stage, the center curtain parted just enough to frame Holman, spotlit in a cherry-pink evening gown. The star was a virtuosa of restraint: "She does not give all of herself at once and never uses the same gesture twice. . . . When she enters . . . her hands are clasped behind her. . . . Gradually she brings up her hands and her voice until, at the finish, she has thrilled and worked her audience, . . . into a madness of emotion."[2] This song and the other hit from the show, "Moanin' Low," made Holman a star. Soon she was hopping after curtain bows to a nightclub, where she mesmerized her audiences with the same smash pair of numbers. In September, Holman waxed a hit record of "Friends." The same month, Bing Crosby used it for his debut solo disc.

Holman and Crosby were among the first performers to be promoted with two new labels: "crooner" (for the intimacy of their approach) and "torch singer" (singing about the flame of love). "Friends" thereby became one of the earliest entries in the "torch song" category of ditties about romantic longings.

"Can't We Be Friends" is the first song examined in this book that features an AABA refrain—a structure that became one of the glories of the Great American Songbook. This pattern became the most common form in 1924 and was soon crystallized into a modern design, streamlined to match the art deco settings in which it first flourished. With "Friends," Swift made a major contribution to the development of that form. Two music writers critique Swift's music, Alec Wilder and her biographer Vicki Ohl. They miss out, however, on how innovative Swift was in designing her melody.

Wilder valued an elusive theatrical refinement. He writes how he "hates to say this," but he feels Swift's tune has "no theatrical flavor" and "has all the earmarks of a pop song"—which he considers a disgrace for a tune introduced on the Broadway stage. He also reveals another of his aesthetic criteria when he includes "Can't We Be Friends" among the majority of songs by white writers of the 1920s that "don't show a great deal of reaction to the increasingly new sounds emerging from jazz bands, dance orchestras, piano players, and blues singers." Wilder feels "Friends" is only "better than average," not truly great, probably "due to notiness or to its verging on cliché." Wilder admits, however, that the verse is "inventive" and that Swift does some "nice things" in the main strain's second and third phrases— "the drop to *d flat* in the third measure" on the exclamation "What a laugh!" and "the run down in the next measure to a low *d flat*" at "This is how the story ends." This is one instance where one might suspect that Wilder's inconsistency about the tune is caused by an unconscious prejudice against women composers.[3]

Ohl hits closer to the mark. She emphasizes more strongly how creative Swift is in handling the Tin Pan Alley conventions of her time: "a winding, meandering line, the melody is highlighted by chromatic inflections and several well-placed skips." Ohl goes on: "The rhythm exhibits moderate syncopation and irregular phrasing to avoid the predictability that Swift so disliked."[4]

The miracle that Swift achieves in her refrain is that, in both the A and B strains, she spans eight measures but never repeats. Her male peers, in their AABA refrains, state a motif and then depend on repetition or near imitation, often moving the phrase higher or lower. So Gershwin does with "Someone to Watch Over Me" (1926), Rodgers with "My Heart Stood

Still" (1927), and Kern with "Can't Help Lovin' That Man" (1927). In "Friends," Swift is far less predictable. Admittedly, she ends two phrases with little chromatic slides, three notes moving down by half-steps. Nevertheless, in all other respects those phrases are so different that this shared trait hardly registers as a repetition. In James's lyric, the protagonist is surprised by the outcome of a romance; fittingly, Swift creates surprise after surprise in her melody.

Innovative and cutting edge for 1929, Swift unfolds what Ohl calls her "meandering line" and "irregular phrasing" as if improvising a jazz solo. In this, she helped to pioneer a kind of compact melodic complexity that would also famously be accomplished by her male peers, such as Carmichael in "Star Dust" (also 1929) and Harold Arlen in "Stormy Weather" (1933). No wonder hundreds of jazz musicians, from Benny Goodman to Jamie Cullum and beyond, have relished Swift's melody. The tune's liquid flow works particularly well on saxophone, and renditions by Sonny Stitt, Benny Carter, Lester Young, Illinois Jacquet, and Houston Person are among the best. Playing it almost as written is enough to create a memorable moment of jazz; their brilliant variations are icing on the cake.

If Swift's main strain is jazz club, her release is Broadway. Because, contrary to Wilder's opinion, the melody of the bridge *is* theatrical. Even in instrumental versions, the drama is clear in its first ascending four-notes, on "Why should I care?"

"Can't We Be Friends" never faded from the repertoire of standards. Nevertheless, its currency subsided somewhat during World War II, when pop culture was split between the dichotomy of hearty morale building and *film noir* bleakness. Jazz musicians resuscitated "Friends" in the early 1950s, along with a new recording from Libby Holman, and the song hit its glory period as the LP format came in.[5] Following their lead, Frank Sinatra included it on his groundbreaking, top-charting 1955 album of torch ballads, *In the Wee Small Hours*. In keeping with the melancholy of this early concept album, Sinatra sings it as the sheet music directs: "Slowly and with much expression." He's especially good in the dramatic verse, and his softly musing refrains are also fine.

A particular champion of "Can't We Be Friends" was the producer Norman Granz. He steered discs of Swift's ditty by Benny Carter, Jane Powell, Woody Herman, and Anita O'Day. In Granz's first teaming of Ella Fitzgerald and Louis Armstrong, each takes one refrain, and it becomes like a conversation over cocktails of two friends relating similar experiences. The result: a best-selling album. Then, a scant three years later, Granz has Ella Fitzgerald essay "Friends" again, solo. Fitzgerald, with and without

Armstrong, takes the ditty at a lively medium-fast tempo. Some singers actually throw in a laugh during their rendition. Fitzgerald doesn't go that far but conveys the protagonist's matter-of-fact insight, regret alleviated by humor. Sinatra dwells on depression; Fitzgerald highlights resilience.

Swift and James were on the cutting edge in creating the "voice" of an era, the urbane sophisticate. F. Scott Fitzgerald creates these kinds of characters in his 1931 short story "A New Leaf," wherein the heroine sings "Can't We Be Friends" to the hero as he (temporarily) withdraws from alcohol dependence. Such dreamers are cultured, literate yet slangy, gallant in the face of deeply felt suffering, and humorously self-aware. They are able to mock their own ecstasy and suffering, exemplified in James's "What a laugh!" phrase that goes so well with Swift's mordant drop down to the *d* flat, the hallmark of the main strain. Just such jaded romantics would become the lead characters in the most treasured Hollywood screwball romantic comedies of the 1930s as well as in a host of the best songs of the upcoming dozen years.

Both Swift and Warburg were themselves that sort of cosmopolitan sophisticate. The lyricist-banker bitterly chastised his second wife for humming "Can't We Be Friends" on their honeymoon, accusing her of taunting him. Yet by the mid-1950s the sting perhaps was healed, for at that time he permanently gave Swift his half of the royalties to the song.

Swift went on to devote herself to the music of Gershwin. She tagged along to his composition lessons and took notes for him. She helped write down his opera *Porgy and Bess* and assisted in its first production without credit. A marriage between Swift and Gershwin was probably mainly prevented by the disapproval of his mother (who did not want a Gentile to marry into their Jewish family) and his bogus psychoanalyst (who grossly manipulated Gershwin, Swift, Warburg, and many in their circle). After his death, Swift always spoke of Gershwin as if she were his widow. She devoted years of her life to resuscitating his unpublished melodies.

Swift also produced her own works, but few entered Tin Pan Alley repertoire. For eighteen months, she and lyricist Al Stillman churned out weekly production music for the Radio City Music Hall. The result for posterity: one publication, "Sawing a Woman in Half," long a staple at the conventions of professional magicians. Her foray as a songwriter in Hollywood for *Never a Dull Moment* (1950) produced one hit ballad, the catchy but uncharacteristically bland "Once You Find Your Guy," for which she wrote her own lyrics. She penned song tunes, lyrics, and instrumental pieces for the successful 1952 one-woman Broadway show of Cornelia Otis Skinner, *Paris '90*, which evoked the City of Lights during the Toulouse Lautrec era. "Calliope," a sweeping, sophisticated waltz, was the take-home ditty. It was published but never widely popularized. Her opuses for two World Fairs and for corporate, community, school, and civic occasions—those few for which scores survive—remain specialist items for Swift fans.

To her last years, Swift remained elegant, vibrant—and composing. At her 1987 concert she performed one of her most recent compositions. At the end of that triumphant evening, she was seen on the curbside, hailing a cab to take her back to her Manhattan apartment, all alone and independent as ever.

Kay Swift's prominent songs
1929: "Can't We Be Friends," lyrics by Paul James
1930: "Fine and Dandy," lyrics by Paul James
1930: "Can This Be Love," lyrics by Paul James
1935: "Sawing a Woman in Half," lyrics by Al Stillman
1950: "Once You Find Your Guy," lyrics by Swift

Some neglected gems
1930: "Up Among the Chimney Pots," lyrics by Paul James; groovy charm song
1930: "Rich or Poor," lyrics by Paul James; sparkling charm song
1930: "Let's Go Eat Worms in the Garden," lyrics by Paul James; jazzy and edged with humor
1950: "Some of the Time I'll Miss You," lyrics by Swift; jagged, sprightly love song
1952: "Calliope," lyrics by Swift; buoyant yet thoughtful waltz

4

"IT HAPPENED IN MONTEREY" (1929)

Mabel Wayne (1890–1978), composer

It was 1925 and Mabel Wayne was age thirty-five when she got reborn as a Tin Pan Alley composer. She was older than most novice songsmiths, but with great élan she simply shaved fourteen years off her age and reinvented herself as a twenty-one year old. For the next three decades, she created well over a hundred songs, with an average of one hit a year, including six enduring standards. Wayne was versatile and adapted to changes in the popular music scene, yet her musical imprint is as definite and firmly etched as any of her more celebrated male peers. Although in her heyday she was covered by the press, her private personality is elusive. The composer is only revealed in small shafts of light shed by the briefest of journalistic entries and the most superficial of interviews. Piecing together shards of information, some of which may not be accurate, a possible outline of Wayne's life emerges.

BIOGRAPHY

Wayne was born in Brooklyn in 1890 to German immigrant parents (the Wimpfheimers). Her ASCAP biographical entry claims that while on a European jaunt with her aunt she trained in classical voice in Switzerland and then went on to study at the New York School of Music. In 1911 and 1912, trade journals reveal that she was active in vaudeville and touring troupes, performing a "pianologue" (a piano playing act, often with spoken patter and bits of singing thrown in). Publicity materials unveil a million-dollar smile, a glorious mane of red hair (later she went blonde), and broad facial features atop a big-boned physique. In June 1912, she married Charles Julian Haas, a manager-salesman from Virginia with an eighth-grade education and, like Mabel, the child of German immigrants. Wayne's occupation in the 1915 census? "Housework."

But, in 1921, Wayne was again in vaudeville, popping in and out of trade journal notices. In 1928, she divorced Charles Haas (who was now going under the last name Harrison). The background for their separation was that, in 1924, Wayne had begun living with a married man, lawyer Benjamin Shiverts. In 1929, Shiverts's wife filed for divorce and also sued Wayne for $100,000 for alienating the affections of her husband.

In July 1933, Wayne and Shiverts were in a car collision with an armored truck. Tragically, a mother strolling with a baby carriage was passing by; while the baby was unharmed, the mother was killed, along with the truck driver. This fatal event seems not to have ended their intimacy, however, for as late as 1936 Shiverts was still acting as Wayne's lawyer.

It was fairly soon after leaving Haas/Harrison and starting the affair with Shiverts that Wayne broke into professional songwriting. In 1925, the Feist publishing house registered Wayne's first copyright, a co-composition with Abel Baer, with lyrics by L. Wolfe Gilbert. Their waltz "Don't Wake Me Up (Let Me Dream)" was a hit—fortuitously, for this "quick click" launched Wayne's Tin Pan Alley career. Feist executive Phil Kornheiser supported Wayne's rise in the company's ranks to the point where she was given an exclusive three-year contract. By the time that agreement expired in mid-1932, Kornheiser had started his own firm, and Wayne immediately placed her next song with him—an affirmation of their mutual loyalty.

Decades later, Wayne spun this story: with her profit from "Don't Wake Me Up," she took a vacation to Southern California. There "she fell under the spell of the old Spanish missions and . . . Indian villages." On her return to Manhattan, she "translated the charm of the American Southwest into music," writing the Latin-tinged waltz "In a Little Spanish Town ('Twas on a Night Like This)" with words by Sam Lewis and Joe E. Young. In 1926, Feist sold a million copies of its sheet music.

"In a Little Spanish Town" established one of Wayne's most idiosyncratic characteristics, which she could manifest in either triple or duple meters. She pours forth cascades of short notes. They are sometimes contrasted with longer notes or more sedately undulating passages. Overall, the effect is like the sinuous swaying and then crack of a whip—or the restless wagging of the tail of a lioness.

In the late 1920s Wayne struck gold with a series of these waltzes with lyrics telling of romance in Latinx regions. "In a Little Spanish Town" was followed by Wayne's most legendary success, "Ramona" (1927). The composer reportedly created it in twenty minutes to convince a room full of Hollywood bigwigs that a catchy theme song would boost the success of the silent film of the same name. The hardheaded businessmen left the meeting singing the tune.

Figure 4.1   Mabel Wayne, composer, in the 1920s. This lioness had a mane. (Photo courtesy of Peter Mintun.)

"Ramona" went on to be the biggest hit of 1928, selling over a million sheet copies remarkably quickly and giving Wayne and her lyricist L. Wolfe Gilbert the biggest single royalty check Tin Pan Alley ever issued, a hundred thousand dollars, two-thirds of which went to Wayne as the composer. (Her share would have equaled over a million dollars in early twenty-first-century currency.) "Chiquita" (1928) followed, also a big hit though not an enduring standard, and then "It Happened in Monterey" (1929).

Through decades, Wayne collaborated with her various lyricists on songs that purveyed Tin Pan Alley stereotypes of escapist exoticism, whether of Italy, France, Hawaii, or a mythic Arcady. Especially, she continued her vein of songs about Spain, Latin America, or the Southwest in the United States, with a dozen pieces from "Indian Cradle Song" (1927) to "All the Way from San Jose" (1948). Most of these were successes, though none on the scale of her big three: "Spanish Town," "Ramona," and "Monterey."

Whatever topic her lyricists chose, Wayne delivered strong, solid melodies. Surveying dozens of her plug tunes from 1925 through 1954, the listener may well respond, "Oh, that's a good melody . . . and *that's* a good melody, but in a completely different style . . . and there's *another* good melody, and *another*, and *another!*" And on and on. Among women composers who were situated at the center of Tin Pan Alley, none attained a career longer, more productive, or more successful than Mabel Wayne.[1]

What is jazz? The definitions and corpus have changed at times—and especially in the mid-1930s. In the mainstream view of the 1920s, to write a fox-trot was to write jazz, and women composers were acknowledged to be "strong for waltzes" but denigrated as being "weak on fox-trots." (Wayne's Black peers, such as Lovie Austin and Lil Hardin Armstrong, wrote great jazz tunes but were not Alley insiders.) Wayne fought being pigeonholed as a waltz writer. The composer bragged that she was not "afraid to let go and put the emotional kick that jazz requires" and was "satisfying a personal vanity" in having her fox-trot melodies published. At the point when Feist signed Wayne as a house composer, *Variety* noted that "not only is Miss Wayne the first femme contract writer in the pop field, but she is disproving the idea about femme composers in also being able to write jazz tunes" rather than just waltzes.[2]

The perspective of time reveals that Wayne could write pointed, punctuated tunes like "Ragamuffin Romeo" (1930) in a genre made famous by Zez Confrey and others like Vee Lawnhurst ("Accent on Youth") and Muriel Pollock. Wayne's own piano playing was probably in this style, which historians like Dave A. Jasen later would categorize as a form of late ragtime. Also, Wayne could write fox-trot melodies like "Indian Cradle Song" that were embraced by hot jazz musicians like Louis Armstrong. Nevertheless, Wayne proved most comfortable with genres prevalent during the era of her maturation, the 1910s: waltzes, tangos, and tunes compatible with the soft-shoe dance.

Wayne developed a knack with the easily moving soft-shoe type of melody starting with her 1934 standard, "Little Man, You've Had a Busy Day." This became her second characteristic style. Two of her biggest 1940s hits convey that kind of pattering ripple: "Why Don't You Fall in Love with Me" (1942) and "A Dreamer's Holiday" (1949).

Wayne's most characteristic melodies tend to be a bit notey, but with "Be Fair," a moderate hit of 1941, she proved she could find success with a less cluttered style. Here she is more sparing in her use of notes and conveys a greater sense of spaciousness. Near the end of her run of hits, she returned to the waltz with the sweeping "On the Outgoing Tide" (1950) and "So Madly in Love" (1952).

In her final plug tunes, Wayne proved that she could convincingly compose for the youth market of the 1950s. "Goodbye, Au Revoir, Adios" (1953), as sung by Johnnie Ray, foreshadowed many aspects of rock-and-roll. Wayne followed up with "Rock and Roll to Heaven" (1956). She then captured the new "Brill Building sound" with "On the Wings of the Wind" (1957). These songs were not hits, but considering that Wayne's first success was in 1925, they are remarkable stylistic achievements.

Wayne described composing melodies this way: "They seem to come right off the ends of my fingers." Her wording suggests she created at the piano. Certainly, her vaudeville success attests to her pianistic abilities. Touring the country, she felt, gave her the "valuable experiences every songwriter should have . . . gauging the public's taste, finding out what people really want . . . bringing her closer to the American people."[3]

Wayne was prolific, but not every composition was notated: "It's only when a tune keeps haunting me, poking itself in wherever I am, and into whatever I do, that I write it."[4] She let a motif prove itself before setting it down on paper and shaping it into song form. She believed—and may have been right—that she achieved a high rate of success through this method of taking her time before putting forward a melody for publication.

When Hollywood moved from silent movies to soundtracks, Wayne wrote songs for the movies. "Ramona" was an era-defining movie theme song, and "It Happened in Monterey" ignited the screen during the first wave of movie musicals. Nevertheless, Wayne soon got into conflict with the Hollywood companies. Harms, one of the music publishing branches of the Warner Bros. movie studio, bought the rights to Wayne's "I Wanna

Woo" (1935). It is one of Wayne's most appealing and innovative compositions, and there was initially great interest from the public. However, almost immediately the Warner Bros. corporation fought with the big radio networks over the use of their entire song catalog. Without performances on radio, "I Wanna Woo" was only a minor hit instead of the blockbuster it deserved to be. Wayne took Harms and Warner Bros. to court for failing to promote the song, asking for $100,000. All the movie studios tended to stick together to punish such insubordination, and Wayne might have found herself locked out of Hollywood for the time being.

Perhaps it was because Hollywood closed its doors to her that Wayne spent much of 1935 and 1936 in England. Her tunes had already been successful there. Indeed, "When Kentucky Bids the World Good Morning" (1930) appears to have been a bigger hit in England than in America. Wayne placed songs in British stage shows and movie musicals, including "Valparaiso" (a dramatically swirling dance number) and "Honey Coloured Moon" (a quintessential Depression ballad, atmospheric, tinged with melancholy). On her return to the States, riding on her success in the British film industry, Wayne sold to the MGM studio one of her collaborations with the British lyricist Neville Fleeson, "Betwixt and Between," a worthy number earmarked for fledgling teenage star Judy Garland. In the end the Wayne-Fleeson ditty was replaced by "In Between," by Roger Edens, a studio insider. Edens, however, lifted at least one line directly from Fleeson, as well as the general concept of the lyric. The result was that in 1940, Wayne once again took a film giant to court, suing MGM over this shifty bit of business. Wayne never worked for Hollywood again.

By being in England during late 1935, Wayne had missed out on a sudden eruption of the craze for big band jazz; the Swing Era arrived while her back was turned. It took Wayne years to approximate the newer streamlined songwriting style needed for swing band treatment. When she finally did tap into this vein, her successes were with the bands that hardcore jazz fans would reject as not really in the swing groove. The Glenn Miller outfit purveyed "A Cabana in Havana": Wayne's danceable Latin melody set a lyric by Tot Seymour ("Accent on Youth") that gave a comic twist to the lost love scenarios of the composer's previous exotica songs. The sweet band of Dick Jurgens had one of the big discs of "Why Don't You Fall in Love with Me." The perfect voice for Wayne's music, however, proved to be that of Jimmy Dorsey and his ballad singer Bob Eberly. Their rendition of the enduring torch song "I Understand" gave Wayne a solid big band hit. It was followed by the lesser but definite Dorsey successes of "Be Fair" and "It Happened in Hawaii."

Wayne left only a few clues to her life outside of songwriting. In the early 1930s, in the wake of her songwriting fame, she returned to performing. Wayne toured as an orchestra leader and for a couple of years had her own radio program. In 1948, she married fellow Tin Pan Alley veteran Nick Campbell. He was a music publisher who seemed to spend more time suing others than promoting songs. By 1952, *Variety* reports that divorce was looming for Wayne and Campbell. Yet in 1953, Campbell was plugging Wayne's "Someone to Kiss Your Tears Away." Perhaps the tune acted as a romantic spur, for in November 1954, Walter Winchell gossiped that the ex-spouses were "togethering again"—but after that Campbell drops out of the picture.[5]

Wayne appears to have been a woman of great strength of personality—spunky and unconventional. She forged a career as a performer not just once but several times. She got divorced twice and in between committed herself to a long-term nonmarital relationship. Feisty and willing to take her complaints to court, she paired with men who were equally litigious. She fearlessly tackled show business giants, perhaps to the ultimate detriment of her career. Her growth as a composer never ceased, yet underlying her compositions is always her own musical integrity.

"IT HAPPENED IN MONTEREY"

In 1929, it was claimed that Wayne "invented the syncopated waltz," marking "the beginning of a new phase in popular music history."[6] Her triple meter ditties did feature more syncopation than comparable earlier hits like "Mexicali Rose." Indeed, many of her swirling musical passages seem to hint at an underlying compound meter, with triple time and duple time happening at the same moment. This aspect has made it all the easier for jazz musicians and arrangers to change Wayne's waltzes into fox-trots. (This is a practice that seems to have originated in the mid-1910s and became more and more common through the decades.) There have been excellent jazz performances of all three of Wayne's "Spanish" trilogy. Nevertheless, "Ramona" has been particularly attractive to the less swinging artists, like Gordon MacRae, Lawrence Welk, and Frankie Carle. Jazz instrumentalists have embraced "In a Little Spanish Town" as a swing or Latin-tinged number, from Chick Webb to Keith Ingham.[7] Meanwhile the singers who emerged out of the big band era tend to similarly transform "It Happened in Monterey" into a duple meter tune.

In 1928, both the movie *Ramona* and its title song "Ramona" swelled to popularity. Where possible, the film was screened with a synchronized soundtrack, still a fresh and sensational novelty, and Wayne's melody was heard throughout the underscoring. Through this titanic success, Wayne won a unique status. By 1929, Kornheiser was reported as "grooming the composeress for production work."[8] At first, Wayne considered doing a Broadway musical, but she ended up contracted with the Universal movie studio to write numbers for the spectacular screen debut of show business giant and bandleader Paul Whiteman. Talking pictures had arrived, and all the studios were churning out musicals. After many false starts at trying to find a storyline, the screenwriters finally opted on a lavish revue built around Whiteman, to be called *King of Jazz*.

In May 1929, Whiteman transported his entire orchestra and retinue from New York to Los Angeles in a special train, giving free concerts at almost every stop along the way. (This was an advertising gimmick for Old Gold cigarettes, who paid for the excursion.) Wayne originally planned "to accompany Whiteman and plot out the songs en route."[9] The composer was denied that opportunity to collaborate, however, when it was decided there would be no women allowed on the train.

Instead of riding with Whiteman in May, Wayne went to California in July. The movie studio was at a loss about how to structure the Whiteman starrer, however, and Wayne had to shuttle back and forth between the east and west coasts before filming began in November. In the end, the bulk of the score for *King of Jazz* was by Milton Ager and Jack Yellen, presumably brought in by John Murray Anderson, the director who had worked with them on Broadway. To their six ditties, Wayne had only two.[10]

Originally Wayne's lyricist was to be L. Wolfe Gilbert, with whom she'd written many songs including "Ramona" and "Chiquita." Gilbert then signed with a rival studio and music publisher, however, and it was announced that instead Billy Rose would team with Wayne. They had already collaborated on several songs copyrighted by Feist. On November 4, 1929, their most famous joint work would be registered for copyright, "It Happened in Monterey."

Rose was one of the great characters of show business—and, in this context, he is worth lingering on because of his role in the career of composer Dana Suesse ("My Silent Love"). Rather like Clarence Williams, Rose had a special gift for promotion, from which sprang his varied careers. Starting as a contest-winning ambidextrous stenographer, he determinedly navigated the transition to Tin Pan Alley lyricist. Then, partly through his marriage to Fanny Brice (the versatile Jewish superstar who is the subject of the musical *Funny Girl*), he expanded into being a prestigious producer, state and world's fair expert, nightclub entrepreneur, newspaper columnist, television host, and theater owner.

Latter day commentators persist in doubting Rose actually contributed much to his song output. They say he claimed credit for things he never wrote, or overly depended on his many colyricists, or was more a cheerleader for their creativity than a wordsmith himself. In certain instances, these accusations may have truth. Yet the testimony of some of his peers reveals that Rose was an indefatigable worker, going without sleep for days while he weighed every word and phrase. His solo credits are far too numerous to have been all falsified. Of his twenty-eight lyrics copyrighted in 1929, twenty were written alone, among them three of his most enduring creations, "I've Got a Feeling I'm Falling," "I'd Rather Be Blue," and, with Wayne, "It Happened in Monterey."

Wayne and Rose first worked together in the spring of 1929, but by the time they reunited to create "Monterey" in the fall, Rose had been given some lessons in sophistication: in the summer, he'd collaborated on Broadway's *Great Day* with college-educated partners composer Vincent Youmans and colyricist Edward Eliscu. The latter describes Rose as crass, uncultured, ignorant, and poorly educated—surprised to learn "home" does not rhyme with "alone"—but "quick to learn." For Rose, writing lyrics was "carpentry." "Creative on his own," he collaborated well, "without making vain objections," but "neither did he express any enthusiasm." He was "hard, unsmiling . . . one hundred percent business." His works were often very appealing products that demonstrated the "common touch," as Eliscu put it.[11] Yet despite his hard work, Rose's lyrics are sometimes a bit gauche, with moments that are straining too hard or seem not quite fulfilled.

Wayne's melody for "It Happened in Monterey" is less tempestuous than those for "In a Little Spanish Town" or "Ramona." The tail of the lioness here leisurely undulates, her pent-up power alert but relaxed. Wayne composed an ABA'C structured refrain. In her main strain, she creates a syncopated effect with dotted notes in the middle of the measure. One note is accented by its placement at the start of the bar and another by its duration in the middle of the bar—"It *ha*-peeend"—followed by a quick spurt of four notes—"in Monterey." In the B-section, Wayne changes tactic, dotting the first note of each measure. This shift creates a little whirlpool within the song. Although the melody seemingly undulates placidly, these tiny patternings create a subtle restlessness that spices up the tune.

Perhaps because Wayne is less quirky in "It Happened in Monterey," the tune has been more conducive to being converted to standard swing style, four-four meter. By contrast, "In a Little Spanish Town" or "Ramona" seem to beg for a more Latin groove, such as the habanera or tango. As if to prove its adaptability to the big band sound, in 1942 the writers of the popular song "Somebody Else Is Taking My Place" stole from Wayne the C-segment melody of "Monterey," and the result was a Swing Era hit.

Rose's lyric tells the story of meeting someone wonderful on a beautiful night in old Monterrey and then leaving, without realizing until too late that one has lost the love of one's life. (Rose spells the city's name as if it was Monterey in California, not Monterrey in Mexico. This is another sign of the naïveté of Rose—and Feist.) In *King of Jazz*, John Boles is the visitor to Monterrey—tall, dark, handsome, smug, cocky, and white-suited. His imperialist story of a brief ill-fated romance with an exotic "other" is typical in some ways—*Madame Butterfly* is the quintessential example—but here is given some twists. First, the Mexican woman, played by Jeanette Loff, is the one who initiates the rendezvous; and, second, it is the male protagonist who ends in loneliness. His luxurious surroundings offer little consolation; all he has left are his memories and the portrait of her he painted. Nevertheless, despite the protagonist's lovelorn status, Wayne's song lacks the drama of the torch songs soon to emerge from other women songwriters.

Through the mid-1920s, Tin Pan Alley lyricists tended to focus on short words, but they were proud when they could introduce longer words. For instance, Jack Yellen gloated when he put "confidentially" into his lyric for "Ain't She Sweet" (1927). Meanwhile, on Broadway, Lorenz Hart was successfully advocating for increasingly sophisticated vocabulary and rhyme patterns. Therefore, Billy Rose was probably proud when he created the verse of "It Happened in Monterey," with rhyme pairs *imagination/consolation* and lines like "sadly I'm reminiscing, / madly again I'm kissing."

Rose is less graceful in parts of the refrain, particularly in his penultimate lines: "My indiscreet heart / Longs for the sweetheart." Despite the perfect rhyme, and despite the sophisticated three-syllable "indiscreet," its connotations simply do not match the dramatic situation. Yet such shortcomings are quibbles: from start to finish, Wayne and Rose successfully create and maintain a delicate atmosphere of regretful memories.

Although two of the Ager-Yellen *King of Jazz* songs were hits, "It Happened in Monterey" beat them in sheet and disc sales. The movie itself disappointed—the production delays made the film miss out on the mass audience's first, brief passion for celluloid musicals, and the Great Depression was already keeping people out of theaters. Never again would Wayne reap financial rewards to equal those earned by "Ramona." Nevertheless, "It Happened in Monterey" was a major hit in the United States and abroad. *King of Jazz* eventually covered its mammoth budget from its international earnings—for instance, it was revived in South Africa seventeen times—further spreading the song's familiarity globally.

When Whiteman's star vehicle was rereleased in the United States in 1933, taking advantage of the brief appearances in it of Bing Crosby, "It Happened in Monterey" gained further exposure. Then Gene Autry sang it (twice) in the 1939 singing western *In Old Monterey*. (Decades later, his colleagues, the Sons of the Pioneers, made one of the most convincing slow waltz versions of the tune.) But while Gene Krupa's big band was changing "In a Little Spanish Town" into a swing number with a hep vocal by Anita O'Day, "Monterey" lay relatively neglected.

Enter the precocious twenty-one-year-old Mel Tormé. In 1943, he had teamed with a vocal group, eventually named the Mel-Tones, who exhibited "an almost extrasensory perception of what their individual notes should be." With them, Tormé was closely following the vanguard in jazzy vocal arrangements, patterning "after a saxophone section" of the big bands, with "open-voiced harmonies, a process of inverting the notes in chords . . . beyond the limits of close harmony." He later reflected that this was "the most carefree, busy, exciting, and, in many ways, happiest time" of his life, "writing arrangements for the Mel-Tones non-stop and loving it." When they finally landed a record contract in 1946, Tormé unveiled his elaborate update of Wayne's 1930 hit.

Tormé swings "It Happened in Monterey" in duple meter. He starts with a swift introduction, "It didn't happen in Montana" or "Havana" or "Atlanta, GA." Then the group phrases the main strain as punchy fragments: "IT! [pause] happened in Monterey." Slangy, slightly parodic, but reveling in the song nevertheless, after the first refrain Tormé then interjects his own material—a narrative about meeting "a little chick from the town of Pomona" along the Rio Grande (he pronounces it to rhyme with "ginger dandy")—Ramona. A lovely, quietly subdued counterpoint section ensues, "Monterey" simultaneous with "Ramona" (plus some new material), for twelve measures. The protagonist—mostly represented by Tormé as the solo voice—claiming to be brokenhearted but sounding full of optimism, anticipates going back to Monterrey to rejoin his love. In 1946, this all must have seemed like cutting edge jive—hep, irreverent, youthful, among the era's foreshadowings of Beatnik culture.

Back in 1929, Wayne had been quoted as disapproving of songs losing their sweetness through being overarranged. In fact, in the 1940s she sued MGM for distorting "In a Little Spanish Town" in the movie musical *Thousands Cheer*. She probably equally loathed Tormé's version of "Monterey."

Tormé's arrangement can be viewed as overdone, but nevertheless it is addictive listening, with infectious good spirits, and in the counterpoint segment delicate and lovely.

Although the Mel-Tones disc was not listed among bestsellers, it seems to have made a deep impression. The Lancers imitated it in a single in 1957. Tormé and the Mel-Tones reunited for an LP in 1959, and "Monterey" was privileged to be one of only two old arrangements that they rerecorded. Also in 1959, the Starlighters vocal group recorded their arrangement, wholly new but just as elaborate and clearly under the inspiration of Tormé's version, by then a classic. Also following Tormé's precedent is the playfully irreverent 1958 version by Bing Crosby and Rosemary Clooney, arranged by Billy May, wherein they declare "they cha-cha-cha in Monterey." Once the cha-cha spread in the United States, arrangers finally found in it a duple meter Latin style that particularly suited "Monterey."

In creating such a noteworthy rendition of "It Happened in Monterey," swinging it in duple meter, Tormé set the stage for the classic 1956 recording by Frank Sinatra, arranged by Nelson Riddle. Sinatra was then at his peak, producing work that for many represents the most perfect embodiment of the glories of the Tin Pan Alley tradition. This was his fourth album with Nelson Riddle, and the first planned as a twelve-inch LP of swinging songs—*Songs for Swingin' Lovers*.

Sinatra takes the tune at a medium tempo, showing the world how to retain the lyricism of Wayne's vocal line while also swinging it. He displays his masterful control of dynamics; for instance, softening his volume at the final lines of the A′ section, on "key to paradise," creating a poignant tenderness that transcends Rose's somewhat clichéd lyric. Then the singer toughens his vocal color for the refrain's final phrase, an assertiveness that leads him into a slightly more aggressive, even more deeply swinging repeat of the chorus.

Sinatra's rendition has become the main touchstone for "It Happened in Monterey." In it, he exhibits virtuoso musicality but also a masterful persona. John Boles embodied upper-class cockiness; Gene Autry, a glamorized cowboy regional authenticity. Sinatra is the working-class hero turned urbane swinger, mixing emotional vulnerability and machismo. To later generations of men, he gives permission to embrace the Great American Songbook in general and "It Happened in Monterey" in particular, through his combining of traditional masculinity with a love for the music.

Riddle writes a flourish of quick notes as a fanfare to start—and, later, end—the arrangement. A segue with delicate castanets in the mix hints at the Latin setting for the lyric. Then Riddle settles into a leisurely groove, confident and hip, proving lessons from the big band Swing Era have been well learned. Accents of brass are restrained, coloring without disturbing an overall streamlined simplicity.

Riddle's arrangement is the basis for the karaoke version that saturates the twenty-first-century internet. Baritones across the world imitate with greater or lesser slavishness Sinatra's variations and attitude. Unfortunately, they fail to capture Sinatra's commitment to the emotional shadings of Rose's lyric and Wayne's music.

In the late 1920s, audiences in the United States accepted the waltzes of Brooklynite Mabel Wayne as "Spanish." Soon, Latina women themselves would be contributing material to the Great American Songbook, but for the moment Wayne's version of Latin music sufficed. For many, the Spanish heritage of the States and of Mexico seemed as distant and alien as a fairy tale; thus, *King of Jazz* offers a fairy tale version of Monterrey. The lyric's misspelling is part of that cavalier dismissal of the details of Spanish traditions in the New World. It seems to say, "Who really cares if this romance took place in Monterrey, Mexico, or Monterey, California? It's all Spanish." Maybe the error was more deeply felt in England (where perhaps they taught geography better), for the publishers there supplied an alternate lyric to substitute for one line. "In old Mexico" became "Where lights softly glow," allowing singers and listeners to imagine the action in Southern California.

Coexisting with its story of a particular, brief, loving interlude in Monterrey (or Monterey), the song also has a general application to human experience: it is a parable about remembering, and the past, and loss. Wayne and Rose created "It Happened in Monterey" just as the Wall Street Crash of 1929 occurred, plunging the nation into the Great Depression. Black Tuesday was October 29, and Feist sent in the copyright registration on November 4, only seven days later. When the song was released to the public in 1930, for its first audiences it was perhaps a lament to the vanishing of 1920s innocence and prosperity. As with the romance in the lyric, the 1920s brought blessings fully appreciated only when forfeited.

Mabel Wayne's major hits
1925: "Don't Wake Me Up (Let Me Dream)," with Abel Baer, lyrics by L. Wolfe Gilbert
1926: "In a Little Spanish Town ('Twas on a Night Like This)," lyrics by Sam Lewis and Joe E. Young
1927: "Indian Cradle Song," lyrics by Gus Kahn
1927: "Ramona," lyrics by L. Wolfe Gilbert

1928: "Chiquita," lyrics by L. Wolfe Gilbert
1929/1930: "It Happened in Monterey," lyrics by Billy Rose
1934: "Little Man, You've Had a Busy Day," lyrics by Maurice Sigler and Al Hoffman
1935: "I Wanna Woo," lyrics by Arthur Swanstrom
1941: "I Understand," lyrics by Kim Gannon
1942: "Rose Ann of Charing Cross," lyrics by Kermit Goell
1942: "Why Don't You Fall in Love with Me?," lyrics by Al Lewis
1942: "South Wind," lyrics by Kim Gannon
1943: "The Right Kind of Love," lyrics by Kermit Goell
1949: "Dreamer's Holiday," lyrics by Kim Gannon
1950: "On the Outgoing Tide," lyrics by Lew Brown
1952: "So Madly in Love," lyrics by Kim Gannon

Mabel Wayne's minor hits
1927: "Cheerie-Beerie-Bee (From Sunny Italy)," lyrics by Sam Lewis and Joe E. Young
1929: "My Angeline," lyrics by L. Wolfe Gilbert
1930: "When Kentucky Bids the World Good Morning," lyrics by Edgar Leslie
1934: "Who Made Little Boy Blue?," lyrics by Don George
1934: "Alone on the Range," lyrics by Mack David
1934: "Butterfly," lyrics by Paul Francis Webster
1935: "His Majesty, the Baby," lyrics by Neville Fleeson and Arthur Terker
1935: "Valparaiso," lyrics by Desmond Carter
1936: "Honey Coloured Moon," lyrics by Desmond Carter
1936: "Through My Venetian Blind," lyrics by Edward Heyman
1940: "A Cabana in Havana," lyrics by Tot Seymour
1941: "Be Fair," lyrics by Kim Gannon
1941/1947: "It Happened in Hawaii," lyrics by Al Dubin
1942: "Under a Strawberry Moon," lyrics by Al Lewis
1945: "When the Sandman Rides the Trail," lyrics by Ed Cherkose
1948: "All the Way from San Jose," lyrics by Kermit Goell
1952: "Guessing," lyrics by Sammy Gallop

Some neglected gems
1929: "Some Day You'll Realize You're Wrong," lyrics by Billy Rose; captivating Jazz Age fox-trot
1931: "When the Clock Is Striking Twelve," lyrics by Edward Eliscu; atmospheric waltz

1939: "Night After Night After You," lyrics by Arthur Swanstrom; top-rate rhythm ballad

1946: "The Language of Love," lyrics by Al Lewis; sexy lyric, intimate melody

1947: "I Just Dropped in to Say Hello," lyrics by Kermit Goell; amiable, spacious tune

1950: "If I Didn't Already Love You, Baby (I'd Certainly Fall in Love with You Now)," lyrics by Al Lewis; delightfully silly soft-shoe

5

THE THIRTIES

By the end of 1928, composer Mabel Wayne and lyricist Dorothy Fields were rising like comets in the sky of Tin Pan Alley, setting the stage for women who flourished as songwriters in the 1930s. In 1928, Wayne was considered an exception in being a woman able to compose a good fox-trot, adaptable to the style of the dance outfits of the Jazz Age. Tin Pan Alley was still being referred to as "one of the few remaining strongholds of masculine dominance."[1] Things changed quickly, and by 1933 women on the Alley had produced some of the biggest jazzy hits of the age. A grove of women tunesmiths and wordsmiths sprouted up. Along with those mentioned in the following sections there were Alberta Nichols, Carmen McRae, Frances Faye, Gertrude Niesen, Lucy "Lu C." Bender, Helen Meinardi, Charlotte Kent, Stella Unger, Madeline Hyde, Edna Fisher, Dedette Hill, Bee Walker, Fanny Baldridge, twin sisters Sue and Kay Werner, and others.

The 1930s were dominated by the Great Depression. After he was inaugurated in 1933, President Franklin D. Roosevelt became something of a national hero by initiating the Works Progress Administration (WPA), alongside other federal programs, giving jobs to many. He got reelected three times, and his wife Eleanor became a national humanitarian figure. Despite their efforts, jobs were fewer, and wages were lower. Many women had to work outside the home to increase the family's income. Nevertheless, the Roosevelts and the popular media helped to raise the morale of the nation.

Radio was supreme as cheap entertainment, and virtually all of it was broadcast live. It depended on music, and the money that the networks paid to ASCAP made a crucial difference to many songwriters. Record sales plummeted in the early 1930s. Only slowly did that industry recuperate, thanks in part to strong efforts, from the mid-1930s onward, to popularize the jukebox.

A new style of dancing—the Lindy Hop, aka the Jitterbug—spun to the fore, alongside a new term for jazz; and thus the Swing Era took flight. Stemming from African American roots, swing invigorated the white mainstream in mid-1935, when Benny Goodman and his big band hit their stride with young audiences. Among the brilliant swing arranger-composers was a smattering of women, such as Mary Lou Williams, Sharon Pease, and Pakistani American Margie Gibson. Each band had a singer, sometimes several, and often at least one was a woman. As for arrangers and singers, representatives from both groups managed to place songs with Tin Pan Alley. For instance, in 1938, from the Chick Webb Orchestra, singer Ella Fitzgerald and arranger Van Alexander added to the nursery song "A-Tisket, A-Tasket," turning it into a swinging musical adventure. The resulting disc sales made history, foreshadowing the upcoming revival of the phonograph industry.

Out in Hollywood, studios almost went bankrupt, but then movies emerged as a panacea for the nation's ills. Among Tinseltown's many escapist tales were musicals and romances that featured spunky heroines— and many hit numbers. Placing a song in a movie starring a pop music idol like Bing Crosby or Fred Astaire was a supreme plug. These movies were full of sparkle and a new bittersweet poignancy. The songs in them—along with equally blithe yet sophisticated items from Tin Pan Alley, the big bands, and Broadway—are still considered the finest works in the Great American Songbook. The lyrics, inspired particularly by the high standard of wit, rhyme, and feeling established in the mid-1920s by Lorenz Hart, were bubbling with spirits and interesting views on human experience— particularly, of course, romance. The music was taut yet swinging, harmonically rich, with melodies that arc like a rainbow. Women songwriters helped to create and maintain a decade of peak artistry that continues to resonate in the twenty-first century.

LATIN MUSIC

Despite the popularity in the 1910s of dances like the tango and maxixe, it was not until the 1930s that Latin music became entrenched in the mainstream worlds of Tin Pan Alley and the prominent "name bands." There were many undercelebrated contributors to this popularization of Latin music in the United States. Ralph Peer, a canny exploiter of musical genres neglected by Tin Pan Alley, entered into a second marriage with Monique Iversen, who spoke Spanish fluently. They moved to Mexico, traveled internationally, and funneled fresh sounds into the Yankee urban mainstream through record producing and music publishing. Only in the twenty-first century was a biography written to celebrate their accomplishments.

Marion Sunshine is another neglected figure. She followed a career as a performer—and writer of lyrics celebrating conservative values such as "An Old Fashioned Garden in Virginia" and the 1914 hit "Mary, You're a Little Bit Old Fashioned"—by becoming a champion of her Cuban husband's cultural traditions. She proved pivotal in cowriting English words for "The Peanut Vendor (El Manisero)" (1931), sparking the rumba vogue; "Brazilian Nights (Amor, Doce Veneno)," popularizing the samba; and "Havana's Calling Me (La Conga)," helping to further the conga dance craze.

More mysterious is the dedication of two Russian Jews to spreading the gospel of Latin music to Yankee audiences. One was Francia Luban, a Tin Pan Alley stalwart and frequent visitor to Mexico. She collaborated in 1936 on the hit lyrics for "A Gay Ranchero (Las Altenitos)," used on screen in *The Gay Desperado* (1936) and later as the title song for a 1948 singing cowboy flick starring Roy Rogers. Her colyricist was another frequent visitor to Mexico, Abe Tuvim, for a time head of the American Zionist Council. He also traveled frequently to Mexico and, in partnership with Mary L. Shanks, published many of that country's top composers.

Sunshine, Tuvim, Shanks, and the Peers were among the many who helped Latin melodies become household favorites in the United States. Discussed here will be lyricists Dolly Morse, Francia Luban, Al Stillman, and Bob Russell, but their worthy colleagues were many, including Carol Raven, L. Wolfe Gilbert, Leonard Whitcup, Charles Carpenter, Ervin Drake, and Ray Gilbert. Even Dorothy Fields and Oscar Hammerstein made stabs at adapting Latinx pop songs. Meanwhile, transnational composers like Margarita Lecuona and Maria Grever, and male peers like Juan Tizol, helped spearhead a new phase of penetration by Latin music.

"SIBONEY" (1931)
Dolly Morse (1883–1953), lyricist

She was born in Brooklyn as Alfreda Theodora Stanberg to Scandinavian immigrants. She published under many names, including Alfred, Theodora,

Dora, Dorothy, Dolly, and D. A., with last names Scott, Esrom, Terriss, and Morse. Her Tin Pan Alley career began with an encounter with Theodore F. Morse, ten years her senior and already a well-known songwriter. Two years later she married him. She frequently supplied him with lyrics, as well as collaborating with others and sometimes composing her own tunes. Together, they ran a publishing house and helped start ASCAP. She avoided publishing under her married name, probably to avoid the appearance of nepotism, until after her husband died in 1924. Then she proclaimed herself Dolly Morse in tribute to Theodore's memory.

Her early lyrics exemplified conventions of the 1910s and the early 1920s. "When Uncle Joe Played Ragtime on His Old Banjo" (1912) reflected the renewed fever for ragtime dances in the 1910s. By contrast, "Sing Me Love's Lullaby" (1917) caught the refinement and poeticisms of the semi-high-class ballad style. Two swooningly romantic lyrics of the early 1920s were popularized by Paul Whiteman in his style of symphonic jazz: "Wonderful One" and "Three O'Clock in the Morning."

"Siboney" started as the 1927 Cuban revue song "Canto Siboney." The composer, Ernesto Lecuona, was to Cuba what George Gershwin was the United States: a virtuoso pianist able to compose successful works in the full range from lowbrow tunes, to middlebrow stage successes, to high-class concert works. His sister, Ernestina Lecuona, was almost equally successful. Their young cousin, Margarita Lecuona, followed in her elders' footsteps. All three made an impact on the US popular song market.

Siboney is an Indigenous group of the Caribbean and also a place name for locations both in and outside Havana. In Ernesto's original lyric "Siboney" functions as the name of an absent beloved whom the singer dreams of and begs to return; and this beloved is probably also a symbol of love of homeland and home culture. This rumba melody began to be popular in the United States before Morse fashioned English lyrics for the tune. As so frequently in such cases, the words she came up with celebrate the music itself. Her lyric describes a haunting strain called "Siboney" that they sing and dance to in Havana.

In writing the lyric to "Siboney," Morse demonstrates that she has learned well the lessons of Lorenz Hart and his college-educated generation. Her words are fitted perfectly to match the phrasing, accents, and atmosphere of Ernesto's music. She tailors beautifully natural interior rhymes that cling like silk to the sinuous contours of the melody: "As they play / 'Siboney' / Every care will fade away."

Morse does draw on conventions about the exotic that are vaguely colonialist or imperialist and thus condescending. Nevertheless, she also partakes of another well-established convention in song lyrics, one that is more positive. She conveys a firm belief in music's power to inspire, heal, and create ecstasy.

In the United States, in 1931, Alfredo Brito and His Siboney Orchestra rode Lecuona's tune to fame. "Siboney" quickly became a staple for the Latin dance orchestras founded and flourishing in the United States during the 1930s and after, such as those of Xavier Cugat and Enric Madriguera. A jazz version by Dizzy Gillespie and Stan Getz in 1953 has been hailed as foreshadowing the latter's influential bossa nova period of a decade later. In 1946, Bing Crosby, accompanied by the Cugat orchestra, luxuriates in singing Morse's rarely heard verse lyric, about music "that made your senses thrill." A jolly 1964 album track by the Mills Brothers offers another of the best vocal renditions. Meanwhile, Lecuona's composition continued its robust existence as a favorite rumba, whether as an instrumental piece; in its original Spanish version; in translations into Portuguese, Icelandic, and Swedish; or in the English-language version. Dolly Morse's well-wrought lyric helped the tune acquire even more charisma than it had before.

"SAY SI SI" ("PARA VIGO ME VOY") (1936)
Francia Luban (1912–1987), lyricist

What took Francia Luban from her birthplace in Kiev to a lifelong career on Tin Pan Alley? A biographer has yet to detail her American Dream story. The year 1933 finds her, at age twenty-one, writing both Spanish-language and English lyrics for the Edward B. Marks publishing house. By 1936, Luban was head of the Latin department at the firm. For the 1940 census, Luban described her job as "interpreter" in the "music" business. It reveals that Francia was the only employed member of her household, supporting her parents and grown-up brother on $1,300 dollars a year (equal to about $30,000 in the early 2020s). She worked for Marks deep into the rock era, with a significant but temporary eight-year break from 1944 through 1952, reputedly for raising offspring, but also at least part of the time helping to lead the Music War Committee, doing vocal coaching, and founding the international department at Leeds Music.

Luban's copyrights were few and mostly confined to the 1930s. Outstripping in impact even the Luban-Tuvim "Gay Ranchero" was another one of her lyrical collaborations, also from 1936, this time with Al Stillman, for "Say Si Si." Stillman was another Jewish American (under George

Gershwin's advice he changed his name from Silverman to Anglicize it). His broad range of hits included a number of Spanish adaptation credits.

The original "Para Vigo Me Voy," copyrighted in the United States in 1935, has words and music by Ernesto Lecuona. By then, Ernesto was a powerhouse in his native Cuba and was known in the United States as a bandleader and the composer of "Siboney." Nevertheless, the 1936 Luban-Stillman adaptation of "Para Vigo" as "Say Si Si," and its eventual success in 1940, was important: it confirmed Ernesto Lecuona's status as a proven hitmaker on Tin Pan Alley.

Lecuona's melody for "Para Vigo Me Voy" has an enchanting and dramatic introductory section. Following this verse, the refrain is short but rippling, with an ABAC structure. It is a bit repetitious: Lecuona creates a similar two-note ending for every phrase. The final C-segment brings a welcome change, with swiftly occurring poignant and then climactic motifs, before ending with an echo of the main strain.

In both "Say Si Si" and "A Gay Ranchero," Luban and her collaborators exhibit a blithe and jolly wit. Both lyrics start with generalizations about love and romance, with an implied sexual aspect not far beneath the surface. Luban and colyricists then move on to particularize. In "Say Si Si," the refrain's first two stanzas offer examples of various ways to say "yes" in multiple languages, bringing to mind Cole Porter's famous list songs like "Let's Do It." Luban and Stillman conclude the refrain, however, with a more personal complaint and a plea to the beloved to yield.

Lecuona's original lyric was suitable for slow ballad treatment (despite mention of conga and bongo drums) with its potentially poignant tale of leaving for Vigo, Spain, and parting from one's beloved. By contrast, Luban and Stillman are playful. They also shy away from the original's racial aspects: Lecuona specifies the sweetheart is "mi negra." This reference to a Black sweetheart is bypassed in the version for Yankee audiences.

In 1936, the first prominent US waxing of the tune, by Xavier Cugat, used Lecuona's original Spanish lyrics. In 1940, two discs that utilized Luban and Stillman's English lyrics transformed the song into a swinging American tune. (This popularity probably gave Luban and her family a welcome income boost.) The Glenn Miller big band, on a history-making roll of success, swung it in their satisfying if tame way, with a brief, cheerful vocal refrain by Marion Hutton. In the other hit version, the Andrews Sisters swing it just as hard. They include two wordless transition sections for variety, as well as an enchanting interlude quietly repeating "si, si," before loudly bursting into a repeat of the B-section.

In 1941, the Edward Marks firm left ASCAP and switched over to the new BMI organization. Therefore, Luban's carefully developed Latin music catalog was able to be heard on radio throughout 1941 during the ASCAP radio boycott. Exposure on the major broadcast networks probably furthered the popularity of "Say Si Si," along with other tunes under Luban's purview, such as "The Peanut Vendor," "Yours," "El Rancho Grande," and "Poinciana." This development made Luban even more key in the spread of Latin songs to the Yankee mainstream.

An enthusiastic 1952 recording of "Say Si Si" by Eugenie Baird, from the small Vinrob company, introduced one and a half refrains of new words (and also a second verse lyric that has never been published). The label on her single reads, "Special new lyric by Al Stillman," and he may have been the instigator for this revival.[2] However, the song's resurrection coincided with Luban's return to Marks, so she may also have been involved. In 1953, Marks printed a new edition with comedy material added for six more refrains, and "Say Si Si" became a hit all over again. The Mills Brothers swung the ditty on the highest-charting disk. They cannily use the verse as a middle interlude and then essay the new second refrain, which talks of how "on every virgin isle, they say it with a smile." History imprinted these renditions of 1952 and 1953 with a slight variation in the words: the phrase "every little Russian says 'da, da'" was considered too politically subversive at the height of the anticommunist paranoia, and instead "every little Danish doll" said the same thing.

"Say Si Si" continued for decades in the repertoires of Dixieland jazz and swing revival bands. Further, the versions by Glenn Miller and the Andrews and Mills siblings have been endlessly reissued, carrying "Say Si Si" into the twenty-first century. Would that Luban's reputation had lasted as long. In the 1960s, she was annually producing the Puerto Rico Night of Poetry and Folk Music in Central Park. In 1969, she was still promoting Latin music with Marks at the height of the rock era. By 1973, she had attained the top status of professional manager, but only at the small Charing Cross Music outfit that specialized in British music. Despite devoting forty years to Tin Pan Alley and helping to sway the fate of American popular music, when Francia Luban died *Billboard* made no note of her passing.

"TABOO" ("TABÚ") (1934/1941)
Margarita Lecuona (1910–1981), composer and Spanish-language lyricist

The swinging horns riff, and a sad voice floats above them, telling of the moon rising on a forbidden rendezvous. It is 1961, and Connie Francis weaves a spell with "Taboo," letting the melody soar. Without pushing too hard, she draws out both the relaxed lyricism and the drama of the song. The tension builds and then breaks forth with an outburst: "Taboo, taboo," bewails the woman, caught between her promise to an old flame and the sudden revelation of a newer, truer love. The song had already been flogged to death as a quintessential item on exotica lounge music albums of the LP era, but Francis redefines it as an American rhythm ballad.

The composer is Marguerita Lecuona. The daughter of a Cuban diplomat, by the time she was ten years old she had already traveled as far as New York City and Europe before circling back to her hometown of Havana. To an even greater extent than her father's cousins, Ernesto and Ernestina, Margarita grew up to be a multitalented artist—dancer, choreographer, pianist, guitarist, singer, actor, producer, costume designer, director, and star of stage, nightclub, radio, and screen.[3]

In 1930, Margarita turned her hand to writing the music and lyrics for songs. Her most successful pair found a firm home in the American songbook, "Tabú" (1934) and "Babalu" (1941). Perhaps inspired by her peripatetic older cousins (whom she called aunt and uncle), Lecuona also toured internationally. She starred in a 1946 movie with Argentinean light comedian Pepe Armil and then married him the following year, moving to Buenos Aires but frequently performing throughout South America and Mexico.

In 1958, Margarita's tours brought her back to Manhattan. Her visit was well timed to coincide with an extended vogue for Latin dance music in the United States. She performed with her Babalu Trio at the Chateau Madrid, a "palm fronted mambo palace." In mid-century, when the communist regime ascended in Cuba, many of Lecuona's relatives transplanted themselves to the United States—for instance, her "Uncle" Ernesto moved to Florida—and, in 1969, Margarita followed suit. She ended her journey in New Jersey, dying there in 1981. Long after her demise, her biggest hits continued to be major money earners in the US market.

By the early 1930s, Margarita Lecuona had developed a mutually beneficial relationship with Ralph Peer. He registered the Library of Congress copyright for "Tabú" in 1934, through his Southern Music imprint. Latin dance bands in the United States began to record the tune, either as an instrumental or using Lecuona's Spanish lyric. Surprisingly, one of the best of these early instrumentals is by the sweet band of Henry King. They set it swaying at a lively tempo, with vigor and zest.

In the early 1940s, Ralph and Monique Peer commissioned "Babalu" from Lecuona. The piece was a quick hit. The title eventually became a household word as the theme song of Desi Arnaz, featured at times on the 1950s television series starring him and his wife Lucille Ball, *I Love Lucy*.

For the main melody of "Tabú," Lecuona spins a dark, brooding strain that undulates in beautiful low-lying curves. The song starts with a concise AABA form, but after that Lecuona introduces new material. The notes of the B-section lie low in the singer's register, acting like a parenthetical statement.

Then the tune veers from Alley norms as a C-segment bursts forth like the chorus of a folk song, a catchy wail that might well get audiences singing along. After this, Lecuona recapitulates to her AAB melodies, but the English-language version omits this repeated material. Instead it jumps straight to Lecuona's D-section: slow, drawn-out notes that build dramatic tension. The suspense is satisfied by another outburst, a repeat of the C-segment, leading to an extended tag, the ultimate exclamation, "Taboo, taboo, taboo . . ." that again subsides for a final ". . . taboo."

Lecuona's original lyric is in the voice of an Afro-Cuban, sadly and reverently invoking the gods and landscape of Africa and bemoaning a land where a Black man cannot look at a white woman—that is "taboo." Tin Pan Alley's version wipes away the poetic, sacred quality of Lecuona's poetry as well as her message of social protest. Intriguingly, however, in the United States, a land ossified in racist attitudes, at a time when the marriage of Black and white was illegal in many states, the Spanish lyric was often performed and recorded. It is open to speculation what those Yankees who understood Spanish thought of it at the time.

In 1941, with most of the established, old guard Tin Pan Alley publishers fighting the radio networks, Peer, as an outsider, was in a good position to get more radio play for his Southern imprint publications. Lyricist Bob Russell was doing a lot of work for Peer at the time, and the publisher got him to write new words for "Tabú." The lyricist was then penning under his original name, S.K. Russell. In a mysterious mix-up, yet to be fully explained, many of the disc labels credited the lyric to Al Stillman (of "Say Si Si"). Perhaps Stillman had written an earlier attempt at giving "Tabú" an English-language adaptation.

At any rate, Bob Russell's lyric became the standard version and under the title "Taboo" has been recorded by many singers.[4] These range from the quiet 1941 rendition by Tony Martin, through the overdramatic 1952 one of June Valli, to the swinging ones of Connie Francis and, in the twenty-first century, Jonny Blu. (In 1959, there was also an instrumental version by the Arthur Lyman Group that charted both as a single and as an album title track.) Russell changes the setting to a nighttime rendezvous between two new lovers, one of whom is already promised to another. Usually it is the singer herself who is already engaged, and at the end of the song the romantic fate of the protagonist is still in doubt; the listener has to guess the outcome. Although he drains the scenario of deeper resonances about oppression and race, Russell captured the dark atmosphere of inner contemplation and pain created by Margarita Lecuona's most compelling melody.

"THEM THERE EYES" (1930)
Doris Tauber (1908–1996), composer

"Doris Tauber, could she play a piano? A double yes to that," affirmed Joe Laurie Jr. in 1940.[5] Tauber was then in the middle of her four-decade career as a mainstay of Tin Pan Alley: pianist, songplugger, accompanist, vocal coach, arranger, and thirteen years as musical secretary to Irving Berlin. Along the way she copyrighted a dozen popular song compositions, with over half of them being at least moderately successful and two enduring as standards: "Them There Eyes" (1930) and "Drinking Again" (1962). Pushed out of the music biz in 1968 when records took over from sheet music, she died almost thirty years later, seemingly forgotten. Like Francia Luban, she was not granted even one line of obituary in *Billboard*.

Tauber was raised in Brooklyn, married Jack Gribin in 1932, and had a son (after a number of miscarriages) in 1946. She was active as a radio pianist from 1926 to 1929, called "The Girl Friend of the Radio," during which time she also worked in the Alley, first for Joe Davis and then for Irving Mills. In 1930, she went over to Irving Berlin's company and later spent 1935 at the Santly-Joy firm before returning to Berlin. From 1944 until retirement, she shifted to the Warner Bros. conglomerate, Music Publishers Holding Corporation.

In 1942, Tauber collaborated intensively with lyricist Sis Willner. There were plans for the two women to do a Broadway show. It never got produced, but they managed to place a single song in the long-running *Star and Garter*. Their collaboration did reap a tune, "Why Remind Me" (1943), that was eventually a hit on radio broadcasts for a month in 1950 and put on the B-side of a briefly charting disc by Frank Sinatra. Three of her other fifties songs were also hits: "Who's Afraid (Not I, Not I, Not I)," "Fooled," and "Livin' Dangerously."

Almost as soon as she transferred to Irving Berlin's publishing house, in 1930 and 1931, Tauber cowrote music and lyrics for two songs with Maceo Pinkard, one of the giants of Tin Pan Alley. Their first was a winner, "Them There Eyes," with cowriter William Tracey. It quickly became a moderate but definite success in both the United States and England.

Pinkard was an African American who made his early career in Nebraska but with great determination built up his songwriting skills—always composing and sometimes also writing lyrics—with the aim of moving to New York. He accomplished this by the end of 1917 and, at age twenty, launched a winning streak on Tin Pan Alley that would last through the 1920s. Unusually for the time, Pinkard's collaborators were almost always white, such as his occasional lyricist William Tracey. His wife, Edna Belle Alexander, also produced songs, often under the pseudonym Alex Belledna, including writing lyrics for Pinkard's 1926 jazz standard, "Sugar." Pinkard's career wound down after 1931 (some sources hint at health problems). By contrast, Tauber was just getting started, with a 1929 sheet music hit, "I Was Made to Love You," recorded by Duke Ellington, and a bluesy 1930 ditty, "Gotta Darn Good Reason Now (For Bein' Good)," waxed by Cab Calloway. The two careers overlapped just long enough for the pair to create a classic.

Alec Wilder's commentary on "Them There Eyes" is worth quoting in full, both for his canny ear for detail and his dismissal of Tauber's potential contribution to the tune. The analyst is as ambivalent about "Eyes" as about Kay Swift's "Can't We Be Friends." He praises it as a "swinging song in which I see Pinkard's as the principal influence." Yet "there are treacherous moments in the melody when you're sure it's going to slide into cliché. But it always just evades it. For example, take the cadential phrase at the end of the first half. It's the octave drop in the fifteenth measure and the c-sharp in the sixteenth that saves it," at the lyric, "Going in a" (drop) "big way, for sweet" (c-sharp) "little you." Dave A. Jasen and Gene Jones also praise that fall, which skillfully occurs just after the lyric speaks about falling (in love). Nonchalant yet surprising, it is typical of the moments that give freshness to this formulaic art. Wilder continues, "And though it's on the thin edge of hokiness, I like the riffish quality of measures twenty-seven and twenty-eight," with the whip-like, "They're gonna get you in a whole lot of trouble."[6]

Notice how with one swift half-sentence, Wilder casts doubt on Tauber's co-authorship of the music. Perhaps Wilder would cite internal evidence, pointing out that "Them There Eyes" resembles Pinkard's strongest standard, "Sweet Georgia Brown" (1926), in their shared form (ABA'C) and jazziness. But why would Pinkard, master of many hits, share credit with a songplugging novice if she had not earned it? And if she had stolen credit—and royalties—why would he then collaborate with her the following year, again sharing cocredit for both music and lyrics? Further, as far as writing in a jazz vein, Tauber had proven she could do it on her own with her solo music credit for the low-down "Gotta Darn Good Reason," copyrighted six weeks before "Them There Eyes." In their turn, Dave Jasen and Gene Jones blithely assume that Tauber was only the colyricist. This is unlikely, as Tauber is credited as a composer on all her other copyrights. Such factors weigh in favor of Pinkard and Tauber genuinely writing the music for "Eyes" together.

The tune that Pinkard and Tauber bubble forth has proven a favorite of jazz musicians from 1930 to the twenty-first century.[7] Gus Arnheim and His Cocoanut Grove Orchestra had the first big selling disc of it, with the Rhythm Boys (including the young Bing Crosby) scatting like mad on their second vocal refrain. At the same time, however, Louis Armstrong also waxed the song, and it was his version that was constantly reissued and even charted as a hit as late as 1936. Characteristically, his vocal refrain rewrote the melody, dropping words here to give the tune more space, adding words there to give it more swing, and flattening Pinkard and Tauber's tiny swinging ripples into rat-tat-tat repeated notes.

Billie Holiday, the famed Lady Day, often acclaimed as the greatest jazz singer, embraced the tune throughout her career. Although Holiday based her version on Louis Armstrong's, hers became the indelible imprint. Her friends considered it her signature tune as early as 1931, but she was not given a chance to commit it to wax until 1939. Her first exuberant recording of it is a classic of small group jazz. Her 1949 single, more sexy and kittenish, with a full brassy orchestra, along with a 1951 live broadcast released in the 1960s, consolidated her ownership of the piece. Holiday leaned on "Them There Eyes" as a staple item, one of the few cheerful up-tempo songs that she kept in her live performance repertoire throughout the decades.

In the jazzy break at the end of the B-section, Armstrong and Holiday both erase the octave drop (alas, for Wilder, Jasen, and Jones, who love it so). Very few singers since have returned to the sheet music to rediscover it. "Them There Eyes" took its place in dozens of nightclub acts reviewed by *Variety* over the course of many decades. It has also supplied the foundation for hundreds of jazz improvisations. It is sexy, lighthearted, full of enthusiasm, and it swings—just what the doctor ordered for performers of the Great American Songbook.

"ACCENT ON YOUTH" (1935)
Tot Seymour (1889–1966), lyricist
Vee Lawnhurst (1905–1992), composer

How does one explain chemistry? Lyricist Tot Seymour and composer Vee Lawnhurst enjoyed successes before and after teaming up, but nothing to match their few years together. From 1935 through 1937, they burst forth with an astounding series of seventeen hit songs. Their forte lay in blithe ditties, featuring swingable melodies and lyrics to match the best of the era in rakish wit, sophistication, and insight into human nature: "And Then Some," "No Other One," "The Day I Let You Get Away," "What's the Name of That Song," "You Don't Love Right," "Alibi Baby," "Us on a Bus," "Cross Patch," and "I'd Rather Call You Baby." The last three mentioned were recorded by Thomas "Fats" Waller, the pianist and singer with irrepressible high spirits; this jazz giant captured the perfect "voice" for some of Seymour and Lawnhurst's best creations. To those lively charmers add a handful of appealing ballads—such as "Please Keep Me in Your Dreams," "Who'll Be the One This Summer," and the atmospheric "It's Dangerous to Love Like This"—and one has a set worthy of a *Seymour and Lawnhurst Songbook* album.

The most enduring Seymour and Lawnhurst number is "Accent on Youth," perhaps the composer's finest ballad tune. The main melody starts with three quick repeated notes and then jumps up to linger on a vulnerable, tender pitch. Seven more notes, back and forth, conclude the first phrase. Lawnhurst imitates this pattern in a lower register, then smoothly toboggans the melody up, down—surprising the listener at each bend. This whole A-section, in an AABA refrain, creates that ineffable melancholy charm and poignancy so characteristic of the 1930s.

The release is equally fine. Lawnhurst creates a seven-note phrase that functions beautifully as the melody line but can also be used as a fill-in phrase, creating a call-and-response pattern. Some canny arrangers and performers use this echoing effect, from the George Hall Orchestra, produced when the song first came out, through to jazz trumpeter Bryan Shaw in the twenty-first century. On top of all this musical excellence, the song features a good verse, rendered in 1935 by Hall and his singer, Dolly Dawn, and by Morton Downey, but heard too seldom since.

"Accent on Youth" has a strong tradition of instrumental versions, starting with an early waxing by the Duke Ellington Orchestra that is full of rich variations. The tune makes a solid foundation for improvisation. Yet it is so well balanced and evocative that jazz greats like Billy Taylor and Bob Wilbur wisely focus mostly on very simple statements that savor Lawnhurst's tasty harmonies and liquid melody.

Seymour and Lawnhurst wrote the song to be used in the 1935 movie *Accent on Youth*, based on a 1934 Broadway play. Lawnhurst's melody is used frequently in the film's underscoring. The plot of *Accent on Youth* tells of a middle-aged playwright, torn by internal struggle as he writes a play about a middle-aged man in love with a young woman. His young secretary then passionately reveals she actually *is* in love with him. Their ensuing on-again, off-again romance is poignantly troubled by their age disparity and constantly flavored by the mirroring of life and art. Although the heroine is momentarily tempted away by a lover nearer her own age, ultimately she returns to the more mature, more deeply feeling man.

A female journalist reported: Seymour and Lawnhurst were "given a hurry assignment to write a song around the title 'Accent on Youth' after other songwriters (male!) had shied from writing a tune around such a title." As well as the harsh sounds of the word "accent" and the near impossibility of singing "youth" mellifluously and not making it sound like "you," there is the mystery of the phrase's meaning. What does it mean to accent youth? Nevertheless, "twelve hours later the girls turned in the song."[8] Perhaps the words are not quite up to Seymour's highest standard—her sophistication is best heard in "And Then Some" and "You Don't Love Right"—but they are still full of interest.

Seymour chooses to paint the scene of a moonlit romantic rendezvous. She cleverly packs the lyric with images and phrases connoting rebirth and renewal, such as "beginning," "spring," "new," and "fresh." Unfortunately, in the final stanza, she tries to pair "dawn" with "born"—a forced off-rhyme that is rare for her in this decade. ("Dawn," however, could simply be a publisher's error for "morn.") In contrast to the self-conscious quality of Billy Rose's use of multisyllabic words in "It Happened in Monterey," Seymour effortlessly climaxes each of her three A-section stanzas with a Latinate word, creating the triple rhyme of *sensation/explanation/inspiration*. It is this level of technique that typifies 1930s sophisticated lyric writing.

Seymour does convincingly generate romantic steaminess but runs into some snags in doing so. In the release, the effect of "intoxicating wine" helps convey the heady delirium of falling in love; but, then, to complete the rhyme pair she recruits the overworked superlative "divine." Finally, Seymour stoops to a reversal of conversational syntax—"With thrills untold"—in order to create a rhyme with the question, "How can we grow old?"

The second strategy the lyricist employs is building the lyric around a series of questions: "Why" this wonderful thing, "How" that, and "What" the other? The answer in each instance is the title phrase: it is all due to the "Accent on Youth." Seymour's skill cannot hide the fact that this overall idea is somewhat peculiar. The notion that a rhapsodic romantic interlude should be the product only of "youth" runs counter to the genre's more usual celebrations of fate, music and dance, zestful libido, or enduring affection.

Seymour's scenario does have a possible close relevance to the narrative of *Accent on Youth*. Her lyric could apply to a middle-aged lover who is overwhelmed by the feeling of revitalization that comes through romance with a younger sweetheart. Further, Seymour's allusions to "the stage is set for love" and "though we may call it inspiration" echo the way the movie's protagonists repeatedly blur the boundaries of two sources of ecstasy: making theater and making love.

As a vocal piece, the song presents some further challenges. If the listener is not familiar with the *Accent on Youth* play or movie, the natural inference is that the lyric is sung by a pair of young lovers. This may be a major reason why the piece did not survive as strongly in singers' repertoires as it should. From the mid-1950s onward, the aging generation of Sinatra, Fitzgerald, Lee, and Cole would have seemed silly claiming to be young. An exception is the excellent 1956 rendition by Dinah Washington, with arranger Harold Mooney using the riff-like motif of the release as a fill-in figure, to fine effect, and Washington giving it her all. Nevertheless, the song has fallen out of currency with most singers, victim of the inevitable senescence of the whole genre of jazz-pop singing. It cries for a younger generation of vocalists to rediscover it.

With a sixteen-year difference in age, the veteran Seymour and the younger Lawnhurst might well have been able to testify to the chemistry and hurdles of such a partnership of middle age and younger years. The veteran Seymour spent most of the 1920s writing songs, skits, and special material for vaudeville, benefits, and industry pageants. She also managed to land a gig as the main lyricist (among several) for the mildly successful 1924 Broadway musical *Innocent Eyes*. Its score is professional and competent but conventional. Seymour's growth between 1924 and 1935 is revealed in a song that foreshadows "Accent on Youth" in its topic, if not in its artistry, "Inspiration (Fountain of Youth)": "Inspiration, beauty is thy name / . . . Inspiration, you have told the truth. / Beauty leads the way / To the Fountain of Youth."

During the 1920s, Lawnhurst was one of an elite group of composers of piano solo novelties, many of them published by Jack Mills. This genre is now seen by some historians as an extension of ragtime but in the 1920s was usually viewed as cutting-edge jazz. Lawnhurst was a virtuosa performer in this style, spinning piano duets for many years with Muriel Pollock and others on records and radio.

Vaudeville faded, and Seymour successfully made the transition to writing hit lyrics for Tin Pan Alley. She partnered for a while with Mabel Wayne, with tunes like "Spanish Dancer." Similarly, the novelty rag genre passed its peak, and Lawnhurst struck up a songwriting partnership with the brilliant Roy Turk. When he unexpectedly passed over, too young, Lawnhurst paired up with Seymour. They proved to be the most consistently successful female songwriting team of the era. What led to the dissolution of their steady collaboration soon after 1937 is uncertain. When they did rejoin in 1942, their one moderate hit demonstrates the shift away from the bittersweet sparkle of the 1930s: "Daddy's Letter" is a wartime period piece, elegant but sentimental, hard to revive. Nevertheless, for a brief period, when the Golden Age style was at its peak, Seymour and Lawnhurst inspired each other as surely as the protagonists of *Accent on Youth*.

"I WISHED ON THE MOON" (1934/1935)
Dorothy Parker (1893–1967), lyricist

Dorothy Parker was the wittiest woman in America, as famous as she was intelligent. She published hundreds of short stories and poems (including the unprecedentedly best-selling 1926 collection *Enough Rope*) and co-authored fistfuls of screenplays. She was at the core of the Algonquin Round Table, a group of writers who, in novelist Edna Ferber's assessment, were "a tonic influence, one on the other, and all on the world of American letters." Biographies about her fill the shelves. They report characteristic moments: writing to her fellow Round Tabler Alexander Woollcott, "Dear God, please make me stop writing like a woman," or being observed by her friend, novelist John Dos Passos, as she told "her usual funny cracks with her eyes full of tears."[9]

The outline of Parker's persona still burns brightly in the early twenty-first century: her mixed Jewish and Scottish ancestry, obsession with death, suicide attempts, many lovers, political activism, constant knitting, dog ownership, and alcoholism. Remnants remain through word of mouth of perhaps her greatest gift—the off-the-cuff barb, often so bawdy it could never be printed in her lifetime, usually a put-down. In 1922, for instance, she supposedly commented on her extramarital pregnancy and the subsequent abortion: "It serves me right for putting all my eggs in one bastard." She quipped that the bastard's contribution of thirty dollars for the operation was "like Judas making a refund."[10] She turned heartbreak into wisecracks. In this way, she was a model for the era's songwriters in works such as Kay Swift's "Can't We Be Friends."

Along the way, she copyrighted two movie songs and two numbers for Broadway. These seemed like an anomaly. Yes, she was sufficiently accomplished on the piano to earn her living, as a youth, playing for a local dance school's classes. Yes, Irving Berlin was a friend, and she played the triangle while he tickled the ivories during bohemian evenings. Yes, she praised the lyrics of P. G. Wodehouse. Yes, lyricist Howard Dietz was among her many lovers. Nonetheless, she is better remembered for her devastating satires of the run-of-the-mill popular song lyric. She considered the scripts she helped write for motion pictures to be "Horseshit," which she spelled with a capital "H." Living by a code of keen aesthetic discernment and rebellion against "bunk," she must have felt ambivalent, at best, about the two lyrics she wrote for Hollywood films. They are both about longing, both were hits, and both endure as jazz standards: "How Am I to Know" (1929) and "I Wished on the Moon" with Ralph Rainger's masterful, evocative ballad melody.

In 1934, Parker and her handsome young husband, Alan Campbell, arrived in Hollywood and soon proved to be an effective screenwriting team, with him supplying dramatic structure and her quickly extemporizing dialog. One of their first studio assignments was to clean up a bawdy Broadway hit comedy, *Sailor Beware*, for the screen. On December 10, the copyright office received a registration for "I Wished on the Moon" with words by Parker and music by Ralph Rainger. Ultimately, the movie was released as *Lady Be Careful* in 1936 and featured no songs. In the meantime, on June 24, 1935, a new copyright was received for the same title, but now the credits read "words and music by Dorothy Parker and Ralph Rainger." Had the writers altered their original work, now more fully collaborating together on all aspects? Or was the new registration merely a corporate manipulation? Either way, the studio got six more months of ownership rights—and perhaps Parker, if she got official cocredit as composer, received a tiny bit more of the royalties—of what proved to be a valuable property.

Parker usually wrote of unfulfillment, but "I Wished on the Moon" ends with fulfillment. Fittingly, she wrote it during a period when her love was reciprocated by a man with whom she was compatible. Her marriage to Campbell was (for a considerable time) stable, her past debts were paid off, and, to her surprise, her suicidal thoughts vanished.

Parker's lyric concludes like a Hollywood script, with a happy resolution. Nevertheless, throughout the verse and most of the ABAB´-structured refrain, the protagonist dwells on what was *lacking* in life. This missing element was ultimately indefinable but in imagination took the shape of a rose, a powder blue sky, a shaft of starlight, a dream. Parker's most telling line comes at the end of the B-section, where the singer remembers yearning for "an April day / that would not dance away." Rainger's melody arcs upward, descends to land on an unexpected note, and then stirs and shifts subtly. The transience of spring, of beauty, of life itself is felt in such a phrase.

Paramount clearly sniffed they had a major hit on their hands, for the studio allotted it to Bing Crosby in his guest appearance in the star-studded *Big Broadcast of 1936*. The plot hinges on an innovative television broadcast, and Crosby is one of the specialties seen over the airwaves. In front of a log cabin, with an invisible chorus, he crooned "I Wished on the Moon."

When Crosby went into the studio to make his single, accompanied by the Dorsey Brothers, oddly enough he fought with producer Jack Kapp to do only a single refrain, as if he were any old band singer. In a rare recorded candid conversation, he says, "I'm very hoarse this afternoon, and I don't think I can do more than one chorus and do it well." Perhaps he was worried about reaching the low note in the B-section and the high note in the penultimate phrase. His delivery *is* husky, but also quite free in how he phrases and adds words, now quieter, now louder. He further argues for the single vocal refrain: "I think it will be an interesting, saleable piece of property." And he was right—it was a hit disc.[11]

As good as Crosby is, his rendition of "I Wished on the Moon" pales beside that of Billie Holiday, doing the vocal on Teddy Wilson's record (also a hit). The whole side swings with that delicious atmosphere of classic 1930s small group jazz—and then comes Holiday with her salty, pouting, sad, exuberant refrain. Her 1955 rerecording of the number luxuriates in having the time to include the verse—a good one, used fairly often by singers. Pianist Carl Drinkard supplies a lovely accompaniment. Although Holiday sounds a bit lethargic and tired, the way she bends the pitch on words like "sky" or "star" is priceless. Her faster tempo 1957 studio recording and 1958 live rendering are less subtle but more wide awake. Holiday loved this tune, as well as another from the same movie, "Miss Brown to You," and often included both in her performance sets.

Ella Fitzgerald also engaged with Parker's lyric more than once. On a 1954 single, reissued for decades on LP and CD, she does a bit of call and response with Gordon Jenkins's choir. Lush with strings, the track ought to be awful, but Fitzgerald is in excellent voice, her grace notes liquid, her variations seemingly inevitable, rising like a rocket out of the launch pad of the chorus's interjections. For her 1963 LP track with Nelson Riddle, she is in even better voice, and the arrangement is fine, but the frisky tempo does not allow them to penetrate to the heart of the song.

Frank Sinatra also recorded the song with Nelson Riddle. Their verse is excellent, but for most of the refrain they choose an inappropriate rumba accompaniment. They are good, and Sinatra handles Parker's lyrics with wonderfully serious intent, but they miss the chance to create a definitive version.

"I Wished on the Moon" seems to have had something of a resurgence in the 1950s, with Holiday, Fitzgerald, Teddi King, June Christy, Billy Eckstine, Patti Page, and others creating a lot of momentum for the song. Many jazz instrumentalists also embraced Rainger's tune. In a performance like that of Coleman Hawkins, one can almost hear him thinking the lyrics as he plays. The ballad's status as a hit of 1935 was firmly overtaken by its role as standard repertoire.[12]

Parker and Campbell split apart, reunited, split apart, and finally reunited as housemates and collaborators until his 1963 death (perhaps suicide, perhaps accident). Meanwhile, Parker's output as an author dwindled but never ceased until a few years before her passing from a heart attack. Hopefully, "I Wished on the Moon" brought some revenue to the writer during those difficult years.

"WHAT'S YOUR STORY, MORNING GLORY" (1938/1940)
Mary Lou Williams (1910–1981), composer-lyricist

Men ran the music business, the music criticism business, and the music history business. It is no surprise, therefore, that men dominate the annals of jazz history. Nevertheless, in that conventional narrative, Mary Lou Williams stands as the Great Exception. All the critics agree that Williams played her piano and wrote her jazz compositions on a level with the most worshipped icons of twentieth-century jazz, from Jelly Roll Morton to Miles Davis. She attained the quality, rose to the fame, and generated the mythos—the rise, fall, and resurrection (which included her conversion to Catholicism)—to match any of them. From her birthplace in Georgia she went on to be a child prodigy in Pittsburgh. It was there she remembered seeing Lovie Austin and taking her as a role model. The launching pad of her mature career was in Oklahoma and Kansas City, with Andy Kirk and

His Clouds of Joy. Their eventual national success led to her international fame. Reportedly, she was proud of "playing heavy, like a man." In the end she attained a stylistic range that was the widest among the great names of jazz piano. She died in New York, not rich but honored.[13]

Her orchestrations are deliciously textured, her harmonies profound, her rhythm unsurpassable. Her jazz compositions flow forth with theme after theme, interesting phrasing, and captivating bits of melody and rhythm. Unfortunately, Tin Pan Alley missed out on a good thing, rarely tapping into the genius of Mary Lou Williams. Although her forte was instrumental pieces in blues, swing, bop, and modern jazz styles, on occasion her songwriting could match that of Duke Ellington, as with the soulful, sensuous, soaring melody of "Ghost of Love" (1938).

Her biggest hit was a rhythm song: a 1942 copyright, "Satchel Mouth Baby," that became a 1946 success in the African American market. It then got tweaked and added to by others and resurrected in 1952 as the mainstream bestseller "Pretty Eyed Baby." It anticipates some of the feeling of rock-and-roll and could well be revived in that style. Yet Williams's most enduring song was a lesser hit that is now a strong standard: the idiosyncratic "What's Your Story, Morning Glory."

"What's Your Story, Morning Glory" is a twelve-bar blues, repeated twice to make a twenty-four measure refrain. Its genesis offers an interesting example of the collaborative process. Williams was pen pals with trumpeter Paul Webster (of the Jimmie Lunceford big band). They wrote letters to each other with words that were like lyrics and sometimes snatches of notated musical notes. Sometime in 1938, Webster wrote to Williams the lines, "What's your story, morning glory? I haven't heard from you," with "two or four bars" of music. Williams remembered, "In about ten or fifteen minutes I wrote this tune . . . he gave me a starter . . . so I put his name on it because otherwise I wouldn't have written it."[14]

Webster's opening phrases are potentially declamatory, often performed loudly as a pair of jazz breaks. Indeed, these measures closely echo the first lines of "Aunt Hagar's Blues" (1921) by blues pioneer W. C. Handy and lyricist J. Tim Brymm, which tell of a preacher's oratory. Webster's title became a catchphrase, used in cartoons, newspaper columns, and around college campuses; and his accompanying musical motifs were later recruited by the composer Sonny Burke as the start of "Black Coffee," with a lyric by (to the confusion of some historians) Paul Francis Webster (no relation to the trumpeter). In 1949, Burke's ditty was a radio dee-jay favorite in discs by Sarah Vaughn and Ella Fitzgerald; and it remains a standard. Its publisher, Leeds, quickly got sued by Remick, who had the rights to

Figure 5.1   Mary Lou Williams, in the mid-1940s, surrounded by music scores, joyfully hard at work as usual. (The Library of Congress, via Wikimedia Commons. Public domain.)

"What's Your Story." There was a settlement, but unfortunately Williams only got three hundred dollars out of it.

From Webster's engaging but conventional kernel, Willliams veers off into uncharted territory. Williams creates unpredictable phrasing and the unexpected appearance of new melodic material. This trait seems emblematic of so many details of Williams's biography: she was a risk taker, in music as in life, and generous, including to her listeners. The focus of the

melodic line becomes more intimate; meanwhile, in the lyric, the protagonist confesses devotion to the beloved. The melody swoops down, coasts on
a long note for half a measure, and rushes forward again. The protagonist
then repeats the words of the title question, but now in two groups of four
notes, which, in the next phrase, gets surprisingly extended into an eleven-
note unit. Finally, Williams unspools fresh melodic material for her ten-
note conclusion.

Williams was most apt to collaborate with lyricists for her occasional
vocal works, but here she writes her own words. Effortless interior rhymes
are created not only by Webster in his title phrase, but also by Williams in
her line, "Gotta feeling there's a lot you're concealing." In an unusual tactic
for a pop lyric, she combines tenderness, concern, sympathy, and affectionate irritation. The saloon staple "My Melancholy Baby" (1911) offers a rare
parallel, in an idea supplied by the original lyricist for that melody, May-
belle E. Watson. Like Watson, Williams creates a protagonist who focuses
on gently coaxing the beloved to reveal their troubles. In the case of Williams, this exploration of somebody else's psyche goes along with her own
extreme sensitivity. She confessed to friends that she was "a born medium,"
declaring, "God gifted me with reading minds."[15] This openness to the
emotions of others was both a blessing and a curse, contributing to her
breakdown and temporary retirement from performing in the early 1950s.

The band with which she won renown, Andy Kirk's Clouds of Joy,
recorded "What's Your Story, Morning Glory" on October 25, 1938, and
Williams copyrighted it two days later as an unpublished composition.
The record company, Decca, must have had little faith in it, however, for
it was not issued until August 1940. The flip side, "Now I Lay Me Down
to Dream," was the charting hit; yet that ballad is now forgotten, while
"What's Your Story, Morning Glory" blooms on and on.

In March 1940, the song was copyrighted again; Williams had sold
the number to the small New Era publisher. In October that year it
was recopyrighted a third time, now with an added credit to lyricist Jack
Lawrence (who wrote many hits for the Clouds of Joy), by Advanced
Music, a subsidiary, devoted to hot jazz, of the huge Warner Bros. music
conglomerate. Lawrence repeated one line and changed another, small but
canny moves that make the lyric easier for the listener to absorb. In the
process, however, two delicious lyric phrases got dropped, including the
refreshingly sophisticated "Give your answer to this patient romancer."
Long ignored, at the shift of the centuries these original lines have been
aired more often (such as by Meredith D'Ambrosio and Carmen Lundy),
under the spirit of rediscovery of the jazz legacy.

Both the Clouds of Joy, with a vocal by Pha Terrell, and the Glenn Miller band, featuring Tex Beneke on both sax and vocals, enjoyed prominent discs of the number. Nevertheless, it was Jimmie Lunceford's instrumental that hit home. Billy Moore's arrangement opens with a baroque flourish and then settles into a sonorous big band accompaniment for an especially fine late-night clarinet chorus. A brief staccato band interlude lends variety, sandwiched between trumpet and saxophone solos.

Anita O'Day and arranger Russ Garcia, on a 1958 album, create a particularly well-balanced version that rings both the intimate and brassy changes on the tune. The same year Ella Fitzgerald, with Marty Paich, smiles indulgently at the taciturn sweetheart. Her version misses being definitive because of an accompaniment that is just a pinch too cool. Two years later, Julie London, not overly interfered with by a riffing chorus, convincingly creates a quietly seductive atmosphere.

In 1961, Teri Thornton, backed by a bop ensemble, delivered her proto-soul vocal with her own additional set of lyrics that is still recruited decades later by some singers. Mary Lou Williams herself recorded "What's Your Story, Morning Glory" many times, each so fine it is impossible to choose between them. The song lives on in the twenty-first century, often in explicitly proclaimed tribute to Williams, and always in implicit tribute to the tradition she exemplified.

"SOME OTHER SPRING" (1939/1940)
Irene Armstrong Wilson Kitchings (c. 1908–1975), composer

In the late 1930s, two brilliant pianists lost their loves. Irene Armstrong lost hers to alienation of affections; Ruth Lowe lost hers when her husband died. In 1939, each wrote and copyrighted a song about their loss. Both of these torch songs were recorded in 1940; and both have endured through the decades in hundreds of renderings. Both women also composed a small corpus of other ballads of almost equal quality, most of them sadly neglected in the twenty-first century.

Irene Armstrong was a superior pianist, heavy playing, and a skilled bandleader. In her one recording, accompanying singer Eloise Bennett in 1926 on "Love Me, Mr. Strange Man," she flows forth with a solo that is gutsy and lowdown, full of the verve of early jazz. In Chicago, she was a favorite of Al Capone and the mob. She got employment and perks from them that allowed her to afford a nicely furnished seven-room apartment.

Then, fellow pianist Teddy Wilson, of the light touch and elegant style, won Armstrong's heart, and the two married. He was lured from Chicago to New York in 1933. Now, as Irene Wilson, she gave up performing, under pressure from her mother-in-law. Teddy Wilson became a nationally known figure: Benny Goodman, shortly after attaining stardom, chose him for his jazz trio. Irene dedicated herself to supporting Teddy's career, maintaining what in Paris would have been called a bohemian artist's *salon*. At almost any time of day or night, musicians congregated for food, camaraderie, relaxation, and music making. Before the decade was out, however, Teddy found another love, and Irene was left trying to keep things going by herself. At this time, she wrote a series of ballads. Eventually Irene was beset with a rare eye illness, Eales disease, which can have many unpleasant symptoms and lead to blindness. She moved back to her native Cleveland, Ohio, where her aunt took her in. There, fortune led her into a lifelong and happy marriage to Elden Kitchings, a minor government official. Her compositions now carry her final name, Irene Kitchings, around the globe.

In the 1930s, Irene became good friends with the singer on Teddy's records: Billie Holiday. Billie gave her new friend the nickname "Renie," and the label stuck. Irene was there as Teddy and Billie went through hundreds and hundreds of Tin Pan Alley sheets, deciding what songs to record. Meanwhile, Irene was accompanying her singing friend during their frequent jamming jazz soirees.

Their chum, saxophonist Ben Webster, observed what an unusual sense of harmony Irene had and encouraged her to compose. When she separated from Teddy, she did just that, copyrighting her first song on April 1, 1939, "This Is the Moment," co-composed with arranger-saxophonist Jimmy Mundy, with lyrics by Charles Carpenter (both men being, at the time, with the Earl Hines Orchestra). Ironically, it was Teddy Wilson who recorded this first plug tune by Irene, his ex-love.

By that time, Holiday had become friends with Arthur Herzog Jr., an erstwhile Tin Pan Alley songwriter who was actively writing words and music for leftist political songs. Holiday sent Irene downtown to meet him: "He's a pretty nice cat, Renie. I want you to meet him, and he writes lyrics."[16] All of Kitchings's songs thereafter would have lyrics by Herzog.

Arthur Herzog Jr. deserves introduction, for not only did he write lyrics for a handful of gemlike melodies by Irene Kitchings, but he also cowrote songs with Billie Holiday, including "God Bless' the Child." He was an Ivy Leaguer, straight out of Princeton University when in 1926 he wrote lyrics for an off-Broadway revue, *Bad Habits*, which yielded a tune that got some attention and was published and plugged by Edward B. Marks,

"Would-Ja?" In 1931, the press announced that Arthur Herzog Jr. had cofounded an investment firm, but it soon disappears from view. In the mid-1930s, Herzog began to copyright songs again, all of them unpublished, for which he often wrote both words and music. These include both Tin Pan Alley–styled titles, like "The Lady Was Lovely," and protest songs, like "We're Veterans of the Future War" and "Jobs, Security, Democracy and Peace." By 1939, he was living close to, and seemingly hanging around (perhaps as its publicist), the downtown politically liberal club Café Society—a venue that played an important part in Billie Holiday's career. In the early 1940s, his collaboration on some unusual popular songs with Kitchings and Holiday brought him back to the fringes of Tin Pan Alley. Herzog then went on to co-author a farce with the saucy title *Mary Had a Little* (1946). This play (despite uniformly bad reviews) managed to have a life on regional American stages and in England on stage and screen.

The 1950s found Herzog in Detroit, as a highly valued movie publicity agent, shuttling back and forth from the heartland to New York City to promote films by Warner Bros. and Universal-International Studio. His son (Arthur the Third) became a successful writer, and his granddaughter (Amy) a well-known film and theater director. Herzog Jr. continued to play an important part in Detroit civic life for decades, even as he focused with pride on his early songwriting output that was gaining new attention in the LP era. He became a widower in 1975 and himself died in 1983, living long enough to be interviewed about his glory years of landmark songwriting with two African American women.

Back in 1939, when Kitchings went downtown to meet with Herzog, she took along Carmen McRae, the young chum of herself and Holiday. Once Herzog had completed the lyric, Irene sprung it on her intimates Carmen and Billie: "Helen Oakley had us for dinner." From Canada, Oakley was one of their best friends. She worked for the Variety record label (a branch of the Irving Mills publishing company) and, more generally, as a publicist for jazz; later she formed a power couple when she married British jazz critic Stanley Dance. Irene said, "Lady, I have this song and I want you to hear it." She recalled, "I played it" for Helen, Carmen, and Billie, "and they said when they looked up Lady was sitting there with tears in her eyes, and she said, 'Renie, I want to make that song.' And I said, 'Lady, you know it's yours.'" After recording the song, Holiday proclaimed, "Renie, don't worry about these songs, you just write 'em and bring 'em to me and I'll make 'em."[17]

Three of the five songs Kitchings and Herzog wrote were torch ballads of lost or longed-for romance: "Some Other Spring," "Ghost of Yesterday," and "If You'd Stay the Way I Dream About You." When Kitchings handed Herzog a melody, he never asked her to change a note, a fact he noted as unusual in his collaborations. In her turn, Kitchings praised him: "I've never had to ask him to change a word." Friends like Carmen McRae and Callie Arter clearly perceived that these poignant works stemmed from Irene's heartbreak over losing Teddy: "That music was just pouring out of her heart."[18] From early in his career, jazz pianist Jimmy Rowles was drawn to these pieces and titled an album *Some Other Spring*. He opined: "Her songs are very special. They're *inside* songs. They make your heart ache. That's what she was—she was a heartache writer."[19] It is this evocation of a deep interior life that marks the finest ballads of the Great American Songbook.

"Some Other Spring" and the other Kitching-Herzog songs have tremendous atmosphere. They are moist, heavy and yet delicate, evoking a climate of fragrant humidity. In "Spring," as in all her compositions, Kitchings features poignant harmonies, never quite predictable. Her melody is akin to Kay Swift's for "Can't We Be Friends" in that it never repeats. Like a fine jazz improvisation, it keeps unfolding in directions fresh and yet inevitable. Even in the release, when Kitchings repeats the pattern of a few notes in a higher register, she then leads in new directions.

Herzog's lyric also surprises, not only in its images but also in its rhyme scheme. He does not take the easy way out and make simple end-rhyme couplets in an *abcb* pattern. Instead he creates the pattern *abac*, opening the possibility for the end-rhymes to be phrased as internal rhymes: "Some other spring, I'll try to love. / Now I still cling, to faded blossoms." He then concludes the main strain with end-rhymes in a virtuoso triple *ddd* pattern: *worn/torn/mourn*. He deftly captures Kitchings's mood of misery, while also medicinally treating the fatigue of romantic defeat with the therapeutic balm of imagined healing. For all the protagonist's questionings about the future, the final message is one of hope for a renewed embrace of life.

The definitive recording of "Some Other Spring" is the first, by Holiday, in July 1939. Almost as special is the September 1939 disc by Teddy Wilson, in what might be a unique case of a musician recording a song inspired by his own infidelity, with a fine vocal by Jean Eldridge. Both waxings received attention and praise in the Black press but did not rate as mainstream hits. Although recopyrighted in 1940 by Regent Music, "Some Other Spring" was not published at that time.

Holiday remembered Benny Goodman's prediction about "Some Other Spring": "Nothing's gonna happen with that tune. It's too beautiful. . . . Maybe in the years to come." He was right: for a decade, the song languished,

but after that the years vindicated "Some Other Spring." In 1950, trade journals announced its first publication by the Edward B. Marks firm, reportedly
spurred by Herzog's urgings. Columbia made plans to reissue the Holiday
and Wilson renderings. *Variety* noted that advance royalties were helping
Kitchings to receive "special treatment" for her increasing blindness: "cor-
tisone and a trip to John Hopkins hospital in Baltimore." For the Decca
label, Austin Powell put out a single, and his big voice heralded a revival of
the piece. He went to Kitchings's hometown of Cleveland, where large ads
proclaimed this new waxing of the song written by "Cleveland's renowned
blind composer Irene Wilson Kitchings." Jazz players Jimmy Raney, Frank
Wess, and Jimmy Rowles essayed the composition in the 1950s, and Holiday
rerecorded it in 1956. In this later version, Holiday digs even more deeply
into the lyrics. As she sings the release, the listener can vividly see the spring
sunshine outside and the coating of ice inside her soul.[20]

In her 1959 debut album, Dakota Staton put her own stamp on "Some
Other Spring," youthful, playful, and jazzy. This is the first time the tune
was on a charting disc, and it seems to mark a watershed for the piece.
In 1960, two Englishmen put their renderings on record: pianist George
Shearing and singer Anthony Newley, enjoying a phase as a pop idol, on
an album that charted in the United Kingdom. His crisp diction and short
phrasings suit the song's delicacy surprisingly well. From then on, the song
was accepted in England and, indeed, throughout Europe, as a standard.[21]
Across the Atlantic, it perhaps assumed a higher ranking than it enjoyed
in the States. British Invasion star Marianne Faithfull reimported "Some
Other Spring" to the United States on her charting 1966 American album,
Faithfull Forever. Meanwhile, jazz heavyweights Anita O'Day and, appropriately, Carmen McRae had embraced the tune. Ella Fitzgerald eventually
came to the song, too, live in 1979, but disappointingly got the lyric wrong.
Tony Bennett took even longer to engage with the Kitchings-Herzog classic, waiting until he paid tribute to Holiday in a 1997 album. The rough
edges of his voice, and the clarity and restraint of the singer and his pianist
Ralph Sharon, serve the song well, with an artificial sounding and irrelevant
string section being the only detraction.

Luckily, Kitchings experienced the rebirth Herzog had hinted at in his
lyrics. Late in life, she said she could hardly believe that "Some Other
Spring" was "written for me." She rejoiced in her second husband: "Elden
keeps me smiling even now my sight is gone."[22] In the creation of "Some
Other Spring," art had imitated life, expressing Irene's pain. But now life
imitated art, reflecting the ultimate hopefulness in the song. Kitchings had,
indeed, found "love with some other spring."

"I'LL NEVER SMILE AGAIN" (1939)
Ruth Lowe (1914–1981), composer-lyricist

In Tin Pan Alley history, there are two famous songs inspired by the death of a spouse. The first story recounts how Irving Berlin lost his new-lywed bride in 1912 and, in his grief, produced "When I Lost You." The second tale is of Ruth Lowe, who wrote "I'll Never Smile Again" in 1939, when her husband passed away. Both songs became number one hits and enduring standards.

Lowe was from Jewish Canadian stock. Her mother's family came from Russia and Poland by way of England. Her father, Samuel Lowenthal, origi-nally a New Yorker, was a gregarious, charming, funny, musical man, the life of the party, filled "with a million ideas." He moved his wife and two daughters to California in search of business success. When that attempt failed, the family (and their piano) were shipped back to Toronto. After more failure, Mr. Lowenthal committed suicide. Pearl Lowenthal, "worn down by life, quiet, unassuming," and cursed with a weak heart, struggled to keep going. Though the household may not have had financial security, they always had a piano.[23]

Ruth studied music during their California years. By the age of nineteen, she was supporting her mother and sister as a performer. As was standard practice, she Anglicized her name to Lowe. Her peers considered her "an exceptional pianist."[24] Around Toronto, she teamed with Ran Daly in a singing act or with pianist-singer Sair Lee on vaudevilles stages, played with local dance bands, and had regular gigs on both local and national radio shows.

In 1935, the most famous all-woman big band breezed into town, Ina Ray Hutton and Her Melodears, and they needed a temporary substitute pia-nist. Lowe got the job and ended up staying with the band for about three years as it toured around the United States. On the road with hardened professionals, Lowe learned to smoke and play poker.[25]

While playing in Chicago, Ruth's fellow band member set her up to be half of a double date. Her blind date turned out to be the tall, dark, handsome—and Jewish—Harold Cohen. The two entered into a swift courtship and marriage. Cohen had been in the jukebox business, for Wurlitzer, for years. Coworkers treasured him as a "hard-hitting salesman," with a "continuous jovial smile" and "kid-like mannerisms," which made him "popular with everyone that he knew." The Lowenthal family was happy too, for he was a "very nice man," and his family were "lovely people" who made everyone "feel very much at home." Thus, by mid-1938, Lowe had found her mate in a stable, successful professional (in that way, a contrast to her father), absolutely devoted to her, and sharing her commitment to jazz and popular music.[26]

From being a coin machine operator, Cohen had made the transition to the music publishing business, centered in Chicago around the Woods Theater, working as a publicist. It is not surprising that Lowe, now being married to a songplugger, started to copyright popular compositions, collaborating at first with local Chicago lyricists Bernice Rosengarden (writing under the less Jewish-sounding pseudonym Bee Arden) and singer Charles "Skip" Farrell. About this time, too, Lowe may have had other encouragement. On a whim, she and her sister visited a fortune teller who predicted, "One day, you will write a song that will be popular all over the world. . . . And as a result, you'll be rich and famous."[27] In April 1939, Lowe attained her first published composition, an instrumental piano piece cowritten with a rising band pianist, Bob Zurke, with the hepcat title "Ode to an Alligator."

Then, on May 15, 1939, Cohen went into the hospital for a routine operation and, completely without warning, died of kidney failure. Lowe went back to Toronto to live with her mother and her sister, Mickey. For days, Ruth just sat looking out the window "watching couples strolling arm in arm in the park." Eventually, she went back to her radio work. One summer day, she told Mickey, "I just don't think I'll ever smile again." That night, she wrote up the idea in popular song form. She played it for Mickey, who remembered, "It was nice . . . but . . . it just seemed like another song."[28]

On August 24, Lowe copyrighted "I'll Never Smile Again" as an unpublished work. Her friend Vida was an arranger for local radio maestro Percy Faith (long before his renowned later career in easy listening), and she played it for him. Faith liked Lowe's song so well he scheduled it on his broadcasts and made a private full orchestra recording. In early September, the Tommy Dorsey band flew to Toronto for the Canadian National Exhibition. Their guitarist (probably Clark Yocum) had as a girlfriend June Hutton, the sister of Lowe's former boss Ina Ray Hutton. Lowe contacted June, who played Faith's recording to the guitarist, who then played it for Dorsey. The bandleader had recently bought a publishing house, newly dubbed Sun Music, and he had them buy the rights to Lowe's tune. On November 27, they recopyrighted it as a published composition.

In March 1940, the Dorsey band gathered around the piano at the Astor Hotel while Joe Bushkin ran through "I'll Never Smile Again." The band's vocalist was Frank Sinatra, and he remembered, "I noticed that everybody was very quiet, the whole orchestra sat quietly when he played it. There was a feeling of eeriness, as though we all knew that this would be a big, big hit, and that it was a lovely song." Freddie Stulce then arranged the song for Dorsey. Mysteriously, the piece was recorded twice, on April 23 and May 23; even more mysteriously, both takes were issued with the same 26628 pressing number. The ultimate rendition is slow and sparse. The Pied Pipers vocal group dominates the proceedings, with Frank Sinatra's solo lines emerging out of the ensemble like a lovely tree seen through the mist. What separates the rendition from the sweet bands of the era is its subtle swing, felt throughout in Bushkin's celeste playing, the wordless riffs of the Pipers, Dorsey's trombone solo, and the fresh, direct, vulnerable singing of Sinatra.[29]

The Dorsey disc of "I'll Never Smile Again" became a bestseller of historic proportions. Although Frank Sinatra shared the spotlight with the Pied Pipers, nevertheless the arrangement was quickly and widely acknowledged as the start of his stardom. Also notable is that, yet again, as with Ella Fitzgerald's "A-Tisket, A-Tasket," a female songwriter contributed to a landmark in the revival of phonorecord sales. Before 1940 ended, Lowe was rewarded by a swift nomination and election to ASCAP membership. The professional friendship between her and Sinatra was cemented in the fall of 1942 when, reportedly on short notice, she wrote the words for his broadcast sign-off piece, "Put Your Dreams Away."

Back in 1940, word quickly spread about how "I'll Never Smile Again" was a product of Lowe's bereavement. By July, articles were appearing about her in trade journals, popular magazines, and newspapers. Suddenly in demand, she moved to New York. By September, she was busy in vaudeville as a solo or in tandem with partners like fellow songwriter Walter Kent. Lowe's life became so hectic that her sister, Mickey, had to join her to function as her secretary. For three years, her days were filled with songwriting, performing, and a life of celebrityhood.

After "I'll Never Smile Again," Lowe's next three plug tunes probably suffered in popularity from the national radio networks banning ASCAP music through most of 1941. Certainly, the very fine "My Next Romance" was just building up momentum as a jukebox favorite as the strike began and never attained the radio play it deserved. Lowe's songwriting luck continued to languish in 1942, perhaps leading her to put aside composing and take up lyric writing for the team of Paul Mann and Stephan Weiss (Austrians who had fled from a Europe in the throes of Nazi takeovers) for "Put Your Dreams Away" and a couple of other tunes.

In 1943, despite the musicians' union ban on recordings, things picked up for Lowe as a songwriter: Sinatra started his radio program, bringing attention to "Put Your Dreams Away," and Lowe wrote words and music for the amiable, soft-shoe styled "More Than Anything in the World," a radio success. By the time autumn rolled around, however, Lowe was fed up with the pace of Manhattan life—and perhaps also with the uphill battle of getting her songs promoted. She copyrighted one more unpublished song on September 8, 1943, and then dropped everything and moved back to Toronto.

By the end of November 1943, Lowe had found and married another tall, dark, handsome, stable, and successful Jewish man, Nathan Sandler. As she entered into her second big romance, a song she had composed with a lyric by Mack David, ironically titled "My First Love," was just rising in radio play and disc sales. Though not an enduring song, it proved to be her second biggest hit, allowing Lowe to say goodbye to Tin Pan Alley on a high note.

In "I'll Never Smile Again," Lowe achieves great simplicity and restraint. Her refrain is in standard ABA´C form, and at first glance the melody seems predictable, with symmetrical phrasings and near repetitions. Within that conventional format, however, there are subtle variations. Allen Forte picks out many of those in his detailed musicological analysis of the song. Unusually, Lowe places the melody's highest note on the first downbeat (on "smile"). She further surprises by then immediately dropping down the interval of a seventh (on "again"). As was customary, she very soon repeats this motif; overall, she sounds it five times. It is, as Forte says, "the hallmark of this song," the hook.[30]

As Forte points out, Lowe's entire C-segment is an eight-measure expansion of those first two measures. In it, the composer displays wit as she first slows and then quickens the rhythmic texture. In her lyrics, the closely occurring rhyme pair beautifully fits her melody: "Within my heart" (four syllables) is followed by "I know I will never start" (seven syllables). This asymmetrical sequence brings the song to a quiet climax.

Lowe makes further striking choices at the ends of the two A-sections. The first time, she plummets down to the tune's lowest note. This corresponds to a query: "What good would it do?" Although it is a question, it does not go up to a high note; therefore, it becomes a defeatist statement: "It won't do any good." Through such small details, Lowe raises the emotional stakes of the song.

At the end of the second A-section, most songwriters would have changed the melody to end on a higher note, in order to lead into the final segment. Lowe herself uses that strategy in two 1941 melodies, "More Than Once" and "It's Raining Memories." But in "I'll Never Smile Again," Lowe repeats the melody exactly as she had stated it just previously. Thereby, she saves her climax for five measures later, and this understated holding back deepens the impression of sincerity.

Lowe is canny: her lyric can apply to her real situation of bereavement or to a less final conclusion to a love affair. Her words can be a pleading love message that leaves open the possibility of reuniting. In the context of 1940, with loved ones starting to be separated by the war—earlier in Canada than in the United States, of course—the song accumulated an even more profound resonance.

The famous Dorsey version is definitive and captures the understatement and air of sanctity of the song. In addition, Lowe's elegy was covered by many other singers and bands. Another popular disc was by the Glenn Miller orchestra, with Ray Eberle on vocals; Tony Martin's waxing also saw sales and jukebox play. The song crossed over to the country-western field, with a disc by Gene Autry and a particularly fine one from Elton Britt.

In 1953, the Four Aces pressure washed "I'll Never Smile Again" with power chords in the barbershop quartet tradition, making it a hit once more. In a charting 1961 version, the Platters, with a lead vocal by Tony Williams, also emphasized its potential to be sweepingly emotional. Instrumentalists from Django Reinhardt to Dave Brubeck caressed the tune, as have vocalists from Vera Lynn to Michael Bublé.[31] Billie Holiday rendered an amazingly effective performance for her final album, proving herself still great even near to her own sad demise. Sinatra revisited "Smile Again" twice; his 1959 Capitol-era track takes the prize for quietly trembling sincerity.

After her second marriage, Lowe composed one more Tin Pan Alley plug tune in 1955, "My Love Came Back to Me," that got good radio play for a couple of weeks; and later the Canadian folk group, the Travelers, recorded her gospel-styled "Take Your Sins to the River." In her personal life, Lowe has been called "rambunctious," but her songwriting is dominated by a different aspect. All of her prominent songs have a quality that is uniquely her own, a very particular gentle warmth and tenderness.

Friends and family describe Lowe as mischievous, perky, quirky, outgoing, and "never standing still for long." Normally, she was "always smiling, always laughing." When her first husband died, and she suddenly lost her smiles and laughter, she must have momentarily felt not really herself. As was the case with Irene Kitchings, Lowe's songwriting became part of the process of overcoming loss. Her life philosophy triumphed, blazoned on a necklace she wore, and passed on to her sons: "Live, Laugh, and Love."[32]

6

"MY SILENT LOVE" (1931/1932)

Dana Suesse (1909–1987), composer

Acquaintances remembered Dana Suesse as "an odd duck," and when she spoke, it could be "with an almost disconcerting air of knowing what it's all about." In photographs from her youthful heyday, her face stares out with a special kind of serious, sober regard. The images radiate the same aura as her music, conveying an inner belief: "I am significant."[1]

Suesse was one of the leading lights of Tin Pan Alley throughout the 1930s. For three decades, she was also a much performed concert composer, a rarity among Americans in the first half of the twentieth century. She should be acclaimed as a pioneer of Third Stream music, a brilliant Neo-Romantic and American Impressionist, a triumphant champion of tonality and melodic lyricism. Yet the brief, dry, and bland entries about her in reference sources offer little hint of the vitality, subtlety, and compelling stance of her compositions. Three of her early popular instrumentals are, arguably, her most quintessential works: "Syncopated Love Song" (1928), "Jazz Nocturne" (1931), and "Blue Moonlight" (1935). In danger of being ignored by the classical and jazz worlds alike, in their drama and elegance these pieces are the musical equivalent of the exquisite 1930s dance duets of Fred Astaire and Ginger Rogers. Themes from all three were given lyrics and transformed into popular songs, including "My Silent Love."

Figure 6.1 Dana Suesse, in the mid-1930s, by then an important face in US music worlds, both popular and classical. (Library of Congress, Washington, DC, Music Division, Dana Suesse Papers, Box 46, Folder 13.)

BIOGRAPHY

Suesse was a child prodigy in her native Kansas City, Missouri, a fate she regretted through decades of adulthood. Her act included ballet dancing, reciting poetry, and improvising at the piano on any musical theme offered by the audience. She first performed in a concert hall at the age of ten (Chaminade, Grieg, Rachmaninoff, and so forth). At thirteen, she began to perform her own compositions, was soloist with her school's student orchestra, and presented her first organ recital. Her parents were Julius, a first-generation American of Austrian-German ancestry, and Nina, from old Southern stock and a member of the Daughters of the American Revolution. Nina changed the family name from the Austrian Suess to the French-looking Suesse and propelled her daughter's career. Seemingly, Julius was largely absent in her upbringing (he traveled for work), and by 1930 he and Nina had divorced.

In early December 1926, Suesse and her mother left the heartland behind forever, moving to New York. Dana had just turned seventeen. By the end of the month, she was performing regularly on radio. She began to study piano with Alexander Siloti (the cousin, and teacher, of Rachmaninoff) and composition with Rubin Goldmark (teacher of Aaron Copland and George Gershwin). Music publishers, however, would not buy her short piano pieces in classical style: "My mother and I went around to all those publishers and found there was no market for this kind of thing."[2]

Decades later, Suesse looked back and claimed that "jazz and popular music" was "unknown territory" to her when she moved to New York. Because historians so firmly label the 1920s as the Jazz Age, some might find her claim hard to believe. For many Americans steeped in the classical tradition, however, jazz would continue to seem alien for generations to come. Suesse quickly realized that not only was there a market for the popular forms but that she found them "very interesting."[3] By the end of January 1927, she had copyrighted words and music for her first popular song (never published); by the end of 1928, music for another, "Razor-Blade Blues."

In July 1928, Suesse copyrighted the first composition with which she would make her mark, "Syncopated Love Song," a short multithematic instrumental work. This genre was partly inspired by the public's widespread embrace of Gershwin's *Rhapsody in Blue*. Paul Whiteman, the decade's most successful bandleader, had commissioned and introduced Gershwin's opus in his 1924 concert, *An Experiment in Modern Music*. In "Syncopated Love Song," Suesse displays her talent for compelling melodies and an expert control of musical components. Nevertheless, from copyright to hit status took two and a half years. This is an example of how composers—especially women composers—had a hard time getting even their highest-quality creations entered into the ranks of Tin Pan Alley plug products.

In the meantime, Suesse forged ahead, doing radio work, performing in the ensemble of a production of *Macbeth* (she had memorized the play as a child), making the rounds of music firms, publishing a few pieces for silent film accompaniment (with titles like "The Get-Away"), and, according to some later reports, working as a private secretary. During these years of struggle, Suesse was encouraged by women of an older generation: Mabel Wayne and composer Jessie L. Deppen (whose songs ranged from high-class to pop). Suesse also remembered Dolly Morse with gratitude: "She was one of the first people in the business I met when I came to New York. She was very, very kind to me, and introduced me to a lot of . . . publishers and all sorts of people."[4]

The publisher, Harms, found belated faith in Suesse's "Syncopated Love Song" and hatched the idea of taking its most catchy melody and making it the basis for a Tin Pan Alley ballad. Leo Robin, already established as a top-flight lyricist, gave it words; Suesse contrived a middle section; and on February 26, 1931, they copyrighted this adaptation, "Have You Forgotten." It proved a happy harbinger of success. The following day, the smaller firm of Olman Music registered Suesse's next song, the woebegone but jaunty "Whistling in the Dark," with lyrics by Allan Boretz. Six publishers had rejected it—to their regret, for "Whistling" became a very quick success. Suesse was now seen as a rising talent, and the firm of Famous Music signed her to a staff contract. By May, Suesse was her own competition, with three hits going at once: "Have You Forgotten" and "Whistling in the Dark" vied for customers with Suesse's initial ditty at Famous Music, "Ho, Hum," with lyrics by Edward Heyman.

Famous Music copyrighted Suesse's next instrumental, "Jazz Nocturne," in late October 1931 and was seriously promoting it by February 1932. Nat Shilkret (the conductor who had championed and then gained cocredit for "Syncopated Love Song") recorded "Jazz Nocturne." By June 1932, his disc was listed among bestsellers. In a process much faster than that for "Syncopated Love Song," Suesse and Heyman adapted her main instrumental melody into a song with lyrics.

On April 14, 1932, the new version was copyrighted, called "My Silent Love." Within two weeks, it was a big hit, with sheet music and record disc sales flourishing from coast to coast. In June, "My Silent Love" was rated the second most popular song in the United States, right behind Bernice Petkere's "Lullaby of the Leaves." At last, female composers had unquestionably triumphed in Tin Pan Alley with jazzy fox-trot melodies. Prejudices might linger, but their ability to shine in this area had at last been strongly established.

Tin Pan Alley believed that dark, brooding, so-called minor key melodies like "My Silent Love," "Lullaby of the Leaves," and the contemporaneous "Hummin' to Myself," by Sammy Fain, could never "click" by Alley standards. Tunes of this sort, like Cole Porter's "What Is This Thing Called

Love" (1929) or Arthur Schwartz's "Dancing in the Dark" (1931), might do well on the Broadway stage, in ballrooms, on the air, or with record sales. In 1932, however, Suesse, Petkere, and Fain broke the barrier and proved such compositions could also fulfill the Alley's most important criterion: amateurs in great numbers would buy sheet music for independent songs of this type.

Suesse had made it. Paul Whiteman premiered her *Concerto in Three Rhythms* with the composer herself at the piano at his 1932 *Fifth Experiment in Modern Music* and her *Symphonic Waltzes* at his 1933 *Sixth Experiment in Modern Music*; her works were played by symphonic orchestras at Town Hall, the Brooklyn Academy of Music, and Boston Symphony Hall; a scattering of her songs were featured on Broadway; she contributed the bulk of a movie musical score (the low-budget *Sweet Surrender*); and so on. She was a guest of the Roosevelts at the White House more than once. Amid all this activity, she produced an ebb and flow of Tin Pan Alley products.

Suesse's estate continues to earn money from the jaunty "You Oughta Be in Pictures" (1934), because its main theme is used internationally in countless documentaries, television shows, and films as a symbol of Hollywood's studio era. Suesse and Heyman claimed to have written it in twelve minutes. At Harms, they were bragging to Henry Spitzer that they could write a hit any time. He said, "All right, there's the piano," and locked them in, giving them a half hour.[5] Heyman grabbed the title phrase from everyday conversation. Suesse plucked from her memory a ten-note ballet theme in triple meter from Riccardo Drigo's famous "Serenade," shaved off the final two notes, put it into four-four meter, shaped it into asymmetrical variations, added a syncopated release melody, and produced a motor-driven American rhythm tune. The writers emerged after twelve minutes with the completed work. Although "You Oughta Be in Pictures" is seldom performed in its entirety, Doris Day proved on a 1959 album that the piece holds up as a singer's standard.

Suesse's third standard is the lyrical, flowing "The Night Is Young (And You're So Beautiful)" of 1936. Like Jerome Kern, Suesse drew on her classical background to create a melody both challenging and inevitable. It marks the start of Suesse's decade-long collaboration with lyricist and entrepreneur Billy Rose; they wrote it for his mammoth spectacle at the Fort Worth, Texas, Frontier Centennial. With colyricist Irving Kahal, Rose creates a lyric with his typical combination of expertise (internal rhymes and delightfully asymmetrical phrasing) and gaucherie (rhyme pairs like *kissable/permissible* and *glamorous/overamorous* do not quite jell, seeming to try too hard).

Writing music for Rose's enterprises was probably a dependable for-hire, bread-and-butter way to earn money for Suesse during those years. She composed for his huge Texas shows during the summers of 1936 and 1937, for his clubs in New York City (the Casa Manana, and then the Diamond Horseshoe), and for his aquacades in Chicago and at the 1939 World's Fair in New York. The last produced her other major hit with Rose, "Yours for a Song," another swooningly romantic melody. It was adopted as the theme song of that fondly remembered exposition. Although, for these, Rose is always listed as one of two lyricists, Suesse affirmed to the end that he was a legitimate contributor.

In 1940, Suesse wedded Courtney Burr. He was from a wealthy family and produced a long string of Broadway productions, bewildering in their almost uniform lack of success. In the marriage, Suesse was the major earner. Not unusually for those in the arts during that era, theirs was an open relationship. Suesse was a bisexual and freely pursued romantic liaisons with men and women during their sixteen-year union.[6]

Although her 1930s songs with Rose received proper plugging by Tin Pan Alley, from 1940 onward the Suesse and Rose collaborations never entered the pop market. For example, in the autumn of 1946, a reviewer of the floor show at Billy Rose's nightclub mentions "A Perfect Love Match" as a catchy tune. Yet it was never copyrighted, let alone published and promoted. It is possible Rose was simply too distracted by what amounted to a media empire, with radio shows, nightclubs, newspaper columns, and producing. Suesse, too, was distracted, composing popular piano instrumentals, issued by Robbins, and works for the concert hall, some distributed in print and recordings by Schirmer. For both Rose and Suesse, their energies were going elsewhere.

Suesse finally escaped the trap of doing hackwork for Rose, with its short-term profits. She cowrote a comedy; in January 1947, it opened and closed quickly on Broadway, but not before Hollywood paid for the movie rights. With this lump sum in hand, Suesse left for three years in Paris, studying composition with Nadia Boulanger, the famed teacher of many of Suesse's male contemporaries, including Aaron Copland, Leonard Bernstein, and Elliot Carter.

Suesse was back in New York by the fall of 1950, to experience a decade of mixed fulfillment and frustration. Two piano concerti and other shorter concert works were premiered; and she did work for the theater, writing musicals and incidental themes for plays. In December 1952, Burr finally produced a major Broadway hit, *The Seven Year Itch*. Suesse wrote incidental music for the production, a multisectional piece that found its greatest popularity in 1954 when given a French lyric by pop singer-songwriter Jean-Claude Darnal as "Toi Qui Disais, Qui Disais, Qui Disais." Suesse knew nothing of this Continental success until the royalties started rolling in.

Suesse divorced Burr in 1954, during the long run of *The Seven Year Itch*. In 1957, on a trip to England, she converted to Catholicism. (Rumors hint at an infatuation with a Catholic Englishman.) Her decade ended with a couple of quick flops: the off-Broadway musical *Come Play with Me* and the Broadway comedy *Golden Fleecing*, produced by Burr and again featuring his ex-wife's incidental music. Then Suesse ceased being visible in the mainstream. Her second marriage, to Charles Edward Delinks, lasted for eleven happy years, from 1970 until his death. Inspired by the enthusiasm of pianist-conductor Peter Mintun, who became her biographer and the heir for her unpublished works, Suesse produced a concert of her compositions at Carnegie Hall in December 1974. She followed this with a 1975 concert at the Newport Music Festival. Since her death in 1987, because of the internet, her works have become more available than any time since her heyday.

"MY SILENT LOVE"

Suesse jam-packs her instrumental piece, "Jazz Nocturne" (1931), with themes that rival the best of Gershwin and Kern. Schematically, it is two AABA structures, the first up-tempo and jazzy, the second slow and moody. Suesse was very proud of the B-section of the latter, because she used three measures of 5/4 time within the overall cut-time meter, perhaps unprecedented in Tin Pan Alley publications of the era. That motif seems innocuous and aimless on first hearing, but repeated listening proves it to be an irresistibly compelling earworm. When Suesse juxtaposes her two main themes at the end of the work, the effect is dramatic and sweeping in a manner that evokes the swelling climaxes of Romantic classical music.[7]

There are two colorful tales about the transformation of the lyrical theme of "Jazz Nocturne" into the popular ballad "My Silent Love" (1932). They are not necessarily contradictory, but one or both might not be true. In one story, the manager of Famous Music, Larry Spier, refused to consider a song version made from "Jazz Nocturne." Therefore, Eddie Heyman waited until Spier was out of town before submitting it to an assistant. In the second anecdote, Suesse and Heyman, in one of the publisher's music rooms, argued "late and heatedly, if good-naturedly, over the lyrics." So concentrated were the collaborators, they were unaware everyone else had left for the night, and they got locked in. The fire department had to get them down on ladders, while "hundreds of people stood around on the sidewalk and the street, gaping and hooting." These anecdotes share the image of an act of creation unknown to others, in that respect paralleling the secret love narrated in Heyman's lyric.[8]

"My Silent Love" has an AABA refrain. Every phrase rises and then falls, creating an arc of despair: love can be aspired to but never attained. The genius of the songwriters emerges in the first phrase: "I reach for you, like I'd reach for a star." Suesse borrows the tune for the A-section quite closely from her "Jazz Nocturne." The melody undulates softly up and down, and then it soars, as Suesse daringly ascends through only two notes (one of them a sharp), up an octave. Heyman matches this flight perfectly: the highest note is on "reach," and the singer stretches their voice as the protagonist stretches in thought.

The chromatic descent (on the words "for a star") reveals how, for the protagonist, all the reaching in the world will do no good. In this A-section, Suesse lends flow to the melody by including seven triplets, yet somehow miraculously avoids turning the tune into a waltz. A final sophisticated touch is the octave drop on the title phrase: "my" (drop) "silent love." The sudden change of vocal register can transform "si-" into a sigh.

Earlier, other composers had ended their A-sections with an octave drop in the final phrase: James P. Johnson and Thomas "Fats" Waller, "Willow Tree" (1928); and Jimmy McHugh, "Exactly Like You" (1930). These were probably accepted by Tin Pan Alley, however, because they were written for Broadway revues and thus allowed a bit more sophistication. Suesse was allowed the octave fall, presumably, because her melody had already impressed the public in its instrumental version. These composers paved the way for Ann Ronell when, later in 1932, she used also an octave drop, in the equivalent spot, in "Willow, Weep for Me."

The B-section of "My Silent Love" bears only a faint schematic resemblance to the corresponding portion of "Jazz Nocturne." Suesse cannily relates her release to the main strain, including in the use of triplets. The melody jumps up an octave, echoing the A-section's octave ascent and drop. Suesse also extends the three-note chromatic descent of "for a star" into chromatic slithers of, first, eight notes, and then, audaciously, nine notes. It hovers on the brink of being excessively obvious but somehow just escapes.

According to one origin tale, Heyman shaped his lyric in close interaction with Suesse, and it is masterful in conception and execution. The language is elegant but conversational. In the first two stanzas, Heyman flavors the entire lyric with his metaphors of vainly reaching for a star or dying out like a campfire in a dampening rain. This is the earliest of the songs covered in the present study that uses a quintessential metaphor of the subgenre that had just recently been labeled "torch song": the flame of love, the fire of affection, passion, and longing. Even more than "Can't We Be Friends," "My Silent Love," with its darkness and drama, bordering on melodrama, is a quintessential torch ballad. Indeed, the song's success, along with others of the era, helped firmly establish this new category.

The protagonist of "My Silent Love" is engaged in an interior mono-logue, directly addressing the beloved but only in imagination. Songwriters had written about love that needs confessing, but Heyman creates an addi-tional layer of complexity. The protagonist makes an avowal that will never be avowed; she sings inside, to a listener who will never hear.

Why does the singer keep her love silent? At the time, the most obvious reason would have been class. The protagonist would be blue collar and the beloved wealthy. That is how the tune is used in the 1953 Hollywood classic *Sabrina*: a chauffer's daughter longs for a millionaire's son, and, meanwhile, "My Silent Love" recurs on the soundtrack. There are many other factors that might keep a love silent, including race, ethnicity, reli-gion, age, levels of fame, society's conventionalized physical values such as weight and looks, or simply shyness. Contemplation of the very fine 1942 recording of "My Silent Love" by Connee Boswell suggests another poi-gnant social barrier: disability. Boswell was a lifelong wheelchair user due to childhood polio.

The era's most closely guarded secret loves would have been same sex. Mintun reveals that not only was Suesse bisexual, but also Eddie Heyman was homosexual. In the post-Stonewall era, the idea of those two, possibly in secret from the publisher and his staff, closeted away together while Heyman formulated his lyric about closeted desire resonates profoundly.

If the singer of "My Silent Love" is female, then the era's gender restraints on taking initiative in a romantic relationship might be the reason for not confessing love. When the song became a hit in 1932, however, the big discs were all dance band performances with a single vocal refrain by a male. (Only one woman recorded it at the time: Rhoda Hicks, on the bud-get Champion label.) The crooners on the otherwise excellent best-selling discs by Isham Jones, Ruby Newman, and Roger Wolfe Kahn are stiff and unremarkable; the appeal in these waxings lies in their rich instrumental textures and gently propulsive fox-trot beat. The Washboard Rhythm Kings delivered a delightfully loose-limbed jazz rendition, with a cheery, relaxed vocal by Eddie Miles. Unusually, the original tone poem, "Jazz Nocturne," enjoyed popularity right alongside the extracted song version, and some recordings combined elements of both.

"My Silent Love" scarcely ever receded from prominence after its first popularity. Frank Sinatra rendered it in a medley during his years with the Tommy Dorsey Orchestra. Even in strict fox-trot tempo, for a single refrain, the singer manages to convey a compelling emotional drama, especially through his control of dynamics, softening the volume on phrases like "You would not understand."

Waves of singles of "My Silent Love" were issued in the periods of 1941–1942, 1946–1948, and, with scarcely a breather, 1950–1951. Over the decades, notable jazz instrumentals came to include Zoot Sims, in a medium-tempo swinging rendition; Erroll Garner, who made it a regular part of his repertoire, always with a new and unpredictable intro; and, with a more delicate approach, Jimmy Rowles.[9] Up-tempo renditions range from Billy May's brassy instrumental to the harmonizing of the Mills Brothers.

Slow vocal versions bring out the best in the piece. Mary Ford, with husband Les Paul on guitar, croons, full of intimate detail, bending notes. The echoing reverberation, typical of the Les Paul sound, helps create a spacey sense of a surreal internal landscape. Peggy Lee, on her charting album *Mink Jazz*, is very similar in conception and ambience and creates an even more subtly detailed soliloquy.

Suesse's Tin Pan Alley career was confined to the 1930s, and in some ways she defines that decade. She creates, in many of her songs, the dark, nocturnal magic so typical of Depression-era ballads. This is often revealed in the titles: "Whistling in the Dark," "Moon About Town," "The Night Is Young," "Gone with the Dawn," "Blue Moonlight."

Heyman's topic of silence holds symbolic power in more ways than one. Suesse was a self-described "acoustiphobe." "I hate noises," she declared.[10] One raucous July 4 evening, she composed "The Night Is Young" with her head buried under mounds of pillows to create the silence she craved. In 1974, she produced her Carnegie Hall concert in an effort to prevent her work and reputation from being silenced. In the twenty-first century, along with her cohort of women songwriters, perhaps her voice can be not silent, but sounded.

Dana Suesse's hits
1931: "Have You Forgotten," lyrics by Leo Robin
1931: "Whistling in the Dark," lyrics by Allan Boretz
1931: "Ho, Hum," lyrics by Edward Heyman

1932: "My Silent Love," lyrics by Edward Heyman
1933: "Moon About Town," lyrics by E. Y. "Yip" Harburg
1934: "You Oughta Be in Pictures," lyrics by Edward Heyman
1935: "Love Makes the World Go 'Round," lyrics by Edward Heyman
1936: "The Night Is Young (And You're So Beautiful)," lyrics by Billy Rose and Irving Kahal
1937: "Gone with the Dawn," lyrics by Billy Rose and Stanley Joseloff
1937: "Happy Birthday to Love," music adapted by Dana Suesse from Austrian song by Fenyes Szabolcs, English-language lyrics by Billy Rose and Stanley Joseloff
1939: "Yours for a Song," lyrics by Billy Rose and Ted Fetter
1939: "A Table in a Corner," lyrics by Sam Coslow
1939: "This Changing World," lyrics by Harold Adamson
1952: "The Girl Without a Name," lyrics by Scott Olsen and Dana Suesse
Also known as: "That Girl" (1954), lyrics by Eddie Bracken; "Toi Qui Disais, Qui Disais, Qui Disais" (1954), French lyrics by Jean-Claude Darnal

Some neglected gems
1933: "Free," lyrics by Edward Heyman; rhythm ballad with few notes but lots of surprises
1934: "Missouri Misery," lyrics by E. Y. "Yip" Harburg; self-conscious but powerful "low down" tune
1936: "You're Like a Toy Balloon," lyrics by Billy Rose and Irving Kahal; sprightly, yet with underlying melancholy
1939: "Blue Moonlight," lyrics by Dana Suesse; groovy and romantic ballad with cleverly phrased lyric; from an instrumental composition, this song version was recorded but never copyrighted or published
1940: "Time for Me to Put My Heart Away," lyrics by Dana Suesse; easy-moving torch song, soigné lyrics; copyrighted and recorded but never published

7

"WILLOW, WEEP FOR ME" (1932)

Ann Ronell (1905–1993), composer-lyricist

Ann Ronell was mentored by George Gershwin, and she was gathered to the bosom of his family like a second sister alongside Frances Gershwin. This did not make it any easier, however, for her to break into Tin Pan Alley. But after three years of making the rounds of publisher's offices, pounding day and night as a rehearsal pianist, and writing special material for performers, she arrived on the Alley in 1930 with her first hit, the blithe and merry "Baby's Birthday Party." Another success followed in 1931, and yet another in 1932, the remarkable ballad "Willow, Weep for Me." Among all songs by women composers, "Willow" is the most performed jazz standard.[1] If Ronell had continued in this vein, she would have even more substantially helped create this unique American art. After 1933, however, her creative life mostly went off in different directions.

BIOGRAPHY

A first-generation American, offspring of Russian-Jewish immigrants, Ronell was raised in Omaha, Nebraska. She declared, "As long as I remember, I've been writing words and music," and in her high school yearbook a friend wrote, "You never think of Ann without thinking of music or dancing." She shipped out to elite colleges in Massachusetts; first to Wheaton where she learned German (which would come in handy later when she translated Viennese operetta). She credited her drama teacher, Violet Robinson, with being "the first to realize—before I did myself—that I had a flair for composing, and it was she who insisted that I study along those lines." She transferred to Radcliffe College, where she could major in music. There she interviewed the musical bigwigs who came to Boston, including Gershwin in the summer of 1926. He ended up questioning her about her ambitions. He liked her songs and, after she graduated, got them to the ear of his publisher and obtained a piano audition for her at the Roxy Theater in New York City, with no immediate result. Gershwin, in the same piece of advice he gave Al Stillman (né Silverstein), recommended Ann change her name from Rosenblatt to the less Jewish-sounding Ronell. Moving to Manhattan, Ronell began her mature career, leading a life of "inexhaustible activity," always working many jobs or pursuing several projects at once.[2]

Ronell's final rehearsal pianist gig was for Great Day by Vincent Youmans, a brilliant song composer with ambitions of becoming a major Broadway producer. Ronell worked on writing a musical he said he would produce, but the complete financial failure of Great Day and the oncoming of the Great Depression foiled that plan. From the project, however, Ronell reaped "Baby's Birthday Party," which she had intended as the show's opening number. In an instance of pure Tin Pan Alley logic, she was responding to the 1929 hit "The Wedding of the Painted Doll": "Songs about dolls and doll parades had been successful. Nothing had been written about babies or baby parties." Featuring a rippling lilt, a hint of the 1920s novelty piano style, the music is comparable to "Painted Doll" as well as Mabel Wayne's "Ragamuffin Romeo." Famous Music bought Ronell's song, and it reportedly reached the Alley's current gold standard for 1930 by selling a hundred thousand sheet music copies.[3]

In 1931, Famous Music issued Ronell's next hit, "Rain on the Roof," another pattering melody mated to a lyric of innocence. With these first two hits, Ronell created a voice as unique and innovative as that of any of her male peers. In her most characteristic mode, she spins giddy tendrils of melody and rhyme, most often in AABA refrains. Both "Baby's Birthday" and "Rain" omit an introductory verse. Instead each features an interlude, also in AABA form, that equals the refrain in melodic invention. For the middle section of "Baby's Birthday," Ronell stomps, still celebratory but in an adult manner conducive to a Charleston dance step. For "Roof," Ronell shifts key and injects, as her biographer Tighe E. Zimmers puts it, "a longing tone." While not overshadowing the choruses, these additional sections deepen each song.[4]

Despite these successes, Ronell still had trouble pitching "Willow, Weep for Me." Irving Berlin himself had to intervene and override his firm's manager, Saul Bornstein, who objected to Ronell's unusual double-time measures in the song's refrain as well as the dedication to George Gershwin. Although the number was not as successful as her previous two pieces, "Willow" still earned some popularity and, in addition, the respect of the songwriting elite.

Nevertheless, Ronell discovered, "You don't make enough money from a popular song to fill in the period between hits." Therefore, like almost every songwriter in the 1930s, she moved to Hollywood. The fifth anniversary of Mickey Mouse gave her the opportunity to create his official birthday song, "Mickey Mouse and Minnie's in Town."

Another Disney product, the animated short *Three Little Pigs*, produced a catchy refrain that quickly took on life in folk culture, "Who's afraid of the big, bad wolf." Ted Sears and Pinto Colvig had written the script and lyrics, and Frank Churchill the music. But Ronell was brought in and, with her savvy, adapted bits of it into popular song form. George Joy, at Irving Berlin's firm, resisted publishing it because "no songs came out of cartoons." When it was published, however, it became a wildfire success all around the world. In a tumultuous time of global depression and increased totalitarianism, the song became a symbol of "laughter at fear."[5]

In essence, Ronell shaped "Who's Afraid of the Big, Bad Wolf" into the mold of her two first hits: an AABA structure followed by a separate contrasting segment. Here, however, these portions take on the roles of lengthy verse and short refrain—in this respect, similar to many folk songs—with, in addition, a transitional theme between the two. Churchill finished his tiny "Who's Afraid" refrain with an instrumental fill of five notes. Ronell set these with the simple verbal phrase "Tra-la-la-la-la" to make a satisfying, carefree conclusion.

Ronell's main work was in the verses and the transitional motif: for these, she contributed 78 percent of the words and patched together four widely dispersed musical themes into one coherent whole. Most impressively, she identified one of Churchill's more fleeting motifs as capable of being used as the release melody of the verse. For this crucial work, Ronell was given credit for "special additional lyrics." This was a better deal than Sears and Colvig received; they got no credit or royalties.

Ronell had one very modest hit with "Beach Boy," from the movie musical *Down to Their Last Yacht* (1934), an unusually structured refrain that alternates her characteristic pattering motifs with sinuous passages. But after that her energies went in new and consuming directions. From about 1937 onward, she became dedicated to the popularization of classical music. Ronell wrote English-language lyrics for both individual vocal pieces and entire stage works, the opera *Marta* and the operetta *The Gypsy Baron*. Her folio with movie soprano Deanna Durbin, *Favorite Songs and Arias*, became a staple of singers for years. In 1935 and 1941, Ronell also created an innovative theater form, which she dubbed "ballet with songs," "ballet-sing," or "ballet-operetta," in which an on-stage dancer and an off-stage singer represented a single character.

Further, in 1935, Ronell married Lester Cowan. He had been a key member of the Production Code office, helping Hollywood achieve self-censorship and avoid interference from the federal government. Now he was embarking on a career as an independent movie producer. Over nineteen years, he produced ten Hollywood movies, and Ronell became his assistant. She reflected, seemingly without the resentment one might expect: "My career was subjugated to his . . . because I felt his was so much more important and significant, his talents so much more integrated with dynamic direction, his worth as a person so much more imperative to be nourished."[6] From a twenty-first-century point of view, her attitude might be seen as the result of brainwashing from a patriarchal society.

On the positive side, through assisting Cowan, Ronell was able to penetrate the American movie industry as no woman had done before. She became the first female to conduct a movie soundtrack (*Tomorrow, the World!*) and to coscore a Hollywood product (*The Story of G.I. Joe*), for which she was nominated for an Academy Award. These accomplishments, however, were single events and did not become part of a larger output for her in either of these fields of endeavor.

Amid all this, Ronell did find some time to write words and music for her own songs. She composed a musical comedy, *Count Me In*, that worked beautifully in its original college production but somehow missed the boat when given a late 1942 Broadway mounting. Historically, it represents another feather in her cap: Ronell was the first woman to write both words and music for a complete Broadway score. (In 1925, Clare Kummer had written words and music for two-thirds of the score—as well as the script—for *Annie Dear*.) Despite the show's failure, some plug tunes might have emerged if there had not been a recording ban in 1943. Ronell had bad luck with the promotion of many of her film songs too. For instance, the stories surrounding "The Merry-Go-Round" in *Champagne Waltz* (1937), the title song of *Love Happy* (1950), and her lyrics for the main theme of *Hondo* (1953) supply a nightmarish litany of lack of support from publishers, movie studios, and record companies. None of this disappointment,

Figure 7.1 Ann Ronell, in 1952, with a songwriter's latest tool, the reel-to-reel tape recorder, listening to her new piece, "Just a Girl" (1952). (Walter Albertin, World Telegram and Sun, Library of Congress, via Wikimedia Commons. Public domain.)

however, detracts from her achievement in writing the classic "Willow, Weep for Me."

"WILLOW, WEEP FOR ME"

For diehard fans of the Great American Songbook, "Willow, Weep for Me" is probably the most respected musical composition focused on in the present study. Two foremost critics, Alec Wilder and Allen Forte, place "Willow" in the top echelon; and musicians like Ted Gioia equally esteem it. That fact makes it ironic—even tragic—that Ronell's later career focused on adapting the music of others and not on her own song composing. Perhaps, in part, her song output decreased out of grief for the death, in 1937, of George Gershwin, the mentor to whom Ronell dedicated "Willow."

Ronell could be deeply philosophic, as in "Funny Little World" or "Love Can Be Dreamed," but in "Willow, Weep for Me" she achieves profundity of *emotion*. Because of this unique status in her oeuvre, as well as her sister-like relationship to Gershwin and the dedication to him, some people suspect that he composed or co-composed "Willow." Nevertheless, a comparison of "Willow" in its original form with "Baby's Birthday Party" and "Rain on the Roof" reveals resemblances among them, supplying internal evidence that "Willow" is Ronell's own work and, indeed, highly characteristic. General aspects are her propensity for the AABA refrain structure and the sense of drama she achieves within the concise pop song genre. More specific clues are the sudden shifts that manifest her fertile musical creativity; the harmonic richness of the release (similar in that way to "Rain on the Roof"); and, most convincingly of all, the short rippling phrases that begin the main strain. All these factors add up to reveal Ronell's individual imprint.

Ronell creates some wonderful touches in the sheet music for "Willow, Weep for Me," ones not often heard in performances. She starts by twice repeating the title phrase, set to a five-note riff that jazz musicians are fully at home with. She sets the word "willow" in a long-short pattern, "WILlow," which helps to keep the title phrase moving through to the end, "me." This is especially important because she courageously starts her refrain with an octave drop, "WIL-" (drop) "-low." Unfortunately, since 1940, most performers reverse this emphasis, making it short-long, "wil-LOW." This alteration can break up the flow and make it heavy and leaden. The exceptions are those who take the tune at a livelier tempo; however, they tend simply to even out the notes, short-short-short-short.

At bar five, Ronell suddenly changes the rhythm, going from triplets and dotted syncopations to even eighth notes, and the accompaniment changes to double-time for just that one measure. As Zimmers points out, this sudden shift conveys "the agitated stress of the singer."[7] The even notes allow the singer to create a sharp attack that contrasts with the flowing patterns before and after. It is very jazzy, the kind of effect that a hip arranger might introduce to any song; yet, oddly, after the song's first year of popularity, it has been very infrequently used.

Similar to what Dana Suesse does in "My Silent Love," Ronell ends most of her phrases with a downward moving gesture, conveying the depression of the protagonist. Also parallel to "My Silent Love," at the end of the A-section, Ronell places another octave drop in the middle of a phrase: "weep" (drop) "for me." She then lingers on "me," a single d note held for more than two measures. Meanwhile, she puts a little three-note hum in the accompaniment, d-f-d. Few utilize it, but Art Tatum built it into his many solos on the tune. Gunther Schuller points out that the harmonies for the A-section are "blues changes condensed" from twelve bars "into eight bars," in an eccentric pattern. To that observation, add that Ronell's lengthy gap at the end of her A-section is also vaguely parallel to the two final "empty" bars of a standard blues stanza.[8]

In "Willow, Weep for Me," Ronell was cutting edge in her A-section melody, with a device that took her beyond her previous work: she exactly repeats her opening five-note riff three times, but the third time she then extends her phrase with an additional eight notes. She thus creates the potential for a thirteen-note unit, if the tempo and the soloist's phrasing allow for it. Ronell's extension of a previously stated motif is akin to what "Fats" Waller had done in "Ain't Misbehavin'" (1929), which Wilder praises as a buoyant "spillover." Nevertheless, in 1932 this approach was still rare. Cole Porter went on to use it in two of his most characteristic tunes: "Night and Day," copyrighted one month after "Willow," and "I Get a Kick Out of You" (1934). Jerome Kern uses the technique in "The Way You Look Tonight" (1936), and, as described earlier, so does Mary Lou Williams in "What's Your Story, Morning Glory" (1938).[9]

The B-section of "Willow, Weep for Me" is, if possible, even more compelling than the A-section. The opening two phrases of the release have almost the same rhythm as the beginning of the A-section, but the melody soars up to its highest note—a flatted sixth—one of the few points where the tune takes flight. Ronell starts the lyric of the bridge with this startling couplet: "Whisper to the wind / And say that love has sinned." The alternations between personification and reification are dizzying, the blue notes increase, and the harmonies become richer. Forte calls the chords of the bridge "unusual . . . very characteristic of big band arrangements in the Swing Era" that was just starting, and thus they represent another cutting-edge element.[10]

Ronell creates a folk-like atmosphere throughout, including through the use of those blues harmonies. Her initial inspiration was nature imagery— her memory of the willow trees on her college campus—and she continues from there, with the stream, the summertime, the wind, the branches, the shadows, and the fall of night. Although she ends each line with perfect rhymes or repetitions, her A-section internal rhymes are folk song–like off-rhymes: *green/stream*, *here/tears*, *down/around*. (The lyric does have one flaw: Ronell might have found a way to avoid the inverted "branches green"—an artsy, nonconversational phrase.) In the release, too, "my heart a-breaking" sounds like a rural colloquialism. In addition, Forte makes much of the way the refrain's first measures focus on notes of the pentatonic scale, a characteristic and symbol of folk music.

Ronell may have been inspired by a 1928 song, mentioned previously, with lyrics by Andy Razaf and music by James P. Johnson and Fats Waller, "Willow Tree." The two songs share traits both general and specific: the AABA refrain, the appeal to the willow tree to weep for the singer, the rifflike nature and repetition of the initial melody, and the prominent octave drop in the last phrase of their A-sections. The Razaf-Johnson-Waller tune was from a Broadway show and represents the kind of song Gershwin was pouring over with Kay Swift during these years; perhaps Ronell was with them during some of their enthusiastic examinations. Ronell's song is more intimate. Unlike Razaf, she specifies in her lyric—including in the lovely verse, heard too seldom—that the protagonist's sorrow is due to loss of love. Here again, in quintessential style, is the torch song genre manifesting itself.

Among the hundreds of renditions, split almost evenly between vocals and instrumentals, it is hard to choose. In 1932 and early 1933, the most successful disc was by Paul Whiteman with a vocal by Irene Taylor. In many ways it remains the definitive performance of the song as originally conceived. The rollicking gentle swing, the sharply emphasized double-time measures, the little wailing figure in the accompaniment between sections, the use of the sinuous verse, and Taylor's fine, bluesy vocal all make it outstanding.

The famous 1946 arrangement by Pete Rugolo for the Stan Kenton band was a feature number for singer June Christy. The quiet, atmospheric opening yields to wilder and wilder chords and sonorities, which Christy, one pioneer of the cool style, vibrato minimalized, serenely floats above. Although the single never charted, when Ronell went on a publicity tour of radio stations around the United States in 1950, she found Kenton's was the one disc of "Willow" that she could be certain the broadcasters owned. In 1954, the Fontane Sisters had a moderate hit single: their respectful but slick, medium-tempo shuffle-beat arrangement of "Willow" bows to changing times by featuring an electric guitar.

A couple of up-tempo band records of the late 1930s hint at where the "Willow, Weep for Me" tradition might have headed. Harry James swings it like mad. Even more fun are Boots and His Buddies, a rollicking regional outfit, who capture better the blitheness found in all Ronell's works, even her most mournful. They called it "The Weep," perhaps to avoid paying royalties. In the 1940s, the Billy Gaines Trio also found the Ronell-like lift hidden in the tune.

As the years rolled by, however, the performance tradition favored slow tempos. For a relaxed, late-night rendition, one cannot better Cozy Cole's All Stars in 1945, with Hank D'Amico's clarinet and Coleman Hawkins's sax lighting the midnight candles. In an equally unshowy but even more deeply felt vein is Mary Lou Williams in 1950; what makes her version so thick with poignant beauty perhaps can never be pinpointed.

Among singers, June Christy kept "Willow, Weep for Me" in her repertoire throughout her career, always singing it well. Billie Holiday beautifully enters into the character of the song. Ella Fitzgerald revels in the music (and she includes the double-time measures) but does not dig deeply into the words. Many others contributed fine renditions: Louis Armstrong, on both trumpet and vocal; Helen Merrill, one of the most intimate versions; and a slew who infused it with soul, including Dinah Washington, Sam Cooke, Lou Rawls, James Brown, and Andy Bey (both solo and with his sisters). Etta James does perhaps the most impressive version of the verse, jettisoning the original melody but keeping Ronell's words, in a stunning *a cappella* bluesy introduction. Perhaps the most satisfying of all is Frank Sinatra, in a 1959 live recording with the Red Norvo Quintet. A hair's breadth faster than his 1958 studio rendition, it is also more carefully shaded; and his voice is as rich as the bowed double bass that accompanies him, with a moving roughness at the edges of those long, low notes with which he ends each A-section. When he quiets his volume on "When the shadows fall," he beautifully evokes the coming of twilight.

The prize for the most danceable version of "Willow, Weep for Me," however, goes to Chad and Jeremy. Their 1965 soft-rock arrangement places a quiet rumba rhythm under Ronell's composition, just as the Beatles had done with "Till There Was You." In the 1960s, this charting disc spurred even more artists to tackle Ronell's classic. The song hardly needed the boost. It had long been recognized as a creation of enduring beauty.

Ann Ronell's hits
Both words and music by Ronell unless otherwise noted.
1930: "Baby's Birthday Party"
1931: "Rain on the Roof"
1932: "Willow, Weep for Me"

1933: "Who's Afraid of the Big, Bad Wolf," by Frank Churchill, with "special added lyrics" by Ronell
1934: "Beach Boy"

Some neglected gems
1934: "Funny Little World"; dark verse, easy-moving, blithe and yet cynical refrain
1940: "Love Can Be Dreamed," music by Johann Strauss II, adapted and with lyrics by Ronell; philosophic love lyric set to a great melody
1942: "Ticketyboo"; cheery, irresistibly contagious rhythm song
1945: "Linda"; Oscar-nominated ballad, short, bittersweet, and Continental in flavor
1949: "Love Happy"; return to Ronell's chipper, Charleston-influenced early style

8

"CLOSE YOUR EYES" (1933)

Bernice Petkere (1901–2000), composer-lyricist

In 1932, Bernice Petkere had a year on Tin Pan Alley unlike that of any-one else. With a propulsive trajectory of five hit songs and ten others also placed with the major publishers, "she burst upon the scene like an explod-ing skyrocket."[1] By the fall of 1933, however, that rocket's trail had faded away. The next five years, containing eighteen copyrights, brought no suc-cess. In 1939, Petkere hit one more bullseye, with the radio hit "It's All So New to Me" (from the movie musical *Ice Follies*). After that, despite a lifetime of songwriting and several bouts of dedicated copyrighting and self-publishing, the party was over. Nevertheless, Petkere's intensely successful twenty-month stretch in the early 1930s yielded two enduring standards, keeping her reputation alive: "Lullaby of the Leaves" and "Close Your Eyes."

BIOGRAPHY

At the height of her fame, Petkere had an Associated Press article about her appear in newspapers around the nation. In Muncie, Indiana (her husband's hometown), the *Morning Star* gave it a title typical for the era: "Writing of Popular Songs Easy for Young Housewife." At this time, the composer was depicted as a "shy little housewife" who writes songs "as a lark," when tunes "just pop into her head." Six decades later, she would convey a very different impression: "You had to be businesslike about music, and I was."[2]

Petkere was not "shy." She was an assertive music professional: when "a couple of music executives . . . got what I call 'fresh' with me . . . I let them have it, smack in the face like you never saw." Further, Petkere was not a "housewife," leading a life of domestic drudgery. Instead she and her husband Eddie Conne (creator of radio programs) "lived elegantly" in "swank" Manhattan hotels like Delmonico's and the Hotel Pierre. In 1940, when her jewelry was robbed, she valued it at $6,000 (in the early 2020s, that would be $127,000). Even in 1933, she would reveal that most of her writing was done "in the early hours of the morning after she and her husband have come home from a party and he has gone to bed." Overall, although Petkere "never smoked" and "never drank," she led a glamorous urbane existence devoted to parties and nightlife—and songwriting. Further, the implication of much of the press about Petkere is that she was an amateur who appeared out of the blue. In reality, Petkere was a show biz and Tin Pan Alley veteran.[3]

Petkere was Jewish: Max Petker and Ethel Fieldman were from Russia via Canada. Bernice was born in Chicago. About 1906, at age five, she won an amateur talent contest in Denver, Colorado; her mother organized a vaudeville act, "Baby Dolls," for her and her young aunt that toured the west coast. Petkere returned to Chicago to complete her school years. She then studied voice with Marvin Henshaw at his music conservatory, meanwhile teaching herself piano. The 1920 census locates her with her father, young stepmother, and two younger brothers in Wyoming, helping the family get along by working as a stenographer. She must have moved out soon, however, for veteran songplugger Ray Walker remembered Petkere in the early 1920s, working as a song demonstrator at the Chicago office of the Irving Berlin publishing company.

By late 1925, Petkere was heading to New York, declaring herself a "well-known" veteran of "the best of cabarets" in "Chicago and other points West."[4] Through most of 1926, she sang (and occasionally played piano) in some prime New York City hot spots: the Club Kentucky, alongside the Duke Ellington orchestra, and the 54th Street Club, alongside naked showgirls in artistic poses. By early 1927, she had married Ed Conne and subsequently fades out of trade paper accounts. Thus, when 1932 rolled around, the press had forgotten her impressive music business résumé.

Petkere notated her melodies using solfege, "do, re, mi," and so forth, as befit her background in voice training. Until her final years, she told the story that she composed her first hit tune on the back of a menu when she was bored in a nightclub one evening. Her companions, including veteran Tin Pan Alley lyricist Joe Young, insisted they return to the Conne hotel suite and hear the composition. There Young wrote a lyric for it centered on the folk rhyme "Star light, star bright, first star I see tonight," a concept reportedly put forward by Petkere herself.

Perhaps the hubbub of the club environment affected Petkere, for the opening motif of "Starlight," the most compelling part of the tune, was copied closely from the unobtrusive middle portion of a famous high-class ballad of 1900, "Violets," by composer Ellen Wright. "Violets" had long entered the pop annals as a major sheet music seller and a favorite on records, and Petkere later admitted she was "influenced" by it. More irritatingly, another pop song composer, William "Bud" Wilkie, had also used this motif in a 1927 song, "Confessing," performed at Hollywood parties but never copyrighted, published, broadcast, or recorded. The resulting legal suit turned into a textbook case concerning whether infringement could be based solely on similarity, making irrelevant any possible access to the supposedly stolen material. In a blow to the music industry, Petkere and her publisher lost. In 1944, after twelve years of court disputes, they had to pay up.

In the final days of 1931, "Starlight" was copyrighted and, whatever bother it brought Petkere later on, its quick success started her on a roll. She soon wrote both words and music for "By a Rippling Stream." Copyrighted on February 10, 1932, it was a hit for Witmark. The very next day, the firm of Shapiro, Bernstein copyrighted "Lonesome Melody," lyrics by Young, a song that got some modest radio play. These were but a prelude, however, to the groundbreaking "Lullaby of the Leaves," lyrics again by Young, copyrighted in March and published in April by the Irving Berlin publishing house. During the worst year of the Great Depression, the public bought over half a million sheet music copies. As discussed earlier, "Lullaby of the Leaves" (with Dana Suesse's "My Silent Love") helped prove two things: that a woman could triumph as a composer of fox-trots in the way that was most important to Tin Pan Alley, with sheet sales, and, further, that dark "minor key" melodies, not associated with any Broadway show, could sell printed music in the hundreds of thousands.

The miracles of the year were not yet finished for Petkere and Joe Young. Their song for male torch singers, the wistfully sado-masochistic "The Lady I Love," triumphed on discs, especially in the vocal by Russ Columbo. Then a follow-up to "Lullaby of the Leaves," with the same Southland setting and general patterning of the refrain, "My River Home," was a fleeting sheet music success. In addition, the pair wrote the radio theme song for Sid

Gary (the boyfriend of Bernice's sister, Renee); they got action on discs for "Hats Off, Here Comes a Lady" and notable radio play for "Did You Mean What You Said Last Night." And an American ex-patriate, pianist Raie da Costa, made a recording of their "Dancing Butterfly" that became a staple item in British culture for years. *Variety* declared that Petkere was "one of those Tin Pan Alley rarities—a femme composer with a consistent batting average."[5] Young's somewhat tired career was given a boost, and Petkere was not only given membership to ASCAP, but also the usual one-year probationary period was waived. Further, she was immediately boosted from the lowest category, the eighth level, up to the fifth class.

Petkere was now a celebrity, with her latest songs being gossiped about in Walter Winchell's columns. Not only that, Petkere survived ulcers in October 1932; within a few weeks of recovering, she journeyed to Chicago to visit her maternal grandmother; and then her husband quit his job and started his own business! By February 1933, Petkere was taking a vacation in Florida, a well-deserved breather from a very busy fifteen months.

Petkere started 1933 by writing words and music for "Close Your Eyes." It was registered for copyright as an unpublished work by the Irving Berlin firm. By July, however, the copyright was transferred to the Sherman Clay publishing house. (Perhaps Saul Bornstein at Berlin's company was feeling petulant after being proved wrong in predicting the failure of Ann Ronell's "Willow, Weep for Me" and therefore willfully ignored Petkere's equally brooding composition?) In the meantime, throughout the summer, "Stay Out of My Dreams," with lyrics by Ned Washington, had become a hit via live and radio renditions.

The success of "Close Your Eyes," in the autumn of 1933, would cap this phase of Petkere's life. By the time an anonymous journalist dubbed her "Queen of Tin Pan Alley" in mid-1934, it was a misnomer.[6] The rest of the 1930s only brought her, as a writer of plug tunes, some mild radio play for "That's You Sweetheart" in late 1935 and the modest hit "This Is All So New to Me." In 1937, Petkere divorced Ed Conne. She wrote a nightclub score in 1938, in Hollywood. Possibly this led to her placing "This Is All So New" in *Ice Follies of 1939*. By the spring of 1940, she was dating Fred Berrens, famous as a conductor of popular music for radio, and at some point the pair got married.

Along with scatterings of other songs over the years, Petkere copyrighted seven titles in 1953. An even more concentrated effort came with the founding of her own publishing firm, Bernice Petkere Music, Inc., and numerous copyrights in 1960 and 1961, not only of her own works but also songs by other writers. At least two heart attacks in the fall of 1960 scarcely

Figure 8.1 Bernice Petkere, in the 1930s, with the traditional tools of the song-writer's trade: piano, paper, and pencil. (Photo courtesy of Peter Mintun.)

slowed her momentum. In 1961, Petkere placed a song written by Lillian H. Crittenden (aka Lillian Bachelor), "So Goes the Story," as the flip of a hit by teen idol Johnny Crawford, "Daydreams," that peaked at position seventy on the *Billboard* chart. Also in 1961, Berrens's new record company issued Petkere's own plug tune, "Christmas Cha Cha Cha," sung by the Merry Macs. Having accomplished these plugs, Petkere phased out her active publishing activities.

Berrens died in 1974; and Petkere spent her later years living "modestly" on "Social Security benefits, an occasional royalty payment and financial help from a relative," content among her neighborhood friends in Los Angeles. She still wrote new songs, but an appointment to plug them to an RCA executive was humiliating: "I got as far as the waiting room, and this long-haired rock 'n' roll type snatched the music from my hand and said to his friends, 'Let's see what grandma wrote.' I grabbed it back and walked out." Perhaps the last journalistic notice of her was by columnist Liz Smith, who reported in 1993 that Petkere had just taken "away from Sony" the rights for one of her two enduring classics, "Close Your Eyes," and was now its publisher. The composer added, "Am I retired? Hell no!"[7]

"CLOSE YOUR EYES"

"Lullaby of the Leaves" and "Close Your Eyes" run neck and neck in terms of popularity, durability, and quality. They enjoy approximately even rankings as jazz standards, with "Lullaby" favored slightly more by instrumentalists and "Close" a bit more by vocalists.[8] In both, Petkere creates an AABA structured refrain, a release that breaks forth with dramatic emphasis, and a brief introductory verse that is not used often enough. More importantly, in both, Petkere alternates major and minor chords. Thereby, she creates a dark, brooding atmosphere that conveys a soulful inner emotional life for the protagonist.

Allen Forte supplies an appreciative analysis of Petkere's music for "Lullaby of the Leaves": the sudden ascent of the opening melody, the arching descents that echo the first motif but in reverse, and the shifts in rhythm both in the A-sections and in the even more highly contrasting release that imitates the sound of a wailing breeze. The notes at the start of the release come so fast that they can be difficult to articulate—or swing—at fast tempos. Forte points to the "minor-major oscillation" in the harmonies, the way the start of the release relates to the start of the A-sections, and how "the basic melodic coordinates" relate closely to the fundamental harmonies. Although he judges it "not a complex song," his analysis reveals how Petkere achieves simplicity, variety, and unity, all within the scope of a small canvas.[9]

The strength of Joe Young's lyric for "Lullaby" lies not in its idyllic nostalgia for the South. Rather, the power comes from Young's images of comfort, the "lullaby" of the title and related phrases—"cradle me," "cover me," "dream a dream or two"—and how those feelings of safety and contentment are felt by the protagonist "in my soul." In 1964, Ella Fitzgerald gave perhaps the definitive vocal version of the song. She includes the seldom-heard verse, setting up the existential feeling of aloneness of the protagonist. Most tellingly, Fitzgerald changes just a few words to remove the outdated Southern clichés. "Southern skies" becomes "summer skies," and "that's Southland" is now "that's heaven."[10]

As always, among the many hundreds of other performances of "Lullaby of the Leaves," it is hard to choose. In 1932, Connee Boswell immediately caught the right feeling for the number. In the 1940s, Mary Lou Williams led a small jazz rendition with typical understated depth. In the 1950s, Anita O'Day and Billy Eckstine delivered fine versions, each swinging in their own distinctive manner. The tune also entered the rock era, with the Ventures taking it onto the 1961 *Billboard* charts with an up-tempo, electric instrumental. In 1969, Mary Hopkin established "Lullaby of the Leaves" as a chapter in the British Invasion, on her charting first album, with a breathy, floating, folky rendition. She cannily avoids tangling with the busy release by wordlessly singing "oo-oo" under the orchestra's bridge.

Petkere and Young followed up "Lullaby of the Leaves" with another song about the South, "My River Home," in which the composer again creates a busy onomatopoeic motif in the release, this time to convey the steamboat "paddles churning." When Petkere came to write both music and lyrics for "Close Your Eyes," however, she distilled the more enduring elements from "Lullaby": the minor key shadings and the comforting images. She does, admittedly, succumb to the temptation to use the tired hyperbolic "divine"; but in this context, to describe a feeling rather than a person, the word is perhaps permissible.

Petkere opens the refrain of "Close Your Eyes" with the poignant title phrase: "close" on *c*, down to *g* on "your," and then up a minor third to *b* flat, to linger on "eyes." Meanwhile, minor harmonies underpin the melody. In the third measure, her second verbal phrase, she sets "Rest your head on my shoulder and sleep" to an undulating pattern of triplets. The warm, settling effect is soothing.

In the release, Petkere restates the opening motif; first, up higher, taking the tune to its top note, and, later, down lower. Petkere expands the A-section's pair of triplets into a series of six, which echo the main strain. This creates both flow and drama.

Alec Wilder felt critical of "Close Your Eyes." He has to admit it is "well written musically." Nevertheless, his "antipathy arises from a sense of the song's self-consciousness." Indeed, throughout his book, Wilder is ambivalent about sinuous, minor key melodies, which he calls at various points "theatrical brooding" and "Mata Hari or canoe music." For "Close Your Eyes," Wilder coins the contemptuous phrase "shopgirl Shakespeare." He uses it to describe what he views as the "incongruous . . . curious juxtaposition" of the "ungloomy, rather lullabyish lyric" with the "dark" music. Wilder, who had once arranged a collection of lullabies, should have known better. As Spanish poet Federico García Lorca observed from his extensive research, folk culture often "utilizes its saddest melodies and most melancholy texts" for lullabies. Further, minor intervals and harmonies are not always for evoking what Wilder calls "safe gloom" but may also connote sensuousness, introspection, or intimacy.[11]

Songs emphasizing the minor rose in prevalence and popularity from the late 1920s onward with the tendency peaking in the 1930s with tunes like "Close Your Eyes." The sense of foreboding and existential questioning carried within such songs must have felt particularly appropriate during the economic agony of the Great Depression. Songs such as "Dancing in the Dark" (1931) and "Brother, Can You Spare a Dime" (1932) made clear the connection between dark music and dark times. Petkere, however, "when asked if she was reflecting the tenor of the Depression in her music" for tunes like "Close Your Eyes," replied, "Absolutely not." She explained that minor-tinged music was "just her 'thing' then." It was, indeed, the "thing" for many other pop song composers of the decade, but this trend among artists surely flourished because people felt it in keeping with the atmosphere of their times.[12]

The 1930s bequeathed their minor-flavored, melancholy, sensual, sophisticated compositions to the ensuing decades; and "Close Your Eyes" has been one of many such tunes that have flourished ever since. Among 1933 waxings, the vocal disc by Ruth Etting is particularly fine, including using the introductory verse as a middle interlude. Among the many dance bands, Ray Noble, with his singer Al Bowlly, renders "Close" especially well. The melody proved to be a natural for Latin rhythmic underpinnings, starting at least with Harry Belafonte's 1948 disc (his first single). Belafonte was one of a series of Black male balladeers who established their own mini-tradition with the song. Herb Lance also helped to start the trend (he issued two singles of it). Johnny Hartman's relaxed rendition is a highlight, and Arthur Prysock capped the series with a moderately charting 1964 single.

Tony Bennett also made two singles of "Close Your Eyes," both in the 1950s, both up-tempo, first with a modern jazz tinge, then with a rhythm-and-blues feel. He inspired a series of white male followers to emulate his swinging approach to the tune. Perhaps the most danceable is Jamie Coe, with the Gigolos, in 1964; they Twist-ed it into a mildly charting single. Doris Day also prominently recorded it twice. The second, on a charting album with the Andre Previn trio, has a solo bass intro that proved influential, being emulated through the decades. Peggy Lee also featured "Close" on a charting album and sang it on television, taking possession of it with all the gentle, sensual intimacy at her command. The prize for a definitive rendition, however, has to go, once again, to Ella Fitzgerald. Her conductor-arranger, as with her disc of "Lullaby of the Leaves," was Frank DeVol. They underpin the A-sections with a light Latin beat, shifting to a subtle swing feel in the release. Fitzgerald is beautifully in tune with Petkere's balance of warmth, tenderness, and drama.

Although "Close Your Eyes" had never fallen out of popularity, in the twenty-first century singers have increasingly embraced it. Kurt Eiling made it the title track of an award-winning 1995 album, bringing it fresh attention. His elaborate arrangement, filled with tempo changes and including a section of lively scatting, has proved influential on others; for instance, Queen Latifah similarly incorporates a scat portion in her 2004 recording. "Close Your Eyes" is the product of an era when an atmosphere of sensuality and even sexuality could be both potent and yet also coexist with innocence, warmth, and feelings of safety and comfort. This vision of romance, as created by Petkere and her contemporaries, has proven powerful for any era.

Bernice Petkere's hits
Both words and music by Petkere unless otherwise noted.

1931: "Starlight (Help Me Find the One I Love)," lyrics by Joe Young
1932: "By a Rippling Stream (Waiting for You)"
1932: "Lullaby of the Leaves," lyrics by Joe Young
1932: "The Lady I Love," lyrics by Joe Young
1932: "My River Home," lyrics by Joe Young
1933: "Stay Out of My Dreams," lyrics by Ned Washington
1933: "Close Your Eyes"
1938: "It's All So New to Me," lyrics by Marty Symes

Some neglected gems
1932: "Hats Off, Here Comes a Lady," lyrics by Joe Young; cheery, cheeky swinger
1934: "A Mile a Minute"; propulsive, irresistible rouser
1934: "Oh, Moon"; contemplative and slightly melodramatic ballad

9

"WHAT A DIFFERENCE A DAY MADE" ("CUANDO VUELVA A TU LADO") (1934)

Maria Grever (1885–1951), composer and Spanish-language lyricist

If you live in Mexico, you are able to see television episodes devoted to Maria Grever, view the 1953 biopic about her starring Libertad Lamarque, buy the best-selling album of Grever's songs that Lamarque subsequently issued, read about Grever in reference books, visit her remains in Mexico City, see her bust in the composer's gallery at Chapultepec Park, and learn how she was awarded a "civil merit medal" by the government two years before her death at age sixty-six. In the United States, where she lived from age thirty-one onward—almost nothing. She reached the top of *Your Hit Parade*, started her own Tin Pan Alley corporation, founded a dynasty of Latinx music in the United States, and yet is practically omitted from the story of the Great American Songbook.

BIOGRAPHY

Grever's youth was split between the native countries of her Mexican mother and Spanish father, as well as travels throughout Europe. Various reports, each of uncertain accuracy, have her composing her first song at the age of four; and then studying in Madrid, at La Scala in Rome, and with various teachers, including concert composer Claude Debussy, operetta composer Franz Lehar, and, on returning to Mexico in her teens, her mother's sister, voice teacher Cuca Torres. In 1907, her sister married a Yankee.

The groom's best man, Leo Augusto Grever, a bigwig in the oil industry, traveled to Mexico for the ceremony. After what must have been a whirlwind courtship, Maria and Leo were married, reportedly a mere "four days after her sister's wedding."[1]

Maria gave birth to their son, Charles, in Mexico in 1910; but, by the end of 1916, the Grevers had moved to New York City. In 1919, a surge of publicity announced her recitals for the military troops in Camp Merritt, New Jersey, and at the Princess Theater, New York. (Reviews were mixed: too much passion, too little vocal control, but good phrasing, good "rhythmic verve.") She also recorded four sides for the Emerson International label. In 1921, age thirty-six, she commences copyrighting songs in the United States. (At about this time, she cut nine years off her age, similarly to, though less extremely than, Mabel Wayne.) Eventually Grever would have about one hundred US copyrights; diverse sources credit her altogether with creating 200, 400, 500, 800, or 850 songs. In Greenwich Village in 1927, she staged what was essentially a one-composer revue, with her cast dancing, acting, and singing, all combined in what she called "song dramas."

In 1930 and 1931, another flurry of press coverage reveals Grever in Hollywood. Her main task seems to have been to help create musical numbers for Spanish-language movie musicals. These films are mentioned in copyright registrations or the era's fan magazines but are underdocumented today: like *Arriba le Telon* and *El Principe Gondolero* for Paramount, the most international of the major studios; or *The Love Gambler*, *The Seas Beneath*, and *Cuando el Amor Rie* for Fox. She also found time for an apparently active social life and a recital of her works. For the concert, she wrote Spanish words for the famous Charles Wakefield Cadman song "At Dawning." Although such Spanish-language versions seem to be only a minor part of her output, a notable later example she wrote was for Cole Porter's "Begin the Beguine."

Through her work for Hollywood, Grever found her first entrée into Tin Pan Alley because the studios had all acquired music publishing branches. Paramount's firm was Famous Music, and Fox Film's imprint was Red Star Music. Unfortunately, none of her Spanish-language numbers for either corporation became US plug tunes. This phase of Grever's output seems to have ended sometime about June 1933, when she briefly returned to Mexico to make radio broadcasts.

For musicians raised in the United States, it was considered abnormal to straddle the worlds of classical music and pop; that is why composers like George Gershwin and Dana Suesse were exceptional and often misunderstood. By contrast, Latinx composers like Ernesto Lecuona and

Figure 9.1 Maria Grever, in the 1930s, posed putting pencil to paper. (Wikimedia Commons. Public domain.)

Maria Grever were free of such strict boundaries. In the 1920s, Grever was published by Mexican firms, or in the United States by classical firms Gus Schirmer or Harold Flammer, or by Ralph Peer's outsider imprint Southern. From at least 1928 onward, classically trained singers in the States were regularly featuring Grever's songs, with her own Spanish-language lyrics, in live recitals, on record, and on radio. Because of this, Grever's peers would have placed her somewhat high in the cultural hierarchy, but this status did not necessarily smooth her way into the pop marketplace.

For instance, in November 1934, classical soprano Jessica Dragonette started featuring a string of six songs by Grever on her radio broadcasts. (The two women were good friends: Dragonette wrote of how, at one of the singer's impromptu dinner parties, Grever whipped up a meal of eggs ranchero. She gushed, "Nobody can do it quite so wonderfully . . . she can cook splendidly.")[2] Dragonette's initial entry was written by Grever as "Noche Misterioso" but was then issued by the Tin Pan Alley firm Harms, with English lyrics by E. Y. "Yip" Harburg, as "Let's Forget Tomorrow, Tonight." A fairly good song, but unfortunately not the best work of either party, and it never became a plug tune.

Just two months earlier, however, Grever had finally landed a song with a major Tin Pan Alley firm Marks: "Cuando Vuelva a Tu Lado" ("When You Return to Me"), which lyricist Stanley Adams reinvented for the English-speaking world as "What a Diff'rence a Day Made." Very possibly,

Francia Luban, who was already involved in creating the Marks catalog of Latin numbers, helped Grever place the tune with the publisher. The firm promoted "What a Diff'rence" into a radio hit for two months and, even more impressively from an Alley point of view, onto the lists of sheet music bestsellers for three weeks—a solid, if not spectacular, success.

Most of Grever's songs had been boleros, tangos, and waltzes, but she had also been trying to find success with fox-trots since at least 1925. "What a Diff'rence a Day Made" could be done to a Latin rhythm (though it rarely was, when sung in English) or as a fox-trot. Its success seems to have further determined Grever to master the Yankee style. She devised a follow up for Marks, "Heartstrings." That was a rare Grever tune that she did not write, originally, as a Spanish-language song; it went straight to English, with another Stanley Adams lyric, and the copyright designation "fox-trot." Grever crafts a spare, smoothly flowing melody, not unlike those of the early 1920s by Irving Berlin and Jerome Kern; but she and Adams stick so closely to Tin Pan Alley conventions that, if it were not for a few original touches here and there, the piece might almost seem a parody. Despite (or because) of this, it was a hit, albeit a milder one than "What a Diff'rence a Day Made."

Grever's biggest US hit came in 1938, "Ti-Pi-Tin," and the lead-up and fallout from it illustrates the struggles of composers on Tin Pan Alley. Grever copyrighted the piece herself, as an unpublished work, in December 1937, with an English translation she commissioned from journeyman lyricist Raymond Leveen. She reported a couple of years later that, at the time, she had been "threatened with blindness as a result of an eye infection." Early on, she seems to have taken the piece to Herb Marks. Despite the success the Marks firm had previously with "What a Diff'rence a Day Made," he turned it down. Fifteen years later, he recalled this as one of his real "boners" but admitted he "still did not particularly care for" the piece.[3] Grever then met with bandleader Horace Heidt and presented a sob story (probably true, knowing Alley ways) about being cheated in the past out of royalties for her creations. Out of pity, on his radio program the night of January 25, 1938, Heidt premiered "Ti-Pi-Tin." It went over well. The Feist publishers grabbed it up and started promoting. From February on, it swept the nation on radio and records and, most of all, in sheet music sales. "Ti-Pi-Tin" reached the number one spot in the prestigious *Your Hit Parade* by late March, staying on top for six weeks, and continuing to excel right through September. Judging by the number of European discs, the tune was immediately popular throughout the Continent, in English, in the original Spanish, and in Italian, German, and Swedish. With a slight delay of six months, it established itself in Mexico too.

"Ti-Pi-Tin" is a lively waltz, telling a lighthearted story of Latin romance. The verse is indispensable and leads into a short infectious refrain that focuses on the nonsense syllables of the title (explained, in Grever's lyric, as the tinkling sound of a guitar). The melody, lilting or giddy depending on the tempo, was waltzed in three-four time; but, almost as often, it was also swung in four-four time, proving its adaptability to the mainstream dance style of the day. Nevertheless, the success of Grever's Spanish waltz, with its simple-hearted lyric, challenges what historians would have us believe, that the late 1930s was a time dominated exclusively by urbane, sophisticated numbers or swinging jazz.

Grever took advantage of the success of "Ti-Pi-Tin" by quickly producing two follow-ups: "My Margarita," a playful duple-meter piece, with an unusual AABAC structure and a witty Walter Hirsch lyric, and "Tu-Li-Tulip-Time," a rather blatant imitation of the "Ti-Pi-Tin" pattern, but this time with a lyric set in Holland. With three hits in a row in 1938, the composer enjoyed her top year in the US song market. Grever leveraged this prominence, guesting at a nightclub's "Tin Pan Alley Carnival" and, in 1940, producing another New York concert that included her short opera *El Cantarito*.

In 1940, the composer experimented with creating her own Tin Pan Alley firm, the Maria Grever Corporation. Under this imprint, she and Leveen produced the captivating "Make Love with a Guitar." Grever's firm copyrighted two orchestral arrangements and then sold the number to Witmark, who plugged it into a three-month radio hit in the United States. Many of Grever's early 1940s pieces were also copyrighted by another firm, one that used part of her maiden name, de la Portilla Publications, presumably also her own imprint. She used this company to publish songs from her 1941 Broadway score, with Leveen, for *Viva O'Brien*. Unfortunately, that musical was a twenty-performance flop.

In 1941, Jack Robbins met with Grever and other Latinx songwriters, hoping to expand their Latin catalog. Likely, top among Robbins's reasons were the increased popularity of BMI songs on radio during the 1941 ASCAP ban, including many Latin numbers, and the shrinking of the European market due to the war. He probably hoped to challenge Francia Luban (at Marks) and Ralph Peer (of Southern) and their extensive accumulation of Latin copyrights. From this point on, Robbins starts to issue many of Grever's newly minted Spanish-language compositions, including one of her most enduring, "Volveré (I Will Return)."

In 1944, the activities of two hustlers coincided to produce Grever's final major year on Tin Pan Alley. After prolonged effort, Ralph Peer succeeded in infiltrating the Hollywood industry and got Grever's 1929 "Te Quiero, Dijiste ('I Love You,' You Said)" featured in a lavish MGM movie musical, the box office winner *Bathing Beauty*. Peer had been trying to get this tune across to mainstream audiences for years, including issuing a failed English translation called "The Echo of a Serenade." Now, in a new adaptation, "Magic Is the Moonlight," given a swooningly romantic if somewhat awkward lyric, Grever's melody finally became a big hit. It gained eight months of serious radio plugs. The rendering on disc by Andy Russell was moderately successful in its own right and even more so as the flip side of "I Dream of You" (by the female team of Osser and Goetschius, discussed in a later chapter).

Simultaneously, Edward B. Marks created a campaign that made "What a Difference a Day Made" an even bigger hit in 1944 than it had been in 1934. (At this point they dropped the apostrophe in "Diff'rence.") Marks promoted it until it was on *Your Hit Parade*—only for one week, but still a major accomplishment. Indeed, for seven months on radio everybody was rendering it, from Bing Crosby on down. Still, some observers felt that Frank Sinatra took special possession of "What a Difference a Day Made" with his many live and radio performances. Luckily, his quiet, fine-grained interpretation survives in a broadcast transcription. Unluckily, however, Sinatra was not among the five artists who went into the studio to commit the song to wax in 1944.

Instead Andy Russell again took the lead on disc with "What a Difference a Day Made," attaining a charting jukebox favorite. Russell was, famously, a first-generation Mexican American. In some of his arrangements he would alternate between English and Spanish, despite the fact he did not become fluent in Spanish until later, during his decade living in Mexico. For instance, in 1945 Russell waxed another Grever song, "My First, My Last, My Only Love," first singing Irving Caesar's English lyrics and then the composer's original Spanish words.

A short-lived 1945 effort to start yet another publishing firm; an unproduced 1946 stage musical with Stanley Adams; and a one-week radio hit, "Wind in My Sails" (1948), wrapped up Grever's US career. A stroke in the spring of 1948 left her partially paralyzed. She received a medal in Mexico for civil merit in 1949, and she passed away in a New York hospital in late 1951. Her legacy to American music did not die, however. Her son, Charles, struggling to glean royalties from a complicated tangle of international copyrights, founded the publishing house Grever International, operating both in the United States and Mexico. By the time he died in 1992, he owned 250,000 copyrights, of which 20,000 were actively in print. In turn,

Charles's son, Robert, founded Cara Records, in San Antonio, Texas, in the 1980s. This label became one of the major movers-and-shakers of Tejano, which mixes Mexican, German, and Czech styles into a special pan-American genre. Maria Grever had expressed how she longed to "present to the American people" Mexican music with all its "cultural richness . . . but with the necessary flexibility to appeal to the universal audience." Through three generations, the Grever family helped to fulfill her mission.[4]

"WHAT A DIFFERENCE A DAY MADE" ("CUANDO VUELVA A TU LADO")

Grever's tunes always sound more compelling when sung with her original Spanish lyrics: the way the sounds melt into one another and flow fits the music best. Her "Quando Vuelva a Tu Lado"—"when I return to your side"—has the singer expecting a troubled reunion with her beloved. There is an implied mystery: she begs him to ask no questions and, whatever she does tell him, to keep it a secret, "for pity's sake." She pleads for—or demands—kisses, embraces, and their hearts beating together. The sounds of the opening title words set the emotional tone: the soft d sounds, the liquid w (in "cuando" and "vuelva") and l sounds, are both seductive and tender. "Cuando Vuelva," after relative neglect in the United States, finally made a stronger impact on the Yankee market as a track on a best-selling 1964 album by the Trio Los Panchos and the Spanish-Turkish-Jewish American singer Eydie Gorme. Their LP also became a touchstone in Mexico, influencing performances of "Cuando Vuelva" into the twenty-first century. Alfredo Gil, of the Trio Los Panchos, was also head of the Mexican publishing firm Campei. In 1965, most probably spurred on by Francia Luban, Gil would sign a complicated agreement with Herbert Marks and Charles Grever to promote each other's catalogs—of course, including Maria's works.

Stanley Adams conjured an entirely different love scenario when creating English lyrics. Now the song is about the sudden discovery of love, as expressed in the title line, used three times in the refrain. English, with its springy, pointed, sometimes harsh consonants, is hard to fit with Grever's swaying melodies. In his title phrase, however, Adams manages to include the w and d sounds that Grever's lyric had featured. His images might be trite—flowers, sunshine, rainbows, skies, and Heaven—but at least they hang together coherently. In the second stanza, Grever had created a linked series of words: "no me . . . nada / Que nada . . . que negaste." Adams strives

for, and just manages to formulate, a similar accomplishment: "yesterday
. . . today . . . nights." He ends this section with the word "mine"—which
is never paired in a rhyme, a move that is fresh, daring, and awkward, all at
the same time. Although one can quibble, Adams successfully conveys the
sense of a new beginning, a life turn around of a miraculous and wonderful
nature. Adams enjoyed a trickle of hits over twenty years and was for several
decades the president of ASCAP, but "What a Difference" would prove to
be his most strongly enduring work.

Grever uses a standard Tin Pan Alley form, ABAC, for her refrain
melody. (The wispy little cloud of a verse is seldom heard in English renditions, though quite often aired in Spanish performances.) The A-section
smoothly flows, starting from five pick-up notes ("What a difference a")
that lead to two drawn-out lengthy words ("day made"). Grever follows this
with a satisfying balance of long and short notes, of triplets and even-notes.
Three descending tones, on "(lit-)-tle ho-urs," are immediately followed by
the same motif in reverse, on "brought the sun." (The descending version
is repeated in the refrain's penultimate phase, "difference a," helping to
create unity within the composition.) The one-step descent to the second
syllable of "ho-urs" is very tender, a facet particularly caught by its earliest
performers. Grever keeps her entire chorus within the small range of an
octave and uses only one tone outside the home key. All these elements
probably contribute to Alec Wilder's praise when he states of Grever's
refrain: "I very much like the first seven measures."[5]

Wilder, however, also states he likes "nothing more" in Grever's tune.
The B-section is dominated by eighteen repeated *a* notes—a device that
Wilder, in general, hates. In this instance, his judgment might be shared
by the performers, for they almost invariably add contours to this rather
emphatic (or flat) development of the refrain. At this point, the singers usually alter Grever's melody, dropping down or going up, a tone or a third, or
bending notes at will to create a conversational flow.

Wilder ignores one of Grever's most compelling moments, a little fill-in
phrase that keeps the momentum going from the second statement of the
A-section melody into the final C-segment. Adams emphasizes this with a
quickly occurring rhyme: "bliss / That thrilling kiss." It can be a noncha-
lantly understated aside, as in Maxine Sullivan's two recordings, both early
(1940, with Benny Carter's band) and late (1981). Or it can be an emphatic,
ecstatic interjection as in Aretha Franklin's 1964 recording. After that, the
undulations of the melody subside gently, including sequencing a seven-
note motif downward, for a quiet, almost reverent conclusion. Meanwhile,
Adams throws in a rhyme pair (*when you/menu*) that is overly self-conscious

yet also clever and audacious. Here, early singers bring out a kind of sensu-ous urbanity, as if eating at a glamorous restaurant in a Hollywood romantic comedy.

In the 1940s, singers added an octave jump on their repeat of the C-seg-ment, on the final "day made"—ruining the diminuendo effect of Grever's original, but adding a stronger climactic element, with a bit of show biz savvy. The 1950s saw an accumulation of more performance traditions for the tune.[6] In recordings, Nellie Lutcher and Chet Baker combined their propulsive jazz phrasing with string sections, and Coleman Hawkins did similarly with a wordless chorus. Lutcher, in her 1952 single, makes "I'm part of you" into "I'm *a* part of you"; she also changes the second statement of the title phrase to "What a difference a day *makes*," harsher sounding but more emphatic. She is perhaps the first performer to establish those changes.

In 1959, Dinah Washington rendered the definitive version for future generations. Her Grammy-winning hit single also became the title track of her hit album. She kept Lutcher's alterations, including "makes" instead of "made" in the second A-section. This has since provided yet another alternate form of the song title; for instance, Washington's album was called *What a Diff'rence a Day Makes!* Her arranger, Belford Hendricks, included strings and ooh-ing voices, borrowed from the Lutcher, Baker, and Hawkins conceptions. These schmaltzy pop elements combined with the subtly swinging propulsion of Milt Hinton on bass, the lightly danc-ing rock triplets in the drums, and Washington's gentle yet biting, bluesy vocals, to create a classic. From then until her premature death at the end of 1963, Washington could not end a performance without "What a Dif-ference." Everyone who has performed it since does so in the light of her brilliant take on the Grever original.

By 1959, Washington was established as the Queen, royalty of jazz and the blues. Nevertheless, her new record producer, Clyde Otis, urged her to move further into the pop field with more strings, and she reluctantly agreed to give him a single take of "What a Difference a Day Made." They nailed it in one. Still, to Otis's disappointment, the Mercury label had no faith in it and would not promote it. Instead Arnold Shaw of the Marks publishing firm personally took it around the country to the white disc jockeys that Mercury usually ignored. Within three months, Washington was on the mainstream pop charts, and another four months brought her high into the top ten.

From then on, Grever was remembered as the composer of "What a Difference," not of "Ti-Pi-Tin." Once again, the Marks firm had performed a crucial intervention that contributed to Grever's legacy in the United States. Thereby, the publishers also helped further the ongoing integration of rhythm-and-blues styles into mainstream white-oriented music. In conquering the pop charts, the Black team of Washington, Otis, Hendricks, and Hinton foreshadowed the upcoming triumphs of Motown.

In 1975, Esther Phillips added yet another wrinkle to the history of Grever's song. In her hit disco arrangement, issued as "What a Difference a Day Makes," Phillips interjected moans and sighs that make clear that the day in question brought something more sexual than just sun, flowers, and rainbows. Washington had combined emphatic theatricality and rhythmic drive, and Phillips takes that mixture to a greater extreme.

Ultimately, however, perhaps more understated versions bring a fresher view of the piece. Corinna Mura, of partially Spanish ancestry, in 1944, included the verse and, perhaps for the first time in an English-language rendition, a section with a Latin beat. Best remembered as the guitar-playing cabaret singer in *Casablanca*, Mura's dignity and the slight flavor of classical technique in her delivery suit Grever's style well. In 1959, jazz pianist Lorraine Geller made the tune hop in one of its most happy renditions. In the early 1960s, jazz saxophonist Hank Crawford goes in the opposite direction, leading a slow version that digs deeply into the soul of the composition. In 1964, just after Washington's death, Bobby Darin was able to merge her influence with his own crooning, tender, intimate conception. The small group jazz of Sonny Rollins in 1996 provides more than ten minutes of riveting, often playful explorations of Grever's tune.

Because it was the theme song and biggest hit of the revered Dinah Washington, "What a Difference a Day Made" will probably live long as a favorite. Hopefully, performers will not fall into the trap of delivering imitations of Washington, inevitably limited, but follow the example of those like Darin and Rollins who have delved into the versatile potential of Grever's most enduring song. She wrote a piece that can be, without conflict, at once a bolero, a jazz standard, and a rhythm-and-blues classic, a composition that helped bring Mexican musical expertise into the US mainstream.

Maria Grever's English-language hits
Music and Spanish lyrics by Grever.

1934: "What a Difference a Day Made (Cuando Vuelva a Tu Lado)," English lyrics by Stanley Adams
1935: "Heartstrings," lyrics by Stanley Adams
1938: "Ti-Pi-Tin," English language lyrics by Raymond Leveen

1938: "Tu-Li-Tulip-Time (Tulipán)," English lyrics by Jack Lawrence
1938: "My Margarita (El Charro)," English lyrics by Walter Hirsch
1939: "Make Love with a Guitar," English lyrics by Raymond Leveen
1944: "Magic Is the Moonlight" (Te Quiero, Dijiste, 1930; aka The Echo of a Serenade, 1941), English lyrics by Charles Pasquale
1948: "Wind in My Sails (Inquietude)," English lyrics by Ervin Drake and Jimmy Shirl

Some of her other Spanish-language standards
1926: "Júrame (Promise, Love)"
1927: "Tú, Tú y Tú (You, Only You)"
1927: "Lamento Gitano (Gypsy Lament)"
1927/1928: "A una Ola" (To a Wave, aka Billow, Under the Moonlight Gleaming)
1931: "Alma Mia" (My Soul, aka Foolish Girl, 1968)
1931: "Por Si No Te Vuelvo a Ver (If You Don't Return)"
1932: "Cuando Me Vaya (When I Go)"
1937: "Que Dirias de Mi (What Would You Say of Me)"
1938: "Celo Tropical (Jealous Moon)"
1941: "Volveré (I Will Return)"
1946: "Así (Like This)"

Some neglected gems
circa 1928: "Chamaca Mia (Sweet Girl of Mine)"; inviting, dancing rhythm tune
1940: "Agua—Agua (Water—Water)," English lyrics by Mack David; dance tune, with both verse and refrain unusually structured
1941: "Cariñito (Sweetie)"; playful, irresistibly catchy earworm
1943: "Mi Guadalupe," English lyrics by Stanley Adams; catchy medium-tempo ballad melody
1945: "Mucho Mas (Much More)"; compelling, lively rumba
date unknown: "Bonita Como las Flores (Pretty as the Flowers)"; lilting medium-tempo ballad
date unknown: "Jamás (Never)," lyrics by F. Manly; gently insistent rhythm ballad

10

"THE WAY YOU LOOK TONIGHT" (1936)

Dorothy Fields (1904–1974), lyricist

Dorothy Fields was the Great Exception, the one woman counted among the elite popular songwriters of the era. Near the end of her life, she was rated "the most important and significant . . . woman writer ever in the history of ASCAP." Dana Suesse affirmed that, among her female peers, "no one could touch Dorothy." To those of the next generation, like Betty Comden, "she was *the* woman songwriter." As a lyricist, Fields was insightful and incisive, wielding the precise skill of a watchmaker. Yet despite her technical expertise, she declared it was "the idea, the thought" that must come first, and that "makes the song." Then "present that idea in fresh, beautiful, eloquent words." For forty-five years, with lyrics such as "I Can't Give You Anything But Love, Baby," "On the Sunny Side of the Street," "I'm in the Mood for Love," "The Way You Look Tonight," and "Big Spender," Fields did just that, placing herself at the top of her profession.[1]

Fields is the best documented of the full-time songwriters covered in this book, the subject of three biographies and numerous essays, all excellent. They tend to situate her as a topflight writer of the American musical, especially on Broadway. For, as well as being a lyricist, Fields was also the colibrettist, with her brother Herbert Fields, for nine Broadway shows. In that role, she created the context not just for her own lyrics (in five productions) but also for those of Cole Porter (in three productions), including his standards "Ev'rything I Love" and "I Love You." Most notably, Dorothy and Herbert created the script for the often revived (albeit usually in altered form) *Annie Get Your Gun* (1946). It featured Irving Berlin's astounding score, containing seven hits; and Dorothy supplied Berlin with title ideas for several of the numbers. As a playwright, she was a major architect of mid-century Broadway musical comedy. However, few historians emphasize the large extent to which Fields made an impact on the pop song marketplace of Tin Pan Alley.

BIOGRAPHY

The early headlines about Dorothy Fields define her as the daughter of Lew Fields, one of the biggest star comedians in American history. For forty-one years, as a performer, producer, director, and playwright, Lew was an important mover-and-shaker in the creation of Broadway musical comedy. Lew pretended to be a first-generation American, but in fact he was a child immigrant with his Jewish family from Russia. This is just one manifestation of how Lew and his wife Rose worked hard to assimilate into upper-middle-class Yankee culture. Another strategy was their determination to keep their children out of show business, with its ill repute and hard-scrabble lifestyle. Their efforts worked with the two older ones. The elder daughter (Frances) married one of the world's most important bankers, and the elder son (Joseph) became a prosperous perfume importer. (Both son-in-law and son went bust after the Great Crash. Frances divorced the banker, and Joseph became a successful playwright.)

The two younger offspring were harder to manage. Herbert bulldozed or wriggled through his father's objections and got into show biz, first as an actor, then a choreographer, then as a musical comedy librettist, especially in partnership with Richard Rodgers and Lorenz Hart. Lew and Rose became all the more determined to prevent Dorothy from developing a career. Upon graduating from finishing school, Dorothy applied to be an actor in a summer stock troupe; and Rose stole the letter of acceptance. In 1927, when experienced songwriter J. Fred Coots was mentoring her as his lyricist, Dorothy went the rounds of Tin Pan Alley offices; and Lew phoned all the music publishers and told them to reject her songs. Only when Herbert, then Dorothy, and then eventually Joseph proved they could be successful in show business did Lew and Rose accept their careers and proudly encourage them.

Despite the pressure from Lew and Rose to be a conventional housewife, Dorothy was insistent: "I wanted to work and be an individual on my own, and from the very beginning, I did work."[2] Her early jobs were as a teacher of music and dance at her alma mater and as a lab technician in her brother's perfume business. On the side, she also wrote witty society verse published in the famous newspaper column *The Conning Tower*. As well, however, Dorothy capitulated to her parents' expectations and, in 1925, married the respectable Dr. Jack Weiner. Yet within weeks she realized it was not going to work. For over a decade, Fields and Weiner were involved in each other's families and even lived together off and on, but it was never a close union and ended in divorce.

Meanwhile, Dorothy had found her professional niche: the Mills Music company took a chance on her as a lyricist. She was quick, delivering songs overnight; and she was talented, attracting the attention (after a slight delay) of hit songwriter Jimmy McHugh. They became nearly inseparable, including as lovers, for eight years of hectic, fun, almost nonstop working.

Of all lyricists, Fields was the one most influenced by Lorenz Hart. His composing partner, Richard Rodgers, was Dorothy's first boyfriend and taught her to play piano. Rodgers and Hart frequently dropped by the Fields home and then formed a Broadway triumvirate with Herbert as their play-wright. Dorothy was a performer—and then the star—of several of the earli-est amateur productions Rodgers and Hart wrote. Looking back, she realized, "I was so impressed with the inter-rhyming and the feminine hybrid rhymes of Larry Hart that I was not writing like anybody but trying to be like Larry." McHugh remembered giving her this advice (or command): "You were try-ing to write up to people, and I told you to write down, give them that which they understood, something that would not tax their intelligence."[3]

Fields's earliest copyrights in 1927 reveal her trying both tactics. "Bon Soir, Cherie" is well crafted but conventional: "Goodbye, don't cry, Cherie / Just save your smiles for me." It's a lyric in the style of a decade earlier. By contrast, "Collegiana" was up to date and erudite—appropriate for a lyric aimed at the college-educated crowd. In it, Fields recruits a device used by many of the Hart-inspired generation but that is perhaps more charac-teristic of Fields than any of her peers: an internal rhyme that breaks up the second phrase, leaving only one or two syllables straggling to complete the thought, thereby creating a strong element of surprise. In "Collegiate," Fields flaunted her virtuosity by uniting this kind of "trailing rhyme" with a three-syllable "mosaic rhyme" (that is, combining more than one word to make the rhyme):

Honor students and every pedagogue,
all go to bed agog
at night.

Forty-six years later, Fields was still an exemplar of this and other techniques associated with Hart. Very quickly, however, she found her own voice: stylish, warm, and yet psychologically probing, poised between the self-conscious wit championed by the young Hart and the comfortable everyday language valued by Tin Pan Alley. In project after project, she was consistent in her touch, technique, and insight, right through to her final hit, "Nobody Does It Like Me" (1973), with its trailing rhyme:

If there's a wrong way to do it,
a right way to screw it
up

In 1935, forces pulled Fields away from McHugh. The RKO movie studio they worked for began to assign her to other composers. One of these was Jerome Kern, the Broadway veteran who was like a god to other writers, including McHugh. Meanwhile, Fields started an affair with another man. McHugh, who was possessive of women in his life, whether lovers, protégés, or relatives, said, "I can't write with a regiment." McHugh enjoyed another twenty-two years of hit songs, but he hardly ever again wrote with the sparkle and fresh energy of his work with Fields. He confessed, near the end, "Dorothy Fields was the love of my life, *musically speaking*." McHugh indicated a special creative chemistry: "Something happened to us both when we worked together. We outdid ourselves." True, neither Fields nor McHugh wrote as many hits and standards after they split up; however, Fields was felt to be an unusually potent inspiration by almost all her collaborators. As Sigmund Romberg extolled, "She draws something out of you."[4]

The year 1935 was the peak of Fields's career as a lyricist, with fourteen hit songs, out of which she reaped four standards: with McHugh, "I'm in the Mood for Love" and "I Feel a Song Comin' On," and with Kern, "Lovely to Look At" and "I Won't Dance." In April, Lucky Strike's *Your Hit Parade* radio program started and quickly became the field of gloating triumph for pop songwriters. Fields opened the first broadcast with songs in positions three ("Lovely to Look At") and four ("I Won't Dance"). Women's songs were rising in the ranks: striding alongside Fields's five 1935 *Hit Parade* entries were Seymour and Lawnhurst's four, including "Accent on Youth," as well as Dorothy Parker's "I Wished on the Moon."

Around 1937, Fields met a New York businessman, Eli Lahm, who shuttled back and forth to California to woo her. They married in 1938, lived happily until his death in 1959, and had two children. Amazingly, Lahm successfully kept out of the celebrity spotlight even while Fields forged ahead as one of Broadway's leading figures.

Dorothy was by then a librettist more often than a lyricist. Herbert Fields had slowly come out of a breakdown of sorts, triggered by the 1937 death of George Gershwin and perhaps aggravated by being a homosexual in a society where that was still against the law. In 1940, Dorothy decided to give up lyric writing to learn the art of scriptwriting as Herbert's partner. From one perspective, she sacrificed her place on *Your Hit Parade* to hold the hand of her emotionally fragile brother; as Dorothy said, "Herbert gets lonesome when he writes."[5] As well, however, perhaps this creative shift also suited her own purposes. The slow development of a script may have complemented her responsibilities as a domestic manager and parent better than the rush and tumble of writing shorter pieces like lyrics, often on overnight deadlines. Nevertheless, throughout her life, Dorothy created quickly, to which was added her routine of waking early to complete her writing in the morning. She woke at seven, arranged the day for herself and the family; at nine, sat down to work with her legal-size pad and blue pencil; and she wrapped up her writing by two or three o'clock. That left her the late afternoon for her social calendar, family responsibilities, and extensive charity work. (Most notably, she headed women's groups that supported Jewish philanthropies and the Girl Scouts.)

Around 1950, Fields once again took up writing lyrics separately from her playwriting. By then, however, the music business had changed. The crumbling Hollywood industry did not properly promote her new songs. For instance, "Today I Love Everybody" was left to die alongside the ill-fated movie it was in, *The Farmer Takes a Wife* (1953). Only after nightclub singers took the number up, starting in 1955, did it take off, culminating in being listed as a television hit for one week in 1957.

Her stage scores also suffered. When Fields wrote the 1954 Broadway musical comedy *By the Beautiful Sea*, the Capitol label committed to issuing the show's cast recording and also EP and LP versions of their pop covers of the numbers. These each achieved a place in the label's own rankings. In the overall *Billboard* charts, however, the score suffered: the cast album did not appear on the magazine's LP sales charts. Though Nat King Cole's single of "Alone Too Long" did chart, it did so only modestly. The other big ballad, "More Love Than Your Love," by Les Baxter's chorus and orchestra, was prominent only as the flip of a bigger hit, "The High and the Mighty." Over at Columbia Records, head honcho Mitch Miller refused to issue *any* singles of Fields's songs. The other record labels, too, almost ignored the score; and the best numbers only skirted the lower edges of the

Figure 10.1   Dorothy Fields. The lyricist, pencil in hand, is surrounded by her Broadway score, with composer Arthur Schwartz, for *A Tree Grows in Brooklyn* (1951). (Walter Albertin, World Telegram and Sun, Library of Congress, via Wikimedia Commons. Public domain.)

radio and television charts. Never again would Fields achieve the string of high-ranking pop hits and enduring jazz standards that she had so effortlessly unspooled with McHugh and Kern in the 1930s.

Following the devastating string of deaths in 1958 of Eli, Herbert, and producer-friend Michael Todd, Fields felt lost. In her generation, a tendency toward alcoholism was often kept in bounds by a balancing tendency toward being a workaholic. When the work dried up, the alcohol filled in. True of Richard Rodgers, Bing Crosby, and many others, this was also true of Fields. From 1959 on, her excessive alcohol intake became a greater problem.

Eager for writing partners, Fields invited the young composer Mary Rodgers to collaborate, but Rodgers refused. Decades later, the composer looked back ruefully: "I remember thinking, 'She's a brilliant lyric-writer,' but I would feel uncomfortable unless I worked with a man. I'd grown up thinking that that's where the authority is." Being the daughter of Broadway patriarch Richard Rodgers partly explains her attitude. When Fields was put forward to be lyricist for what became the 1964 hit musical *Funny Girl* starring Barbra Streisand, its composer Jule Styne rejected the idea, fearing "a female star and a female lyricist might gang up on him." Ironically, for the first time since her parents' early interferences, Fields found her gender working against her. Perhaps this is no wonder, for society was in the thrall of what sociologist Betty Friedan would soon define as "the Feminine Mystique," when sexist attitudes were intensely pervasive.[6]

Four years went by. When another young composer, Cy Coleman, approached Fields and asked to collaborate, she quickly accepted. This led to one of the great comeback stories of Broadway. They wrote the score for *Sweet Charity*—a hit in its 1966 production, spawning four numbers that ranked on the *Billboard* Easy Listening charts and an equal number of audience favorites. This musical play has been often revived in New York and London, and its 1969 movie version rolls merrily along on home entertainment systems in the twenty-first century. Throughout her career, in interview after interview, Fields deflected praise from herself to her composers; and so she declared with verve: "The Coleman magic got this old gal to write the kind of contemporary words that settle so well" with the modern script and characters.[7] In the 1970s, charting dance versions of "If My Friends Could See Me Now" (a single by Linda Clifford) and the score's greatest hit, "Big Spender" (an album track by the Ritchie Family sisters), carried Fields's lyrics into the disco era. In 1973, a further musical comedy with Coleman, *Seesaw*, was a respectable (and respected) near miss. Fields was working on casting its post-Broadway touring company on the day she died, suddenly, unexpectedly, in 1974.

"THE WAY YOU LOOK TONIGHT"

Jerome Kern was a friendly colleague of Lew Fields, but Dorothy had never met him. When putting together the movie version of Kern's Broadway hit *Roberta*, as a starring vehicle for Fred Astaire, Ginger Rogers, and Irene Dunne, the RKO movie studio assigned Fields to rewrite the lyrics for "I Won't Dance" (as discussed in chapter 1) and to create lyrics for a new tune by Kern. Overnight, she produced the words for "Lovely to Look At." The studio held its breath until they heard that Kern loved it. Fields recalled when she finally met the composer: "I walked into the room kind of shaking a bit; he left the piano and came up and kissed me."[8] They were off to a good start, and, very quickly, she nicknamed him Junior (she was taller than he was).

She described their routine: "I would run over in the morning" and spend the day, having coffee with Eva Kern, playing confidante to daughter Betty Kern, working off and on, and then playing Monopoly deep into the night: "There was always a—I don't know—a kind of family feeling about my association with the Kerns."[9] Decades later, Fields chose the favorite among the composers she had worked with: Kern. Arguably, their work together was the best of their respective forty-five year careers, even though they collaborated for only four years. Of their six films together, the 1936 movie musical *Swing Time*, starring Fred Astaire and Ginger Rogers, was their fullest, most successful, and most satisfying score. From it, "The Way You Look Tonight" was the biggest hit. It sold sheets, it sold discs (five hit versions), it got radio play, and it was fourteen weeks on *Your Hit Parade*. At the turn of the new year, it won the Academy Award for Best Song. It is Fields's most recorded standard (and, for Kern, second only to his "All the Things You Are").

Over the course of many years, critic Mark Steyn asked songwriters "to name their all-time favorite song." The result was a tie, "It Had to Be You" (1924) and "The Way You Look Tonight." Of "The Way You Look," Steyn extolls, "The first eight bars comes in as naturally as walking." Alec Wilder is of the same mind: "The song flows with elegance and grace"; further, Fields matches the melody with a "lovely, warm lyric." Fields vividly remembered first hearing the tune: "I had to leave the room because I started to cry. The release absolutely killed me. I couldn't stop, it was so beautiful."[10]

The hallmarks of Kern's main strain are two long whole notes that drop wide intervals at the start (down a fifth) and middle (down an octave—a daring move). These alternate with a five-note pattern, tenderly flowing, that is sounded, repeated higher, and then repeated yet higher and extended by another four notes. Thereby, Kern unexpectedly lengthens his motif, just as does Ann Ronell in "Willow, Weep for Me" and Mary Lou Williams in "What's Your Story, Morning Glory."

British journalist Nicky Campbell ranks "The Way You Look Tonight" as one of the half-dozen greatest love songs. Speaking to Fields's son David Lahm in 2015, Campbell exults: "It changes the way I feel. It changes my biochemistry. I get love coursing through my entire body." Campbell and a random passerby agree, it's "beautiful." He asks, "What's the best thing about it?" Without hesitation, the woman answers, "The lyrics!"[11]

In the title, Fields further expresses the central idea of "looking" from her first hit with Kern, "Lovely to Look At." (The two would follow up in 1938 with "Just Let Me Look at You," and two decades later Fields and composer Harold Arlen would offer "Let Me Look at You.") Here, however, Fields builds her climaxes to emphasize, on two of Kern's lengthy whole notes, the words "lo-ve (drop an octave) *yo-u*." The lyricist implies that the protagonist does not merely admire the way the sweetheart *looks* but, rather, adores the beloved as a *whole*.

Fields would proclaim, "The best lyric writing is the simple lyric writing."[12] Yet in songs such as "The Way You Look Tonight," she combines simplicity with complexity. In analyzing her work, she emphasized the importance of "the idea," the "good initial thought." Here, the overall thought is unsophisticated: you're looking great and I love you. The miracle is in the details and the subsidiary notions along the way.

More than other elite lyricists, in her corpus Fields returns again and again to four central words: "passion," "glow," "tender," and "warm." She uses the latter three in "The Way You Look Tonight." Also characteristic of Fields is her use of adverbs to modify adjectives, as seen in some of her song titles, like "Terribly Attractive" and "Merely Marvelous." In "The Way You Look," her first stanza quickly introduces one of these, "awf'ly low," immediately creating the down-to-earth, conversational tone.

That first stanza does something else that is worth noting: the singer looks ahead in time to when he will look back and remember the present. Oscar Hammerstein II used this gambit repeatedly in his lyrics, from "You Will Remember Vienna" (1930) to "So Far" (1947). Fields colors this idea with a sense of foreboding that is particularly characteristic of the Great Depression: in that imagined future, the world will be "cold," the singer will be "awf'ly low." Thereby, Fields raises the emotional stakes, making the glowing joy of the present all the more potent, the savoring of each moment all the more important.

In each A-section she uses a slightly different type of rhyme at the crucial point where Kern trickily extends his phrasing. The first is straightforward: *low/glow*. In the refrain's final stanza she features her characteristic device, an internal rhyme followed by an essential final word: *change/arrange it*. In the second A-section, Fields does the same thing but with even more complexity: *warm/for m(e)*.

In her release, Fields creates one of her most surprising images: "Your tenderness grows / Tearing my fear apart." To envision something so soft and yielding as "tenderness" engaged in an act so violent as "tearing" is startling. Rarely do Tin Pan Alley–era songs acknowledge that people fear intimacy; but Fields does tip her hat to this reality, here and in "Don't Mention Love to Me" (1935) and "Alone Too Long" (1954). She also makes the violent act of "tearing" paradoxically dispel fear rather than create fear. This swift succession of clashing connotations, packed tightly into two lines, amounts to a creative gesture that is odd, is bizarre, is *genius*.

Throughout her career, Fields made such oppositions work. Her pairings acknowledge the complexity of love:

"That marvelous baby, a ruin to me" ("Baby," 1928)
"To meet my sweet and lovely doom" ("When She Walks in the Room," 1945)
"Nice to laugh with, nice to fight with" ("Nice to Be Near," 1958)

Some of her most upbeat lyrics are shaded with cheerfully violent imagery:

"I'm in the ring, Mr. Rainbow / With a horseshoe in my glove" ("Hey! Young Fella," 1934)
"Stardust will hit me kerplunk in the eye" ("The Sea Song," 1954)
"You feel so high / You could rip the sky apart" ("The Happy Heart," 1957)

Through such juxtapositions, along with other devices, Fields avoids being saccharine or trite.

Astaire and Rogers films, like Fields's lyrics, avoid the overly sentimental, and *Swing Time* is no exception. For example, the movie's second biggest hit, "A Fine Romance," is subtitled "A Sarcastic Love Song." "The Way You Look Tonight" was sung by Astaire at the piano, as he tries to make Rogers forgive him (he ruined their chances for an audition). She is in the other room, yet his love song draws her to him. She slowly crosses the floor and tenderly touches his shoulder—and then his reaction makes her realize she is a mess: she is in the middle of shampooing (originally, she was going to be cooking, her hair sticking out and smudges on her face). So much for the way she looks tonight. Astaire's vocal is excellent, both in the movie and in his best-selling 78 single. His articulation of the first word, on that drop of a fifth, "Some – day," is just right—enchanted, melancholy, and poignant.

The melody of "Way You Look" returns, played instrumentally, for their final dance duet. This reprise is bitterly ironic, for at that point it seems that their romance is doomed. A last switcheroo allows them a happy ending, when he reprises "Fine Romance" and she croons to him "The Way You Look." Amazingly, Kern and Fields wrote these two contrasting numbers so they can be sung in counterpoint.

Fields starts the second and fourth A-sections with the word "Lovely." One could quibble that this redundancy is taking the easy way out. It is, however, the kind of choice Fields made in some other songs too. For example, in "I Feel a Song Comin' On," she uses both "glorious" and "glory." The implication is that Fields felt such repetition was a positive element. The word "lovely," however, also causes anxiety to some female singers, because, to an extent, it is a word reserved for describing women. In *Swing Time*, when Rogers sings the lyric at the end, Fields substitutes the hero's name, "Lucky." Over the decades, women have come up with some alternatives: "sweetheart" (Dixie Lee), "lover" (Doris Day), or "charming" (Ella Fitzgerald).

Fred Astaire takes preeminence among the earliest interpreters of the song; whether on screen or 78 disc in 1936 or on LP in the 1950s, he is wistful, tender, gallant, and affectionate. Billie Holiday, as the singer with Teddy Wilson's small combo, is in her happiest early mode as she reshapes the melody expertly but with seeming ease, to allow for her remarkably natural phrasing of the words. Other worthwhile 1936 versions are by wife-and-husband duo Dixie Lee (with her striking, straightforward, characterful singing) and Bing Crosby (in good voice), and Rudy Vallee, with his serious regard of the song, his sensibility saturating the whole arrangement. Those two discs incorporate the final humming passage, not always used.

In the 1940s, Benny Goodman and Peggy Lee waxed a briefly charting rendition of "The Way You Look Tonight" under notable circumstances. They recorded it in the Carnegie Hall recital room, late at night; they were anxiously under pressure, anticipating the forthcoming music union's recording ban. Their sustained, hushed intimacy is superlative—and hard won: the soloists had to climb past each other onto a table to get close enough to the ceiling microphone. Lee may not yet be fully matured, but she could already weave a spell. Frank Sinatra's V-disc rendition, recorded for use by the military, is also touchingly intimate—at least, at the start; but then he and an intrusive chorus reach for climaxes that are showy but not needed. Through the decades, this tendency mars the renditions of too many other artists. Yet the way Sinatra softly shades Fields's most tender phrases is exemplary.

The LP era brought three predominant approaches, one slow and two up-tempo. Ella Fitzgerald, with arranger Nelson Riddle, made what has to be the slow version of choice. It's perhaps a shade *too* slow, but both are in top form, and they include the final humming tag. The vocal versions with the fastest tempos are influenced by modern jazz, that is, the bop and cool jazz traditions. Anita O'Day, Mel Tormé, and Betty Carter are exhilarating as they race through Kern's melody, but they hardly dig deeply into Fields's lyrics. The more swing-influenced renditions add a new twist to Fields's lyrics: a kind of romantic or sexual confidence. Doris Day lends her upbeat coyness to a lightly swinging version. Her "lover" makes her exclaim, "Oh, it was lovely," in a vaguely postcoital state of cheerfulness. In the early 1960s, Nat King Cole, on British television, and Sinatra, with Nelson Riddle on LP, typify the ballad-with-a-beat tradition. The swinging medium-fast tempo and brassy big band backing allow them to imbue Fields's lyric with an alpha male swagger.

Arguably even more interesting is the rock-and-roll tradition that developed around "The Way You Look Tonight." The Jaguars likely first mined this subvein in 1956. With its doo-wop solo-and-group vocal, and a piano riff styled after "Moonlight Sonata," it became one of the best-distributed renditions as part of a 1959 *Oldies But Goodies* LP that eventually charted for an astounding 183 weeks. The real landmark, however, was the 1961 hit single by the Lettermen, borrowing the "Moonlight" riff, and with the quartet giving a richly harmonized half-cadence at the end of the A-sections that was widely imitated by later male groups. One imitator, Danny Seyton and the Sabres, charted in England in 1964. Two years further along in the British Invasion, Chad and Jeremy added to their half-cadences a bit of the Beatles's "Do You Want to Know a Secret."

The prize for danceability, however, goes to two 1961 singles. The Jarmels soar above a semi-rumba rhythmic backing. They feature an enthusiastic doo-wop backing vocal group and free-wheeling melismas from the soloist. In a rival disc, the Crests are rollicking as Johnny Maestro coasts above them with his own high-flying elaborations. Both are *echt* rock-and-roll ballad arrangements. All of these youth market versions convey the idealistic facets of the lyric. They approach Fields's words with a jejeune innocence, interjecting "whoa, whoa, whoa" and "gee" and changing various words and phrases as they choose.

Fields's son, jazz musician David Lahm, reports that the royalties for "The Way You Look Tonight" began to climb, then soar, starting with its use in *The Father of the Bride*, the 1991 Steve Martin midlife crisis sentimental comedy. A drawling vocal by Steve Tyrell floats on the soundtrack during the bride-and-groom dance at the reception and then soon after, in the end scene, as Martin draws Diane Keaton (as the mother of the bride) into a slow dance as the movie ends. On the film's soundtrack CD, it was Tony Bennett's lightly swinging version with jazz trio that spread the song's popularity. This hit movie "established it as a wedding favorite," and in the 2000s "The Way You Look Tonight" flourished, with new recordings coming along at the rate of two a month in some years.[13] While previously Fields was probably most associated with her hits with McHugh—"I Can't Give You Anything But Love, Baby," "On the Sunny Side of the Street,"

and "I'm in the Mood for Love"—now "The Way You Look Tonight" out-
stripped all her other standards.[14] Her collaboration with Kern triumphed
in the end.

  Fields never stopped missing Kern. In 1945, she planned to reunite with
him on Broadway for *Annie Get Your Gun*, but he collapsed on a New York
sidewalk. For a week, at the hospital, she and Hammerstein shared the final
bedside vigil with his family. She remembered, "That was the worst week of
my life."[15] After his death, Fields wrote new lyrics to Kern melodies for the
1952 movie musical *Lovely to Look At* (a hit soundtrack album), and then,
to three more previously neglected tunes, for the 1958 album *Premiere Performance* by Eva Kern's second husband, singer George Byron. The result
was a new Fields-Kern standard, beloved by aficionados and critics, "April
Fooled Me." In 1961, Fields hoped to create a stage musical with further
unused Kern compositions, but her central idea of a story about the Peace
Corps was preempted by a rival producer. Thus, the world's chance for more
gems from one of the most compatible pairings of the Great American
Songbook dissolved away into nothingness.

Dorothy Fields's major hits
° *The asterisk indicates mainly popular in instrumental versions.*

1928: "I Can't Give You Anything But Love, Baby," music by Jimmy
McHugh
1928: "I Must Have That Man," music by Jimmy McHugh
1928: "Doin' the New Low-Down," music by Jimmy McHugh
1928: "Diga Diga Doo," music by Jimmy McHugh
1930: "On the Sunny Side of the Street," music by Jimmy McHugh
1930: "Exactly Like You," music by Jimmy McHugh
1930: "Blue Again," music by Jimmy McHugh
1930: "Go Home and Tell Your Mother," music by Jimmy McHugh
1931: "Cuban Love Song," music by Jimmy McHugh and Herbert Stothart
1932: "Don't Blame Me," music by Jimmy McHugh
1932: "Hey, Young Fella! (Close Your Old Umbrella)," music by Jimmy
McHugh
1933: "Dinner at Eight," music by Jimmy McHugh
1934: "Lost in a Fog," music by Jimmy McHugh
1934: "Thank You for a Lovely Evening," music by Jimmy McHugh
1934: "Serenade for a Wealthy Widow," lyrics with Jimmy McHugh, music
by Reginald Forsythe°
1934: "Goodbye Blues," music by Jimmy McHugh and Arnold Johnson

1935: "I'm in the Mood for Love," music by Jimmy McHugh

1935: "I Feel a Song Comin' On," music by Jimmy McHugh

1935: "Every Little Moment," music by Jimmy McHugh

1935: "I'm Livin' in a Great Big Way," music by Jimmy McHugh

1935: "(Then You've Seen) Harlem at Its Best," music by Jimmy McHugh

1935: "I Won't Dance," lyrics with Jimmy McHugh, Otto Harbach, and Oscar Hammerstein II, music by Jerome Kern

1935: "Lovely to Look At," music by Jerome Kern

1935: "I Dream Too Much," music by Jerome Kern

1935: "I'm the Echo (You're the Song)," music by Jerome Kern

1935: "Don't Mention Love to Me," music by Oscar Levant

1936: "The Way You Look Tonight," music by Jerome Kern

1936: "A Fine Romance," music by Jerome Kern

1936: "Pick Yourself Up," music by Jerome Kern

1936: "Bojangles of Harlem," music by Jerome Kern

1936: "The Waltz in Swing Time," music by Jerome Kern*

1937: "Our Song," music by Jerome Kern

1938: "You Couldn't Be Cuter," music by Jerome Kern

1938: "Just Let Me Look at You," music by Jerome Kern

1939: "This Is It," music by Arthur Schwartz

1939: "It's All Yours," music by Arthur Schwartz

1945: "Close as Pages in a Book," music by Sigmund Romberg

1951: "I'll Buy You a Star," music by Arthur Schwartz

1951: "Make the Man Love Me," music by Arthur Schwartz

1954: "Alone Too Long," music by Arthur Schwartz

1966: "Big Spender," music by Cy Coleman

1966: "Where Am I Going," music by Cy Coleman

1966: "You Wanna Bet," music by Cy Coleman

1966: "Baby, Dream Your Dream," music by Cy Coleman

1966/1978: "If My Friends Could See Me Now," music by Cy Coleman

Dorothy Fields's minor hits

1928: "Porgy," music by Jimmy McHugh

1928: "Baby," music by Jimmy McHugh

1928: "Let's Sit and Talk About You," music by Jimmy McHugh

1930: "One More Waltz," music by Jimmy McHugh

1933: "My Dancing Lady," music by Jimmy McHugh

1934: "I Love Gardenias," music by Jimmy McHugh

1934: "I'm Full of the Devil," music by Jimmy McHugh

1935: "Speaking Confidentially," music by Jimmy McHugh

1935: "I Got Love," music by Jerome Kern*
1935: "Out of Sight, Out of Mind," music by Oscar Levant
1936: "Never Gonna Dance," music by Jerome Kern
1936: "Stars in My Eyes," music by Fritz Kreisler
1937: "The Whistling Boy," music by Jerome Kern
1950: "You Kissed Me (He Kissed Me)," music by Morton Gould
1950: "A Cow and a Plough and a Frau," music by Morton Gould
1951: "Look Who's Dancing," music by Arthur Schwartz
1951: "Love Is the Reason," music by Arthur Schwartz
1951: "If You Haven't Got a Sweetheart," music by Arthur Schwartz
1951: "Andiamo," music by Harold Arlen
1951: "Young Folks Should Get Married," music by Harry Warren
1953/1957: "Today I Love Everybody," music by Harold Arlen
1954: "Hang Up," music by Arthur Schwartz
1954: "Happy Habit," music by Arthur Schwartz
1954: "Coney Island Boat," music by Arthur Schwartz
1957: "Junior Miss," music by Burton Lane
1966/1969: "The Rhythm of Life," music by Cy Coleman
1973: "Nobody Does It Like Me," music by Cy Coleman

Further performer favorites
1928: "Magnolia's Wedding Day," music by Jimmy McHugh*
1937/1940: "Remind Me," music by Jerome Kern
1939: "I'll Pay the Check," music by Arthur Schwartz
1951: "He Had Refinement," music by Arthur Schwartz
1954: "I'd Rather Wake Up By Myself," music by Arthur Schwartz
1958: "April Fooled Me," lyrics for previously unused music by Jerome Kern
1966: "Taffeta Pink Sample Size 10," music by Cy Coleman
1966: "I'm a Brass Band," music by Cy Coleman
1969: "My Personal Property," music by Cy Coleman
1973: "It's Not Where You Start, It's Where You Finish," music by Cy Coleman

Some of the many neglected gems
1928: "Futuristic Rhythm," music by Jimmy McHugh; jagged-edged early jazz dance song
1931: "Singin' the Blues," music by Jimmy McHugh; loose-limbed swinger
1933: "Let's Sit This One Out," music by Jimmy McHugh; soft-shoe tune, saucy lyric

1937/1940: "Back in My Shell," music by Jerome Kern; folksy, urbane, jovial bitterness

1939: "Just a Little Bit More," music by Arthur Schwartz; melancholy quasi-protest song

1939: "A Lady Needs a Change," music by Arthur Schwartz; celebrating female sexual agency

1945: "April Snow," music by Sigmund Romberg; contemplative, delicate ballad

1950: "My Love an' My Mule," music by Harold Arlen; groovy tune, with perfectly fitting lyric

1951: "It's Dynamite," music by Harry Warren; slithery rhythm tune and forceful, intricate lyric

1951: "Don't Be Afraid," music by Arthur Schwartz; poignant, inspirational character song

1953: "With the Sun Warm Upon Me," music by Harold Arlen; loping melody, nature-loving lyric

1954: "The Sea Song," music by Arthur Schwartz; happy, infectious waltz

1957: "Have Feet, Will Dance," music by Burton Lane; swinging tune, wittily telegraphic lyric

1959: "Merely Marvelous," music by Albert Hague; self-deprecating, triumphant, dreamy waltz

1959: "Two Faces in the Dark," music by Albert Hague; mystery-filled torch ballad

1973: "Seesaw," music by Cy Coleman; melancholy waltz, with bittersweet, philosophic lyric

11

THE FORTIES

By 1941, those women who had risen to the top of Tin Pan Alley in the previous decade, who might be called the "class of 1930," had almost all faded from the scene: Lil Hardin Armstrong completed her Decca contract, and Kay Swift, Dana Suesse, Bernice Petkere, Ann Ronell, Vee Lawnhurst, and Tot Seymour were no longer on the pop song honor rolls. Even Dorothy Fields had temporarily retreated from the popular song field in favor of writing librettos. Of the female pioneers of the peak 1930s style, only Mabel Wayne remained in high profile. To take their place, however, and foreshadowed by Irene Kitchings and Ruth Lowe, came an influx of newly prominent talents.

The 1940s were split in two by the atom bomb, the first half dominated by World War II, the second half by the Cold War. A new fear of nuclear disaster undergirded everyday life. The arts, including pop music, struggled to confront that anxiety with two strategies. Works of darkness were exemplified by Hollywood's *films noirs*; Tin Pan Alley matched those movies with night-shaded torch ballads. The other approach was to soothe the world's fears with escapism through songs of cheer, playfulness, romance, and security.

In wartime America, women were recruited in large numbers into formerly male-only jobs. In postwar America, the men took back those jobs; and, for the first time in twenty-five years, the media focused on propaganda designed to keep women in the home. Women, through their

unpaid, underacknowledged labor, conceived, gestated, and raised the larg-
est generation in history—the Baby Boom. For twenty years the birth rate
never dropped.

There are recurring threads that run through the history of many 1940s
women songwriters, some of them common since "Sugar Blues" and
"Down Hearted Blues." First, there are many uncertainties about authorship and credit. Second, many of the women were not just songwriters but
also performers.

Third, several of these women songwriters were managers of men who
occupied the spotlight and popularized their songs. Fourth, many were
married to instrumentalists and bandleaders. At the time they would
have been identified as "the wife of so-and-so—the famous musician."
Now it would be as likely that the men would be identified as "the husband of so-and-so—you know, she wrote that famous song, 'Such-and-
Such.'" Despite shared circumstances, each woman spun her fate in her
own way.

The music industry was wracked with changes. The head of the musician's union, Petrillo, clumsily tried to stop the widespread use of canned
music with two recording bans. This tactic was disruptive and ultimately
worked against live music. Indeed, the recording industry revived, despite
the wartime rationing of the shellac that discs were made of. By the end
of the decade, disc jockeys playing a recording on the radio had become
the most important yardstick of a song's success. Who controlled what got
recorded? Usually, Artists and Repertoire executives, called "A&R men"—
always "men."

In 1941, ASCAP tried to double its fees to the radio stations. Refused,
the association banned their songs from most airwaves. In retaliation, the
networks started Broadcast Music Incorporated (BMI), which became the
haven for the underdog—country-western writers, African Americans, the
poor, the novices, the Latinas. Some of these BMI songsmiths were women
who managed to sustain careers for decades.

The American public found they could do very well without the elite
ASCAP writers. Military personnel, wafted like dandelion seeds from their
hometowns to locales around the globe, either spread or were exposed to
regional blues, Latin, and country music, often for the first time. Among the
writers in these veins were some women who made a splash on the national
scene, such as the African American blues singer Lil Green ("Romance in
the Dark"); country-western writers Jenny Lou Carson ("Jealous Heart")
and Louise Massey ("My Adobe Hacienda"); and, from Mexico, Consuelo
Velázquez ("Besame Mucho").

Partly because of the legacy of the New Women—and New Deal Women, including the subjects of the previous chapters—and partly because of the support of BMI, the proportion of female songwriters slightly increased. Kay Twomey exemplifies the new era. In many ways, her career paralleled that of Joan Whitney ("Far Away Places"). In contrast to Whitney, however, Twomey stayed tied to BMI throughout her twenty-year career.

The Irish Catholic Kay Twomey deserves an entire book devoted to her because of her stylistic range and longevity, which spanned from the peak of the big bands to the era of bubblegum rock. She usually worked in pairs and trios, often with Jewish men, sometimes with other women, nearly always cocredited for both music and lyrics. Her corpus often leaned toward the influences of folk music, country-western, and rhythm-and-blues.

Twomey and her peers furthered an Alley tendency toward simplified music, or lyrics, or structures, or concepts, or viewpoints. This new trend was, in part, nostalgic, because writers often self-consciously emulated the styles of earlier, pre-jazz Tin Pan Alley. These could be described as "neo-simple." Novelty songs also thrived, many of them family friendly.

In 1954, Johnny Mercer wrote that he viewed most new songs as "cheap and tawdry." In a rare moment of frankness, the lyricist admitted that "the best men" (typically, no mention of women) "we have writing today" (presumably including himself) "are not writing as well as they did ten years ago." For him, a "golden age" had passed.[1]

The songs of the late 1940s and 1950s are less taut than those of the 1930s. Nevertheless, they radiate a kind of competence and confidence, a sense of superiority, suitable for the era. Some of these works form the category criticized by David Jenness and Don Velsey as an "infantilized" "bleat pop."[2] Still, twenty-first-century audiences often greet with delight such critically ignored products as lyricist Betty Peterson's "My Happiness" (1948) and composer Inez James's "Vaya Con Dios" (1952).

Twomey contributed more than her fair share of these neo-simple products. For instance, with Bee Walker and Sammy Cahn, she penned "Hey, Jealous Lover." In a hit single Frank Sinatra swung it hard, but to live audiences he would humorously confide, "I absolutely and unequivocally detest this song."[3] Indeed, despite thirty-one hit songs stretching from 1943 to 1962, Twomey added nothing to the elite repertoire of jazz and cabaret standards. Perhaps future artists will rediscover her finer forgotten works, such as the swinging "Two Pair of Shoes" (1941) and the atmospheric "Melancholy Minstrel" (1948). Such examples give just a taste of what awaits the revivalist: amid the dross, many women songsmiths of the 1940s and 1950s wrote some neglected high-quality works. The songs in the following sections, however, need no apologists or defenders, for they are still prized treasures of the Great American Songbook.

"HOW HIGH THE MOON" (1940)
Nancy Hamilton (1908–1984), lyricist

In 1934, Irving Berlin for the first time heard the work of Nancy Hamilton—she had supplied more than a third of the lyrics for the Broadway revue *New Faces*. He went backstage and told her, "If I had written that song, I would die happy."[4] But Hamilton's potential fame got buried. Why so?

Many factors worked against Hamilton. She was a mildly anti-Semitic WASP female, in musical theater and film industries dominated by Jewish males; a conservative Republican amid colleagues who were liberal or left wing; an upper-class Ivy Leaguer whose ingrained attitudes kept her aloof from both the popular and *avant garde* arts; an Anglophile who created musicals based on English literature even while the long-running shows celebrated Americana; "a high functioning alcoholic" (in her niece's words); a ghostwriter for her famous friends; a prolific author who nevertheless had trouble completing projects; a lesbian in a heteronormative society; and the longtime lover and helpmate of one of the most famous women in American theater, the star actor Katherine Cornell—a devoted, self-sacrificing role that subtracted years, even decades, from Hamilton's career.

Despite all these obstacles, Hamilton managed to create three intimate Broadway revues, writing sketches and lyrics to music by Morgan Lewis. Chappell underpromoted the few songs they printed from each of these, leaving future generations to uncover blithe and jolly items like "Teeter Totter Tessie" (celebrating an assertive female) and "A House with a Little Red Barn."

For *Two for the Show*, Hamilton and Lewis wrote "How High the Moon." Perhaps for once Chappell got behind one of her numbers, for "How High the Moon" was a hit, including in sheet music sales. Hamilton's strongest magic might have lain in scoffing at things: critics were most enthusiastic about her satirical songs. Yet Hamilton found her most enduring success in a simple Tin Pan Alley ballad lyric.

Or perhaps "How High the Moon" is not so simple. True, as her biographer Korey Rothman points out, Hamilton uses the most basic, not to say clichéd, rhymes: *soon/moon*; *true/you/too*. And Rothman critiques Hamilton as too often following the same phrasing pattern, with the syntax thumping

along, each line independent of the other. In her B-section stanzas, however, Hamilton creates longer phrases that nevertheless have articulation
points where the singer can break them into shorter units. These wrinkles
hinge on swiftly occurring internal rhymes: "above / when love" and "until
you will / how still." Time has revealed that Hamilton's phrasing holds a
valuable quality; her lyric swings.

Morgan Lewis composed a refrain in ABAB′ form. Instrumentalists
are fascinated by his harmonies, which unpredictably shift back and forth
between major and minor. As Alec Wilder points out, Lewis daringly
doesn't return to the tonic chord for thirteen measures. Therefore, almost
immediately, "How High the Moon" was embraced by young, innovative
instrumentalists, becoming "the 'bop' hymn" and thus helping give birth
to a new phase of jazz.[5] Charlie Parker famously used Lewis's chords as the
basis for his instrumental "Ornithology," in effect doubling the number of
instrumental renditions of "How High."[6] Singers that aligned themselves
with bop found, happily, that Hamilton's words were as easy to inflect with
jazz feeling as Lewis's music.

Hamilton uses metaphors that were not new: the beloved is symbolized
by music and celestial lights—all of them distant, out of reach. Within the
convention, however, Hamilton creates her own clever ambiguity. For
example, in her first A-section, Hamilton tantalizes the listener: Are the
phrases exclamations or questions—"How high the moon!" or "How high
the moon?" In her second A-section, she uses both punctuation options:
"It's where you are!" and "How near, how far?" Hamilton sets these
phrases on top of some of Lewis's most poignant harmonies. Hamilton's
ambiguity has power: the protagonist is uncertain, and the listener is uncertain. Lyrics and music together create a powerful sense of being unmoored,
of floating in a disorienting void of darkness.

The original staging for "How High the Moon" externalized this dis-
oriented inner landscape: the number was set during a London wartime
blackout. The forebodings of a dark future, felt in Great Depression songs
from "My Silent Love" to "What's Your Story, Morning Glory," have come
true. Because the United States was not yet involved in the war, however,
Tin Pan Alley could still safely indulge in combining this fear of the future
with romantic longing.

Yet "How High the Moon" proved relevant to later audiences. The biggest hit recording, a 1951 up-tempo romp by husband and wife Les Paul
(guitar) and Mary Ford (vocal), furthered that duo's innovative techniques
of overdubbing and sonic manipulation. That arrangement became the
basis for Emmylou Harris's 1981 Gold-selling LP track. Gloria Gaynor

brought "How High the Moon" into the disco era, with her 1975 charting single, just as that upbeat style was crystallizing.

Back in 1947, a number of singers bopped their way through "How High Is the Moon" on disc, proving themselves in step with the new vogue in jazz: Anita O'Day, Bibi Johnson (in imitation of O'Day), June Christy, and Ginnie Powell shift tempos and scat enthusiastically. Paul Bascombe's band chanted a hepster's variation of Hamilton's lyric that makes it clear that not just the moon but the singer, also, is high—on marijuana or alcohol. The sense of soulful but tipsy disequilibrium created by Hamilton and Lewis fit well with both the jazz world's new musical style and the larger society's postwar unease.

It is Ella Fitzgerald, of course, whose bop version became the touchstone. She performed it live in endless variations throughout her long career, and reissued recordings propagate it beyond her death. In the classic 1947 waxing and in her charting 1960 live version in Berlin, Fitzgerald sings Hamilton's lyrics and then launches into her own stanzas ("We're singing it / Because you asked for it"), followed by refrain after refrain of scatting and a brief return to words for the conclusion ("We hope you liked high, high, high, high / High is the moon"). She, and others who sing the tune in a fast tempo, render Hamilton's words in a throwaway fashion.

The most tender version of Hamilton's lyrics, however, is also by Fitzgerald. As the final encore in her 1964 concert at Juan-les-Pins, she slowly and lovingly croons a single simple chorus of "How High the Moon" the way it was originally conceived, as a love ballad. It is startling and effective, a *coup de théâtre*. Mel Tormé comes close to matching Fitzgerald in his 1961 studio recording. He includes the excellent verse and, with a pared down instrumentation supporting him, manages to convey all the mystery and romance of Hamilton and Lewis's creation. In the 1950s and 1960s, Pat Suzuki, Morgana King, and Johnny Tillotson were among the many others who featured slow-tempo arrangements of "How High," and all three emphasize the ballad's lost-in-space atmosphere.

"I DREAM OF YOU (MORE THAN YOU DREAM I DO)" (1944)
Marjorie Goetschius (1915–1997), composer-lyricist
Edna Osser (1919–2005), composer-lyricist

Edna Osser and Marjorie Goetschius met on the Staten Island Ferry. Goetschius later wrote, "I'd never felt anything click like that."[7] Besides living in the same borough of New York City, the two women had other things in common. Both could write either words or music for popular songs, although Osser was primarily a lyricist and Goetschius primarily a composer. Both were Jewish and married to Jewish arranger-conductors: at the time, Abe Osser (professionally known as Glenn) was the arranger for the Coast Guard band, and Goetschius's husband, Emery Deutsch (in civilian life, a radio and society bandleader), was its conductor. Both women occasionally collaborated with their husbands on songwriting.

Their first joint copyright, "I Dream of You (More Than You Dream I Do)," was registered by Embassy Music on February 15, 1944, as an unpublished work, and on April 17 as a published work. Embassy was a small firm but was 10 percent owned by Tommy Dorsey. The firm worked hard to promote this new plug tune, but spring, summer, and most of the fall passed before it won popularity. Finally, they attained a disc by Andy Russell that began to chart in November. Embassy's unusual perseverance in promoting what seemed to be a nonstarter was celebrated by the industry.

Also unusually, every hit single of "I Dream of You" had another hit on the flip side: Andy Russell (Maria Grever's "Magic Is the Moonlight"), Tommy Dorsey ("Boogie Woogie"), Frank Sinatra ("Saturday Night Is the Loneliest Night of the Week"), and Perry Como ("I'm Confessin'"). But "I Dream" did not ride on the coattails of more successful numbers; in every instance, it was at least as equally successful as its disc mate. It got equal or greater radio play, and, most importantly, in the sheet music market it sold and sold and sold.

Goetschius (pronounced GET-shee-us; a pretentious ancestor had added the Latin "us" to the Austrian name "Geotschi") and Osser liked verbal quibbles. In the title phrase of the first stanza of "I Dream of You (More Than You Dream I Do)," "dream" is used in two different meanings. Then, in the lyric's second stanza, "mean" is used in two different denotations, echoing the 1928 hit "Mean to Me." Both women would use similar formulations with success in the future. For instance, together they wrote the hits "I Long to Belong to You" and "The Last Time I Saw You," which starts, "Was the last time I saw you the last time?" Goetschius then wrote a lyric for a tune by her neighbor, classical violinist Jascha Heifetz, titled "When You Make Love to Me Don't Make Believe," a hit in England. In "I Dream of You," the writers cannily use other strategies in their release (where they instead focus on the contrast of "close" and "far" and the tongue-tied dilemma of the singer) and most of the final section (with its final powerful confession, "I want you so").

Rarely does such a modest tune evoke such a powerful atmosphere of warmth and longing. Melodically, the AABA refrain of "I Dream of You" flows with calm ease, kin to Jerome Kern at his most gentle. The momentum is kept going by tied notes that span the metrical bars: "I dreee-am of you." This is a common device that can be lively or forceful but here instead creates tender insistence. The pain of uncertain love is conveyed through the minor harmonies underpinning almost half the measures. Most admirably, from the recitative-like verse onward, the conversational fit between words and music is about as perfect as any example in the Great American Songbook.

Although Andy Russell had the initial hit record of "I Dream of You" and Tommy Dorsey the best charting one, it is Frank Sinatra's rendition that has proved to be the one for the ages. It was one of the first songs of his solo career to be recorded with an orchestra (the musician's union strike dictated choral backings for his earlier discs). Arranger Axel Stordahl creates one of his better introductions, a miniature sinfonietta in itself. Unusually, Sinatra includes the verse, perhaps to distinguish his arrangement from those that preceded him. Endlessly reissued, Sinatra's free, sensitive take on "I Dream of You" easily surpasses the lackluster, slow, string-laden 1960s album tracks of Jerry Vale and Johnny Mathis (who uses the verse, probably in tribute to Sinatra); even Ray Charles failed to break that pattern. Only Teresa Brewer, on a 1986 album, infuses the song with a jazzy bite. Brewer and cornetist Ruby Braff, with their breathy, expertly focused mic techniques, tap into the intimate power of the Goetschius-Osser tune.

Goetschius and Osser continued to create hits, together and apart, for the next ten years. Their follow-up ballad to "I Dream of You" was nearly as popular and begs for revival: the poignant, soaring "I'll Always Be with You." They found success right into the age of neo-simplicity, represented by their joint "Can I Canoe You Up the River" (a big hit in England) and Goetschius's "This Is My Confession" (the flip of a Joni James hit, the singer revisited it later in her career).

Goetschius came from a distinguished musical family. Her mother was a concert pianist, and her grandmother was an opera singer. The grandfather, Percy Goetschius, was Julliard's first authority on classical composing, teaching many, including Kay Swift. Marjorie became the only female student of Joseph Schillinger, composition teacher to Henry Cowell, George Gershwin, Glenn Miller, and many others. It was Deutsch who, naturally enough, recommended that she try her hand at pop music, but she continued to write classical music as well, including sonatas for Heifetz.

Osser was a first-generation Polish Jewish American, one of four raised in poverty in New York City by a widowed mother. Edna's brother, Lennie Meisel, was a Tin Pan Alley songplugger who unfortunately did not work for any of the firms that issued his sister's works. He acted as matchmaker for Edna and Abe, encouraging Osser to go to the bookstore where Edna worked. (Abe bought a Grove Dictionary of Music.)

The Ossers ran Glenn's career as a joint enterprise. His supreme competence, quickness, and reliability in all musical matters contrasted with his ineptness in any social interaction. Edna, by contrast, "was superb at interpersonal skills." She took care of the necessities of Glenn's high-profile music career, fulfilling their duties in "all sorts of cocktail parties, negotiations regarding what's going to be done, when it's going to be done, what it's going to cost." From 1966 onward, Abe and Edna together wrote production numbers for the Miss America competition. Edna, described by her son as "an early feminist," "felt that the pageant really did promote a better future for women." She "argued that most of these women were really in" the contest "to go to college, to make careers, to make an important contribution to society."[8]

Nevertheless, it is telling how domestic details dominate some of the anecdotes from these songwriters' lives. In 1952, Goetschius and Deutsch had their first child, and the composer became haunted by "an old Italian folk song that her opera star grandmother used to sing to her." She "let the melody run through her head," but "I was too busy to do more, what with midnight feedings and such." Two years ticked by before she had time to collaborate with Al Hoffman to transform the folk strain into the hit "My Bambino." Meanwhile, Osser started a successful stretch of writing advertising jingles. One, "Alice in Philco Land," lasted exactly sixty seconds. Therefore, Osser would sing it as a timer when she had to take her son's rectal temperature. Such vignettes illustrate how, during the tyranny of the Feminine Mystique, women's professional activities had to be forced into the tiny fissures in the bedrock of patriarchy.[9]

Osser functioned as an informal counselor and therapist to a wide circle of family members and acquaintances. She and Goetschius remained lifelong friends. In 1945, about the time they were collaborating on "The Last Time I Saw You," the composer wrote to the lyricist (who was a dedicated lifelong Democrat):

God, I'm trying so hard to develop real understanding. You know, whether you realize it or not, you did worlds for me that night. You caught me up short when I needed it, though I'd rather die than admit it at the time. Most of my furious arguing was because I knew you were right in so much you said, and I was mad that someone should know so much about my faults. You even opened my eyes politically. And you'd be surprised what my viewpoint is now, that I can see both sides.[10]

This letter between two female songwriters is of a kind not found in the biographies of their male peers. It brims with rapport, self-reflection, and the transformative power of interpersonal communication. The profundity this missive reveals is mirrored in the depth of the collaboration of Goetschius and Osser in songs like "I Dream of You."

"THE MAN WITH THE HORN" (1946)
Bonnie Lake (1916–1992), composer

Bonnie Lake got lucky with theme songs. Her first big plug tune, "Sandman," with lyrics by Ralph Freed, was swung at a gently loping speed as the signature song of the Dorsey Brothers band. They recorded it in 1934 with a vocal by Lake's songwriting peer Kay Werner. When the brothers split apart, Jimmy Dorsey kept the band and (for a while) Lake's tune. "Sandman" was made even more famous as the up-tempo opening instrumental theme for the 1935–1936 radio broadcasts of Benny Goodman. Arranged by Fletcher Henderson, it helped signal the start of the Swing Era. Goodman's disc was among the top sellers, paired with his closing number, "Goodbye." Lake went on to write more themes: for reed-player Fud Livingston; for her first husband, trombonist Jack Jenney; a closing theme for her third husband, conductor Russ Case; and an opener for singer Julius La Rosa's television series. With her sister Ann Sothern, she cowrote the swinging "Katy" to play under the credits of *The Ann Sothern Show*. *Variety* described it as a good racket: "Publishers give their right arm to plant a theme song. This, because of the constant plug."[11] So, although she never had a truly big hit number, Lake did all right.

Lake's mother, Annette, an immigrant from Denmark, was a touring classical singer; her father was the son of immigrants from England. Annette, after a stint in Hollywood coaching actors for the talkies, taught in a Carnegie Hall studio; there, Bonnie began her songwriting. She received encouragement from Jerome Kern; and Oscar Hammerstein II gave her a specially imported rhyming dictionary. Although songwriting remained her focus, Bonnie also led vocal groups, played piano, and was a singer, with a thin but resonant, matter-of-fact voice, flavored with a touch of vinegar. Her 1940 disc of two sophisticated Vernon Duke songs is treasured by musical theater aficionados.

Over the course of her long career, Lake created about two hundred songs, along with a dozen instrumentals and several dozen unfinished fragments of lyrics and music. She wrote with over three dozen collaborators, including seven women. Among these was Ruth Freed (and her brother Ralph Freed but never their more famous sibling, Arthur Freed) as well as her own sisters Marion Lake and Ann Sothern.

For the first twelve years, Bonnie Lake wrote songs solidly rooted in Swing Era jazz. These were purveyed by that style's exponents: "I've Got Your Number" (the Dorsey Brothers), "Red Nose" (Louis Armstrong), "Smile Your Troubles Away" (Connee Boswell), "Cuban Boogie Woogie" (Charlie Barnet), and "Sad Eyes" (Erskine Hawkins).[12] Teamed on disc with the Nat King Cole Trio, Lake waxed her own "Harlem Swing." Fittingly, the lyric set to her most enduring melody celebrates the jazz milieu in evocative terms, "The Man with the Horn."

Journalist-novelist Adela Rogers St. John became Lake's friend in mid-life, describing her as a "short, trim, vivacious . . . meticulous person, fastidiously neat about herself, her home, everything." Lake was "a professional, practical, realistic woman," St. John relates, which made Lake's unexpected advent of psychic mediumship skills in her fifties seem all the more incongruous. Lake married four times. She divorced radio program executive Hugh Murray (husband number two), conductor Russ Case (number three), and public relations man John J. Dickman (number four). Lake stuck with husband number one, Jack Jenney, through five years while he soared as a top bandleader and trombone soloist (featured as a nationwide audience favorite in the finale of the 1942 movie musical *Syncopation*)—and then bumbled, stumbled, and tumbled down through bankruptcy, two failed bands, and discharge from the army after "a fever." Ray Conniff, fellow trombonist, remembered Jenney: "A helluva musician. But gosh, he just ruined his life with that booze." Singer Bea Wain agreed: "He was smashed a lot." Meanwhile, Lake was singing and arranging for Jenney's bands, doing vocals for Artie Shaw when Jenney got hired by him, guesting on the radio, performing for military troops, and always writing songs. At the end, Jenney was doing pick-up jobs in Hollywood when he died from "kidney trouble" and "appendicitis" in December 1945. Lake probably needed every ounce of the practicality that St. Johns describes to get through that rollercoaster of a marriage.[13]

From 1945 through 1948, Lake collaborated with Eddie De Lange on several songs. De Lange had thrived both as a lyricist since 1932 and, for four years, as a cobandleader of the Hudson–De Lange big band. After that outfit broke up in 1938, De Lange entered into his four most successful songwriting years, producing lyrics for the standard "Darn That Dream" and a string of other hits.

In February 1946, a Lake–De Lange creation, "The Man with the Horn," was taken up by a new small Los Angeles imprint, Crystal Music. In May, the firm copyrighted the song. The registration reads, "Music by J. Jenney and Bonnie Lake; words by Eddie De Lange." Jenney had been dead five months by that time; the story was that he had co-composed it before his demise. (Jenney had been credited with only one previous song copyright, with his first wife, also a prolific songwriter, Kay Thompson.) Had he helped write this tune, or was the credit merely an honorary tribute to him, or even a marketing ploy? Another authorship question is raised by the sheet music. On it, the publisher listed De Lange not just as the lyricist but also as a third co-composer of the music. De Lange had lots of "words and music by" cocredits but no "music by" solo credits. In this case, did he contribute to the music or not? Of the three, Lake was the most experienced composer; therefore, it's likely that she was the dominant force in creating the music.

"The Man with the Horn" was taken up immediately by the big bands and horn players, with discs by Boyd Raeburn (bass sax; he waxed it on indie labels in 1946, 1951, and 1953), Harry James (trumpet; the flip of his 1947 hit "Jalousie"), and Randy Brooks (trumpet). Nevertheless, De Lange's lyric was ignored for several years. Early in 1950, on one of her many recordings for the Armed Forces Radio Service, Lake banters with singer Mark Smith as a prelude to his performing what they claim is the first vocal rendition of "Man with the Horn." She also mentions that by this time it was—yes—the theme song for two bandleaders, trumpeters Jimmy Zito and Ray Anthony. The latter was soon to rise with the most popular big band of the 1950s, with a slightly over-obvious but immensely appealing style. Anthony's rendition of Lake's tune was soon widely distributed to the public with the altered name of "Young Man with a Horn" to capitalize on the popular 1950 jazz-based movie of title.[14]

"The Man with the Horn" is one of the earliest songs to emerge in parallel to the nocturnal world of Hollywood's *films noirs*. While De Lange's lyric is not his best—there are some awkward spots—he does powerfully evoke the late night atmosphere of jazz clubs. De Lange's second stanza is particularly unusual in the Great American Songbook with its vivid details of the horn player closing his eyes, pouring out heartfelt music, taking his solo apart (with two possible meanings: stepping slightly away from the rest of the ensemble and also dissecting and rejoining the musical elements). The words are almost a romantic love song for the horn player but not quite. The love, ultimately, is for the music, not the man.

At the start of the AA´BA˝ refrain, Lake and her collaborators rivet the attention with seven pick-up notes hinging on compelling ascending half-steps: "You'll al- (half step) ways find (half step) me near the." The following dramatic jump up a fifth (*e* flat to *b* flat) to land on the word "man" works marvelously, highlighting the song's title phrase, and foreshadowing the two dramatic octave leaps in the bridge. The start of that release also enchants with bittersweet chromatic half-steps, descending this time.

Trumpeter Ivan Hunter points out that "The Man with the Horn," like many of Lake's Swing Era songs, "reacts to, and is therefore dependent on, the chordal harmony."[15] (And what harmonies they are—chock-full of juicy chords!) This is the opposite of the kind of pure, independent melody line that Alec Wilder repeatedly praises, but it is very much the way a jazz musician works. As De Lange's lyric says, jazz soloists "take apart" the harmonies and create a melodic flow out of the components of the chords. Lake does the same.

Singers eventually discovered "The Man with the Horn," starting with a 1951 single by Hadda Brooks (hip, and tender as peach fuzz). The 1957 album track by Anita O'Day is perhaps the definitive vocal version; she lived jazz and knew its after-hours milieu inside out. A number of the twenty-first-century jazz singer renditions show signs of being in tribute to O'Day.

In 1960, the Four Saints vocal quartet harmonized the blazes out of the song, with a window in the middle of the arrangement for the horns. In 1966, Nina Simone (astringent) and Della Reese (sermon-like) both recorded it. Reese's conversational conception plays out beautifully in live performance, as in a 1985 concert with trumpeter Al Hirt playing obbligato beside her; the entire number becomes a tribute, her to him, and them both to music. As long as horn players are playing jazz and singers dig them, Lake's "The Man with the Horn" is apt to live on.

"IT'S A GOOD DAY" (1946)
Peggy Lee (1920–2002), lyricist

As the 1940s spun into the 1950s, Peggy Lee emerged as one of the singers whose output defined the Great American Songbook, taking her place alongside Ella Fitzgerald, Frank Sinatra, and Nat King Cole. She also readily adapted to some of the styles that came after rock-and-roll, partly because of her steady dedication to songwriting. As a star singer who wrote many of her own hits, she foreshadowed the singer-songwriter era.

Lee wrote 270 songs with sixty-nine collaborators, four of them women. She did not just write for herself: not only were her songs widely recorded by others, a couple of dozen of them were *only* recorded by others. Primarily a lyricist, nevertheless Lee also composed music for thirty-one of her pieces. She saw 137 of her works published; during her heyday, three or more a year, often through her own company, Denslow Music.

From 1944 to 1966 Lee gestated twenty-four hit songs, yielding more than a dozen standards. Plus, Lee is commonly granted unofficial credit for two other standards. "Don't Smoke in Bed" is credited to friend Willard Robison, but she claimed it was mostly created either by herself alone or with her then-husband Dave Barbour. For "Fever," by Otis Blackwell and Eddie Cooley, Lee and Sid Kuller wrote extensive additional material that is now published as part of the score; ironically, those uncredited elaborations represent her most often–performed writing. As well, some of Lee's final lyrics, from her one-woman Broadway show *Peg* (1989), are singers' favorites that show signs of becoming standards. Her hit-writing peak was achieved from "I Don't Know Enough About You" (1945) to "I Love Being Here with You" (1960) and includes an enviable five hits from her score for the Disney animated musical *Lady and the Tramp* (1955).

Lee, a Scandinavian American from North Dakota, transformed herself from an insecure survivor of abuse (verbal, physical, and emotional, from her stepmother) to an icon of both feminine sensuality and feminist independence. She took on dozens of voices when she sang, but somehow her art always expressed one coherent sensibility: a slightly dreamlike, otherworldly, quiet intelligence that fed her sense of humor and took her deeply inside and yet kept her separate from her own public persona and her song protagonist's joys and sorrows. Lee's aesthetic integrity and versatility were perhaps fed by her songwriting, for in her lyrics she created a wide variety of characters and moods.

"It's a Good Day" was copyrighted in August 1946 with lyrics by Lee and music by her husband, the brilliant, quiet, soulful, alcoholic guitarist-arranger Dave Barbour. Lee was not a dependable reporter on her own life; she spun two accounts of writing "Good Day." In both, she was at home housecleaning when she spontaneously exclaimed the title phrase, but other details of the circumstances vary. During the late 1940s, the Feminine Mystique was coalescing; therefore, it is no surprise that Lee's first version emphasizes domesticity and motherhood. She proclaimed that she was "always happy" when housecleaning and, on top of that, was early in a pregnancy: "Then I started to hum, and Dave came out with his guitar, and before we knew it we had written the words and music for a song."[16]

Figure 11.1   Peggy Lee, in the 1950s, with another tool of the lyricist's trade: the typewriter. (Photo courtesy of Peggy Lee Associates, LLC.)

Forty years later, after a lifetime as a *bon vivant* and highly paid career woman, Lee claimed instead that the "good day" brought gifts of wine, a pheasant, and job offers. In this vignette, relayed decades after her divorce from Barbour and a quarter century after his death, Lee deemphasized her husband's contribution:

> As I busied myself with housework, I began to sing a little "dummy" melody, and, as the words kept popping in, I put down the vacuum or whatever and wrote them down. When it was finished, I put Nicki in her baby buggy and practically ran down to my sister's apartment house, called up to her window and sang my song. . . . When David came home, . . . he got some manuscripts and worked out the harmonies for what would be our first big hit.[17]

The same enigma occurs here as with "Down Hearted Blues": did the singer-songwriter's collaborator actually compose the melody or merely notate and harmonize it?

Lee and Barbour shape an AA′BA″ refrain with a driving momentum that matches the theatrical sweep achieved in Broadway classics like Vincent Youman's "Hallelujah" (1927) or the title song from Rodgers and Hammerstein's *Oklahoma!* (1943). In her lyric, Lee might well have been influenced by that landmark stage musical and its opening number, "Oh, What a Beautiful Morning," which set the pattern for more than a decade of optimistic ditties. These were often waltzes like "It's a Most Unusual Day" (1948) and "Wonderful, Wonderful Day" (1954) but sometimes were duple meter tunes like "It's a Good Day" or Mel Tormé's "County Fair" (1948). Lee organizes her A-section stanzas around lists: it's a good day for this, and for that, and for the other. (Many of Lee's early song successes are list songs to one extent or another.) She creates triple rhymes, albeit mostly of simple one-syllable words: *shoes/blues/lose*. The little miracle of the lyric is the B-section, when the singer reports on how she scolded the sun to arise and get moving.

Biographer Peter Richmond rightly views "It's a Good Day" as a reflection of the postwar era, a harbinger of "the fifties' string-spangled lush-life vision of a new America": the songwriters seem to be saying: "Come on, America. . . . Get up and get to it: Grab a piece of the brand-new dream." However, Richmond's conclusion that the piece is "a blithely naïve feel-good song" with a "complete lack of irony" is too limited. As Irving Berlin proclaimed early in his career, "sunshine" and "sadness" need to be mixed together to create a truly popular song. Minor chords in the main strain and flatted notes in the release, including a bluesy slur on "sun," hint at heartache. Meanwhile, as the lyric evolves through the stanzas, Lee creates a protagonist who has known the darker side of life—been saddened by the blues, burdened with unpaid bills, and dependent on pills to cure her ills. These shades of trouble give poignancy to the optimistic, galvanizing energy of the song.[18]

Lee's own "good day" foreshadowed her later sorrows. The pregnancy was followed by the diagnosis that she could not bear more children. The work offers led to a frenetic career that drove a wedge between Lee and Barbour. The pheasant she received could be seen as symbolizing the overeating she struggled with for decades; and the gift of the wine, the substance dependencies that came to dominate the lives of first Barbour and then Lee herself.

The disc that Lee and Barbour waxed of "It's a Good Day," with a jazz group, was a mild hit in 1947. (It long remained a disc jockey staple, and performers still copy Barbour's flickering guitar lines and Heinie Beau's motor-driven arrangement.) Yet the song's status in 1947 is better measured by other markers. "Good Day" received tremendous exposure on live radio broadcasts; in that field it was ranked number two for the year. Most importantly from Tin Pan Alley's perspective, the song spent weeks on the sheet music best-seller lists for both the United States and England. For twenty years, "Good Day" remained a surefire applause-getter in night-clubs and stayed a broadcast favorite, including as Lee's radio theme song, ranking among the most performed standards of the 1950s. The television renditions abound, with Betty White delivering one of the most charming and the duo of Frank Sinatra and Dinah Shore perhaps the most swinging.

Among the many studio recordings, Kay Starr is full-throated and galvanic; Billy Daniels, inventive; and Jonah Jones, jazz textured. The tune tends to sound frenetic when taken at the usual fast tempo. Therefore some of the more relaxed versions are the most engaging, such as by twenty-first-century jazz singers Sarah DeLeon and Matthieu Boré. A rendition by the country-swing band Asleep at the Wheel, who made it a 2010 album title track, testifies to the song's cross-genre appeal. As a singer and as a songwriter, Lee surpassed boundaries.

"A SUNDAY KIND OF LOVE" (1946)
Anita Leonard (b. 1922), composer-lyricist
Barbara Belle (b. 1922), composer-lyricist

For "A Sunday Kind of Love," the copyright claims are tangled. This is true, however, for many favorites of the Tin Pan Alley era. There are some notable examples among songs credited to women songwriters, and these others set "A Sunday Kind of Love" in context.

For instance: Two men claimed that Fleecie Moore did not write "Caldonia" (1945), one of the pivotal songs in the formation of rock-and-roll. Their stories are never questioned, even though they were hardly disinterested reporters. Lou Levy, who ran the Tin Pan Alley publishing house Leeds Music, probably got decades of after-dinner storytelling from his saga about how rhythm-and-blues star Louis Jordan cheated him: the bandleader promised to publish exclusively with Leeds for two years but then published instead with Preview Music, getting away with it by having the songs he wrote copyrighted under the name of his wife, Fleecie Moore. At the time, Jordan denied writing "Caldonia," but three decades later he declared: "'Caldonia' was by . . . me. Fleecie Moore's name is on it, but she didn't have anything to do with it. . . . She didn't know nothin' about no music at all. Her name is on this song and that song, and she's still getting money."[19] Moore registered twenty-six song copyrights during the years of her marriage to Jordan; with this interview, Jordan denied her authorship of any of them.

If Fleecie Moore "didn't know nothin' about no music," then how is it that she continued to copyright song compositions for several years after her bitterly acrimonious divorce from Jordan? Some of those later ones were copyrighted by Preview Music (the firm owned by her ex-husband's manager), and some of them were cocredits with Claude Demetruis (her frequent collaborator and one of the era's most prolific and respected African American songwriters).[20] Because it seems that she was capable of writing songs after her divorce, presumably she could write songs during her married years too. This being the case, maybe she did write "Caldonia." Levy and Jordan each held strong financial and emotional stakes in denying Moore's authorship; therefore, posterity can never really be certain.

In other cases, the cocredit to women appears, disappears, and reappears like the rabbit in a magician's act. "Well, All Right (Tonight's the Night)," which the Andrews Sisters rendered into a hit, was copyrighted three times in 1939, in April, May, and June. The registrations in April and June (when it was finally published) credit two men (Don Raye and Dan Howell) plus the jazz singer Frances Faye. The May registration, however, omits Faye and substitutes clarinetist-bandleader Artie Shaw. In the end, Shaw was permanently dropped from the credits, and Faye goes on record as the cocreator of this Swing Era anthem; and, certainly, the "voice" of the piece is very much in Faye's rambunctious style.

Here's another story involving lyricist Don Raye. On July 3, 1941, the newly formed team of Raye and composer Gene De Paul copyrighted "I'll Remember April," earmarked for the movie musical *Ride 'Em Cowboy*. By the time the film premiered in February 1942, the song had been recopyrighted with Pat Johnston added as a cowriter. Little can be found about her other than that she suffered from the lingering effects of infantile paralysis and wrote lyrics to tunes by Teddy Wilson, Eubie Blake, and Sonny Burke. The exquisite "I'll Remember April" proved to be her only hit and standard.

A fourth example: Starting in February 1955, singers began to record "Alright, Okay, You Win," written in a style that hovers on the cusp between swing and rock-and-roll. In August, Munson Music in New York copyrighted it, crediting it to Sid Wyche. By that time, however, two of the four covers of the tune had listed on their labels another African American as cowriter: Mayme Watts. Both Wyche and Watts were prolific writers in the decade, and they collaborated on a dozen copyrights registered from

March 1955 until April 1961. Another of their joint works seems on the path to become a standard in the early twenty-first century, "Don't Be on the Outside (Looking at the Inside)." In 1959, "Alright, Okay, You Win" was recopyrighted, with some new words and music, now credited to both Wyche and Watts. This registration made official what record labels had already proclaimed: Mayme Watts was a co-author of the piece.

The history of "A Sunday Kind of Love" and its writers reveals those same kinds of mysteries. In August 1943, Barbara Einhorn and Anita Rothblum began to register unpublished copyrights together. Occasionally Barbara would be credited with the words and Anita with the music, but usually their credits read "words and music by," indicating that the two women collaborated on both elements. They also worked apart, sometimes solo and sometimes with other writing partners. In 1945, when they finally began to get their songs published by established Tin Pan Alley firms, the two women permanently dropped their ethnic-sounding last names and became Barbara Belle (Belle was her original first name) and Anita Leonard (Leonard was her older brother).

Most of their breaks in the music business came from collaborating with—or perhaps merely cutting in—bandleaders. (The "perhaps" being the main point.) The two women got published with credits shared by maestros Louis Armstrong, Doc Wheeler, Al Trace, and Lucky Millinder. The pair themselves copyrighted the unpublished "The Boy-i-oy and the Girl-i-irl" on September 27, 1945. In November, they succeeded in getting it published by Enterprise Music, the company of music star Louis Prima; and along the way (surprise, surprise) Prima became credited as a co-author of the piece. Soon, the same process occurred for another Belle-Leonard copyright, "The Bee Song."

Around this time, Belle became part of Louis Prima's management team, and her career became bound to his for seventeen years. Prima was a jazz trumpeter and singer who became a great showman, known for bouncing all over the stage with irrepressible physical energy. (In 1967, he supplied the voice and the model for the king of the apes in Disney's animated *The Jungle Book*.) Prima rose to top pop star status, fell from that height, and then, with his wife, singer Keely Smith, rose again in the 1950s to make history as a kingpin of the Las Vegas nightclub scene. Throughout, Belle was right alongside with him. But when Smith split up from Prima, Belle (and her husband Lee Newman) left with her and helped the vocalist revive her career several times.

Belle was orphaned at age nine and grew up in the foster care system. In juvenile court, she became childhood friends with Fran Warren, both being high-spirited rebels. After running away from her foster home, Belle entered the Tin Pan Alley workforce; meanwhile, Warren became a singer with the Claude Thornhill big band. When the two encountered each other as adults, Belle immediately took on the role of Warren's personal manager. As well as guiding Warren through her years of success as a recording star, Belle (eventually joined by Newman) took on a roster of other show business clients, becoming a force in the industry. As with many other female songwriters, despite a lifetime in the entertainment business, Belle received no obituary in trade journals.

Returning to 1946: the stage was set for the strange history of "A Sunday Kind of Love." On February 26, the song was registered for copyright as an unpublished work, credited to Belle, Leonard, a novice songwriter Stan Rhodes (he later had a major career in advertising, jingle writing, radio, and television), and—you guessed it—Louis Prima. The odd thing is that when it was recopyrighted as a published work, by Enterprise, on April 25, 1946, Prima's name had been *dropped* from the credits. In previous cases, his name had been *added in* later, but, extraordinarily, "Sunday Kind of Love" reversed the pattern. Most of the song's first recordings list Prima as a cowriter—and in the decades since he is credited on sheet music and records—but three of these early disc labels do *not* include Prima's name. One of those was the premiere recording, in October 1946, by Claude Thornhill with a vocal by—you guessed it again—Fran Warren.

Prima enjoyed many copyright registrations over the course of thirty years. Some of the best and most successful were solo credits like "Sing, Sing, Sing" (1936) and "Oh, Babe" (1950). As with most music stars of his day, however, how many of his cocredits were really products of his own creativity is a question that may never be answered. His biographer, Gary Boulard, interviewed Barbara Belle, and, perhaps tellingly, in a discussion of Prima's songwriting he never mentions "A Sunday Kind of Love," which (along with "Sing, Sing, Sing") is Prima's most performed copyright. The very omission hints that Belle revealed to Boulard that Prima was merely cut in on the song.

The AABA refrain of "A Sunday Kind of Love" starts with three striking pick-up notes (one of which is a bluesy third). Many singers take advantage of that lead-in, holding onto each note to create suspense. The tune then alternates, first diddling on repeated notes and whole steps and then swooping up and down. Like Kay Swift in "Can't We Be Friends," in designing the strains of both the A-sections and the B-section, Belle and Leonard (and Rhodes) never exactly repeat a melodic idea. A flatted third near the end of the A-section lends a richness to the title phrase (on "*Sun*-day").

The verse of "A Sunday Kind of Love" sets up the song as part of a conversation, a pleading to a prospective love partner. By contrast, the refrain's lyric, when taken by itself, is a convincing inner monologue. It is a taking stock, a self-assessment by someone who feels "on a lonely road that leads . . . nowhere."

Perhaps the most interesting line is "I'd like to know it's more than love at first sight." In a genre that often celebrates "love at first sight," this is a remarkable flouting of convention. (Compare it with such songs as "The Man I Love," "Have You Met Miss Jones," "The Moment I Met You," "I'll Know," et cetera.) Throughout, the protagonist seems to hover on the border between youth and experience, naïveté and maturity.

"A Sunday Kind of Love" is well crafted and creative. Nevertheless—and this is hard to pinpoint—the song is also a bit blaring and obvious, a factor that hints at the trends of the next ten years. Perhaps one problem is the central idea of the lyric: the protagonist's longing for the security of "a Sunday kind of love" is staid, perhaps even a bit sanctimonious. Still, the song works so well, has so many nifty touches, with a particularly good first half of the release, and the lyric and melody fit so closely, that it sweeps away all quibbling.

Fran Warren left an indelible mark on "A Sunday Kind of Love." Her style is emotional, with an intensity that approaches that of Judy Garland. Warren uses her prominent vibrato, lots of slides, and little sobbing effects. Not just the song, then, but her rendition also foreshadows the overly sentimental trend of the next few years. Nevertheless, the effect is sensational. The Thornhill band plays a crucial role in the appeal of the disc, with rich, bluesy figures weaving in and out of her vocal. In 1947, Jo Stafford had the other charting single. As so often, her pure, cool voice paradoxically combines with her swagger and wholeheartedness. Paul Weston, her husband, supplies an arrangement that punctuates and swells—a crucial element to the track's success. Although many others waxed "Sunday" in 1947, not even the jazz-inflected versions of Ella Fitzgerald or Frankie Laine—or Louis Prima—could match Warren and Stafford.[21]

The tune adapted to many styles that followed in the wake of rock-and-roll. There developed a doo-wop tradition for "A Sunday Kind of Love," starting with the slow-tempo 1953 version of the Harp-Tones and the up-tempo 1957 arrangement by the Del Vikings, irresistibly danceable. (Unusually, about half of these renditions use the verse.) Jan and Dean chose the lively option for their hit 1962 single, taking the song into the realm of California vocal surf music. Dinah Washington delivered one of the best versions (on her charting *What a Diff'rence a Day Makes* album), and Etta James another (on her charting *At Last* album). These two infused "Sunday" with a full measure of soulfulness. In 1976, Kenny Rankin made the tune sound like a product of the singer-songwriter era; and, in 1988, Reba McEntire turned it into a country-western hit and standard.

In 1948, Leonard entered into a lifelong marriage to character actor Louis Nye. Belle and Rhodes united to create two more minor hits, the ballads "Early Autumn" (1947) and "Monday Again" (1948).[22] By the end of the 1940s, Leonard, Belle, and Rhodes had all bowed out of the Tin Pan Alley scene. Although each resumed copyrighting pop songs in the mid-1950s, they never collaborated again, and none of them regained the hit-making momentum promised by the success of their "A Sunday Kind of Love."

"IT'S TOO SOON TO KNOW" (1947)
Deborah Chessler (1923–2012), composer-lyricist

Weekdays, Shirley Chessler worked selling women's clothes at the Hixby's department store in Baltimore. The rest of the time she spent writing songs and peddling them backstage to the stars on tour. Chessler couldn't write music or play an instrument, but transcribers made her lead sheets and she sang well enough to plug her tunes. She sold a song to the local theater, advertising its new air conditioning; she placed a song with Desi Arnaz; and she sold Lionel Hampton on a Yiddish novelty piece and then cowrote a song with his wife Gladys. As the budding songsmith labored to enter the music profession, singer Buddy Clark (né Samuel Goldberg) advised her to change her given name to something that sounded less Jewish, so Shirley became Deborah.

Eventually, a radio disc jockey nudged Chessler toward singer Martha Tilton, who gave her an introduction to someone in the Brill Building on 49th Street in Manhattan, where Tin Pan Alley had come to roost. By this time, in the late 1940s, the pop song industry was increasingly oriented toward recordings; and Chessler realized the publishing companies "don't do anything unless there's a record." The result: in late 1947 and early 1948, two indie record labels covered Chessler's unpublished "Tell Me So." These discs got her a bit of a Baltimore reputation, which drew the notice of a Black vocal group, the Vibra-Naires, and their recording engineer-manager, Abe Schaeffer. They called to ask for her advice, sang her a sample over the telephone, and Chessler was hooked. She spent the next six years as their manager, as the group got a contract with Jerry Blaine and his new Jubilee record label, changed their name to the Orioles, became imitated by every teenage vocal group in the United States, and thereby helped invent doo-wop and rock-and-roll.

The partnership of the woman and the five men was highly effective: they were all clean-living, hardworking, and honest. Deborah Chessler and her mother Irene toured with them for some years. Deborah would tell the clubs, "Don't cheat my group, and I'll be *wonderful* to work with."[23] Historian Greil Marcus reports: "She learned every club owner's trick and how to beat them." Reminiscing into a tape recorder decades later, lead singer Sonny Til declared, "You were like a *sister* to us, and we *loved* you. And Mom Chessler was *our mom*, too." Their saga of cross-racial teamwork is so compelling that it is the basis for the 2018 stage musical *Soul Harmony*.

Unfortunately, 1950 brought tragedy to the team: touring incessantly took its toll on Irene Chessler, and she died at age forty-eight, and an auto accident on the way back from a gig killed guitarist Tommy Gaither—and injured bass Johnny Reed and show-stopping baritone George Nelson, both of whom soon left the group. By 1954, Deborah Chessler had finally got a belated divorce from her first husband (whom the military had rejected as "psychopathic"); and her desire to give new romance a chance led her to retire from show business. She went back to her old job in sales: "It was like I had never left."

Being manager to the Orioles did not guarantee Chessler an outlet for her songs. She had to audition each new piece for the group. The songwriter recalled: "Most of the times I didn't have" any songs on their disc releases; "I just had them on the sessions where I had written something and the boys liked it . . . the main thing is that they had to like it. And if they liked it, it usually came out good."[24] Chessler had three big hits and one minor one with the Orioles and ended her pop charts stint in 1953 by writing two hits (with Fanny Wolff) for Sunny Gale.

Chessler and the Orioles broke through with "It's Too Soon to Know." The disc was a huge jukebox success, a live radio and dee-jay program hit, and charted on the newly named Rhythm and Blues sales charts in *Billboard*. Remarkably, in an era when sheet sales had become subsidiary, particularly for R&B tunes, Chessler's song was also a sheet music success. It remains a lively standard into the twenty-first century.

Chessler copyrighted "It's Too Soon to Know" as an unpublished work in late December 1947. She told a colorful story about its creation. A New York man wooed her, told her he loved her, and said he could arrange a split from her husband. Her mother encouraged her to accept him, but Chessler in exasperation exclaimed, "Aw, Mom, it's too soon to know." She then went to the bathroom, where inspiration struck. Her mother found her a pencil, and Chessler wrote out the lyric on toilet paper. Whether true or not, the story hints at how stimulated the songwriter was by being in the Big Apple and how entwined her mother (a widow and single parent) was in her life.

For "It's Too Soon to Know," Chessler wrote a catchy melody, quiet but building dramatically, in the unusual form of AA′BA″B′C. It is most exemplary as a fit for her searing lyric. The protagonist enters into a remarkable interior monologue in which she speculates about the ultimate fate of a possible love affair. Except for the title phrase, the first two stanzas are all questions. In the second stanza, the contrast of being a fire or merely a flame is a clever twist on the central image of the torch song genre. It was this line that caused Jerry Leiber (who wrote "Hound Dog," "Jailhouse Rock," and many others) to exclaim admiringly to Greil Marcus, "She was one *bitch* of a songwriter!"

The remainder of the lyric focuses on how the affair might go wrong. Perhaps the most remarkable lines come near the end: "Though I'll cry when she's gone / I won't die, I'll live on." Many more conventional Tin Pan Alley songs would insist "if my love is unrequited, I *will* die." Up to that point, listeners might have been wondering whether the protagonist was getting a bit hysterical in so vividly imagining the worst, but now they are reassured: this character has her feet on the ground, is resilient, will survive. Chessler also does something remarkable with the melody for these lines. First she builds dramatically to the tune's highest note, on "die." Then she descends slightly to set the phrase "live on" to a repeated note that just hangs there, gently unresolved. The melody is in suspense (like the protagonist) and glides off into the unknown, embodying the lyric's idea of living on into an uncertain future.

For fans of rock-and-roll, the definitive version will remain the original, by the Orioles. None of the big labels who covered the tune in 1948 could beat this upstart indie disc on the charts. The slow tempo brings into prominence the relaxed diction of lead tenor Sonny Til ("me" becomes "mih," "die" is "duh"), which matches the slangy touches of Chessler's lyric ("if she don't love me"). The beautiful unity of the vibratos of all the singers is otherworldly, as if in a dream landscape or on some strange, empty, alien planet. In live performance, the Orioles added innovative, much copied touches: dance steps for the backup singers, histrionic emotionalism from the sexy Til, and sudden electric breakouts by baritone soloist George Nelson.

For fans of jazz singing, the touchstone version is that by Ella Fitzgerald, the first cover to be waxed. Not a *Billboard* chart item at the time, nevertheless it has been continuously in print, especially as part of the often reissued *Best of Ella Fitzgerald, Volume 1*. Fitzgerald is at her most intimate, her voice slightly husky and midway toward her mature style. As with her version of "I Wished on the Moon," Fitzgerald creates a remarkably tasteful interaction with her supporting vocal group, a call and response that fits the discursive nature of the lyric and that many later arrangements imitated.

The Orioles made "It's Too Soon to Know" an essential repertoire item for beginner doo-wop groups. Those who straddled rock-and-roll and the Great American Songbook have taken it up repeatedly. Very soon after Fitzgerald in 1948, Dinah Washington followed with her own cover. (She was an early booster of Chessler, reportedly telling the struggling songwriter, "You write like a Black woman," and making "Tell Me So" the flip of a single that was a hit in Harlem in the summer of 1948, just before the Orioles took off.)[25] Tony Bennett had some success with a heavy-beat version that charted in 1955 (the flip of his "Close Your Eyes"). The most notable revival was by Pat Boone, who sold a million copies of his straightforward, appealing, intimate but pallid single in 1958. Renditions with more bite followed, by such as Etta James (another charting single), Timi Yuro, Esther Phillips (perhaps best of all), and Linda Ronstadt. The 1993 article by Greil Marcus revived Chessler's reputation by asking, "Is This the Woman Who Invented Rock and Roll?" A face was given to the myth when Chessler appeared on television to emcee the 1995 induction of the Orioles into the Rock and Roll Hall of Fame. Only bass singer Johnny Reed was still alive to share the stage with the woman with whom the Orioles had engineered their success.

"SCARLET RIBBONS (FOR HER HAIR)" (1949)
Evelyn Danzig (1902–1996), composer

By composing "Scarlet Ribbons," Evelyn Danzig helped further the folk music vogue that would feed the pop market for decades. Jewish, born in Texas, and raised in Brooklyn, she did her advanced studies at the Convent of the Holy Name in Albany, New York. She had several famous piano mentors, most notably Zygmunt Stojowski (teacher of Antonia Brico, Oscar Levant, and many others), and became a classical pianist for concerts and radio. (Her older brother, Allison, became a famous sports journalist and historian of the game of tennis.) In her first forty-five years, she copyrighted only one instrumental piece, "Reversioners" (1926), under her married name, Evelyn Janet Levine. (Her husband, Manuel, was a prominent lawyer, eventually judge and Republican District Attorney, based out of his Long Island hometown of Port Jefferson.) Finally, in 1947, with her eldest son having left for college (he became a lawyer too), Danzig sent in her second copyright, words and music for "Soft Shades of Night."

From at least the early 1940s on, Danzig was very active in local music events, public and private; and it was in that context that her fellow Port Jefferson resident, disc jockey (later, celebrity interviewer) Fred Robbins, heard her compositions. (The jazz standard "Robbins Nest" was named for his broadcast show.) He encouraged Danzig to write pop songs and gave her contacts. Her first pop tune had lyrics by Lucille Robbins (Fred's wife) and Nancy Farnsworth. (Farnsworth's "Here Come Those Tears Again," written with son-in-law Jackson Browne after her daughter's suicide, would chart in 1977.) This was "Temporarily Blue," a well-crafted torch ballad that Robbins and Danzig quickly maneuvered into the hands of the manager and the record producer for Billy Eckstine. Unfortunately, for unknown reasons, the MGM label did not release Eckstine's track until 1954.[26]

By spring 1949, Danzig was collaborating with Kay Twomey, who recently had success with two songs about miracles, "The Serenade of the Bells" (1947) and "The Legend of Tiabi" (1948). Sentimentalized mysticism was in vogue, seen in movies like *The Enchanted Cottage* and *The Miracle of the Bells*. When Danzig teamed with Jack Segal, in their second copyright together they hit the jackpot with another such fable about a wondrous event, "Scarlet Ribbons (For Her Hair)." Thus, at the age of forty-seven—later than any other women in this book—Danzig entered the Tin Pan Alley market with a bang.

In his lyric for "Scarlet Ribbons," Segal creates a protagonist who overhears the tail-end of her young daughter's prayer: the wish for scarlet hair ribbons. By that time of night, there is no chance to find any ribbons, let alone scarlet ones. But as the sun rises, the mother looks in again and sees there is an array of ribbons on the child's bed—an unexplainable miracle. Mills Music picked up the number, and by October they got Jo Stafford, Dinah Shore, Dick Haymes, and others to wax it. Yet they worried: Would this story of a child's gift request become "lost in a flood of Christmas disks"?[27] They tried to hold back release of the records until the New Year, to increase its chance of success. Mills's strategy worked, for in January the song became a solid if unspectacular hit: eleven weeks of radio life, with both live broadcasts and disc jockey programs purveying the song.

The radio disc jockeys favored the Stafford version. Shore's rendition was admirably simple and heartfelt, but the accompaniment was perhaps too restrained for the tastes of audiences in 1950. By contrast, the Vic Schoen arrangement for Haymes was overarranged, far too complex. The Paul Weston arrangement for Stafford struck a happy medium. Stafford is at her most tender, and her slight air of detachment lets the story tell itself.

Segal and Danzig first create an AABA refrain. But then, with further lyrics that conclude the tale, they repeat the B-section and a shortened version of the A-section with a new cadence. So the overall structure is AABABA´ (unusual, though not unique). A further wrinkle is that all but the last of the A-sections are eight measures, but the B-sections are only four measures.

Musically, what is most astonishing is how Danzig builds the majority of the song on a pattern consisting of only four notes; this motif is then repeated lower and lower, ending with a three-note resolution. That process takes four bars and is then repeated. Overall, that four-note pattern forms the basis for two-thirds of the song. The release is almost as simple: eight notes in a dramatically ascending motif that is over just as the ear is trying to grasp it. Danzig's economy of means matches Irving Berlin at his best. The overall effect is elegant and magical.

Segal mates Danzig's even, sedate musical phrases with uneven groupings of syllables, three or four or five or eight, in unpredictable patterns. The writers avoid being trite and complacent through this vibrant dynamic between the security of the melody and the insecurity of the way the words are set to that melody. This can be viewed as a parallel to the paradoxical stability and restlessness of postwar US society.

"Scarlet Ribbons" was a definite but modest hit in 1950. In 1952, the rising star Harry Belafonte recorded the tune, creating a lot of industry interest but only fleeting public success during the 1952 Christmas season. He then, however, used the song as a foundation stone of his act as he rose to stardom. For almost four years, he blanketed the country with "Ribbons," in nightclubs, live on television, and in the revue *Three for Tonight* as it toured and then played Broadway. During this period, amid Belafonte's repertoire of Caribbean and folk songs, "Scarlet Ribbons" was his only Tin Pan Alley number. In 1956, his label included it in his million-selling album *Belafonte*. In 1957, his single of it became a charting hit in England. This, plus a spate of other recordings of "Ribbons," boosted the piece into a British 1957 sheet music bestseller.

Belafonte's rendition can be seen as definitive. A single guitar supplies the main accompaniment, and though a choir (all too often found in arrangements) eventually sneaks in, it is (for a change) unobtrusive. The singer, with a light grain in his timbre, lends to the piece all the sincerity and restraint that he had learned from bringing the folk music tradition into the pop music market.

From then onward, people usually referred to "Scarlet Ribbons" as a folk song, or at least in the folk style. Alec Wilder's praise for the piece reveals its hybrid nature: "It's very simple and very evocative in the manner of a true folk song." But the critic is confused: "It's not truly a pop song. But it was published by a pop publisher and it's not 'got up' in an art song copy."[28] (Nevertheless, "Ribbons" found a comfortable place in the repertoire of some classical singers performing in an entertainment context.) As so often when evaluating songs by women, Wilder is slightly off the mark: in fact, in 1950 "Scarlet Ribbons" was a timely pop entry.

Five postwar trends in the pop song marketplace overlap in "Scarlet Ribbons." The first was a Baby Boom phenomenon: parents wanted songs either about children (like Kay Thompson's 1956 hit "Eloise") or that could be enjoyed alongside their offspring (like Helen Deutsch's 1953 success "Hi-Lili, Hi-Lo"). Second was an explicit or implicit religiosity. This was hinted at in lyrics such as "Sunday Kind of Love" and more explicit in big hits of the day like "Robe of Calvary," which brought success to Kay Twomey, Elaine Rivers, and their two male cowriters (who had to shift to Christian-sounding pennames on the credits: Fred Wise became Fred White and Ben Weisman became Robert St. Clair).

Third was the increased incorporation of folk music traits into Tin Pan Alley products; for example, "(Ghost) Riders in the Sky," a 1948 pop phenomenon, which Stan Jones, a park ranger, based partly on the traditional melody of "When Johnny Comes Marching Home." (He plugged the song to Hollywood location scouts. Result: a show business career.) The fourth trend was a tendency toward greater simplicity. Some songs became cruder for it—others, more pure and distilled, such as with Doris Fisher's "Please Don't Kiss Me" (1948), Joan Whitney's "My Own Bit of Land" (1950), and Polly Arnold's "Wind Song" (1954). Danzig and Segal wrote a title that tells it all: "Simple, Simple, Simple" (1950). (It is actually a sadly neglected, audaciously pared down gem.)

Fifth, and closely connected to this last, was the rise of songs that would be appropriate to intimate nightclub settings. At such venues, audiences demanded the off-beat, such as three numbers from the Broadway revue *New Faces of 1952*: Elisse Boyd's poignant, confiding "Guess Who I Saw Today," or June Carroll's sprightly, witty "Love Is a Simple Thing" and quirky "Penny Candy." Amazingly, "Scarlet Ribbons" caught the zeitgeist so well, it was able to exemplify all five of these vogues.

Although not a huge hit at the start, for the next twenty years there was scarcely a break in the popularity of "Scarlet Ribbons." Almost as soon as one vogue subsided, another took its place. A particularly big year for the Danzig-Segal opus was 1959, when the Browns (a country-western sibling act) had a hit single; so did Enoch Light and the Light Brigade (in an instrumental version), and the seminal folk act the Kingston Trio, establishing it once and for all as a folkie standard by its inclusion in their million-selling album *The Kingston Trio at Large.* Even Joan Baez recorded it, although her taping got only bootleg pressings until 1978.

Almost all performers, whether pop, country, or folk, retain the song's air of quiet sanctity. Peter Nero, in an instrumental version, was able to achieve more variations on the melody, making it a fugue, a cool jazz theme, and an easy listening tune all in one track. Rock bands like Gandalf or the Cats (in a hit European version) give it more of a beat but still manage to respect the song. Only the 1991 disco arrangement by Cliff Richard (though sincerely meant and widely popular) seems to violate the atmosphere of the piece. Never mind, for in her evocative 1992 version, Sinead O'Connor restored the song's spare purity. (*Billboard* granted Danzig an obituary, seemingly on the strength of the O'Connor revival.)

Continuing their collaboration, Danzig and Segal displayed their versatility with a brassy blues, "Warm-Hearted Woman" (1951). It was a fleeting and modest hit. Probably more helpful to their bank balance (in that era of increasing disc sales) was "Little Café Paree" (1951) appearing on the B-side of a Vic Damone hit. Their neglected gem, "Where I May Live with My Love" (1952), was perhaps their most sophisticated plug tune. Segal went on to team with Marvin Fisher (brother of Doris Fisher) for the standard "When Sunny Gets Blue" (1956) and a dozen other aficionado favorites.

Danzig also went on to write with other collaborators, such as lyricist Sammy Gallop. With Sylvia Dee ("Too Young") she captured some of the same innocent spirit as "Scarlet Ribbons," with "Teddy Bear" (1955)—another short-lived hit.[29] Danzig wound up her most active composing years with another Segal collaboration, a stage musical produced regionally in 1962, *Hester,* based on *The Scarlet Letter.* Its numbers, along with Danzig's later song copyrights through 1967, await rediscovery.

"GOD BLESS' THE CHILD" (1941)

Billie Holiday (1915–1959), composer-lyricist

Billie Holiday set the high-water mark for jazz singing, digging emotionally deeper than anyone else into the Great American Songbook, bending notes heartbreakingly, and swinging joyously. Ella Fitzgerald and Peggy Lee worshipped her; Frank Sinatra proclaimed she was the most important influence on his singing. A collection of the more than eighty books about Holiday would fill several shelves. Hollywood has distorted her life to spectacular effect in two major biopics; and three stage plays similarly use her as a tragic icon.

Yet one can search in vain in the indexes of the major publications on Holiday for the words "songwriting" or "as songwriter." The creative process behind her songwriting is clouded. Holiday, along with many celebrities, was inconsistent and inaccurate about the facts of her saga. As far as everyday life goes, she was described by her long-time accompanist Carl Drinkard as "a pathological liar—she could tell herself something enough times so she'd believe it."[1] Further, decades after the event, when Holiday was long deceased and could not debate the matter, her major writing partner, Arthur Herzog Jr., disputed her role in the creation of their collaborations. But was *he* reliable? Well, see the discussion that follows.

BIOGRAPHY

By the standards of her era, Billie Holiday could hardly have started from a more disempowered position. She was a woman. She was Black *and* Irish

Catholic—a double whammy. She was dirt poor. Moreover, because Billie was conceived and born out of wedlock, her family despised and abused her and her mother, Sadie Fagan. Still a child, Billie survived rape and unfair and cruel institutionalizations. From such oppressed beginnings, she rose to be one of America's greatest artists, internationally acclaimed, and a star of the media. The flip side of such prominence was that she became the single most hounded celebrity scapegoat of the government's misguided tactics for fighting heroin addiction. Because of this, for years she could not perform in a New York City nightclub, and television sponsors fought to keep her off the air.

Holiday was a person of even greater contradictions than most. Toughness coexisted with vulnerability; elation with depression; violent temper with tenderness. She was dubbed "Lady Day," at first jokingly because of the contrast to her foul language but very soon in all seriousness because Holiday radiated a profundity and an inner integrity that were undeniable.[2]

The facts of Holiday's life have become familiar, even perhaps overfamiliar to fans of jazz singing: her birth out of wedlock in Philadelphia; her years being raised by distant relatives; her absent jazz-guitar-playing father; her mother's hardscrabble work life with the railroads, as a domestic servant, and (her preferred career) as a neighborhood restaurant owner. At about age fourteen, Holiday joined her mother in New York City, where the teenager's singing career budded and blossomed. From then until she was twenty-six, Holiday mostly lived with her mother—a staid domestic setup easy to forget in light of her later tragic image. After that, even though addictions and dysfunctional marriages took hold, she still enjoyed many good times, with friends, fans, pet dogs, and godchildren bringing joy. In 1956, when interviewer Mike Wallace asked her "why so many jazz greats seem to die so early," Holiday gave a revealing answer:

> Well, Mike, the only way I can answer that question is, we try to live one hundred days in one day and we try to please so many people, and we try to—like myself, I wanna bend this note and bend that note, and sing this way and sing that way, and get all the feeling and eat all the good foods and travel all in one day, and you can't do it. [Laughs] So I think that's why.[3]

She was a woman who would offer as a prime example of a happy song "Yesterdays," with its Otto Harbach lyric declaring "sad am I, glad am I." Her music, too, is imbued with an intermingling of sadness and gladness.

Many music and political critics heap scorn upon Holiday's Tin Pan Alley repertoire, while praising her way of singing them. Yet Holiday loved these

Figure 12.1   Billie Holiday, 1947, with a woman's best friend. (William P. Gottlieb, Downbeat, via Wikimedia Commons. Public domain.)

songs and wrote ones like them. In the 1930s, preparing for a single recording session, she and Teddy Wilson would routinely go through forty songs to choose three or four to wax. She knew the genre inside and out.

BILLIE HOLIDAY, SONGWRITER

Holiday, Irene Kitchings, and Carmen McRae were part of a close-knit group of female friends in the late 1930s. All three began to write pop songs at about the same time in the first half of 1939, encouraging each other. Holiday seems to have been actively working to hone her style and voice, partly by selecting older songs with serious lyrics and rendering them in slower tempos and partly by filling her repertoire with material created by herself and a trusted circle of songwriters.

As a songwriter, Holiday has eighteen titles in her corpus, five with bylines for lyrics only and the rest with "words and music by" credits.[4] The range of styles is wide, including simply structured twelve-bar blues; multisectional, more complex blues; and conventional Tin Pan Alley songs. Holiday displayed new abilities in her two 1950s songs with Jeanne Burns. "Preacher Boy" is a gentle folk-inflected waltz, ideal for audiences at an intimate, sophisticated boîte, while "Who Needs You" is an agitated bop-inflected waltz, ideal for a modern jazz club. All of Holiday's works share a certain quirkiness: the lyrics (and sometimes the musical lines) contain interesting, slightly off-beat touches. It fits her taste: Holiday liked unusual songs—"something nobody else does"—that were not big immediate hits, like "Yesterdays," "Deep Song," and Kitchings's "Some Other Spring." The fact that her own song credits reflect that sensibility argues that she might well be responsible at least in part for their creation. Her songs are also consistent in their high quality. Even the most obscure are worthy of being performed.

Kim Purnell, in her dissertation on Holiday, supplies a related clue. All of Holiday's lyrics express a personality "far from the one-dimensional creature we have been taught to pity." Instead the song texts show her as "a complex individual with insight, wit, and a desire for a better life."[5] Holiday achieved what Irving Berlin said was essential to a good popular song, the mixture of sorrow and happiness, as in her first Tin Pan Alley–styled work, "Everything Happens for the Best." She addresses it to a once idolized but now unfaithful sweetheart, conveying goodbye and good riddance through unusual juxtapositions: "You're running my heart so deep in the ground. / That's okay, it happens for the best." Almost twenty years later, in what may be her final lyric, "Left Alone," Holiday does similarly. After three stanzas of despair, the protagonist suddenly affirms: "Perhaps we'll meet before I die. / Hearts will open," then quickly shifts back to aching loneliness for the title phrase, "but until then, I'm left alone." Purnell points out that, in Holiday's songs, alongside the "sadness [and] depression" runs these strains of "optimism . . . resilience, courage, and hope."

Notable, particularly, are her final ten years, when Holiday wrote lyrics that are salty and assertive. The titles speak for themselves: "Now or Never," "You Gotta Show Me," and "Who Needs You?" are prime examples, and almost as clearly in this category are "Please Don't Do It in Here" and "You'd Do It Anyway." In other words, despite a small songwriting output, the songs Holiday is cocredited for display the usual signs of authorship: a guiding aesthetic, consistent high quality, recurring themes, artistic periods, and artistic growth.

Yet Arthur Herzog claimed Holiday "has never written a line of words or music." Specifically, he tells of her taking credit for two songs she hardly contributed to at all. Herzog said he wrote "God Bless' the Child" and that Holiday only supplied the title, the central idea, and the change of a single note. He claims he gave her credit because a publisher would only take the number if Holiday would record it. On the other hand, Holiday made the opposite claim, that she alone wrote the words and music. When she got Herzog involved, she related, they merely "changed the lyric in a couple of spots, but not much." Possibly, Herzog and Holiday were both simply being credit hogs; the song might well have been an equal creation.[6]

Speaking years after Holiday's death, her former accompanist, Bobby Tucker, testified that he wrote the tune of "Somebody's on My Mind," which is credited to Holiday and Herzog. The singer supplied the notion of turning Tucker's melody into a song, and she gave it a title. Then, having difficulty with the words, Holiday nagged Herzog into drafting "twenty-seven different sets of lyrics." Later, Tucker found a letter among Holiday's bills in which her publisher, Marks, wrote "as per your request we have removed Bobby Tucker's name."[7] The irony is that, in the end, the melody credit (which, under a normal contract, would receive two-thirds of the royalties) was assigned solely to Herzog. But Herzog never relayed *that* story.

There are other facts, too, that counter Herzog. For one, Holiday shared official cocredits with ten collaborators. None of the other credited writers complained that she did not contribute to the creation of these songs. Two lived long enough to have plenty of chances to speak up: Jeanne Burns (d. 1982) and Mal Waldron (d. 2002).

Even Tucker credits Holiday with the title to fit his tune "Somebody's on My Mind," and even Herzog credits her with the concept and title of "God Bless' the Child." For that alone, Holiday would deserve the credit and co-ownership that Herzog begrudges her. For instance, Sadie Vimmerstedt earned equal credit and royalties with Johnny Mercer because she mailed him these two lines: "I wanna be around to pick up the pieces / When somebody breaks your heart." This was seen to be fair because (as Dorothy Fields and Sammy Cahn affirmed) a Tin Pan Alley lyric grows from the idea and the title.

We know from many testimonies that Holiday was loose with the truth, but Herzog's character is much less documented than Holiday's. In his favor, Herzog and Irene Kitchings were in agreement about the harmonious way they wrote songs together in 1939 and 1940. On the other hand, by 1953 Herzog was a movie publicist—not a profession known for sticking precisely to the facts. Further, by 1961 Herzog was actively promoting his own image and reputation as a songwriter, often with exaggeration, such as stating he was "the author of fifty-seven lyrics now on records," when he could have more correctly claimed to be the author of seven lyrics that, together, enjoyed fifty-seven diskings.[8] By 1971, when he was interviewed about his collaboration with Holiday, Herzog had spent the preceding decade puffing up his reputation as a songwriter.

All this does not diminish Herzog as a powerful creative force. Even his 1926 plug tune, "Would-Ja," which he wrote when fresh out of college, is a superior lyric. Herzog's poignant, pungent lyrics for Kitchings are of much higher quality than the lyric that other people wrote for her first tune "This Is the Moment." The four songs Herzog created with Holiday are among her most compelling, including her most performed opus, "God Bless' the Child."

"GOD BLESS' THE CHILD"

Holiday recorded "God Bless' the Child" in May 1941, and the disc was released in July, the same month the Edward B. Marks firm published it. On both the sheet music cover and copyright registration the work is described as a "swing-spiritual"—odd, for the melody is not intrinsically swinging and the lyrics are not very spiritual. The cover gives this detail: "Based on the authentic proverb 'God Blessed the Child That's Got His Own.'" Nobody has found such an expression in American folklore.

The Gospels state in several places, "For he that hath, to him shall be given." (Most interpreters think this means that a person who hath true understanding of religious teachings shall then be given spiritual growth.) By at least 1919, these passages had been transformed into the slangy expression, "Them that has, gits." Holiday and Herzog start their refrain with a variation of that phrase.

Unlike other songs with this title, such as Shania Twain's 1996 hit, the Holiday-Herzog "God Bless' the Child" is not about God or children. It is about adults being independent of charity and their relatives. Further, it is about money and the inequities and hypocrisies it creates. There was a slender string of Tin Pan Alley lyrics that ruminate cynically on the nature of life, money, and fate, running from "Life's a Funny Proposition After All" (1904) through Ann Ronell's "Funny Little World" (1934) and further. The one that Holiday and Herzog follow most closely is a 1923 song that

Bessie Smith made famous in 1929, "Nobody Knows You When You're Down and Out."

In telling how "God Bless' the Child" was created, the only thing Holiday was consistent about was that it came out of her asking her mother for money and Sadie refusing. The story Herzog remembered was the opposite: Holiday refused money to Sadie. Either way, at the root of the lyric's origin is the central relationship between daughter and mother. At the time, Sadie was angry at Holiday because of Jimmy Monroe, the slick and attractive bad boy who got the singer hooked on heroin. In a defiant gesture, Holiday married Monroe in September 1941, six months after recording "God Bless' the Child." Finally, Holiday stopped living with her mother—independence at last. (With consequences: the singer was tortured by guilt about Sadie's death, at age forty-nine, in 1945. Holiday then divorced Monroe in 1947.)

In 1941, during the ASCAP radio ban, Herzog wanted to get a song on the market while BMI was giving opportunities to underdog songwriters, like himself and Holiday. Fittingly, the song they wrote can be seen as celebrating the resilience of the underdog. Herzog also wanted to write a song that evoked Black folk culture of the South. His impulse can be viewed as part of an era when the political left strove to celebrate Americana. Although Holiday drew from her life in conceiving "God Bless' the Child," Herzog might have too. He was an Ivy Leaguer who seems to have failed as a Wall Street broker. It is possible his fall from fortune was a turning point, politically, because by 1936 he was writing tributes to the worker like his "Farmer-Labor Party Song."

"God Bless' the Child" is in AABA form. The A sections are a bit longer than usual, ten measures instead of eight, because of the repetitions of the phrase "that's got his own." A similar repetition had been used by Harold Arlen and Ted Koehler in "Stormy Weather" (1933). For the most part, the tune for "God Bless'" ambles along easily, akin to Hoagy Carmichael at his most relaxed in songs like "Moon Country" (1934) and "Bread and Gravy" (1935). The release, however, breaks out with a sudden exclamation, "Money, you got lots of friends," starting on and then returning again and again to the song's highest note, as, meanwhile, the harmonies linger on the minor. It is startling to hear the singer suddenly talk to "Money"; Bernice Petkere creates a similar effect when she starts the release of "Close Your Eyes" by commanding, "Music, play!"

Ted Gioia complains that the melody of "God Bless' the Child" is "a bit too sing-song."[9] That effect occurs because the melody is based on repetitions in units of two measures—predictable or inexorable, depending on how one hears it. The pattern is kept from being overly predictable, however, by slight variations. For instance, during what seems like it will be repetition, Holiday and Herzog instead drop down to an unexpected flatted note. Even if Herzog's claim is true that Holiday only asked for the change of a single note, within this context of melodic repetition such a detail might well amount to a major contribution.

Billie Holiday made four official recordings of "God Bless' the Child," three in the studio and one for a short film. She always varies the melody extensively, and she also sometimes varies the lyrics. Each rendition is different and superb in its own way. The prize, however, must go to her first waxing, in 1941, which was inducted into the Grammy Hall of Fame in 1976. Backed by a brooding, soft-edged small group jazz accompaniment headed by Eddie Heywood, Holiday is at her peak, her voice mellow and fresh but mature, with poignant downward slides on words like "friends." Her final tag, "He just don't worry 'bout nothin' / 'Cause he's got his own," which she also used in her final recording of the tune, is typical of her ambiguity. Holiday may have felt this was a happy song celebrating those who stand on their own two feet. Or she may be sorrowing for those who must hold on to money to be free from worry. Or acidly critiquing society. Or all three.

The melody works best, perhaps, as a hand-in-glove fit for the unique lyric. Nevertheless, "God Bless' the Child" ranks high among jazz compositions.[10] A long list of instrumentalists embrace the tune. Two saxophonists created extra-special versions: Eddie Harris, quiet and spare on a low-charting 1961 single, and Eric Dolphy, fluttering and flying unaccompanied in a 1964 live solo. Among the quietest renditions are those by Anita O'Day and Ethel Ennis; among the most rhythmic are from Bea Wain (after Holiday, the first to record it, starting it toward becoming a standard) and Kay Starr (with Count Basie and His Orchestra). Among the strangest are Yeardley Smith as the cartoon character Lisa Simpson (an oddity that ironically remains one of the best-selling renditions) and a 1997 duet of Tony Bennett and the digitally revived Billie Holiday (her portion extracted from her 1950 short film).

"God Bless'" evokes folk wisdom, so it is appropriate that two of the most well-balanced renditions come from outside the jazz world, from pop-folk singers Harry Belafonte (the first to feature it on a charting LP, in 1958) and Jimmie F. Rodgers. Diana Ross, playing Holiday in the 1973 biopic *Lady Sings the Blues*, rendered the piece with restraint. Ross's version charted not just as part of the soundtrack album but also as the flip side of the hit single of "Good Morning Heartache."

The best-selling version of "God Bless' the Child" came in 1969, however, with a rendition by the eight-member rock-jazz fusion band Blood, Sweat & Tears, featuring blue-eyed soul singer David Clayton-Thomas. (The lyric probably held a powerful meaning for this Canadian vocalist who had been a homeless teenager.) Their rendition is long (almost six minutes) with more than half a dozen shifts in speed (from an up-tempo Latin feel to a slow out-of-tempo coda) and instrumentation (from brass choir to organ to electric guitar to harmonica). Altogether, on the original album and "greatest hits" compilations, this rendition has probably sold more than twelve million copies. Some would see the situation ironically: in a society dominated by white males, find a young, good-looking white guy (or in this case, eight of them) to sell your product and you'll make pots of money. As if to prove, "Them that has, gits."

Billie Holiday's standards
Words and music by Holiday and any collaborators, unless otherwise noted.
1936: "Billie's Blues (I Love My Man)" (first version)
1939: "Fine and Mellow"
1941: "God Bless' the Child," with Arthur Herzog Jr.
1944: "Billie's Blues (I Love My Man)" (extended second version)
1944: "Don't Explain," words by Holiday, music by Arthur Herzog Jr.
1956: "Lady Sings the Blues," words by Holiday, music by Herbie Nichols
1957: "Left Alone," words by Holiday, music by Mal Waldron

Some neglected gems
1939: "Everything Happens for the Best," with Tab Smith; end of a love affair, curt yet tender
1939: "Our Love Is Different," words by Holiday and Rance J. Conway, music by Sonny White and Benton Lee Alba; idealistic love lyric with unusual touches
1949: "Now or Never," with Curtis R. Lewis; jump blues with three distinct strains
1955: "Preacher Boy," with Jeanne Burns; wistful folk-like ballad
1957: "Who Needs You?," with Jeanne Burns; jazz waltz with assertive lyric

⒔

"GOOD MORNING HEARTACHE" (1945)

Irene Higginbotham (1918–1988), composer-lyricist

In August 1938, twenty-year-old Irene Higginbotham walked into a room in Manhattan to meet with other African American songwriters. Ten were newcomers, like her, and four were old-timers, like Eubie Blake, but all of them were struggling to find a place in Tin Pan Alley as Black tunesmiths during the Swing Era. They hoped to form an organization to advocate and make conditions better, but the idea never took root. Among them all—thirteen men and two women—only Higginbotham would flourish during the coming decade. By the summer of 1944, Higginbotham was a member of ASCAP. By the end of 1945, she had cowritten the song that would carry her reputation into the future, "Good Morning Heartache."

BIOGRAPHY

Higginbotham was born in Worcester, Massachusetts. Her mother died soon thereafter, and her father, Garnett, moved the family back to Georgia, probably his home state. (Garnett's younger brother, and thus Irene's uncle, was the famous jazz trombonist Jay C. Higginbotham; and he had been born in Social Circle, Georgia, in 1906. Garnett himself is described in Irene's early 1940s publicity blurbs as a former "Atlanta teacher"—moreover, a "musician-teacher-journalist.") Irene's ASCAP biographical entry fills in some details of what happened then. She attended the elite, Black, progressive Atlanta University Laboratory School (Martin Luther King Jr. later attended it), studied piano intensively, and began to perform in classical music concerts. It is easier to find information about her music teachers than about her: Frederick Douglass Hall was given tribute in the congressional record, and his teacher, Kemper Harreld, founded the internationally famous glee club of what is now Morehouse College in Atlanta. For that time and place, Higginbotham was studying at the highest levels possible.

By 1935, Higginbotham had shifted her base from Atlanta to New York City and, reportedly, attended business school, becoming a stenographer. As late as New Year's Eve, 1941, she was still living with her father, just north of Harlem in Morningside Heights. Meanwhile, again reportedly, she was composing classical concert works. She was probably writing under the guise of Hart Jones (in a 1938 article, the pseudonym is given in parentheses after Higginbotham's name). A brief biographical note in one of her 1944 publications claimed she had written "more than a thousand tunes," starting from the age of five.[1]

Sometime in late 1939, Irene hooked up with her uncle Jay to create "Harlem Stomp." Just after New Year's Day, 1940, Lewis Music copyrighted the tune, and on March 14 it was recorded by (drum roll, please) Louis Armstrong. Through 1943, Armstrong continued to perform "Harlem Stomp," and placing this number with him truly launched Irene's career as a writer of pop music.

Unusually for an African American woman of her era, Higginbotham attained what might be viewed as a conventional Tin Pan Alley trajectory. Other Black women, from Alberta Hunter to Billie Holiday and beyond, supported themselves at famous performers; Lucy Fletcher and Irene Kitchings hovered at the fringes of the sheet music industry. But Higginbotham thrived at its core, sustaining a steady output as a songsmith for more than ten years. By the mid-1950s, Jesse Mae Robinson ("I Went to Your Wedding," 1952), Rose Marie McCoy ("Tryin' to Get to You," 1954), and a host of other African American women would follow Higginbotham's lead.

From 1940 through 1957, Higginbotham copyrighted about 112 pieces through thirty publishing houses. She collaborated with thirty-four other writers, including three women, but usually worked alone. Higginbotham registered a handful of instrumental works but focused on songs, almost always with "words and music by" credits. For the sixteen songs where the credits for music and lyrics are separated, she is listed as the composer in all but one instance.

Higginbotham captured the quintessence of the early 1940s. Whether jump ("Lenox Avenue Jump"), jive ("Are You Livin' Ol' Man"), timely war ditties ("Mama Putcha Britches On," which celebrated the Rosie the Riveter type), novelty ("It's Got a Hole in It"), blues ("Cold Winter Papa"), or boogie ("The Boogie Beat'll Getcha If You Don't Watch Out"), Higginbotham made it to order. In all this, too, can sometimes be sensed a small drop of artificiality: she fulfills the era's conventions while also keeping a slight distance from them. At times, she hints at a broader range than she was fully allowed to explore: she imbues "Mrs. Finnigan" with a polka-like feeling and snuck into many a work a brief moment of the "*da*-dum" Charleston rhythm, as in "Grand Central Station" or "Boogie Woogie on a Saturday Night."

At times Higginbotham wrote with a depth and theatrical sweep that should have earmarked her for Broadway or Hollywood musicals. Pieces like "Bobby's Trombone Blues" seem designed for some collegiate movie musical with young dancers wearing out the gymnasium floor. (The closest Higginbotham came was "adding music choir features" to *Born to Swing*, a 1944 Andy Razaf–Donald Heywood stage musical that closed quickly in Philadelphia.)[2] Her songs teem with interesting, vividly drawn characters: the gossips in "Liver Lip Jones" and "Loud Mama"; the square converted to a hepster in "That Did It, Marie"; or the lug of a sailor in "Hello, Suzanne," who reunites with his sweetie by greeting her with comedian Phil Silvers's famous catchphrase, "Glad ta see ya." Higginbotham's works are springy and full of life.

As early as 1941, when Nat King Cole recorded her "This Will Make You Laugh," Higginbotham proved she could also convey the delicate heartbreak of the best torch ballads. This song has become her second-best-known work, thanks to champions such as Carmen McRae and Natalie Cole. Oddly, the piece was not copyrighted until 1943, by Peer International; and then it was recopyrighted in 1945, by Preview Music, with J. Mayo Williams added as cowriter. In Higginbotham's body of work there are several such discrepancies, rivaling any of the copyright mysteries involving Barbara Belle and others discussed previously.

By mid-1942, Higginbotham had earned recordings by big names like Benny Goodman ("That Did It, Marie," the popular flip of a hit, with a vocal by Peggy Lee) and placed works with a dozen Tin Pan Alley imprints. One of those publishers would prove to be of primary importance to her productivity: Joe Davis, who ran a series of sheet music firms from 1916 onward. In 1940, Davis was the second publisher to take on a Higginbotham tune. Altogether he ended up being responsible for almost half her copyrights.

Never one of the elite of the sheet music industry, Joe Davis nevertheless persevered and adapted, surviving into the 1970s. Along the way he issued many hits and wrote a few of them himself. Most notably, he launched, befriended, exploited, and nurtured many African American writers and performers, from Thomas "Fats" Waller to Otis Blackwell. He was described as both "hard-nosed" and "genial"; and, in 1953, a letter from lyricist Andy Razaf to Davis testifies to the publisher's ability to maintain a cordial relationship even with a Black collaborator whom he had at times taken advantage of.

In the early 1940s, with World War II raging, Davis faced a dilemma. There was a shortage of shellac to make phono records, so the publisher was missing out on chances to get his publications recorded. The solution: start his own independent label, send the records to radio disc jockeys, and hope airplay would boost sheet music sales. In the end, some of the discs did well as standalone products. At first named Beacon Records, it became Davis Records in 1946, before he phased out the business as sales patterns shifted. From mid-1942 through 1945, Beacon was the second most important New York City independent record label (after Savoy). The label's star songwriter was Irene Higginbotham.

Beacon Records and Higginbotham put themselves on the map with a recording of her "Fat Meat Is Good Meat." It was Higginbotham's only certifiable hit during her active songwriting years. Her refrain is built on a simple repeated riff (like many of Higginbotham's songs for Beacon) with a modest AA structure, but a more sophisticated interlude section gives the piece a pinch of complexity. The whole is infectious and contains some wit, and Higginbotham's lyric was timely during wartime food rationing. With the lines, "Don't take no back seat / Don't take no lean meat," it was also a metaphor for the rights of African Americans to the bounty of US prosperity. On disc, the tune enjoyed a rip-roaring Dixieland swing rendition led by clarinetist Jimmy Lytell but more truly centered on a scintillating vocal by Savannah Churchill; it helped make her a star.

As the owner of a small indie label with limited distribution, Joe Davis would have been glad to have a disc sell twenty thousand copies soon after release, but "Fat Meat Is Good Meat" reportedly quickly sold the way a Bing Crosby hit might have, with a hundred thousand copies shipped in two months' time. It was tremendously popular in jukeboxes that served African American customers. By March 1943, even *Billboard* sat up and took notice, as they ranked "Fat Meat" among the best-selling records in Southern states. Davis reissued it twice: in 1945, under the Joe Davis label, and in 1948, under his short-lived Celebrity label. Each pressing added to the sales record of "Fat Meat."

In 1952, Joe Davis was recruited by the MGM record company to produce rhythm-and-blues discs for that rather square label to distribute,
under a short-term lease arrangement. Davis wanted to hire Higginbotham
to create material, but there was a hitch. Davis was focusing on his Beacon
Music publishing business, affiliated with BMI, but Higginbotham was by
then firmly established as a member of ASCAP. The solution was a common
one: copyright and issue Higginbotham's new songs under a pseudonym.

Davis's biographer, Bruce Bastin, examined the publisher's files and
discovered that, in 1952, lead-sheet manuscripts clearly written by Higginbotham were issued with record labels crediting them to the pseudonym
"Glenn Gibson." What Bastin did not know was that those works were
copyrighted under the name of Bert Davis. This was Joe Davis's second
wife, Bertha Ruth Thalheimer, always called Bert, who was a composer and
lyricist in her own right and, judging by stray notes in her husband's hand-
writing, under a number of pseudonyms. For instance, at times she used
the professional last name shared with her brothers, Dave and Jack Kapp,
record executives for Decca.

Bastin credits Higginbotham with all of the 1952 Glenn Gibson records
that were Bert Davis copyrights. As if to prove Bastin right, one of the thirteen "Bert Davis" registrations of that year, "Don't Sing Me No Blues,"
had been copyrighted six years previously as written by Irene Higginbotham. Contrarily, as if to prove Bastin wrong, while he states that "For You
I Have Eyes" is by Higginbotham, nevertheless the copyright is registered
in the name of Eugene Stapleton, a member of the Crickets who recorded
the number—a highly likely credit. Despite an occasional slip like that,
Bastin is probably mostly correct because he looked through Joe Davis's
actual business papers. Confusingly, Bertha was copyrighting mostly as
"Glenn Gibson," and Irene was copyrighting mostly as "Bert Davis" but
being issued on record as "Glenn Gibson." This flurry of activity in 1952
was almost Higginbotham's final fling at the Tin Pan Alley business. It is
sad that her contribution to that batch of early rhythm-and-blues discs was
hidden for so many years.

Higginbotham's songs for MGM Records, later reissued on Davis's Jay-
Dee label, only sold moderately. Nevertheless, she supplied the dynamic
singer Beulah Bryant with a career-long theme song in the vibrant "Fat
Mama Blues." With lines like "I'm proud!—to be / Sweet three-oh-three,"
Higginbotham foreshadows the twenty-first-century era that affirms body
pride.

Though her music still speaks clearly to audiences, posterity has little
other means to sense Higginbotham's personality. Publicity photos from

her heyday reveal a face made beautiful by its expression of warmth and dignity, a soulfulness imbued in part by a gentle sorrowfulness. In September 1945, Higginbotham had a son by East Indian immigrant Moetehar Padellan—junior was given the same name—but it was not until 1952 that the couple tied the knot.

In the summer of 1945, Higginbotham experienced health problems, which she reported to Joe Davis were caused by food poisoning. Perhaps so, but she was also in the middle of her pregnancy—because it was out of wedlock, she probably wanted to keep it secret. Her experience was part of a trend, for births out of wedlock increased greatly during World War II, signaling the start of the sexual revolution.

A hint at Higginbotham's private voice emerges from two letters she sent Davis at this time. On July 8, the songwriter wrote from her home: "I'd appreciate it if you still have that work for me, to drop it in the mail, as I could do it easily while convalescing. . . . I certainly could use a little check." Higginbotham shows that she was hardworking, polite, witty, and short of money. (What kind of work could Davis have possibly sent to her? Copying parts? Writing arrangements? Or was Davis supplying specifications about new songs needed for his label's performers?) In August, Higginbotham wrote from St. Luke's Hospital concerning manuscripts she was enclosing: "If you can use them . . . OK if not, just save them for me." This displays an easygoing, trusting relationship with Davis. The publisher had Wingy Manone record her "That's a Gasser" and Walter Thomas her "Black Maria's Blues"; about these, Higginbotham wrote from her hospital bed: "If you have records . . . could you mail me them . . . my head nurse seems to be interested."[3] Even in a hospital bed, Higginbotham was plugging her tunes.

"GOOD MORNING HEARTACHE"

In the last quarter of 1945, after giving birth, Higginbotham achieved a new depth to her ballad writing, collaborating on her most enduring work, "Good Morning Heartache." All three cowriters were lesser-known sprigs of famous family trees: Irene, niece of Jay C. Higginbotham; Ervin Drake (a first-generation Jewish American, né Druckman), younger brother of Milton Drake (writer of the hits "Java Jive," "Mairzy Doats," and others); Dan Fisher, youngest brother of both Doris Fisher (writer of many mid-1940s hits; see the next chapter) and aspiring newcomer Marvin Fisher (whose success would peak in the 1950s with "When Sunny Gets Blue"), all

Figure 13.1   Irene Higginbotham, in the 1940s. (Garnett Higginbotham Sr., Creative Commons BY-ShareAlike 4.0, https://creativecommons.org/licenses/by-sa/4.0, via Wikimedia Commons.)

three being children of Fred Fisher (the Tin Pan Alley pioneer who wrote "Chicago," "Peg o' My Heart," and many others). Ervin was getting a lot of work giving English-language lyrics to Spanish and Portuguese tunes, including the hit "Tico-Tico," many of them for the Marks or Peer firms. Dan was starting his lifelong double career as an executive of Tin Pan Alley firms and backer-producer of Broadway plays. Eventually Dan managed the companies of both his late father and brother Marvin, but in 1945 he worked for Northern Music. This was a publishing house of Decca Records, which was run by Bert Davis's brothers, the Kapps. There were many inter-connections: Irene, though producing a flood of songs for Joe Davis, had also been selling compositions to Northern since the spring of 1944.

Until the end of his days, Ervin Drake told a romantic story about the genesis of "Good Morning Heartache." The lyricist was suffering through sleepless nights after having ending a love affair with beautiful Edith Bein, who was being courted by wealthier men. When Drake heard Higginbo-tham's melody, "It hit me—smack! This is exactly what I felt when Edith left me." He claimed he then wrote the words in twenty minutes. The payoff: decades later, Ervin and Edith met again and, both having lost their spouses, in 1981 they finally married.

"Good Morning Heartache" was copyrighted shortly before Christ-mas in 1945; Billie Holiday recorded it a month later for Decca. Drake remembered the session: "She was standing at the microphone, and I was on a chair, within arm's length. She did it in one take." "Heartache" was paired on the flip side with another Higginbotham-Fisher credit, this time with lyricist Sammy Gallop, "No Good Man." The disc may have sold well—exact figures no longer survive—but was not a blazing success. Throughout the period when it was being reviewed and advertised, the two songs vied with each other for kudos, with advertisements listing one or the other as the A-side. "Heartache" had the benefit of being included in a low-budget all-Black movie musical *Beware*, sung by the film's star, Louis Jordan. Yet when Higginbotham listed works for her 1948 ASCAP bio, she included "No Good Man" but left out "Good Morning Heartache," as if it was not important.

Stuart Nicholson claims that Decca producer Milt Gabler commissioned songs to be custom designed for Holiday, including Dan Fisher's "Good Morning Heartache" and "No Good Man," as well as Doris Fisher's "That Ole Devil Called Love." By contrast, the implication of Drake's story is that it was Dan Fisher who got "Heartache" into Holiday's hands, but that Dan did not contribute to the actual writing of the music or lyrics. Certainly, Dan was not prolific like the rest of his family. He copyrighted scarcely more than a handful of songs, and most of those were with Higginbotham. Yet there was certainly talent in the Fisher family, and Drake may have been unfairly slighting Dan's contribution.

Never before had Higginbotham spread her notes as elegantly across an eight-measure span as in "Good Morning Heartache." She creates a series of little surges, almost but never quite repeating herself. Higginbotham soon extends her initial five-note phrases with an additional seven notes—a spillover effect similar to what Ann Ronell does in "Willow, Weep for

Me"—and then a tumbling eleven-note phrase. A recurring blue flatted seventh haunts the melody, just like the "heartache" haunts the singer.

In the release Higginbotham creates a dramatic contrast. This is often the case in the composer's AABA-structured refrains, but never more satisfyingly than here. She still retains unity with the main strain by continuing the varied repetitions and five-note groupings, but with longer gaps between them. At the end of the release, she upsets the apple cart with a quick melodic couplet that uses a new syncopated rhythm.

Meanwhile, lyricist Drake has the protagonist treat an inner feeling— heartache—as if it were a person, greeting it as "you old gloomy sight" and, at the end, bidding it "sit down." Drake mixes contrasting elements in a balance that descends from sophisticated 1920s songs like Kay Swift's "Can't We Be Friends." The singer is deeply depressed, even angry and bitter, but also has whimsy, humor, and a kind of gallant resignation. Music and lyrics combine to sketch a scene of urbane loneliness straight out of a *film noir*.

Holiday kept performing "Good Morning Heartache" (for instance, a live rendition in 1949 was recorded). When her autobiography was published in 1956, amid a surge of publicity, producer Norman Granz had her record the number again, along with "No Good Man" and other songs that helped define Holiday's mature persona. From then on, a handful of other singers adopted "Heartache" (although only Nina Simone took up "No Good Man"). "Good Morning Heartache" got another boost when Holiday died in 1959, as singers and instrumentalists paid tribute to the late singer. By the end of the 1960s, however, the flow of new recordings of it had petered out.

"Good Morning Heartache" changed from being maybe a semistandard to a most decidedly definite standard when Diana Ross sang it in the 1972 biographical film about Holiday, *Lady Sings the Blues*. Ross's soundtrack album sold millions, and the big single was "Good Morning Heartache" (backed by "God Bless' the Child"), improbably rising into Top Forty radio. Now "Heartache" was seized upon by the older jazz singers (Rosemary Clooney did a fine version), soul singers (Natalie Cole enjoyed a Gold record with her album track, and Freddie Jackson topped that by going Platinum with his), and jazz instrumentalists (in the disco era, Lou Donaldson managed to break into the Hot 100 chart with his LP track).[4] It begs the question: So this was not a good song before? Indeed, "Heartache" supplies a prime example of how a powerful plug will suddenly reveal the high quality of a somewhat neglected song, boosting it into the pantheon of works considered "exquisite" and "great."[5]

Billie Holiday gave the definitive renditions of "Good Morning Heartache." Her tender, vulnerable, and down-to-earth 1946 vocal is compellingly backed by a lightly swinging orchestra, softened with reeds and strings. Her 1956 rendering is less fresh but carries even more mature weight, her voice now quite different, flavored with a coppery taste. Diana Ross offers a fine, straight-ahead take, avoiding seventies embellishments. Over the decades, Ella Fitzgerald, both in the studio and live, always supplied a wonderful repeat of the release but otherwise does not quite capture the atmosphere of the song. Tony Bennett is best on the final A-section, when he quiets down to a chilling hush. Andy Bey created one of the most consistently downhearted renditions. Chris Connor has a rhythmically vital take on the piece that more clearly connects it with Higginbotham's jazz instrumental works. Carmen McRae, slightly sardonic, supplied one of the most well-balanced renditions.

Happily, all three of the songwriters lived to witness the resurrection of "Good Morning Heartache." Yet despite the prominent roles they had filled in the pop music industry, none was given an obituary in *Billboard*. Drake lived to age ninety-five and managed to go into history with interviews that tell his part of the "Good Morning Heartache" story. No one bothered to gather Higginbotham's memories.

Irene Higginbotham's hits
Words and music by Higginbotham and any collaborators, unless otherwise noted.
1942: "Fat Meat Is Good Meat"
1945/1973: "Good Morning Heartache," with Dan Fisher and Ervin Drake

Other prominent songs
1940/1943: "Harlem Stomp," with Jay C. Higginbotham; later, Buddy Feyne credited with lyrics
1941: "That Did It, Marie," lyrics by Fred Meadows
1941/1943/1945: "This Will Make You Laugh," solo effort; later, J. Mayo Williams also credited
1942: "Tell Me Your Blues and I Will Tell You Mine"
1942/1945: "Are You Ready Ol' Man/Are You Livin' Ol' Man," with Abner Silver and Redd Evans
1944: "Boogie Woogie on a Saturday Night"
1944: "Lenox Avenue Jump"
1945: "No Good Man," with Dan Fisher and Sammy Gallop
1946: "Mean and Evil Blues," with Claude Demetruis[6]
1953: "Fat Mama Blues"

Some neglected gems

1941: "Bobby's Trombone Blues"; galvanic special material for Bobby Byrne's band

1941: "The Boogie Beat'll Getcha If You Don't Watch Out"; swirling with Caribbean undertow

1943: "Grand Central Station"; solid World War II swinger, tinged with Charleston rhythm

1944: "Hello, Suzanne," lyrics by Cye Baron; lovely, concise release

1944: "In the Quiet of the Dawn"; joyful lyric, hushed melody, described as "ethereal"[7]

1947: "It's Mad, Mad, Mad," lyrics by Sydney Shaw; rich, juicy torch tune

1950: "Fair Jennie's Lament"; sprightly, snaking, sad-tinged instrumental begging for a lyric

1953: "Put a Little Bug in My Ear"; scolding, playful charm song

(14)

"PUT THE BLAME ON
MAME" (1945/1946)

Doris Fisher (1915–2003), composer-lyricist

Two vignettes illuminate the personality of Doris Fisher.

First anecdote: In Washington, DC, the summer of 1953, "she sat down before a Senate subcommittee and began to pound the table." She was tanned and costumed to hold the attention of the male politicians in "a chic dress" and a "canary yellow hat" that probably made a good contrast to her dark brown hair. She demanded "a law to make juke box operators pay her royalties." Unfortunately, she and the other Tin Pan Alley representatives there that day did not have much luck, and it would be years before any recompense was put into effect.[1]

Second anecdote: Miami, winter of 1965, Eden Roc Hotel, the Mona Lisa Room, with Charlie Cochran playing piano and serenading Fisher with a song she wrote, the sophisticated cult favorite "Let's Stay Young Forever." After the usual nightclub crowds had gone home, Fisher and a coterie of aficionados hung around while Fisher took over the piano and performed her own "Put the Blame on Mame" from the movie *Gilda* (1946). She unspooled secret stanzas of "wonderful, slightly racy, unpublished lyrics"—now probably lost forever.[2]

Fisher left the music business at the top of her game. After an astonishing run of nineteen hit songs in the space of three years, 1944 through 1946, Fisher had become a bigwig, called a millionaire in write-ups. She was also the daughter of a bigwig (Fred Fisher, composer of "Chicago," "Peg o' My Heart," etc.) and the older sister of bigwigs (Dan Fisher, "Good Morning

Heartache"; Marvin Fisher, "When Sunny Gets Blue") and became the wife of a bigwig (Charles Gershenson, Detroit auto parts industrialist). Michael Feinstein met her and described her as "feisty, tenacious and talented." She herself bragged, "When I sold" a song, "believe me, nobody could leave the room. I sold so *strong*." Behind her highly variegated output lay that strength.[3]

BIOGRAPHY

Her father, Fred Fisher (1875–1942), was an adult Jewish immigrant from Germany, a colorful character who never lost his thick accent, absentmindedly burned dollar bills during the intense debates he loved, and after three painful years with an incurable disease ended his own life. Over the course of forty years on Tin Pan Alley, he wrote in a wide range of subgenres. Fred fostered Doris's career, cowriting her first copyright in 1936, a comedy song in *Fisher's Funny Folio*, "That's Why I Bring You Roses." (The reason for the roses: the singer can't pronounce "chrysanthemum.") Later, Fred helped Doris deepen her oeuvre by writing the lyrics for her first enduring ballad, the darkly shaded, enigmatic "Whispering Grass."

Doris started at age eighteen singing on radio. Later recordings reveal her confident piano playing and the rich timbre of a flexible voice. At twenty, Fisher married ne'er-do-well I. Jay Faggen, press agent and nightclub and theater owner. She stuck with him while he was jailed for nonpayment of alimony to his previous wife; wrote songs for his club, the Harlem Uproar House; and was the secretary for his corporation at the time of his bankruptcy in 1937. Perhaps this signaled the end of the marriage, for he fades out of her life about then. The Faggen episode is ignored in write-ups about her two later marriages and divorces.

Throughout the late 1930s, Fisher continued her radio work, striving for a desirable nighttime slot and then being featured on Eddy Duchin broadcasts. Eventually she began to make records with her own small band under the name Penny Wise and Her Wise Guys. She enjoyed her first songwriting hit, teaming with jazz bassist Slim Gaillard, revising one stanza and creating a new release to turn his riff tune "Tutti Frutti" into a standard Tin Pan Alley product. While pursuing her radio work, Fisher continued churning out the occasional copyright. As well as writing with her father, she also collaborated with others, including Arthur Gershwin (younger brother of the more famous Ira and George). She earned her own membership to ASCAP at the end of 1941, just after that society's ill-fated radio ban. At about this same time, she entered into marriage with businessman Paul Wald and gave birth to a daughter.

In early 1943, Doris Fisher yoked up with Allan Roberts, an Alley veteran ten years her senior. The result was the same as with Tot Seymour and Vee Lawnhurst: the creative chemistry of Fisher and Roberts unexpectedly made two moderately successful songsmiths into a dynamite team of hit writers. The pair achieved a short intense period of the highest success. Further, Fisher was able to take a prominent place in the glamorous, high-profile world of Hollywood, with a multiyear contract at Columbia Studios.

Which is not to say that success was immediate. Fisher and Roberts did the usual drudge work of the struggling songwriter: special material for club performers, singing commercials, et cetera. "We were too hep," Doris said. "Musicians swooned over our tunes, but nobody ever bought any of them."[4] Among these early works was "Invitation to the Blues," cowritten with Arthur Gershwin, mentioned in trade papers as early as May 1943, but not copyrighted until a year later. In the long term, the quirky melodic jumps, matched to some eccentric verbal images, have made "Invitation to the Blues" a favorite with "hep" performers and thus a semistandard.

Fisher and Roberts shared the ability to write both music and lyrics, and they are always cocredited for both aspects during their years together. Roberts stated, however, that "Doris usually writes the music." In interviews, the pair liked to brag about how they "dashed off five numbers" at a party. Roberts swaggered: "A songwriter should never take more than an hour and a half on a popular song."[5] Fisher reported, "We're wacky." Her evidence: they created their hit for Louis Prima, "Angelina (Waitress at the Pizzeria)," from an Italian café menu. She also stated, "Allan is the tear-jerker of the team, and I specialize in light stuff."[6] Fisher inherited from her father a penchant for comedy songs, including two of her earliest plug tunes: the country-flavored "Sidekick Joe" (which she herself recorded) and "Dolly Doolittle" (with old-timer Al Bryan and her father), partly about the labor of housekeeping.

After a year of failure with hep material and hack work, Roberts must have experienced a moment of taking stock, for, in late winter 1944, he suddenly gave free rein to his taste for sad songs. Roberts jumpstarted the team's first major hit, "You Always Hurt the One You Love." Fisher reported, "He kept yelling, 'Schmaltz it up, kid. Schmaltz it up.' After it was finished, I burst out crying and moaned. 'This is corn. You can have my share for five dollars.' . . . Then we sold it, and before I knew what hit me we had made $25,000."[7] This waltz was a huge success for the Mills Brothers on the Decca label, and it was printed by one of Decca's publishing imprints, Sun Music. The songwriters might have griped because Sun Music did zilch to promote the song on the radio and to other record companies. Yet despite that, sheet music sales soared. A follow-up was in order, and Fisher and Roberts supplied Sun Music with "Into Each Life Some Rain Must Fall." Although "Hurt" is in three-four meter and "Rain" is in four-four, the two songs are so similar in phrasing that either lyric fits either tune. The result of this self-imitation: another huge hit for Decca Records, this time featuring the Ink Spots with Ella Fitzgerald.

With these two 1944 successes, Fisher and Roberts helped to usher in a return to the simplicity and sentimentality that reigned before the mid-1920s. "You Always Hurt the One You Love" seems deliberately to evoke a bygone era, specifically the sobbingly repentant 1916 waltz "I'm Sorry I Made You Cry." What musicians had quickly discovered, however, was that this triple-meter tune and others like it were easy to turn into duple-meter swingers. This is just what singers and bands quickly did with "You Always Hurt." The Mills Brothers followed a slow waltz chorus with a medium-fast, duple-meter jazzy refrain. "Into Each Life" proved just as swingable. Fisher was probably relieved to discover her pair of tearjerkers could also be "hep." Over the following decades, dozens of arrangers confirmed the adaptability of both songs. Fisher and Roberts followed that pair of ballads with an even bigger hit, the playful (but mostly forgotten) "Good, Good, Good," a lively Latin novelty. By mid-1945, the team could (and did) brag of eleven plug numbers out on major record labels.

Fisher and Roberts got the job at Columbia because of this amazing track record of hits. The character of the studio was probably another factor. A penny-pinching underdog in the Hollywood hierarchy, run by vulgarian Harry Cohn, a former Tin Pan Alley plugger, assisted by music director Jonie Taps, who was also an ex-Alley plugger and manager, Columbia could not afford to put under long-term contract the established elite writers; instead they turned to these two newcomers. At the same time, in a parallel instance, at the other underdog Hollywood studio, Universal, another inexpensive pair got hired: composer Inez James and lyricist Sidney Miller.

It may have helped Doris Fisher and Inez James that they were so inextricably linked to male writing partners. Note a parallel: Dorothy Fields initially entered Hollywood by being firmly fused with Jimmy McHugh. A final factor in the winning of a Columbia contract might have been Doris's status as the daughter of the late, much beloved Fred, one of the celebrities of Tin Pan Alley history.

For both Tin Pan Alley and Hollywood, Fisher and Roberts created a profusion of rhythmic novelties, exaggeratedly sentimental saloon ballads, humorous Latin-tinged pieces, and country-western-styled comedy songs. Amid this smorgasbord, they also bequeathed to posterity a dozen love-themed works that infuse downbeat melancholy with a tang and a jaunty, resigned humor. In these, they streamline for the mid-1940s the urbane bittersweet quality of the best 1930s standards, creating song protagonists who face heartache with defiance or humor.

Most prominent among these is "That Ole Devil Called Love" (1944), which Sun Music and Decca Records arranged to feature as the flip on Billie Holiday's first single for the label, the hit "Lover Man." With its personification of an emotion, Doris's "Devil Called Love" is a clear forerunner of brother Dan's "Good Morning Heartache." Both remained staples for Holiday and, especially since her death, for many others. In later decades, "Devil" has spread internationally, particularly in recordings by Alison Moyet (1985), Grace Knight (1991), and Rebecca Ferguson (2015).

The lyrics of Fisher and Roberts's tough-fibered ballads are set apart from the run-of-the-mill by quirky or salty verbal phrases buried within the refrain. The team created examples that stretch from their beginning together right through to their end:

"My heart was all dressed up to go dreaming. / I had a brand new shine on my views" ("Invitation to the Blues," 1943)
"Now you can't see me for dust. / How can you be so downright callous?" ("Now You Tell Me," 1945)
"We're through—so what? / Was you so hot?" ("It's So Easy," 1946)

While other writers evoked the atmosphere of *films noirs* in jazz songs—Bonnie Lake, the nighttime world of "The Man with the Horn"; Irene Higginbotham, the bleak urban isolation of "Good Morning Heartache"—Fisher and Roberts had the rare chance to compose movie numbers for actual *films noirs*. In these, their singers focus on the dangers of love. World weary, they assert "Either It's Love or It Isn't" (from *Dead Reckoning*). They warily beg "Please Don't Kiss Me" (in *The Lady from Shanghai*). Sometimes the lover seems to be on a knife's edge, as in "Amado Mio" (the love ballad in *Gilda*) in which, previously, the singer was "acting a part" in romances, but in this new affair she urgently insists "it's now or never."

Fisher and Roberts's first film assignment, in August 1945, was for *Gilda*, a starring vehicle for Columbia's one major asset, Rita Hayworth. In March 1946, the movie was released. The two songs they had written for that *film noir* became such an important part of its success that, in May, the studio doubled their salaries.

In August 1946, Fisher divorced Paul Wald. She stated, "I discovered that a career and marriage didn't work out." Yet within four months, Fisher was again engaged to be married. This time it was to Charles Gershenson, the Jewish auto parts businessman of Detroit, a forty-eight-year-old bachelor, "one of [the] original jetset, 1930 version" who "romanced internationally known movie stars and heiresses" in glamorous "New York and Hollywood nights spots." They had a stylish wedding in Florida. Alongside Doris's mother and brother Dan were many of the Gershenson family and others from Detroit—and also Rose, the Gershwin brothers' mother. With this marriage, Fisher decided to retire. Nevertheless, through 1948 a string of previously written Fisher and Roberts songs continued to hit the charts.[8]

Doris settled into a life of domesticity, raising two children, frequenting nightclubs and opera premieres, golfing with up-and-coming celebrities like the young Barbra Streisand, and producing charity events. Newspaper articles and copyright registrations reveal that every couple of years Fisher would create a new song, some of them with Roberts. Her old numbers kept being revived, but never again would one of her new pieces rise to prominence.

Fisher became an expert on American antiques, eventually donating her collection to the US government. She bestowed her expertise on Jacqueline Kennedy's historical restoration of the White House. In 1967, she ran off to Europe on a spree with a handsome younger man, divorcing Gershenson. Then she moved back to Los Angeles and successfully opened two retail stores selling kitchen and dining room goods. Doris was vigilant in taking control of her copyrights as they came up for renewal. Although Marvin and Dan sold the song catalogs of themselves and their father, Doris kept control of hers. She lived long enough to be interviewed about her role in the creation of the classic *Gilda*.

"PUT THE BLAME ON MAME"

Arriving in Hollywood in early August 1945, still trying to orient themselves, Fisher and Roberts were handed the shooting script for *Gilda*. Fisher remembered: "Al came up with that title," "Put the Blame on Mame," "because of the script." They saw that the plot was about a woman who has blame put upon her because she appears to be oversexual, so they wrote a song about that very thing. The songwriter reminisced: "At about three a.m. we went into a publisher's office on Vine Street, since we had no office of our own, sat down by a piano and, I don't know, it just happened.

We'd already been playing around with that feeling for a song so it just worked." Because they had already been experimenting with that type of melancholy, swinging, bluesy sound, they were able to create a classic in two hours. The filmmakers needed the number to be sung either slowly and pensively or up-tempo and brassy, so Fisher and Roberts delivered a song that can be both. When Fisher auditioned the number for the studio bosses, she confessed to Hayworth, "I'm petrified." The actor replied, "So am I," because this was Hayworth's first full-length dramatic role since she achieved star status in 1941.[9]

It's a rare song that redirects worldwide vogues in sexual imagery, the history of cinema, and the life and career of a famous Hollywood star, but "Put the Blame on Mame" did all that. The image of Rita Hayworth plus the dubbed singing voice of Anita Ellis created a cultural touchstone. Through the role of Gilda, Hayworth influenced everyday life (setting a new benchmark for glamorous female sexuality), film (in Europe, particularly, becoming a model for writers, directors, and stars to imitate), Hayworth's career (her later roles were almost always good-bad women, like Gilda), and Hayworth's personal life (her third husband, Ali Kahn, disappointed in the real Hayworth, watched *Gilda* over and over). The movie now regularly ranks among the thirty best *films noirs* of all time. Central to the impact of *Gilda* was Fisher and Roberts's "Mame."

"Put the Blame on Mame" is a twenty-four-bar song. Though not labeled as such, the first twelve measures feel like a verse, and the second twelve measures feel like a refrain. The refrain, for a couple of bars, seems about to become a blues, harmonically, but then it veers off into its own unique pattern. Cleverly, the final four bars of the verse melody are repeated almost exactly as the penultimate melody of the refrain. The songsmiths were also clever in evoking song forms of both the past and the present. The verse and refrain are of almost equal weight, as in a folk song of the 1800s. Further, the verse is similar to many of about 1910 in its four-bar transition phrase to the chorus. The refrain has a four-bar break for a comic couplet just before the final repeat, evoking early 1920s tunes like "How Come You Do Me Like You Do." Yet, overall, the minor-key comic narrative is in line with 1940s examples like "The Saga of Jenny" (1941) and "One Meatball" (1944).

In the lyric, Fisher and Roberts dwell on famous events of American history—natural disasters (earthquakes, blizzards, fires), murder (of Dan McGrew), and the California Gold Rush. The punchline is that Mame is the true cause of all these events through her power and sexuality. In live performance, the exaggerations provoke laughter. On record, the sadness can peep through. The melancholy minor strains remind the listener that throughout history women have, sadly, all too often gotten the blame. On the screen, the song becomes an opportunity for a woman to convey her own individual sensuality—first for Hayworth, and later for others, among them Jane Russell and Gypsy Rose Lee (because Columbia kept reusing the song).

In the plot, set in Buenos Aires, Gilda is the wife of the sinister casino owner Ballin Munson, who is also the boss of her ex-lover Johnny Farrell. Gilda and Johnny, whose past estrangement is never fully explained, spend an hour and a half being supremely nasty to each other. Finally, Ballin having died, the pair forgive each other and walk off happily.

"Put the Blame on Mame" slips into the soundtrack of *Gilda* at several points. Gilda's voice is heard humming it off screen to introduce the character. It is, clearly, her favorite tune, her theme. Later, at the casino at 5:00 am, she wakes Johnny by strumming her guitar and singing "Mame" to the older, wise washroom attendant, Tito. Her slow rendition of the two verses—about a kiss igniting the Chicago fire, and a cold "No!" causing the New York blizzard—are sung first with rueful amusement, then with thoughtful introspection. The moment offers a window on her soul.

Finally, Gilda uses "Put the Blame on Mame" to taunt Johnny, performing a sexually suggestive up-tempo version of "Mame" for the crowds at the casino. Designer Jean Louis created for Hayworth a gleaming black sheath with a slit skirt, hair stylist Helen Hunt groomed her auburn tresses into a cloud that dances with her, and the camerawork frames her for optimum glamour. Most of all, choreographer Jack Cole created for Hayworth a routine for the ages. (They rehearsed it on the fly, in short time slots stolen between takes of the dramatic scenes.) The movie censors would not allow bumps, grinds, or stripteases. But Hayworth eats up the space, striding, twisting, tossing and lifting her hair, shifting weight side to side to thrust a hip here, a hip there, lifting her shoulders, spreading her arms. Meanwhile, the Fisher and Roberts lyric tells of Mame doing a shimmy that caused the San Francisco earthquake and dancing the hitchy-koo to "murder" Dan McGrew. The climax of the dance comes in the latter verse, when Hayworth slowly peels off one long glove, then uses it in the dance like a baton or an extra limb.

Fisher made a good point about this sequence: "When you look at that number and analyze it, there are broad strippy gestures that Cole gave her to do. But the voice when you separate it is a little voice because that's the way Rita was"—a shy, reserved, soft-spoken person. Anita Ellis was able to bring these same qualities to her dubbing for the singing of Gilda, with what Fisher described as an "elf-like, breathy voice."[10] Ellis was legendary both for her stage fright and for her impeccable artistry, a true singer's singer. Although her timbre on the *Gilda* soundtrack evokes innocence, in 1960 Ellis made her own recording of "Put the Blame on Mame," and by then she was able to make her voice as swaggering and sexy, aurally, as Hayworth had been visually in the movie. Ellis's album version is perhaps the definitive vocal performance of "Mame."

Gilda surprised the Columbia brass by being not just a successful film but a phenomenon, and "Put the Blame on Mame" was central to the advertising campaign. Nevertheless, neither of the two Fisher-Roberts songs from *Gilda* ever appeared on the popularity charts of *Variety* or *Billboard*. Again, Sun Music neglected to obtain many recordings of "Mame" beyond the two by its parent company, Decca Records. The Milt Herth Trio featured the Jesters offering a jolly, uninflected, up-tempo group vocal. Cass Daley applied her rowdy, comic personality in a slightly slower rendition, which reportedly sold over 125,000 in less than two months but was only charted by regional papers, not the trades. (As icing on the cake for Fisher and Roberts, the flip side was one of their earliest collaborations, "The Truth of the Matter.") Monica Lewis delivered a much more carefully modulated rendition of "Mame" on the independent label Signature, starting slowly to give a taste of the moody mystery of the tune before picking up the tempo. The fate of Lewis's disc may hint at why the trade journals were silent on the success of "Mame"—it was banned from radio in conservative Philadelphia. Oddly, "Amado Mio" was also invisible in the US popularity charts. Perhaps both songs were simply too sexy for the 1946 American pop music market.

Gilda made a powerful impact in Europe—for one thing, appearing at the first Cannes Film Festival—and both "Put the Blame on Mame" and "Amado Mio" took firmer root there than in the United States. In 1946, "Mame" appeared on England's Top Twenty lists for one week, and "Amado" charted for four weeks. Amazingly, at the same time Fisher and Roberts enjoyed two other British bestsellers, "Into Each Life Some Rain Must Fall" and "Good, Good, Good," thus earning four spots in England's Top Twenty.

The melody for "Mame" was used for an Italian hit "Non v'innamorate" ("Don't Fall in Love"). A Polish version translates as "Mom Was to Blame," revealing an always hinted at Freudian interpretation of who "Mame" really represents. Orson Welles had been Hayworth's second husband; though long divorced, in Europe he found wherever he went crowds would chant "Gilda! Gilda!" and the band would blare out "Put the Blame on Mame."

Although "You Always Hurt the One You Love" outstrips Fisher's other works as a standard, "Put the Blame on Mame" continues to capture performers and audiences in more recent decades. In 1985, Caribbean-French-Belgian Viktor Lazlo featured it on her first album, an international success. The finger-snapping intro and big band arrangement pays tribute both to Peggy Lee's "Fever" and *Gilda*. British Joanna Eden delivers a nicely balanced jazz treatment with the Chris Ingham Quartet. The more soulful qualities of the song are brought out in two slower versions. Sunny Crownover with guitarist Duke Robillard pay tribute to the "guitar" version in *Gilda*. Another is a surprise instrumental rendition: Portuguese guitarist Paolo Dias Duarte duets with, on flute, Brazilian American modernist classical composer Paulo C. Chagas. Thus, they demonstrate the international spread of "Put the Blame on Mame," as well as the respect of one composer for another. Performers appreciate it as a strong song, about a strong woman, by a strong woman.

Doris Fisher's major hits
1938: "Tutti Frutti," with Slim Gaillard
1940: "Whispering Grass," lyrics by Fred Fisher

The following have words and music by Doris Fisher and Allan Roberts.
1944: "You Always Hurt the One You Love"
1944: "Angelina (The Waitress at the Pizzeria)"
1944: "Into Each Life Some Rain Must Fall"
1944/1985: "That Ole Devil Called Love"
1945: "Good, Good, Good (That's You, That's You)"
1945: "I Wish"
1945: "Tampico"
1945: "Gee, It's Good to Hold You"
1945/1947: "You Can't See the Sun When You're Crying"
1946: "Put the Blame on Mame"
1946: "Amado Mio"
1946: "Either It's Love or It Isn't"

Doris Fisher and Allan Roberts's minor hits
1943: "Invitation to the Blues," with Arthur Gershwin
1944: "Fifteen Years (And I'm Still Serving Time)"
1945: "Tired"
1946: "I Never Had a Dream Come True"
1946: "They Can't Convince Me"

1946: "That's Good Enough for Me"
1946/1948: "Please Don't Kiss Me"

Some neglected gems
1944: "Saltin' Away My Sweet Dreams"; rich, groovy melody
1944: "Up! Up! Up!"; simple but infectiously singable back porch waltz
1945: "I'm Happy Being Me"; philosophic, folksy song
1945: "Who'll Lend Me a Rainbow"; magical, metaphorical ballad
1946: "Copa-Cabana"; mourning the end of a fleeting, cosmopolitan affair
1946: "Let's Stay Young Forever"; waltz with difficult, delightful melodic curves
1946: "Warm Kiss (And a Cold Heart)"; cheerful torch lament

15

"FAR AWAY PLACES" (1947)

Joan Whitney (1914–1990), composer-lyricist

In the spring of 1940, Joan Whitney went to Washington, DC, to work as a dance band singer at the lounge in the Mayflower Hotel with the Dick Koons orchestra. Within a couple of weeks, however, she announced her plans to go back to New York City. She was going to become a songwriter. Her new collaborator would be Alex Kramer, bandleader and vocal coach from Canada.

Nine years later, in February 1949, Whitney walked back into the Mayflower Hotel. She was now the cowriter of a long string of successful songs. In fact, that month Whitney and Kramer's "Far Away Places" was the number one hit song in the United States. She was revisiting Washington with Kramer to perform for bigwig businessmen and politicians at the annual banquet of the elite Alfalfa Club. During the evening, they delivered a selection from their large output. Their coperformers were two legendary colleagues: W. C. Handy (writer of "The St. Louis Blues," the most-performed popular song of the first half of the twentieth century) and Herman Hupfeld (whose "As Time Goes By" became an evergreen when woven into the movie *Casablanca*). In such circumstances, with such companions and audience, Whitney's return to one of her old stomping grounds must have felt triumphant.

In a newspaper photo taken that day, Kramer is at the keyboard and Whitney leans on the piano. They catch each other's eyes and grin broadly with almost palpable delight. From 1940 to 1949, the pair collaborated under a strict agreement never to ask about the other's private life. Yet the following year, in 1950, the two collaborators broke that long-standing compact and married each other. They soon developed the habit of walking hand in hand down the sidewalks of Manhattan, singing duets as loudly as possible. During the next four decades, until Whitney's death, they happily fused their professional and private worlds (see figure 1.2).

BIOGRAPHY

Joan Whitney started life as Zoe Parenteau, named after her father, first-generation French American Zoel Parenteau. He was a conductor-pianist-composer, for decades prominent in the American music scene. In the 1910s Parenteau *père* was the composer of flop Broadway musicals. In the 1920s, he found greater success writing for comedies. In 1921, he wrote "Some Day I'll Find You" and other incidental music for *Kiki*, which enjoyed a lengthy Broadway run. In 1922, in *To the Ladies*, Helen Hayes introduced Parenteau's song "Happy Day." This pseudo-spiritual enjoyed a considerable vogue for several years.

Whitney's son, Doren Voeth, vividly recalls his maternal grandmother, of Pennsylvania Dutch ancestry, Emma "Jerry" Summersgill; he knew her long after her divorce from Parenteau. Summersgill was "unbelievably bright and very sharp-tongued." She had her own well-paid singing career as a "professional church soloist" who "travelled the country doing cathedrals," sometimes riding "in private rail coaches with men of wealth."[1]

Zoe was raised in Pittsburgh, Pennsylvania. After high school, she was sent to New York City to go to Finch College. That institution was sometimes derided as being just a finishing school. Nevertheless, despite its atmosphere of luxury and refinement, it was a forward-thinking women's vocational college, especially for the arts. By September 1934, however, Zoe was in the huge chorus of the Broadway operetta *The Great Waltz*. A fellow ensemble member was Harold "Hal" Voeth. He was often part of a dance sextet called the Debonairs. By the end of the 1930s, Zoe was Mrs. Hal Voeth.

Despite the success of *The Great Waltz*, Zoe soon left its cast to become a show girl in the musical revue *Calling All Stars*. At this time, she changed her stage name to Joan Whitney. She may have chosen her new moniker in tribute to the prominent heiress Joan Whitney Payson, her slightly older contemporary who achieved enduring renown as an art collector and cofounder of the Mets. "Joan Whitney" was easier to spell than her given name, avoided confusion with her father's similar name, and reeked of class by association. The songwriter also went by other pseudonyms during her varied career as a band, nightclub, and radio singer and then as a songwriter. Besides her married name of Zoe Voeth and stage name Joan Whitney, she also used during this period the professional names of Zoe Day, Nellie Day, Renee Day, Beverley St. Ives, and Joan Allen.

Calling All Stars folded within a couple of months, but the show's title may have inspired Whitney's clever 1941 song "Calling All Hearts." During the rest of the 1930s, she was a singer on radio, in hotel lounges, and with dance bands. In 1937, she toured with the Will Osborne orchestra, with whom she recorded a couple of songs. Whitney's singing may have lacked the distinctive qualities of Billie Holiday, Ella Fitzgerald, or Peggy Lee, but she easily held her own among her peers. The years 1938 and 1939 found Whitney paving out a career as a singer in swanky midtown New York nightclubs, especially at the Hotel Pierre.

Sometime in early 1940 Whitney sought vocal coaching from Alexander Charles Kramer, a Jewish newcomer from Montreal. Born in 1903, he was eleven years older than Whitney and, like her father, a bandleader and radio conductor. Whitney had already been writing some of her own original material for her club and radio work, and the woman who owned the coaching studio suggested that she and Kramer try songwriting together. Their partnership would prove remarkably stable and long lasting. Only very, very rarely would one write without the other. Sometimes the duo collaborated with a third writer, such as their close friend Hy Zaret. While Whitney was pregnant in 1944, Kramer and Zaret wrote one hit without her, "Counting the Days." Kramer must have, indeed, been anxiously "counting the days" until Whitney safely delivered.[2]

Tin Pan Alley could be intimidating. Whitney and Kramer nervously took their first great song, "High on a Windy Hill," to Saul Bornstein, ASCAP board member and Tin Pan Alley veteran:

> Bornstein tried to make them feel at ease, sat them down and said: "Kids, before you play your song, I want you to hear my latest plug." He went to the phonograph and played . . . "Imagination." Whitney and Kramer were so embarrassed at the thought of comparison that they fled.[3]

The Johnny Burke–James Van Heusen standard "Imagination" is still considered one of the masterpieces of the Great American Songbook. Whitney and Kramer were now expected to match the high standards of this prevailing style.

As with many others, especially women songwriters, the chance for Whitney and Kramer to break into Tin Pan Alley came about because of the fight between the well-established ASCAP old guard and the upstart BMI who welcomed with open arms novices like Whitney. With ASCAP tunes banned from most radio networks through much of 1941, the BMI writers found success—and Whitney and Kramer more than any others. In their sprightly medium-tempo works, filled with interior and multisyllable rhymes, and poignant, brooding ballads, they captured the sophisticated style of ASCAP stalwarts such as Cole Porter and Dorothy Fields. Whitney had recently been recording this very type of song as a band singer. In 1942, almost as soon as the radio ban was over, Whitney and Kramer shifted allegiance from BMI to ASCAP. Over the next decade, they became very involved with the operations of both ASCAP and the Songwriters Guild of America.

Doren Voeth gives an eyewitness account of his mother and stepfather collaborating:

> They both played piano. Alex was classically trained and had a more thorough understanding of the subject. My mother had piano and singing lessons and played only popular music but was proficient enough to accompany herself in performances. They might both take the keyboard when writing, although Alex was more proficient at taking her vocal ideas and blending them musically into the work. Lyrics were by both all the time.

Voeth concludes that in both "parenting and writing, it was an equal partnership." They pursued the creation of songs "as a business," evenly dividing responsibilities. Whitney handled promotion; contacts with labels, artists, and A&R men; and the calendar. Kramer became an ASCAP director, kept up his show biz contacts, and arranged musicians, technicians, and studio time for their demonstration recordings. Whitney and Kramer were among the first to document every stage of a song's creation with reel-to-reel tape recording (as in figure 7.1). Kramer also cofounded a nationwide charitable organization to create hospital broadcast programs for (and with) military veterans. At various times, the pair also expanded into publishing, running a record label, and managing younger singer-songwriters. They felt under constant pressure, "always mindful," Voeth recalls, of "how many" songs "you could have" out on the market "that didn't rise on charts in *Billboard* before your calls went unanswered."[4]

Within a few years of their first hits, Whitney and Kramer broke away from imitating the likes of Cole Porter and instead developed their own style—light, fresh, streamlined. They broke fresh ground with their innovative 1943 rhythmic novelty song "It's Love, Love, Love," which became a hit the following year. The love-and-marriage Tin Pan Alley lyric is set to music compatible with a calypso rhythm. This was the first time US writers adopted this Trinidadian style in a hit song. The ensuing popularity of calypso among Yankees was one harbinger of the upcoming spread of roots music and internationalism. Whitney and Kramer wrote several more calypso-inflected melodies, including "Money Is the Root of All Evil (Take It Away, Take It Away, Take It Away)," "Curiosity," and "Man, Man Is for the Woman Made."

The team also arranged the shape of "It's Love, Love, Love" to give almost equal weight to the verse and refrain, harkening back to a folk music and nineteenth-century pattern. Recent hits had already foreshadowed this practice, such as "You Are My Sunshine" (1940) and "Oh, What a Beautiful Morning" (1943). But "It's Love, Love, Love" consolidated this trend, and the team's similarly structured follow-ups greatly furthered it. Among the most popular were "Love Somebody," "You'll Never Get Away," and "No Other Arms, No Other Lips." Nevertheless, Whitney and Kramer's most enduring songs were in the typical Tin Pan Alley AABA structure, including the big band charmer "Candy" (1945), the rhythm-and-blues comic novelty "Ain't Nobody Here But Us Chickens" (1946), and "Far Away Places" (1947).

"FAR AWAY PLACES"

"Far Away Places" avoids any mention of romance and instead focuses on unsatisfied wanderlust. Because of this, it must have seemed like a breath of fresh air in the late 1940s hit parade. The topic had been rare, but in the wake of "Far Away Places" other songwriters would find success with it: Tot Seymour (her last hit, "Watchin' the Trains Go By," 1950), Harold Rome ("Restless Heart," 1954), and Carolyn Leigh ("Stowaway," 1954). The lyric conjures up the image of a character stuck in some backwater, probably a small rural town. The melody moves in slow waves, as if into undefined distant spaces of air and cloud, land and sea.

The main strain of "Far Away Places" hinges on the three tones accompanying the title words "far aw-ay." These notes occur in four successive phrases, each one ending the pattern in a different way. This recurring motif creates steadiness, which might represent the pull of the daily routine in which the protagonist is confined. Yet this repetition beautifully coexists with the restless variety of the different phrase endings, perhaps represent-ing the impulse to wander. The phrase "calling, calling" at the end of the first and final stanzas evokes a distantly echoing summons. Whitney and Kramer's subtle artistry shines in such details.

The release is more urgent and, as the lyric says, "restless." The melody moves upward. Meanwhile the lyric evokes one of the hallmarks of the twentieth century: the train whistle, a haunting symbol of longing. The hoot of the distant railroad taunts the protagonist, intensifying an awareness of her bleak stay-at-home existence. One line in the release stanza contains a triple rhyme (*pray/day/underway*), a fancy yet unobtrusive device that subtly adds to the sense of urgency. In contrast to the soaring melody of the release, the return to the A-section melody feels like a confirmation of all the factors that confine the protagonist.

In an economical fashion, the final stanza adds new notions to the lyric: the singer is viewed by others as being spacey and impractical. Yet inside her is a "burning," a fire that may well fuel the protagonist someday to burst out of her constricting environment, into the adventures of the new and unknown. The lyrics ride the undulating melody downward to resolution and rest.

The protagonist of "Far Away Places" seems like a close cousin of that of "I'm Always Chasing Rainbows," a 1918 hit that enjoyed a major revival in 1946. Philip Furia describes the protagonist of that song as a "thoroughly American rainbow-chaser [who] would become the perfect 'voice' for wit-tily turned lyrics that balance nonchalance and sophistication, slang and elegance."[5] The Whitney-Kramer dreamer is a late Tin Pan Alley transfor-mation of that "voice," but in this case regional naiveté is balanced by inner fire.

Waltz hits of the late 1940s tended to be rousing, like "It's a Most Unusual Day" (1948). By contrast, this Whitney-Kramer dreamy, muted waltz holds more in common with older pensive waltzes that were being revived to new popularity, like "I Wonder Who's Kissing Her Now" (a 1909 song revived in 1947) and "Now Is the Hour" (a 1914 instrumental, adapted by Dorothy Stewart and others into a hit of 1948). In adopting this slightly old-fashioned feel, "Far Away Places" was in line with trends within the country music field. Pee Wee King's "Tennessee Waltz" was a similarly plaintive, nostalgically staid country-western hit in 1948, the same year that "Far Away Places" was published. (It was copyrighted as an unpublished composition in the fall of 1947.) After "Far Away Places" paved a way to success with urban audiences in 1949, "Tennessee Waltz" became a cross-over hit all over the nation in 1950.

The slightly rural feeling of "Far Away Places" suited the late 1940s, when country music was increasingly influencing and overlapping with the urbane Tin Pan Alley modality. Whitney and Kramer were *au courant* with this vogue, writing for country-western artists as early as 1946. Pop music was stirring toward new syntheses: first rockabilly and then the Nashville Sound.

The dynamic between suffocating inertia and squirming restlessness contained within "Far Away Places" was a harbinger of some aspects of the 1950s. There were many who were restless. An African American caught in a racist Southern town could be the song's protagonist, longing for escape to "Far Away Places." Or the piece could be a metaphor for many women's dissatisfaction with household confinement dictated by the Feminine Mystique.

The most visible troublemakers of the 1950s, however, burning to escape confinement, were the young, the juvenile delinquent, the teenaged "rebel without a cause." The lyric of "Far Away Places" foreshadowed their nameless discomfort with the settled life of their elders, even as the composition's gentle, melancholy waltz melody may have seemed to capture the essence of staid conservatism. In music, it was African American rhythm-and-blues, turning into rock-and-roll, that gave teenagers catharsis. In the next decade, Whitney and Kramer would both mentor rock-and-roll singer-songwriters and themselves capture the new style in their 1957 jump blues hit "Cool Shake."

To the protagonist of "Far Away Places," the names of China and Siam are "strange sounding." (The latter nation seesawed between *Siam* and *Thailand* during the years "Far Away Places" was written. Because *Thailand* has endured, singers often insert substitute place names. There are many options that scan properly: Taiwan, Brazil, Japan, Iran, Peru, Nepal, Kuwait, et cetera.) This can be seen as a reflection of US ethnocentrism during an era when audiences were mesmerized by the stereotyped exoticism of Hollywood movies like *Anna and the King of Siam* (1946) and *Calcutta* (1947).

"Far Away Places" was a quickly spreading hit in early 1949, firmly establishing a spot on *Your Hit Parade* for many weeks. The piece attained four charting recordings, topped by that of Margaret Whiting, followed closely by Bing Crosby and Perry Como. Neglected were the appealingly understated singles recorded by their fellow crooners Vic Damone and Donald Peers.

In 1949, Dinah Shore's hit disc was lower-ranked, placing fourth. Yet as the decades rolled on, Shore perhaps became more closely identified with the ditty than Whiting, Crosby, or Como. She rerecorded the tune for an

LP and also featured it on television. With her regional origins and down-home Southern friendliness, she made a natural fit with the song's poetry of provincial longings and its languorous melody.

"Far Away Places" embodies late 1940s Tin Pan Alley craftsmanship as it gently leaned toward a country-western feel. Fittingly, in later decades the song found one of its most persistent champions in country star Willie Nelson. His three recordings are mainstays in the age of the internet and streaming. The first, in collaboration with eclectic musician-producer Leon Russell, was on a hit LP in 1979. Two others—even more mature renditions—followed in 2013: a studio version with Sheryl Crow, on a charting album, and a live performance.

Johnny Cash also brought the piece solidly into the country tradition, in a recording that waited many years for release. He frames the song with an autobiographical anecdote: "Far Away Places" was the first song he sang publicly as an aspiring performer, at an amateur night. He only got two votes, he reminisces. Decades later, his recorded version is sober and restrained—and very popular in the twenty-first century.

As with most Tin Pan Alley waltzes, "Far Away Places" is sometimes converted into duple meter. Thusly, Ethel Ennis gave it a stimulating kick, with organ and percussion punctuating her swinging rendition with syncopated interjections. In England of the early 1960s, the Springfields made it into a rumba, with Dusty Springfield's vocal backed by the group chanting exotic names in an appealing riff. The Bachelors had a UK hit with "Far Away Places" in 1963, in four-four meter and medium tempo, sparked by the soloist's somewhat exaggeratedly articulated singing. Over in the Netherlands, the Black Dynamites transformed the ballad into an Indorock twist tune, with a vocal flavored with Elvis Presley–isms.

In 1970, "Far Away Places" found an enduring place as an up-tempo rock tune: the Embers, a North Carolina band, mainstays of surfer-rock and the "shag circuit," made it their trademark song, a regional hit. The Embers changed a few words, threw out the B-section, and invented a new middle interlude. The band borrowed a restlessly driving bass line from a 1968 hit "Tighten Up." This transformation proved so compelling that rival groups have covered their arrangement. For instance, the band August Tide makes this version a boasting affirmation that manages to be both wistful and rousing. Their interpretation leaves little doubt that this man's wanderlust (and other kinds of lust) will someday be satisfied.

When Whitney and Kramer wrote "Far Away Places," the technology for jet planes was just around the corner. Within the next decade, Americans longing for a faraway place could hop on an international flight and go there. The anthem for this new era was Frank Sinatra's album title track "Come Fly with Me." Nevertheless, "Far Away Places" with its soothingly mesmerizing rhythms and salute to old-fashioned railroad travel continued to find a place in American culture.

Joan Whitney and Alex Kramer's hits
1940: "So You're the One," with Hy Zaret
1940: "High on a Windy Hill"
1940: "It All Comes Back to Me Now," with Hy Zaret
1941: "My Sister and I," with Hy Zaret
1941: "Yo Te Amo, Oh! Baby," with Hy Zaret
1943: "It's Love, Love, Love," with Mack David
1945: "Candy," with Mack David
1945: "Money Is the Root of All Evil (Take It Away, Take It Away, Take It Away)"
1946: "Ain't Nobody Here But Us Chickens"
1946: "That's the Beginning of the End"
1947: "Curiosity," lyrics with Sam Ward
1947: "Love Somebody"
1947: "Far Away Places"
1949: "Comme Ci, Comme Ca," English lyrics, original French lyrics by Pierre Dudan, music by Bruno Coquetrix
1951/1966/1970: "No Man Is an Island"; the Van Dykes, 1966, soul adaptation; Dennis Brown, 1970, reggae adaptation
1952: "You'll Never Get Away"
1953: "Man, Man Is for the Woman Made"
1954: "Pupalina"
1955: "How Lonely Can I Get"
1957: "Cool Shake"
1959: "No Other Arms, No Other Lips," with Hy Zaret
1966: "What's This World a-Comin' To"

Some neglected gems
1945: "Make Me Know It"; entreating lyric, brooding melody
1946: "(It's Gonna Depend on) The Way That the Wind Blows"; atmospheric ballad
1947: "I Only Saw Him Once"; quiet, conversational ballad
1949: "Deep as the River"; lyrical, metaphoric torch song

1950: "My Own Bit of Land"; quiet tune, opposite topic of "Far Away Places"

1954: "Going, Going, Gone"; slow torch waltz, the feel slightly similar to "Far Away Places"

1960: "Come Back Home to Roma," with Rod McKuen; Continental-flavored, quiet pleading

THE FIFTIES

"Female songwriters—they're mostly lyricists, right?" Not so. Two-thirds of the women covered so far were composers of music. However, in the upcoming sections all the creators were, indeed, writers of lyrics only. With the coming of the 1950s, a new preponderance of female wordsmiths is probably the reason for that common mistake.

The Great American Songbook is enhanced by first-rate songs of the 1950s. Some achieve a more mature depth than those of the previous decades. Further, compared to classics of the 1930s and 1940s, these pieces often speak even more directly to latter-day listeners. Nevertheless, the mass audience of the 1950s mostly embraced a simplified version of the Tin Pan Alley style; for instance, "(How Much Is) That Doggie in the Window?" (1952). Usually, more sophisticated works had to wait years before enthusiastic insiders—and lucky chances—spurred them on to a wider popularity. One example is "I Left My Heart in San Francisco," a 1953 song that pianist Ralph Sharon (who was a friend of its songwriters) left forgotten in his shirt drawer until he unearthed it for a Tony Bennett gig in California in 1961. Another is "Fly Me to the Moon," a 1954 song featured by many singers on albums before it finally charted as a single in 1962. Indeed, several of the songs mentioned in the upcoming sections were first popular with niche audiences and then reached the mass audience only after a delay.

This contrast between simplified mass audience styles and more distinctive specialized tastes is echoed in the general US culture of the 1950s, in the conflict between conformity, on the one hand, and, on the other, nonconformity, rebellion, and individualism. Many factors chipped away at the smug complacency of mainstream values: more nonmarital sex; the Civil Rights movement; the fall from grace of anticommunist McCarthyism; the introduction of yoga and an increased interest in Eastern philosophies in the United States; the white drop-out Beats; the Black urban hipsters; the *avant garde* of the visual and performance arts; and, in popular music, bop, modern jazz, the rawer strands of rock-and-roll, and the further popularization of traditional folk styles. Those trends, plus a surge in environmentalism, naturism and nudism, and health food advocacy, all fed the eventual creation of late 1960s counterculture. The pioneer generation born between the wars paved the way for the Baby Boomers who began to reach puberty in 1959. Both generations felt the dynamic of the day, a desire to fit in with the prosperous postwar era versus an urge to escape its confines.

At the start of the 1950s, live performances—and live broadcasts on radio and television—were still crucial to measuring a song's popularity. By the decade's end, however, a tune's ranking depended entirely on how well a recording did. For adult audiences, a song's appearance on a best-selling album was at least as important as, maybe more so than, a pop single. Many songs of this era became standards by flourishing on a series of charting albums.

Although 1955 is usually seen as the start of the rock-and-roll era, for Tin Pan Alley the year 1957 was a more fateful turning point. Sheet music suddenly disappeared from magazine stands, and sales dipped permanently. By then, many children as young as nine years old chose rock-and-roll as their favorite music. Within ten years, that juvenile audience had reached adulthood and become the driving force of popular music. On Broadway, rock-and-roll would gradually take over, becoming the foundation of a new theatrical sound. Over the years, the styles of the jazz decades would dwindle, almost die, and then be revived as an enduring—often even profitable—niche market.

The 1950s were the most intense period of what Betty Friedan labeled "the Feminine Mystique" that dictated women existed only for sex, reproduction, child rearing, and domestic duties. Dedicated career women like Betty Comden and Sylvia Dee delegated household chores or childcare to others in order to give time to their work. Nevertheless, journalists wrote about them as "housewives." To be a married woman or even a single mother was, by the era's definition, to be a "housewife."[1]

Many female songwriters of the 1930s and 1940s quit the pop song marketplace at a point that could be viewed as premature. Ruth Lowe, Irene Kitchings, Anita Leonard, Doris Fisher, and Deborah Chessler gave priority to their personal relationships—as did, in their own ways, Kay Swift, Ann Ronell, Nancy Hamilton, and (from 1940 to 1944) Dorothy Fields, and probably many others made the same choice. This was a major pattern of the era; and men found in it an excuse for not valuing women songwriters. In December 1945, "several Tin Pan Alley guys were sitting around Lindy's at three a.m. knocking women composers."[2] Women had proved they could write jazzy hits, but the men argued that they did not have staying power—other than Dorothy Fields, always the great exception. Supposedly this showed they were inferior as songwriters.

A better-informed historian might have pointed out to the smart-alecks at Lindy's that if Jerome Kern had retired in 1913, ten years into his career, he would have been completely unknown. Even in 1923, after a twenty-year career, Kern had produced only two truly enduring standards, "They Didn't Believe Me" (1914) and "Look for the Silver Lining" (1921). If childcare and housework had overtaken Kern when he was in his thirties, as it did for many of his female colleagues, he would be as obscure today as they are.

Even speaking from a supposedly more enlightened late twentieth-century perspective, Stephen Sondheim could pronounce that "the peak" of artistry arrives in one's forties, when songwriters achieve a "combination of their most vigorous and . . . mature" abilities.[3] Amazingly, he could make such a declaration, seemingly without considering the consequences such a factor might have to a woman's career. What if Sondheim had been female and had retired in time to have children, focusing on domestic duties after only ten years in the pop song marketplace? Then he (or, rather, she) would probably be seen today as a good lyricist but rather limited composer who overall simply did not have what it takes to sustain a lengthy career, as proved by an ultimate series of failures: *Anyone Can Whistle* (1964); *Do I Hear a Waltz?* (1965); *Evening Primrose* (1966); and the uncompleted, embarrassing *The Race to Urga*.

Indeed, if Kern and Sondheim had been women, they might not have been given a chance in the first place. Dana Suesse recalled, "I do remember meeting a couple of composers and producers who were discussing a projected musical. My name was brought up when they started to look for a collaborator. Their feeling was that a woman would not be suitable for that kind of job."[4] Even if Suesse had been given the opportunity to compose a complete Broadway score, she would have had to succeed right away, as did Dorothy Fields (with *Blackbirds of 1928*) and Betty Comden (with *On the Town*, 1944), or she would not have been given a follow-up opportunity.

Sylvia Dee (*The Barefoot Boy with Cheek*, 1947) and Stella Unger (*Seventh Heaven*, 1955) failed when given their shot for Broadway success. But so did the team of Jerry Bock and Sheldon Harnick: their first show, *The Body Beautiful* (1958), did not run. They were men, so they were privileged to get *Fiorello* (1959) on stage. Result: a long run and a Pulitzer Prize. Similarly, the pairing of John Kander and Fred Ebb: their *Flora the Red Menace* (1965) flopped, but they still got to do *Cabaret* (1966). Remarkably, Frederick Loewe had *three* Broadway failures but kept being given more chances, and thus the world eventually got *My Fair Lady* (1956), the most popular musical of the mid-century. No women were given that much slack.

In the light of such trains of thought, the accomplishments of the women in this study, and their many female colleagues, are revealed as even more remarkable. The wiseacres at Lindy's in 1945 could not foresee that the upcoming decades would reveal that not just Dorothy Fields but many others, including Joan Whitney, Kay Twomey, Sylvia Dee, Betty Comden, and Marilyn Bergman, would prove that, despite the odds, female songwriting careers could last for more than a decade.

"TOO YOUNG" (1949/1951)
Sylvia Dee (1914–1967), lyricist

Sylvia Dee was born Josephine Moore. Her mother Elizabeth Moore was also a lyricist, and in their era they were the only mother-daughter pair in ASCAP. From 1920 to 1964, Elizabeth Moore (1890–1980) wrote the texts for hundreds of concert songs and choral pieces. She proclaimed, "My songs are arty, and arty songs are not profitable." Moore reported that, conversely, "my daughter resolved from the start that she was going to write for money, not art."[5] Elizabeth published songs using the last name of her first, late husband, air corps Lt. Duncan Moore. But for her work as a journalist (food, garden, and social columns, and ultimately women's editor), she used her second married name, De Sylva. Josephine may have rebelled against Elizabeth's noncommercialism, but in tribute to her mother she slightly transformed "De Sylva" to create her own pen name, "Sylvia Dee."

Described as "an indefatigable worker" with an always busy "agile brain," Sylvia Dee was "obsessed with ambition." In interviews, both Sylvia and Elizabeth emphasized the hard labor and scant rewards of songwriting. Moore affirmed, "You write, and write, and write some more, fail miserably a hundred times . . . take the rebuffs and discouragements and in time you may break in," with an emphasis on the *may*. Dee agreed: "You must plan to write fifty songs for every one published," get put "through the mill," and "haunt the publishers by day and the bandleaders by night." Both agreed, there was no "get rich quick" path in songwriting.[6]

In a twenty-eight-year career on Tin Pan Alley, Sylvia Dee demonstrated her work ethic by copyrighting almost two hundred songs. She witnessed twenty-five become hits—big, little, and in between—and then, after her death, her collaborators guided another handful to prominence. In late 1940 she entered Tin Pan Alley, thanks to the ASCAP radio ban, as a staff writer for BMI's own publishing imprint. Like Joan Whitney, however, Dee jumped ship to ASCAP as soon as possible, earning membership in 1943.

In the late 1930s, a stint in Minneapolis got Dee a poem and a write-up in the famous regional news column of Cedric Adams. Out of this emerged the suggestion that Dee make contact with Sidney Lippman, a Minnesotan who was staff manager at Irving Berlin's firm. From at least 1940 onward, Dee and Lippman wrote songs together, though not exclusively, until her death.

For a number of years, Dee worked for a department store publicity department in Rochester, New York, so at first her collaboration with Lippman was often via long distance, especially during his years in the military in World War II. Lippman vaguely remembered a childhood nursery doggerel that Dee slowly shaped into their pivotal success, the novelty "Chickery Chick" (1945), a number one tune that sold both sheet music and over a million discs. It "really was junk," she opined, but its success enabled Dee to move herself and her seven-year-old son (by her first marriage, that had ended in divorce) to New York City. [7]

"Chickery Chick," plus their connection with Minnesota, won Dee and Lippman a Broadway score, *The Barefoot Boy with Cheek* (1947), with a story about the University of Minneapolis. The show was a failure with a three-month run, but Dee and Lippman delivered a hit, "After Graduation Day." Dee's lyric defiantly celebrates young love: "They say romances break up after graduation day," but the co-ed sweethearts "can keep our love as lovely and prove there's nothing in what they say." Dee and Lippman returned to this topic for their second number one hit, "Too Young."

In an oft-used method, Dee would come up with a title, Lippman would write the melody to match, and then Dee would flesh out the full lyric to his tune. In 1949, Dee's half-brother was a twenty-year-old college boy eager to get married. "Everyone told Don he was too young to know what he was doing," she said, and that conflict inspired the title "Too Young." "Just as in the song," she pointed out, he entered into a happy marriage, and the decades proved it to be a lifelong one.[8]

Lippman reported that the pair peddled "Too Young" "to every music publishing house in New York" and got scoffed at by each one. The only nibble was from Redd Evans, but he ran a tiny one-person operation; therefore, the team "felt he might not be able to put the song over." (Dee and Lippman were rare among songwriters: they always emphasized that the success of a piece depended on the publisher's efforts.) Late in the fall of 1950, "in desperation," Dee and Lippman let Evans have "Too Young."[9] By Thanksgiving, the publisher won a disc by the orchestra of Victor Young, released in time for Christmas. At the tail end of December, Evans rather belatedly mailed in the copyright, and the song was registered on January 1, 1951.

Evans must have put his all into plugging "Too Young" because early 1951 witnessed a boom in sheet sales (over 300,000 copies) and a spate of recordings, several of which rose in the charts. Of them all, Nat King Cole delivered the landmark version. The extravagantly lush Nelson Riddle arrangement, conducted by Les Baxter, swells and subsides and swells again. The strings and decorative piano fill-ins surge with sentiment (or sentimentality, depending on the listener). Cole's confiding voice rides the waves with expertise. With his intimate, slightly dry, down-the-middle delivery, he supplies a canny counterbalance to the excesses of the arrangement. At age thirty-one, Cole was a bit old to embody this protagonist, but he brings what his younger colleagues did not: a touch of defiance alongside the sensitivity. The record sold a million copies, thankfully saving Cole from the IRS (who were set to take away his home for overdue back taxes) and giving Dee and Lippman their second top song—twelve weeks as number one on *Your Hit Parade*.

In "Too Young," Lippman created a gently curving, spare melody, only seventy notes, in ABA'C form. In the lyric, Dee cannily repeats words in the first two sections, as if the lover is hesitant, stumbling over his own thoughts. Oscar Hammerstein II used that device for the same effect in "Some Enchanted Evening," written at almost the same time as "Too Young" though hitting the market two years earlier: "Somehow you know, / You know even then." Both lyricists then drop that technique as they spin out new stanzas in which their protagonists become more confident and assertive. The quiet craft of Dee's art is revealed in mellifluous but conversational phrases, as in her ending: "And then some day they may recall / We were not too young at all." She excels with unobtrusive internal rhyme (d*ay* th*ey* m*ay*; re-call/*we*), the linking *t* (no*t t*oo), and alliterative repetitions of *th* (*then/they*) and *w* (*we were*), all intertwined, yet sounding completely natural.

Of course, the real brilliance is the conception. Blending romanticism with quiet courageousness, the singer and the beloved demand the right to have a committed love relationship. Except for their age (though it's never stated how young they are), this was a goal comfortably in line with society's values. But through their assertions, the protagonists foreshadow the rebellious youths of the upcoming decades who fought for the right to vote, hold political office, and, ultimately, enjoy equality and free choice in all things.

Dee's lyric also foreshadowed the emergence of teen idols in the upcoming three decades, who relished the opportunity to sing this age-appropriate classic. In 1957, nineteen-year-old Tommy Sands proved the tune could rock. Even younger were the Lymon brothers, Tommy (thirteen) and Frankie (fifteen). This underaged tradition flourished in the 1950s and dwindled a bit in the 1960s, but in 1972 fourteen-year-old Donnie Osmond revived it with a flourish. The arrangement was a huge hit both as an album title track and a single, as smoothly textured and popular as Wonder Bread. Osmond's exclamations after the first chorus ("Oh. Oh!") seem designed to arouse his fans. The next year, inevitably, fourteen-year-old Michael Jackson had his turn with "Too Young," a track on a charting album. He quavers with earnestness; meanwhile the arrangement approximates the Cole-Riddle model, one of many such tributes that carried through into the twenty-first century.

Jerry Lee Lewis offers a different, and poignant, application of Dee's lyric. His 1966 take on the song, underpinned by a lively quasi-Latin rhythm, featuring his inventive, nubbly piano figurations, is poignant only in light of his marriage, in 1958, to his thirteen-year-old cousin Myra. The scandal changed the course of Lewis's career and, therefore, rock-and-roll history.

Dee's range was enviable. She caught the bittersweet sparkle of the Depression in "Have You Changed" (1941), saucy cheer of postwar society in "My Sugar Is So Refined" (1946), and rollicking humor of rock-and-roll in "Robot Man" (1960)—hits, all of them. In the 1960s, Dee could still manufacture vehicles for performers from the Swing Era. "Look for Me (I'll Be Around)" was an atmospheric ballad for Sarah Vaughn on a torch song concept album. "Bring Me Sunshine," swung by the Mills Brothers, was soon taken up as a jazzy hit for Willie Nelson and as the closing theme for British television's beloved *Morecambe & Wise Show*.

A Dee lyric issued posthumously, "Toll the Bell for Henry Holloway" (1969), is like a companion piece to the Beatles's "Eleanor Rigby," which had just come out in the months before Dee's death. In "Toll the Bell," Dee satirizes the suburban culture she thrived in; for a while she made her home in the (in)famous Levittown on Long Island. This allowed her to be "in close contact with the very people" who were her audience.[10] Dee's protagonist "winds up his clock and goes to bed / and sleeps among the living dead."

In 1950, with "Too Young," Dee and Lippman found the precise location between the controlled purity of the Jerome Kern tradition and postwar neo-simplicity. It is the kind of balancing act that Dee achieved again and again. Perhaps her most accomplished work is her biggest hit, "The End of the World" (1962), with composer Arthur Kent. With this sorrowful ballad, youthful country singer Skeeter Davis soared into the top five of all the major charts—country-western, rhythm and blues, pop, and adult contemporary—the only recording to accomplish this.

At the time of her death, Dee was in a happy second marriage to Dr. Jere Faison, a proponent of natural birth methods; and the lyricist died at home of a heart attack, after being ill for some time. Afterward, Dee posthumously won the ASCAP country-western award for "I Taught Her Everything She Knew." In true Dee fashion, however, this was also a hit on the adult charts for Ella Fitzgerald. That jazz singer had made perhaps the best rendering of Dee's first hit, "I'm Thrilled," almost thirty years before. In the interim, like Fitzgerald, Dee had helped define mid-century American popular music.

"TWISTED" (1952)
Annie Ross (1930–2020), lyricist

While Sylvia Dee situated herself in Levittown, that quintessence of American suburbs, singer-lyricist Annie Ross steered clear of the conformity of US society in the 1950s. As Ross said late in life, "I've never gone with anything that is the 'popular' belief. I think I was a bit of a rebel. And I was searching, searching."[11] She was a respected jazz singer, revered for her four-year partnership with Dave Lambert and Jon Hendricks. Valued by some as the greatest jazz vocal group of all time, the trio broke up in 1962 when Ross settled in England to kick her heroin addiction. There, her circles overlapped with those of another lyricist, expatriate Fran Landesman, another nonconformist, covered in the next section. Already, the two were linked by both having had affairs with the countercultural comedian Lenny Bruce. Landesman wrote lyrics for an unproduced musical revue for Ross to star in, with a new song she was excited about called "Piss Off, My Love." The title alone is revealing: while these two women wrote lyrics with all the wit and craft of the Broadway greats of the 1930s, they did so in a world of radically changed social mores.

In another contrast, Sylvia Dee and her Tin Pan Alley colleagues were trying to simplify the pop song formula, while their peers like Ross and Landesman were trying to complicate it. As David Jenness and Don Velsey point out, from the mid-1940s onward, some songwriters for Broadway, cabaret, and jazz "stretched" the Tin Pan Alley model.[12] For instance, they might create more sections, or lengthier ones. Further, they wrote lyrics with increasingly complex attitudes and thoughts. In its form and content, Annie Ross's "Twisted" is an example of that greater sophistication.

The outlines of Ross's life are well known, thanks to various profiles, interviews, and a 2012 BBC documentary. Her parents were Scottish (originally Irish on her mother's side) and in show biz. Her older brother became the famous UK comedian and television personality Jimmy Logan. Her aunt, Ella Logan, moved to the United States, where she became a respected jazz singer and Hollywood supporting player in the 1930s and then a Broadway singing star in the 1940s.

When Annie was four, her family came to the United States for a visit, and she won a trip to Hollywood in a talent contest. Her mother dumped her there to be raised by Aunt Ella, an unsympathetic and "complicated" woman.[13] Annie spent her school years in Hollywood, seen in a few small parts in movies. Ross retained her American accent the rest of her life; and, in 2001, she became a US citizen.

Reaching adulthood, Ross was dismissed by Aunt Ella Logan, "You can't sing, you haven't got the magic," who sent her back to Scotland.[14] Very quickly, Ross escaped to Paris, joined its thriving color-blind jazz scene, recorded with saxophonist James Moody, and had an affair and a son with African American bop drummer Kenny Clarke. Ross and Clarke both led a touring jazz lifestyle, not designed for rearing children. The son, rejected by Ross's Scottish family, ended up raised by Clarke's relatives in Pittsburgh. Ross visited as often as possible, weeping at every parting, probably remembering her own abandonment by her parents.

Since about 1944, Ross had been crafting lyrics. She remembered mostly writing torch songs in her teens, reflecting the unhappiness of her upbringing. In early 1949, she won a recording by Johnny Mercer—and a publication by Capitol—of a cheery, slightly sexually suggestive up-tempo song, "Let's Fly." In 1952, the Prestige record label asked Ross to fit some lyrics to one of the jazz instrumentals in their catalog. This practice was soon to be labeled "vocalese." Ross chose "Twisted," a 1949 piece by Wardell Gray, the African American bop saxophonist. Gray had created four themes, structured ABCD, followed by improvised solos (on the themes of the BCD sections), then a double repeat, AA, and a final short coda. Ross added another repeat of A, ending up with AABCDAA and coda.

In her A-sections, Ross creates a confrontation between the song's narrator and a psychoanalyst. Ross never had been (and never would be) in analysis. Nevertheless, the United States was captivated by the charisma of psychoanalysis, manifested in numerous Hollywood movies that distorted psychotherapy into glamorous melodrama. Ross created a famous opening lyric: "My analyst told me that I was right out of my head." The protagonist is having none of that, proclaiming with a skillful internal rhyme, "I knew that he *thought* I was crazy, but I'm *not!*"

In the three inner segments of BCD, the singer recalls her rebellious, nonconformist childhood, getting high on vodka, and shunning double-decker buses because there was only a driver steering on the bottom, not on both levels. With the return to the A-sections, the narrator returns to the psychoanalysis session. She brags that she has two heads, which (as every one knows) are better than one. No wonder she thought the bus should have two heads steering it. It is an open question whether the singer is referring cleverly to Freud's theory of the Ego and the Id, or has a split personality disorder, or is instinctively foreshadowing the 1960s discoveries about the right and left hemispheres of the brain. Throughout, Ross immaculately shapes her words to the sprightly, groovy contours of Gray's melody. At the same time, she offers a character study as clear and compelling as famous Broadway examples such as Rodgers and Hammerstein's "Soliloquy" from *Carousel* (1945).

The definitive versions of "Twisted" are by Ross herself—she put it on record three times as well as on television tapings. Ross was strongest in exactly this type of medium-to-fast tempo piece that allowed her intelligent humor to gleam through. Her reed-like, quicksilver voice with a range from mezzo-soprano to stratospheric staccato high notes eventually aged into a deep and gruff instrument. Young or old, however, she had an immaculate sense of time. She could drop a single note on top of a riff, or into a pause, with expert assurance.

Ross's 1952 disking of "Twisted" put her on the map with jazz insiders, as well as with some more general African American audiences. In March 1953, *Billboard* reported: "Bop vocal by thrush is doing well in the Midwest. It's solid for the jazz market and getting a good R&B ride in Cincinnati, St. Louis, and Chicago." For the 1959 album by Lambert, Hendricks and Ross, *The Hottest New Group in Jazz*, she again rendered the piece for posterity. The song works even better here, with Ross's partners interjecting brief responses to her protagonist. For seventeen-year-old Joni Mitchell, this album became a "musical epiphany," one of "only three or four in my life . . . the record . . . wore thin . . . I learned every song on it."[15]

Although Ross's various takes on "Twisted" were immediately valued as classics by the discerning, the song did not show up on *Billboard* charts until much later—and then, in a typical pattern, only as an album track. Joni Mitchell sang it on her best-selling album *Court and Spark*, recorded in 1973. Mitchell's reed-like timbre, confiding style, and light touch perfectly suit the piece, hinting at how deeply this idiosyncratic singer-songwriter's "voice" was influenced by Annie Ross. *Court and Spark* sold two million copies, and later renditions of "Twisted" are often done in tribute to Mitchell. Simultaneously, Bette Midler also achieved a charting album with "Twisted" on it, in a wacky version in which the singer takes on the role of both the protagonist and her confidantes. "Twisted" had finally arrived as a mainstream favorite.

Between recordings and a few copyright registrations, Ross left evidence of having written only about a half dozen lyrics and melodies. Ironically, she never wrote words for her own haunting jazz ballad tune, "Annie's Lament." Posterity might wish for more songwriting from her, but Ross put her energies into maintaining sobriety, managing a nightclub, numerous acting jobs, and then reviving her career as a singer.

One night, Ross found herself singing the opening line of "Twisted" as "my aunt always told me." She realized that the song was really about her own childhood, in particular the lack of understanding and support from her aunt, Ella Logan. These powerful emotional roots helped the lyric become "a wry anthem for hipsters who spurned normality or healthy adjustment." Indeed, the piece has been a touchstone for many who feel out of step with society and the values of authority figures. To the end, these audiences embraced Ross singing "Twisted," her signature piece.[16]

"SPRING CAN REALLY HANG YOU UP THE MOST" (1955)
Fran Landesman (1927–2011), lyricist

In contrast to Annie Ross, Fran Landesman probably wrote over a thousand lyrics during her fifty-nine-year career: more than 200 with her first composer, Tommy Wolf; over 350 with her final composer, Simon Wallace; and, in between, uncounted additional ones with at least two dozen other collaborators. Wallace called her "modus operandis . . . a furious pace." Her elder son, journalist Cosmo Landesman, described how she "stays up all night writing songs." Wolf described how they collaborated: "The lyric is paramount and always precedes the music." He went on: "She writes with incredible speed, in curious flashes of intense concentration, as a stenographer taking sudden, urgent dictation from a personal, omnipotent muse."[17]

Out of this bountiful creativity, Landesman harvested over a dozen aficionado favorites; two semistandards; a handful of late works headed toward becoming standards, particularly "Scars" (1997); two works that were tracks on charting albums; several flip sides of pop hits; one British pop-rock hit, Georgie Fame's "Try My World" (1967); and two favorites that, after years of building into strong jazz standards, eventually featured on hit recordings—"The Ballad of the Sad Young Men" (1959) and "Spring Can Really Hang You Up the Most" (1955).

Fran and Jay Landesman were as famous for their countercultural lifestyle as for their work. Jay was the first to publish the Beat writers; ran the hippest nightclub-cabaret-theater in his hometown of St. Louis, Missouri; and helped establish health foods and macrobiotics in England. Fran and Jay's relationship became the most famous example of an open marriage, and their lovers were many.

In 1964, Fran and Jay moved from the United States to England with their two sons. There, she began to be treated not as a lyricist but as a poet, so that is what she became. (Landesman recalled that the male Beat writers in the United States "weren't interested in women doing anything but emptying ashtrays." They were "never even aware that I did anything" as a writer.)[18] She ended up publishing volumes of her poems, often reading them on BBC radio, and being a frequent guest at the Royal Academy of Dramatic Arts. By the end of the 1970s, she was flourishing as a performer in small venues, reciting poems and speak-singing her songs, alongside her younger son, musician Miles Landesman.

Cosmo Landesman reports that his mother's goal was "to write songs for big musicals," the Broadway blockbuster. Fran had all the skill and productivity of Dorothy Fields and Carolyn Leigh ("Witchcraft"), but, frustratingly, "her career was always taking off and then stalling." Jay would tell her, "Success destroys your soul," and she would snap back, "I wouldn't know. I never had any."[19]

With Tommy Wolf, Fran and Jay wrote a musical based on their lives—upper-middle-class Jewish woman from Connecticut meets literary Jewish hipster in New York, and their worlds collide—called *The Nervous Set* (1959). It was a sell-out success in their intimate cabaret theater in St.

Louis. The show probably would have run for years in a small off-Broadway venue, but all its experimental, quirky charm got lost in a cavernous Broadway theater, where it only ran two weeks. A compensation: from it came "The Ballad of the Sad Young Men," which gradually proved to be one of Landesman's two strongest standards, featured on late 1960s charting discs by Steve Lawrence, Miriam Makeba, Petula Clark, and Roberta Flack.

In 1993, an intimate London revue built from Landesman's songs and poems, *Invade My Privacy*, got good reviews. But, perhaps because of her unhappy experience with *The Nervous Set*, Fran rejected the changes demanded by the producer interested in taking it to New York (who happened to be Jay's nephew, Rocco Landesman). Nevertheless, a few years before her death, Fran assessed her life: "In my wildest dreams, it's exactly what I would have wanted. It's as if God looked down and designed a future for me that gave me everything I would have wanted." She added, with typical frankness, "And I can't think why. I'm not kind or considerate."[20] In the end, Landesman was understandably satisfied with a résumé that included acclaimed one-woman shows, nine musical theater works, four volumes of poetry, and over two hundred recorded songs.

Despite her grand ambitions, Landesman wrote songs that seemed deliberately to flout mainstream values. For one thing, almost all her major collaborators were pianists in the modern jazz idiom, like Wolf and Wallace. These composers were rarely concerned with the singability or danceability desired in popular songs. Instead they worked toward an engrossing listening experience, filling compositions with unexpected twists, turns, and phrasings.

Further, Landesman wrote lyrics about not conforming. Two of her better-known pieces define her stance. In "Night People," from *The Nervous Set*, she refers to "the trite people . . . you gray people," who, unfortunately, were the bulk of Broadway ticket buyers. Perhaps it was not a good idea to court success by insulting her audience. Over a quarter of a century later, in "Small Day Tomorrow" with music by Bob Dorough, Landesman's protagonist brags, "I'm a drop out, who'd rather cop out, than run with all the sheep"—lines that to an extent define the lives that she and Jay led.

Landesman's hero was Lorenz Hart. In song after song she captured much the same bittersweet wit as Hart had—but with her own flavor: cynical yet innocent, existentially lonely yet playful. What she could not do, that Hart could, was write a sweetly sentimental love song. Even at the start, in one of her first copyrights, "This Little Love of Ours," she praises noncommitment: "We love just a little, but not too much." The decades proved that no one could match Landesman in writing about the pains, pleasures, and comedy of transient affairs. When she did apparently write about her relationship with Jay, it was also in bittersweet terms, as in "I Should Have Been Dancing": "When I should have been making sense of my life / I was busy messing up yours." Landesman's keen ability to write about longing and lost love is displayed in her most recorded song, "Spring Can Really Hang You Up the Most," with music by Tommy Wolf.

Fran and Jay met Wolf as he played in the lounge of a St. Louis restaurant. In between watching the Democratic Party presidential nominees debate, they charmed him by requesting songs he had never heard of. Offered the lofty sounding position of "musical director" of Jay's new nightclub, the Crystal Palace, Wolf grabbed it. There, the jazz group he led inspired Fran to create her first lyrics. By the summer of 1953, Wolf was sending in batches of copyright registrations for their collaborations. In November 1955, the copyright for "Spring Can Really Hang You Up the Most" was registered; for the first time, not by Wolf as an individual but by a publishing firm, Buckeye Music. This was a new imprint, linked to Fraternity Records who, not surprisingly, were the first to get a recording of "Spring" on the market in 1955. The next year, they issued an album of Wolf playing and singing his collaborations with Landesman. The songwriting pair were on the map.

At the same time, George Shearing played St. Louis and then took "Spring Can Really Hang You Up the Most" to Jackie Cain and Roy Kral, the married singing pair—they became lifelong friends of Fran and Jay— and from them the song went to Roy's sister, singer Irene Kral. Jackie and Roy, and later Irene, recorded the tune; its momentum began to grow. In early 1959, "Spring" finally appeared on a major American record label, by June Christy on Capitol. That year, too, the number appeared in the St. Louis version of *The Nervous Set*—but was cut from the Broadway version. The omission hardly mattered, for the song became a staple item for a cohort of singers who rose in the 1950s. These performers helped trailblaze bop (Betty Carter), cool jazz (Rita Reys), and an understated style that counterbalanced the emotionality of the era (Julie London). Ella Fitzgerald became a particular champion of "Spring," recording it three times.

Landesman was inspired to write "Spring Can Really Hang You Up the Most" after rereading T. S. Eliot's quintessential Lost Generation poem, *The Wasteland*. (In St. Louis, Fran and Jay lived across the street from Eliot's birthplace.) She asked herself: "How would the jazz crowd phrase Eliot's thought 'April is the cruelest month'?" When she came up with an answer, the musicians said, "You're crazy" because "people just didn't write songs with titles like that in those days."[21] Typically for Landesman, she went ahead anyway, disregarding convention. Also typically for sophisticated writers like herself, she wrote not just a simple AABA chorus but a verse, two complete sets of lyrics for the refrain, plus a lengthy second ending that amounts to a whole additional C-segment. Wolf, in his turn, varied the third A-section to such an extent that it throws listeners off balance just when they think resolution is at hand.

The protagonist tells of having a happy "little fling" throughout the winter and then losing love in the spring. As Jenness and Velsey point out, Landesman creates almost every stanza so it first tells of the customary beauties of spring in one breath, and in the next breath dispels the joy with a wry, lonely, and depressed conclusion. Paralleling Landesman's lyric, Wolf writes a slow, dreamy melody that ascends up hopefully and then gently ripples down, defeated. Together, they create one of the most powerful evocations of the melancholy, lazy restlessness of spring fever.

Landesman makes a key statement at the end of the more dramatic B-section: "I know the score, / And I've decided that spring is a bore!" As Cosmo Landesman wrote, describing his parents' social circle: "In that world to be a bore was the greatest of sins."[22] In this view, heartbreak is just too, too trite; treat it with a shrug of the shoulders, some dry wit, and a bit of colorful slang. The protagonist is clearly a descendant of Kay Swift's rueful sophisticate in "Can't We Be Friends," wry in the face of emotional devastation.

It is hard to find a bad rendition of "Spring Can Really Hang You Up the Most."[23] It carries a dreamy, quietly witty life of its own. Perhaps the definitive renditions are by singers who matured during the cool jazz decade: June Christy (backed by Pete Rugolo) sang the first set of lyrics; Chris Connor (backed by Maynard Ferguson) sang the second set of lyrics; and Carmen McRae sang both sets of lyrics, cannily increasing the tempo slightly for the second refrain. The best-selling recordings, however, are by women of the next generation: Bette Midler (in 1990) and Barbra Streisand (in both 1991 and 2009), selling millions of discs. Happily, Landesman lived to reap the royalties.

"JUST IN TIME" (1956)

Betty Comden (1917–2006), lyricist

For sixty-four years, Betty Comden teamed with Adolph Green to write lyrics and scripts, contributing to what many call the Golden Age of the American Musical. Yet Comden noted: "We've written dozens of songs" (actually, probably well over a thousand) "but had only three big hits."[1] By "big hits," she meant tunes that were immediately embraced by the public, stayed on the charts for a month or more, quickly accumulated dozens of recordings, and endured in the repertoire. Comden and Green's lucky three were all created with composer Jule Styne: "Make Someone Happy" (1960) and, from their foremost Broadway show *Bells Are Ringing* (1956), "The Party's Over" and "Just in Time."

But that hardly tells the whole story about Comden and Green's contribution to the Great American Songbook. True, the career of Comden and Green is usually viewed as part of theater or movie history. That is the emphasis in show business annals and in two biographies about the pair— even in Comden's memoir, *Off Stage*, that focuses on her personal life. Nevertheless, it is time to celebrate their status as the creators of songs that enjoy an independent life of their own, outside of musicals. Their output offers the perfect example of lyrics that at first appeal mainly to dedicated Broadway audiences and sophisticated supper club singers but that slowly become among the most performed songs of all.

The pair themselves plugged their lyrics by performing their two-person show, *A Party with Comden and Green*, for many decades. Also, revivals of their stage shows, or reissues of their movie musicals, helped to keep alive many Comden and Green numbers. Alternately, when an idolized performer took up a song, it might spread to others; for instance, Judy Garland kept performing the lively "Comes Once in a Lifetime" (1962) for more than five years, and in 2012 Barbra Streisand issued her rendering of "Being Good Isn't Good Enough" (1967), which was then covered by Michele Lea on *Glee* in 2014, further boosting the ballad's status in the repertoire.

Comden and Green wrote mainly lighthearted comedies filled with, as Thomas Hischak puts it, "Broadway types . . . sketched quickly, broadly and clearly." The lyrics have a clean, fresh air quality, and one imagines enthusiastic exclamation points after titles like "It's Love!" or "I Met a Girl!" Yet in almost every musical they placed at least one contemplative ballad, like "The Party's Over," that cuts right to the heart. Whether poignant or upbeat, their lyrics convey a message about the human condition, one that cannot be pinpointed but feels like it desperately needed to be said and yet had never been said before.

Figure 17.1   Theater, movies, and life always felt like *A Party with Betty Comden and Adolph Green*. The colyricists are shown here performing that two-person revue in 1958. (New York Public Library.)

BIOGRAPHY

Born in Brooklyn, Baysa Cohen changed her name by the time she started her theater career. *Baysa* was a variation of Bess (think *Bess-ya*), that is, a short form of Elizabeth, and thus came *Betty*; and she turned *Cohen* into the less Jewish-sounding *Comden*. At her progressive school, she and twelve other seventh graders worked as a team to adapt *Ivanhoe* into a stage production that they then performed locally, a harbinger of her later group collaborations and her ultimate career as half of a writing duo.

While earning her bachelor's degree in drama from New York University, Comden met Adolph Green, who was hanging around downtown theaters looking for acting work. After graduation, Comden eked out the start of a performing career in regional playhouses, repertory companies, and the subway circuit of theaters scattered around the boroughs of New York. With Green, she helped form a short-lived theater troupe of six. Then Green's friend Judy Tuvim—who later translated her name to the less Jewish-sounding Holliday—found a weekly gig at a poets' hangout, the tiny Village Vanguard. A new sketch comedy troupe formed around Green and Holliday: Alvin Hammer (a budding actor and monologist), John Frank (who was a skilled multi-instrumentalist), and Comden (who, along with acting and singing, could play a few chords on the piano). Penniless, they had to write their own scripts and songs collectively, ribbing popular culture—movies, plays, newspapers, advertisements, pop music, and radio. Throughout the winter and spring of 1938, audiences slowly grew and word spread until, finally, a rave review in a newspaper made them the toast of the town.

The Revuers went over sensationally with elite sophisticates in intimate clubs but not always so well with more general audiences. By the middle of 1944, after a lot of ups and downs, the other three Revuers had dropped out, leaving only Comden and Green. When their career ship seemed to be drifting, Green's friendship with composer Leonard Bernstein got them the chance to write the script and lyrics for a Broadway musical. The result, *On the Town* (1944), about three sailors on a one-day leave in New York City, was a landmark critical success and ran for more than a year. Comden recalled, "We were nightclub performers writing material one day—and the next we were suddenly musical dramatists, with a publisher and membership in ASCAP, getting four checks a year!"[2] At last, they went from the fringes to the center of show business.

Comden and Green also crafted tailor-made roles for themselves in *On the Town*: an anthropologist and a sailor who confess, in a duet satirizing

operatic style, that they get "Carried Away" by enthusiasm. The pair performed this trademark piece until the end of their careers. For special
comedy material like this, that fit character or situation and satirized either
human nature or artistic genres (or both), Comden and Green could not
be bettered. In fact, while creating the show with Bernstein and choreographer Jerome Robbins, Comden "filled a yellow legal pad with their
'credo': that the action should be integrated; that music and dance and
book must be all of one piece and never stop telling the story, each number
being part of the action; that nothing should be permitted that was 'cheap
or crummy.'"[3] Thus Comden and Green joined the vogue of the integrated
musical started by Rodgers and Hammerstein with *Oklahoma!* a couple of
seasons earlier.

Because they emphasized situation and character, Comden and Green
remained a step removed from the independent pop song beloved by Tin
Pan Alley. They were, as Comden later put it, from "a different world."
The veteran publisher Witmark printed songs from *On the Town*, and
they earmarked the ballads "Lucky to Be Me" and "Some Other Time" as
the plug tunes. But perhaps the aura of the elite hung over the numbers.
The cheery, lyrical "Lucky to Be Me" was the most conventional number
in the *On the Town* score and yet only got a measly two recordings. It did
not appear on any charts. Live, only performers in "smart, intimate" "class
cafes" took it up.[4]

The other ballad from *On the Town*, "Some Other Time," a poignant
leave taking, got neither recordings nor club renditions (at least, none that
got reviewed). Although the LP era brought a couple of handfuls of renditions, at the time of the 1971 Broadway revival of *On the Town* Comden
could still remark that "Some Other Time" was "much less well known than
the other" numbers in the score.[5] Yet starting about the time of Tony Bennett's 1975 recording with jazz pianist Bill Evans (a longtime champion of
the tune), the song's momentum slowly grew. During the 1990s, the trickle
became a deluge: in 1999 alone there were eleven recordings of "Some
Other Time" released.

"Some Other Time" is now Comden and Green's second-most popular
song, with hundreds of renditions, including by Barbra Streisand on several
of her charting albums. In 1944, "Some Other Time" ranked low (if at all)
among popular songs. Since 1944, however, thanks to decades of renditions, it has achieved a ranking as the sixteenth most often recorded song of
1944—far above many works of the mid-1940s that, back then, beat it by a
long shot. This case is not unique; nevertheless, it is still an unusual fate for
a jazz-and-cabaret standard. Add it to other songs from the show—"Lucky

to Be Me" (currently ranked thirty-four for 1944), the haunting "Lonely Town" (position forty-six), and the swinging "I Can Cook Too" (position eighty)—and *On the Town* has proven to be the most successful score of its season.[6] It's a common pattern for Comden and Green's numbers: neglected at the start but eventually triumphing.

With rave reviews and a fourteen-month run, *On the Town* set Comden and Green off and running on a fifty-year Broadway career. Although they had their share of failures, those were always well-respected failures; and their successes came along in regular succession. The pair would go on to win five Tony Awards for their Broadway musicals; earn Hollywood studios millions of dollars with their witty screenplays; write the script (and one song) for *Singin' in the Rain* (1952), rated the best movie musical of all time; and become elected into halls of fame and bestowed with lifetime achievement awards.

Ironically, Comden and Green's most popular Broadway work was not only their least characteristic but also a shared credit with other writers (particularly lyricist Carolyn Leigh, covered in the next chapter). This was a new fully musicalized stage version of *Peter Pan* (1954), telecast live twice, taped for annual television replays, and revived often, notably for a sixteen-month Broadway run in 1979 and a two-year tour starting in 2011. With Jule Styne, Comden and Green contributed not only hilarious comedy and situation numbers but also uncharacteristically delicate, mellow, nostalgic songs like "Distant Melody" and "Never Never Land." In the 1990s, the latter song suddenly became a staple item in the repertoires of musical theater and cabaret singers (who perhaps, as children, had been fans of the 1979 *Peter Pan* revival), acquiring dozens of recordings.

Comden and Green worked together every day. She (an early bird) and he (a night owl) compromised on meeting in the early afternoon. Comden recalled: "As I had foolishly learnt to type, I was the one who had to write it all down." Most of their projects "started with us," Green said, "we usually create our own." The experience? "Agony. Just read, kick around things, meet every day and stare at each other and say no to something for a year, then suddenly say 'Let's try it.'" A song's conception could come from all the usual methods—melody first, lyric first, title first—but always emerged out of character and situation.[7]

When working, Comden could be found sitting with her legal-sized pad and pencil, the calm in the storm, while Green paced feverishly around the room. Later, she'd be at her typewriter consolidating their final draft. Green praised Comden: she had "ready-at-hand, a well-digested fund of erudition, a dazzling sense of humor, and a concise, wit—sharp, but never unkind." In turn, Comden described her partner: "Adolph Green gives a new meaning to the word *eccentric*." One of his chief characteristics was walking through Manhattan, his arms loaded with newspapers, magazines, and books, never looking up from his reading but somehow never getting run over. After more than fifty years, Comden reported: "We can still make each other laugh. He can still amuse, surprise, even astonish me with his knowledge, his insight, his compassion." Critic Rex Reed opined that, as respectable as they were in their domestic lives, "when they are together, as they usually are, they are both quite mad."[8]

Comden entered a lifelong marriage in 1938 to handsome Siegfried Schutzman, an artist turned home products designer, who anglicized his name to Stephen Kyle. His company, Americraft, remained a modest but steady business, while Comden's success burst its seams, even as she gave birth to a daughter and son. Like Dorothy Fields's second husband, Kyle seems, for his era, to have been unusually secure in himself. All reports concur with Comden's tribute to him: "Steve loved what I did, and admired it, and always wanted me to go on with my work. He was always there for me to discuss my work with, and his judgment was perceptive, creative and helpful." In the end, inevitably, "Steve had a lot of responsibilities for running the family as I went about my business, loving my children but feeling inadequate, and happy to let others take over." Comden confessed, "I felt I had no gift for mothering at all, and was bewildered and scared by the daily problems." Her self-doubts only increased as her son adolesced and developed lifelong addictions that led to his early death.[9]

Through such life experiences and their support of liberal causes, Comden and Green's work noticeably deepened and matured, step by step, over the decades. They never lost their scintillating talent to write satire, comedy material, character songs, and situation numbers. They developed, however, new abilities. They grew to write lyrics, as Comden said, with "heart . . . *pretty* songs," like their ballads in *Wonderful Town* (1954): "Ohio" (a substantial hit for a couple of months) or "A Quiet Girl" and "It's Love" (both, like many of their lesser hits, charting for a week or two). In the 1960s, they matured through writing social consciousness pieces like their art song with Bernstein, "So Pretty" (a child's bewilderment at the Vietnam War), and their final pop hit, "Now!" (a call to action for African American rights). Their new-style Broadway power ballad, "Being Good Isn't Good Enough" (from *Hallelujah, Baby!* in 1967); a monologue of internal struggle, "Together" (Lily's solo in the *On the Twentieth Century* sextette, 1977); and a lament for environmental change, "Look Around" (from *The Will Rogers Follies*, 1991)—these offer just a few demonstrations of their artistic growth.

"JUST IN TIME"

Jule Styne committed to full-time songwriting starting at the relatively late age of thirty-four. (Thus Styne offers another example of a male who, if he had been a career woman who retired just in time to bear children, would be forgotten today.) He was a Ukrainian-British-American Jew who gave classical concerts as a piano prodigy but grew up to talk "like the pug in a Warner Bros. gangster movie." He'd blurt out, "I like to yell. So what?" Styne was a king of the pop song in the 1940s, but his goal was to be a Broadway composer like Richard Rodgers, and to do so he needed someone like Lorenz Hart for lyrics. So, in 1951, he was happy to be teamed with the erudite satirists Comden and Green, figuring he could learn from them, and they could learn from him. They came from opposite camps, as Comden observed: "Whenever I say in Jule's presence that all the songs and words come out of a situation and character, Jule says 'But we want to look for a hit song, too.'" Despite such differences, over the course of twenty-three years the trio introduced new numbers for eight Broadway productions. Comden reported. "We don't know how we get along with Jule . . . and yet it all matched. We laughed a lot. . . . We shared a sense of the absurd." All three were bursting with ideas and enthusiasm.[10]

In the mid-1950s, Comden and Green were brainstorming musical play ideas to star their erstwhile cowriter and stage partner, Judy Holliday. Since leaving the Revuers, Holliday had become a theater and movie star playing variations on the good-hearted, naïve blonde with an everywoman touch that helps her to a happy ending. An advertisement illustrating an answering service operator led Comden and Green to visit a phone answering office. They discovered an elite clientele served from shabby premises, a perfect setting for humorous encounters of different subcultures and classes. Because Holliday had once earned her living as a telephone operator for Orson Welles's Mercury Theater, it seemed a natural fit. They took the idea to Styne, and he loved it.

Sensing a hit show, Styne led Comden and Green into forming a new publishing company, Stratford Music, devoted to their scores together. Appropriately, out of this show the lyricists yielded more charting hits than from any of their other musicals. "Long Before I Knew You" is, arguably, Comden and Green's tenderest, most fully realized love ballad; it was a live radio hit in the United States for five months, a successful Steve Lawrence single, and a charting sheet music seller in England. The swaggering yet melancholy medium-tempo swinger "Independent (On My Own)" was the flip of a major Rosemary Clooney hit (this was "Mangos," composed by a woman, Dee Libbey). Jo Stafford's single of the waltz title song, "Bells Are Ringing," charted for two weeks (as well as being the flip of a hit). Doris Day's disc of "The Party's Over" charted for almost three months; later, Nat King Cole (1958), Peggy Lee (1960), Bobby Darin (1962), and a host of others right through Seth McFarlane (2019) rendered it on best-selling albums, turning the torch ballad into one of the strongest standards. And then, the leader of the pack, "Just in Time" was a hit single for Tony Bennett before *Bells Are Ringing* even opened on Broadway and charted on live radio for over a year.

Comden described how she and Green shared "radar communication," a kind of mental telepathy. She refused to analyze creativity: "You cannot describe this process in so many words. . . . in the middle and surrounding all of it is a very mysterious thing . . . a tremendously accidental, unanalytical thing." The pair said to Styne, "Wouldn't it be nice to have something in the show like an old Youmans tune, where there's two notes, but the bass keeps changing and moving under the notes?" It seemed like another instance of mental radar, because, years before, Styne had the same idea and therefore was able to produce the melodic kernel immediately: back and forth between two notes, a tiny half-step apart—mesmerizing. Yet as with Vincent Youmans's "I Know That You Know," the incessant repetition seemed to resist lyrics.[11]

Styne knew he had a hit melody, and for three months the trio sang it at parties as "Da-Dee-Da"; it went over great, but where was the title? In frustration, Styne called Frank Loesser for help. Depending on the source, Loesser either invented the title or, alternately, merely offered some advice: "It has to have a rolling title." Comden recalled: "We came to a place where the leading male character feels that his life has been saved by the arrival of this curious girl, Judy Holliday." In this telling, Comden and Green invented the title phrase: "Suddenly it came to one of us—don't ask me which one—the right words for that situation and that character. And they fitted the melody Jule had been playing at parties: 'Just in Time.'"[12]

Comden and Green do keep the title "rolling," as Loesser advised. The music is structured AA′BA″, and in the first stanza the lyricists end three lines in a row with the word "time," letting it roll around again and again, like the spoke on a wheel. In the second stanza, with unostentatious craft, they shift their strategy: a sequence of three metaphors—rather complex—and a triple end-rhyme scheme of simple one-syllable words: *lost/tossed/crossed*.

In the release, Styne continues the Youmans-like pattern, and then breaks it with a few pairs of repeated notes that take the tune to its highest pitches. In the final stanza, Comden and Green encapsulate the happy turning point in the character's life: "You found me just in time / And changed my lonely life, that lovely day." The unobtrusive alliterative *l* sounds (*lonely, life, lovely*) and the emphasis on time and related upbeat ideas (*change, life, day*)—all these help to create a quiet cohesion.

It is easy to point to Comden and Green's skills with satire and comic situation, and *Bells Are Ringing* has its fill of such numbers. "It's a Perfect Relationship" outlines how the heroine, Ella (Judy Holliday), has fallen in love with the voice of one of the answering service's customers, Jeff, a blocked playwright. Over the phone, she gives him advice, pretending to be "Mom," a sympathetic old lady. Forbidden by the police to converse on personal matters with the clients, she resorts to seeing them in person. Pretending to be "Melisande Scott," she meets Jeff and rescues him from drink and despair. Near the end, when Ella realizes that she has never learned to be herself, she declares (in a *tour de force* showstopper) "I'm Going Back" to her former job (at the Bonjour Tristesse Brassiere Company—one of the show's big laughs). Both pieces were tailor-made for Judy Holliday's brilliant, mercurial shifts in style and mood, yet they have also nicely served the many women who later played Ella. Thus, the two numbers have become standard repertoire as senior recital pieces, audition songs, and cabaret applause-getters. Those are only two items in this gem-filled score.

Along with satire, Comden and Green also created less easily discernible threads running through their oeuvre. One is *time*, in all its wrinkles. Is there any other corpus that has so many titles that use that word? Look at "Some Other Time" (*On the Town*, 1944), "Bad Timing" (*Billion Dollar Baby*, 1954), or "Now's the Time" (*Hallelujah, Baby!*, 1967). Some of their scores even have two examples: the movie musical *It's Always Fair Weather* (1955) features both "The Time Has Come for Parting" and "Once Upon a Time," and the Broadway score for *Subways Are for Sleeping* (1961) has "I'm Just Taking My Time" and "Comes Once in a Lifetime." This topic stretches from their opening songs for *On the Town*, "I Feel Like I'm Not Out of Bed Yet" (as the new day starts, longing to be back asleep) and "New York, New York" (the urgency of having "just one day" to see New York while on leave) to *The Will Rogers Follies* (1991), their final Broadway score, with "Look Around" (which contrasts the natural beauties of the past with the ruined environment of the present). Add songs with titles like

"Everlasting" (*Two on the Aisle*, 1951), "Never Never Land" (*Peter Pan*, 1954), "Now!" (1963), and "Never" (*On the Twentieth Century*, 1979), and it becomes clear that Comden and Green's meditations on time form a topic ripe for some future doctoral thesis.

"Just in Time" fits nicely into Comden and Green's recurring concern with the passage of time. The recitative-like verse, seldom used (Carmen McRae does the best job with it), sets up the stakes: the protagonist faced hopeless failure. But, in the nick, she or he has been saved. Despite the simple, easy-going melody and straightforward, impeccably conversational lyrics, the song builds tremendous drama. As with Peggy Lee's "It's a Good Day," the shadows of the past lurk at the edges of this cheerful, tender, triumphant, grateful proclamation.

Tony Bennett owns "Just in Time," if anyone can be said to. He had the first hit single with it. Less than three years later, Bennett recorded "Just in Time" again, now with the Count Basie orchestra. In 2006, he returned to the song in duet with Michael Bublé, on the double-Platinum seller *Duets: An American Classic* album. As a single, that track was a charting Adult Contemporary hit too. As if that wasn't enough, in 2012, Bennett returned to "Just in Time" in duet with Juan Luis Guerra (who sings the lyric partly in Spanish) on yet another charting album, *Viva Duets*. To all renditions Bennett brings his charismatic mixture of drama and swing.

Indeed, the true home for "Just in Time" proved to be on albums, many of them charting, ranging from the 1956 original Broadway cast recording to the 2023 take by Rickie Lee Jones. The top purveyors of the Great American Songbook pounced on "Just in Time," clearly gleeful at having such a good, new, swinging song. Frank Sinatra swung it hard, helped by Billy May. Peggy Lee swung it delicately, helped by Nelson Riddle. Live, Ella Fitzgerald raced through it without losing her sense of fine detail. Jazz instrumentalists recorded it as often as vocalists, fully embracing Styne's melody and harmonies.[13]

Dean Martin owned "Just in Time" almost as fully as Tony Bennett, for not only did Martin render it on LP, slightly more slowly and sincerely than some of his peers, but he also played the hero of *Bells Are Ringing* for the 1960 movie version, starring opposite Judy Holliday. The crooner sings it even more tenderly on the soundtrack; and then the pace picks up to a soft-shoe tempo and the mood becomes lively and playful as Martin and Holliday romp through a comedy routine, before a return to intimacy at the number's end. The song's capacity to be a slow ballad is sometimes brought out even more fully: by Barbra Streisand, in 1964, in one of her most restrained performances of that era; and by Nina Simone, live in

1962, whose piano playing delivers one of the most profound variations on Styne's tune and whose intense vocal makes this story of salvation utterly believable.

In some ways, "Just in Time" perfectly captures the essence of Comden and Green. As Comden explained, "We try to help audiences feel the way they should when they leave the theater—that is, glad to be alive. The windows have been opened, fresh air has been let in, and they're . . . happy people."[14] Exactly like the protagonist of "Just in Time."

Betty Comden and Adolph Green's hits
1949: "The Right Girl for Me," music by Roger Edens
1951: "Everlasting," music by Jule Styne
1951: "Hold Me, Hold Me, Hold Me," music by Jule Styne
1953: "Ohio," music by Leonard Bernstein
1953: "It's Love," music by Leonard Bernstein
1953: "A Quiet Girl," music by Leonard Bernstein
1956: "Just in Time," music by Jule Styne
1956: "The Party's Over," music by Jule Styne
1956: "Long Before I Knew You," music by Jule Styne
1956: "Bells Are Ringing," music by Jule Styne
1958: "Dance Only with Me," music by Jule Styne
1958: "Say, Darling," music by Jule Styne
1958: "Something's Always Happening on the River," music by Jule Styne
1960: "Make Someone Happy," music by Jule Styne
1962: "Comes Once in a Lifetime," music by Jule Styne
1963: "Now!," adaptation by Jule Styne of "Hava Nagila"

Further performer favorites
1944: "New York, New York," music by Leonard Bernstein
1944: "Lonely Town," music by Leonard Bernstein
1944: "Lucky to Be Me," music by Leonard Bernstein
1944: "I Can Cook Too," lyrics cowritten by and music by Leonard Bernstein
1944: "Some Other Time," music by Leonard Bernstein
1951: "If You Hadn't, But You Did," music by Jule Styne
1953: "A Little Bit in Love," music by Leonard Bernstein
1953: "The Wrong Note Rag," music by Leonard Bernstein
1954: "Never Never Land," music by Jule Styne
1954: "Distant Melody," music by Jule Styne
1955: "Thanks a Lot, But No Thanks," music by Andre Previn

1956: "It's a Perfect Relationship," music by Jule Styne
1956: "I'm Going Back," music by Jule Styne
1967: "Being Good Isn't Good Enough," music by Jule Styne
1991: "No Man Left for Me," music by Cy Coleman

Some of the many neglected gems
1944: "I Feel Like I'm Not Out of Bed Yet," music by Leonard Bernstein; pretty, lazy, hazy
1949: "It's Fate, Baby, It's Fate," music by Roger Edens; slinky ballad disguised as comedy
1950: "You're Awful," music by Roger Edens; charm song, loving and ironical
1951: "Give a Little, Get a Little," music by Jule Styne; groovy melody, cheerful witty lyric
1951: "So Far, So Good," music by Jule Styne; charm song, realistic lyric
1955: "I Like Myself," music by Andre Previn; cheery rhythm ballad in classic style
1958: "Try to Love Me Just as I Am," music by Jule Styne; a topic simple but complex
1960: "Take a Job," music by Jule Styne; jazz solo melody, spot-on lyric
1960: "Cry Like the Wind," music by Jule Styne; spare lyric, folk-like lament
1964: "Call Me Savage," music by Jule Styne; comically boasting rhythm song
1967: "Talking to Yourself," music by Jule Styne; slow interior monologue
1967: "Watch My Dust," music by Jule Styne; galvanizing, lively boast
1978: "Our Private World," music by Cy Coleman; love ballad in two meters
1978: "Together" (Lily's solo in Sextette), music by Cy Coleman; poignant interior debate
1991: "My Unknown Someone," music by Cy Coleman; meandering but compelling ballad

18

"WITCHCRAFT" (1957)

Carolyn Leigh (1926–1983), lyricist

More than any of her peers, Carolyn Leigh flourished between 1955 and 1964 by writing popular songs for adults, at a time when rock-and-roll was mostly for teenagers. Betty Comden attracted Broadway theatergoers, Fran Landesman's most characteristic work was for hip connoisseurs, and Sylvia Dee addressed the mass audience. Carolyn Leigh, perhaps uniquely, was successful in all three modes. Leigh's stage musicals delighted packed audiences: *Peter Pan* (1954) and *Little Me* (1962) are revived again and again. With composer Cy Coleman, she wrote lyrics for sophisticated cabaret shows, such as "You Fascinate Me So," or for intimate singers like Blossom Dearie, such as "I Walk a Little Faster"; and these turned out to be among her most recorded creations. Simultaneously, Leigh and Coleman crafted works that bypassed Broadway and cabaret and shot straight to the pop charts, like "Firefly" for Tony Bennett and "Witchcraft" for Frank Sinatra.

Stephen Sondheim praised Carolyn Leigh as "the most brilliant technician" of her generation, combining the best of predecessors Cole Porter and Dorothy Fields.[1] Leigh's intricate rhymes always flow naturally with the music and supply an elated lift to the listener. Yet, ultimately, it is her complicated *esprit*—cynical, sweet, melancholy, exuberant—that gives her works depth.

Leigh proclaimed, "I can't write a song unless I feel it." She drew—and her younger sister, June Silver, still draws—many connections between her life and lyrics. Silver reflects, "I think every one of her songs had a little bit of 'I want' in it, her own desire"; indeed, "every single thing that happened to her related to some of her wording, some of her lyrics." Perhaps more than most, Leigh wrote many lines, and many songs, that act like bookmarks of her own biography and inner life.[2]

BIOGRAPHY

She was born in New York City, as Carolyn Paula Rosenthal, to Jewish parents. The young Carolyn tested as having an IQ of 140, that is, in the top 2 percent of the nation's brightest. Her parents, ill advisedly, then began to treat her like a grown-up. When she later wrote "I Won't Grow Up" for *Peter Pan*, it bore the weight of this remembered dilemma. That emotional depth has helped the lyric transcend its Broadway origins, taking its place on charting LPs in a hard-rocking version by the Fools (1980) and an easy-moving rendition by Rickie Lee Jones (1991).

At age sixteen, Leigh found herself unwed, with child—part of the wartime trend, the start of the sexual revolution. Leigh was rushed to the hospital: an ectopic pregnancy. Leigh survived, the baby did not; and she perhaps lost the ability to bear children. In 1967, Leigh would become the only Broadway writer of her generation to plot a musical built around a young woman's unmarried pregnancy, *How Now, Dow Jones*.

Leigh went on to graduate from Queens College and New York University. In 1947, seven weeks before turning twenty-one, she married Julius Levine. In 1959, she divorced Levine, but presumably she did not regret the interlude, for in that year she copyrighted the song "Marry Young."

Until 1951, the details of Leigh's career are hazy—including when and why she changed her last name to Leigh—but she seems to have been involved with radio scripting and advertising, presumably including jingle writing. The story goes that, one day in 1951, Leigh made a business call and, by mistake, dialed the number of Armo Music Publishing. The publisher said he needed writers and asked her to come for an interview; she did, and she left with a new job.

For various BMI firms—first Armo and Jay-Cee, later Sunbeam and others—Leigh copyrighted a couple dozen lyrics. Her third copyright was a hit: "I'm Just Waiting for You," set to a bluesy tune by famed African American songwriter and record producer Henry Glover. Not just a hit, it was a home run with bases loaded, with three 1951 discs in the charts for rhythm-and-blues (the Lucky Millinder Orchestra), pop (Rosemary Clooney), and country-western (Hawkshaw Hawkins). In 1957, Pat Boone revived it—and, again, it charted high. Leigh must have felt ambivalent about this simple, serviceable lyric, for she tended to ignore its existence in later interviews.

By her own estimation, Leigh wrote "over three hundred" songs—twenty-five of them being copyrighted—before she "finally hit" with "Young at Heart."[3] This charming, elegant piece was recorded by Frank Sinatra in December 1953 and belatedly copyrighted by Sunbeam in January 1954. Leigh was inspired by a visit to her father, in the hospital for his heart condition. (Rosenthal would die of a heart attack in late 1956, at age fifty-one, living long enough to witness Leigh's success.) She wrote the lyric to a pre-existing instrumental, the delicate "Moonbeam," by Johnny Richards (born Juan Cascales, he had been a child immigrant from Mexico and was best known for his angular, bop-influenced jazz arranging). "Young at Heart" sailed to the number one spot on *Your Hit Parade* and then got taken up by Hollywood as the title for Frank Sinatra's 1955 *noir* musical. What between Sinatra's original Capitol single, a movie soundtrack LP and EP, a rerecording for Reprise, and various compilation albums selling Gold or Platinum, the crooner's version keeps marching on. Many other singers have also made their mark with "Young at Heart." Jimmy Durante, gruff and buoyant, is notable for his 1963 charting album track, the flip of a hit single as well.

With "Young at Heart," Leigh came into her own. In it, she gives power to a fairly conventional positive life philosophy through bubbling triple and quadruple rhymes and unusual vocabulary: "And if you should *survive* to a hundred and *five*, / Think of all you'll *derive* out being *alive*!" What other lyric in this repertoire uses the word "derive"—and so naturally? Leigh was among those who could easily fit uncustomary vocabulary into the Tin Pan Alley genre; for example, "filled with dark *resentment*" ("The Chosen Few," 1956), "if *telepathy* serves me true" ("Say No More," 1965), and "the way you *effervesce* all over the place" ("Here's Looking at You," c. 1982).

Though it was not all smooth sailing for Leigh after the success of "Young at Heart"—she had to continue her share of hack work like operetta translations for television and writing jingles—she was on her way. Overall, in the first twenty-one years of her Tin Pan Alley life, she achieved eighteen hit singles and fourteen flips of hits and, come the LP era, seven new hits as album tracks. A number of other pieces became standards through repeated performances. She worked with over fifty composers, including three women (and she wrote a few melodies herself). Leigh achieved some degree of success with over twenty of those tunesmiths, yet her most valued contribution to the Great American Songbook remains her work with composer Cy Coleman.

In 1954, when Mary Martin and her husband, producer Richard Halliday, heard "Young at Heart" on the radio, Leigh's combination of skipping innocence and playful rhyming immediately convinced them that she was the right lyricist for their revision of *Peter Pan*. With composer Moose Charlap, she contributed favorites cherished by generations of audiences, including the exuberant plug tunes "I've Gotta Crow" and "I'm Flying." In 1954, too, Leigh began to transition from BMI to ASCAP. Further, she met perhaps the most influential person to her subsequent career, publisher Edwin H. "Buddy" Morris.

Twenty years older than Leigh, puckish-faced with an extropic left eye that wandered outward, Buddy Morris was well established on Tin Pan Alley. He had helped the Warner Bros. movie studio create a powerhouse conglomerate of music publishing imprints. Then, having started his own independent publishing company in 1941, he sued his old bosses for the monopolistic situation he himself had created! Most importantly, he made it his task to nurture young writers, guiding them into Broadway careers; for example, in the 1940s, Jule Styne and Sammy Cahn, and in the 1950s and 1960s, Jerry Herman, Charles Strouse, and Lee Adams. None expressed as much gratitude as Carolyn Leigh, perhaps because it was rare for a male to boost a woman songwriter with such faith. She extolled, "My publisher is a wonderful person and has treated me almost too well. Actually, I believe I could count on a sizable yearly income without ever writing another word. This is nice to know."[4]

To thank Buddy Morris for his support, Leigh wrote "It Amazes Me" (1958): "It simply amazes me, / What he sees in me, dazzles me, dazes me." When she and Coleman were creating the Broadway score for *Wildcat* (1960), they wrote the first half of "Hey, Look Me Over" and gave the publisher a preview. He teased, "I guarantee you I will break every contract I have with you and I will not publish that score unless you put that song in it." Leigh thought, "Since I think Buddy Morris is the greatest man I know at this stage of my life, why don't I just use his name for good luck?"[5] Therefore she put him into the song: "Up like a rosebud, high on the vine, / Don't thumb your nose, Bud, take a tip from mine." However grateful Jerry Herman or Lee Adams might have been to Morris, Leigh is the only wordsmith to pay him such lyrical tributes.

After collaborating together (though not always exclusively) since 1956, Leigh and Cy Coleman decided to break up at the end of 1962, after the traumas of getting *Little Me* to Broadway. She recalled, "We came away from that not speaking to one another and with a music publisher [Buddy Morris] in tears. He built an office for us and the day he wanted to show us the office, we had split up."[6] In one way, Leigh and Coleman were just one of several pairs trying to extend the Tin Pan Alley tradition into the era of the LP and rock-and-roll by writing sophisticated songs for singers like Sinatra, Bennett, Dearie, and Peggy Lee. They had peers: Jack Segal and Marvin Fisher (brother of Doris Fisher) who wrote "When Sunny Gets Blue"; Stanley Styne and Donald Kahn (son of Grace LeBoy) who wrote "(This Is the End of) A Beautiful Friendship," and others. Of that cohort, though, Leigh and Coleman were perhaps the most successful. The impact of their breakup after a swift six years of high productivity is still felt among aficionados. It's as if Richard Rodgers and Lorenz Hart had broken up at the end of 1925, after only a few Broadway shows.

Leigh's personality was as vivid and troubled as those of Lorenz Hart, Dorothy Parker, and Billie Holiday; and though she is less well documented, various interviews, essays, and the memories of those who knew her offer glimpses. Leigh was "complex," full of contradictions. June Silver recalls how her sister was "very emotional" with "really big emotional problems" and "always in a state of apprehension." Leigh would repeat and repeat, "I don't know what's going to happen." Yet "she was *fun*." Leigh wore thick glasses (nearsighted) and, physically, was tall and hefty; her heart attack at age fifty-seven was partly attributed to "gross obesity." She fought often—"legendary fights"—with Coleman, who called her "tough." She was blunt to the point of insulting and drew the same behavior from him. They split up rather than keep "snarling" at each other. Yet they remained good friends, repeatedly returned to their collaboration, and, as Silver remembers, "they had fun together—when they were talking to each other." Similarly, her final composer, Jule Styne, growled, "She was doing women's lib before there was any women's lib," and reports that "they had a lot of great arguments and bust-ups and clenched-teeth showbiz showdowns." Nevertheless, in the end, she and Styne and Coleman gathered to play poker every Wednesday, good chums. Silver reports that "despite the fights she had in the industry," she "was well loved" by her collaborators.[7]

Deborah Grace Winer describes Leigh's lyrics as "hip, sexy, and optimistic." Ironically, Leigh wrote her hip lyrics despite seeing herself as "something of a square." Silver says that Leigh "was old-fashioned in a lot of ways," including about nonmarital sex, though admittedly she lived a contradiction: "She was a very traditional person in a very untraditional role"—a go-getter career woman who rose to the top echelon of Tin Pan Alley and Broadway. Leigh wrote some of the most buoyant, rousing songs in the Great American Songbook. Yet Silver also reports, "I think most of the time she was depressed. So much of her inside *wanted* to be happy, and so the exuberance; it always came out in a happy way."[8]

Most tellingly, Silver remembers her sister as "anxious about things that were minute, were minutiae," on a level beyond the norm. This created stress in Leigh's personal life; in her craft, it made her lyrics perfectly shaped and intricate. To some listeners, her complex rhyming is what makes her songs worthwhile, delightful, deep, and uplifting. To others, Leigh overrhymes, leaving them saying, "Oh, no, here comes another one." Compare the ends of the following two ballads about youthful romantic commitment, with Leigh's rhymes italicized:

Sylvia Dee's "Too Young"
And then someday they may recall,
We were not too young at all.

Leigh's "Marry Young"
Let it *slip* off the *tip* of your *tongue*,
"I love *you*, you love *me*, people *do*, why can't *we* marry *young*?"

Or compare the opening lines of the following two waltzes on the topic of wanderlust:

Joan Whitney and Alex Kramer's "Far Away Places"
Far away places, with strange sounding names,
Far away over the sea.

Leigh's "Stowaway"
I'd like to *go away*, be a *stowaway*,
Take a *trip*, on a *ship*, let my worries *blow away*.

That last quoted line is very typical of Leigh: a quick rhyming pair (or, often, three or four rhyme mates) followed sometimes by a trailing syllable or two (like Hart and Fields), more often three syllables, or occasionally (as in "Stowaway") so many syllables that it creates its own phase. Through this recurring technique, she creates a magical spring and sparkle all her own, albeit at the risk of overwhelming the listener's ear.

Leigh can be both compared and contrasted to Fran Landesman. Both were technically brilliant, bittersweet, and cutting-edge in dealing with sexual matters. But Landesman's characters usually want to "drop out" of the status quo; Leigh's protagonists usually want to join it. Further, although both have been described as "hip," Landesman was more "cool" (in the slang sense). Compare Landesman's "Spring Can Really Hang You

Up the Most" to Leigh's "Spring in Maine." Both deal with the melancholy of springtime when love has been lost. But for Landesman, spring without love is "a bore." For Leigh, spring without love brings "pain." For Leigh, life may be painful but is *never* a bore.

Leigh developed her characteristic themes over the course of her first eight years or so on Tin Pan Alley. She wrote a modicum of 1950s standard fare—lyrics for teens, calypsos, country-western tunes, ballads of all kinds (rhythm-and-blues, bleating pop, neo-simple sentimental pieces). She crystallized her rhyme-intensive technique with "Young at Heart" (1953). In that hit, too, she developed a flair for uplift. This mode fed into her string of assertive, affirmative lyrics from "I've Gotta Crow" (1954), through "Hey, Look Me Over" (1960), to "Myrtle's Parade" (c. 1970). About 1956, Leigh began tapping a bittersweet strain that saturates some of her best ballads, like "Spring in Maine" (1957) and "On Second Thought" (1961).

Most of all, starting in 1952, Leigh begins to produce titles on the topic of sexual eagerness, anticipation, and desire—the theme for which she is most celebrated. That these were created by a woman, and often sung by women, marked one step in advancing sexual freedom. Examples were many, including "Come Here, You" (1952), "I Want My Love Right Now" (1955), "You Bring Out the Lover in Me" (1955), "The Call of the Wild" (1956), "The Best Is Yet to Come" (1959), and so on. The most famous of these is "Witchcraft."

"WITCHCRAFT"

Before the Brill Building became the symbol of teen music of the late 1950s and early 1960s, it was already the home for many well-established Tin Pan Alley firms. It was in the Brill Building that Leigh ran into Cy Coleman. Some versions of the story make it in the corridor, some the elevator, some the bar on a lower floor. It was a typical Brill Building encounter, leading to an immediate songwriting session.

Cy Coleman was a thriving jazz pianist who wrote one song, had a hit, and was thereby encouraged to keep on writing songs. (Another Jewish American from New York City, he Anglicized his birth name of Seymour Kaufman.) Though his piano style was modern jazz, Coleman managed to write singable, danceable melodies for Tin Pan Alley and Broadway in a range of styles beyond the scope of many of his jazz peers. He was always afraid his songwriting and show writing would eclipse his jazz performing—this was one of the conflicts he had with Leigh, who wanted to keep writing songs all the time.

In later years, Coleman used "Witchcraft" as an example of how lyricists inspired new ideas from him. Along with "Hey, Look Me Over," it was a song "helped into life by a like-minded words person." Leigh reminisced: "I did have an idea I was dying to do with Cy. I told him about it and that it was called 'Witchcraft.' My feeling was that we shouldn't do a typical AABA song because it seemed to me it would take away the excitement and meaning of the word, *witchcraft*." For this lyric about irresistible sexual attraction, Leigh wanted "a new form, . . . a totally different construction." Coleman came up with a preliminary tune, "very exotic." Leigh, however, knew he could do better. At a work session, Coleman recalled, "We were playing around, and I came around with another opening strain, and she said, 'That's Witchcraft!'" Leigh recognized that the new tune had the "excitement" she was looking for.[9]

The first section of "Witchcraft" is built on a six-note riff, repeated three times. Here, Leigh ends each line with a single syllable rhyme: *hair/stare/bare*. The second section takes that riff up a third and extends it by two notes. These added notes allow Leigh to change to her characteristic multisyllable rhymes: *defense for it/intense for it/sense for it*. The third section emphatically leaps up octaves, then builds to the melody's highest note. Then comes a new melody, a slithering eight-note pattern sequenced downward twice; this creates the opportunity for another of Leigh's multisyllable triple-rhyme schemes. And back to the first riff, with another high note, just before the end, to round it off.

The structure becomes, therefore, AA´BCA˝. Richard Rodgers took Cy Coleman out to lunch just to congratulate him on its originality. The Broadway patriarch wouldn't have realized that it was lyricist Leigh whose vision drove the song's creation and form.

The songwriters cut a demo record and sent it to Voyle Gilmore to play for Frank Sinatra. The singer, busy with the filming of *Pal Joey*, challenged Gilmore to choose just one song out of a huge stack of demos. When Gilmore spun the "Witchcraft" disc, Sinatra's music manager Hank Sanicola shook his head, "No." But Sinatra insisted, "This is the song I want to record."[10] Nelson Riddle supplied one of his classic arrangements, and Sinatra spent two and a half hours in the studio fine-tuning his vocal. Result: an easy-swinging, dramatically building, sensual and seductive track that climbed into the top ten in the United States and top twenty in the United Kingdom. The song itself graced *Your Hit Parade* in its last months of existence, supplying a fitting bookend to match the first *Your Hit Parade* broadcast, way back in 1935, which featured "I Won't Dance" by Dorothy Fields, another lyric about resisting (or not) temptation.

Leigh creates protagonists who are simultaneously seduced and seducing. In her lyrics about desire, she often refers to how conventional morality keeps sexual urges in check. To offer just one of many instances, in "You Bring Out the Lover in Me," the singer states, "Me of all people, morally strong, / Throwing the fight, saying it's right, right to go wrong!" In "Witchcraft," the protagonist sings about "common sense," "conscience," and a "wicked" "taboo." But the attraction, the impulses, are so strong that they override all repressions—that's what makes Leigh's songs so sexy. At the same time, the supposed anxiety concerning intimate pleasures is also a playful game. The music, the rhyme schemes—everything indicates the singer's zestful anticipation.

If these songs draw on Leigh's own life, those experiences remain veiled. It was while developing this part of her art that she divorced her first husband and married, in December 1959, her second—a lawyer who, her sister remembers, was Carolyn's "true love." Perhaps these songs grew out of their courtship. (After ten years, they got a divorce—it seemed everybody was, in the early 1970s. As for Leigh's third husband, she wed him on a whim, because she liked his name, then had the marriage annulled within six weeks.)

Leigh was bold and deliberate in what she was doing. She quipped, "I always tried to go as far as I could go. I always knew when my mother's friends wouldn't talk to me I went too far."[11] In "Witchcraft," her protagonist talks about "when you arouse the need in me," stretching the boundaries of what was then permissible in pop song lyrics. But Leigh had her finger exactly on the pulse of the times. The two Kinsey Reports had been published with revelations about sexuality in men (1948) and women (1953). Marilyn Monroe and Elvis Presley brought new images of sensuality into the center of popular culture. In 1957, when Leigh wrote "Witchcraft," several of the top-grossing movies featured characters involved with premarital, nonmarital, and extramarital sex; pregnancies out of wedlock; even incest and rape. *Playboy* magazine had started publishing four years before; within a couple of years, *Playboy's Penthouse* variety television show would feature Cy Coleman playing and singing "Witchcraft." For this series, Coleman was chosen to compose "Playboy's Theme," issued as a single on the Playboy record label—and who would write the lyric for it? Carolyn Leigh, of course, using her typical interlocking multisyllable rhymes to praise the playboy's canny wife, who "when he plays it *indiscreetly*, / Never takes the *play completely away*." Leigh manages to express a male-dominant viewpoint while also subtly undercutting it with descriptions of the male as undiscerning, gullible, and "ornery."

"Witchcraft" flourished not just in Sinatra's single but also as a favored album track.[12] Notable are its swinging renditions by Rosemary Clooney (who, clearly feeling "witch" was a gendered term, alters the lyrics at a couple of points) as well as Chris Connor and Sarah Vaughn (neither of whom feel a need to change the words). Ella Fitzgerald, caught live on more than one occasion, liked to start with the short but clever verse. Matinee idols of the early 1960s—the Playboy era—happily borrowed its potential for macho swagger; for instance, George Maharis (1962), George Chakiris (1963), and Robert Horton (1964). In 1963, Sinatra himself rerecorded it for his Reprise label. His two renditions featured on plenty of Gold- and Platinum-selling albums; and when he placed "Witchcraft" on his 1993 *Duets* set, with his aged voice paired with Anita Baker's crystal clear tones, it went triple Platinum.

A few performers break away from the swinging approach. In 1960, Mark Murphy stretched out the tune as a medium slow, behind-the-beat hipster piece. In the 2010s, Europeans like Tommy Andersen and Vian Izak reconceived it in super-slow tempo, conveying the spacey haziness of being enchanted.

Twenty-six years after Sinatra recorded "Witchcraft," Leigh wrote her last song, created with Jule Styne as they waited for Cy Coleman to join them for poker: "Killing Time," a reflection of her frustration with years of writing unproduced musicals for Broadway. Her sister reflects, "Somehow, she sensed she was not going to live—so she was killing time." Leigh died suddenly of a heart attack on November 19, 1983. Twenty-one years later, Coleman died, equally unexpectedly, just before midnight, mere minutes before the anniversary of Leigh's passing. Leigh and Coleman were linked in death as they had been in life.

Carolyn Leigh's hits
* *The asterisk indicates mainly popular in an instrumental version.*

Songs that made their mark with charting singles
1951: "I'm Waiting Just for You," music by Henry Glover
1953: "Young at Heart," music by Johnny Richards
1954: "Stowaway," music by Jerry Livingston
1955: "My Son John," music by Sammy Fain
1956: "(How Little It Matters) How Little We Know," music by Philip Springer
1957: "Swinging Sweethearts," music by Ron Goodwin*
1957: "Spring in Maine," music by Steve Allen

1957: "My, How the Time Goes By," music by Cy Coleman
1957: "Witchcraft," music by Cy Coleman
1958: "Firefly," music by Cy Coleman
1958/1963: "A Doodlin' Song (Doop Doo-De-Oop)," music by Cy Coleman
1960: "Hey, Look Me Over," music by Cy Coleman
1960: "Tall Hope," music by Cy Coleman
1962/1965: "Real Live Girl," music by Cy Coleman
1963: "Stay with Me," music by Jerome Moross
1964: "Pass Me By," music by Cy Coleman
1965/1967: "Afterthoughts," music by Gene De Paul
1967: "Step to the Rear," music by Elmer Bernstein
1967: "Walk Away," music by Elmer Bernstein

Some songs that made their mark on charting albums
1954: "I Won't Grow Up," music by Moose Charlap
1954: "First Impression," music by Moose Charlap
1958: "It Amazes Me," music by Cy Coleman
1958: "I Walk a Little Faster," music by Cy Coleman
1959: "Marry Young," music by Cy Coleman
1959: "The Best Is Yet to Come," music by Cy Coleman
1961: "The Rules of the Road," music by Cy Coleman
1962: "I've Got Your Number," music by Cy Coleman
1964: "When in Rome (I Do as the Romans Do)," music by Cy Coleman

Other standards and performer favorites
1954: "I'm Flying," music by Moose Charlap
1958: "You Fascinate Me So," music by Cy Coleman
1961: "On Second Thought," music by Cy Coleman
1962: "On the Other Side of the Tracks," music by Cy Coleman
1962: "Here's to Us," music by Cy Coleman
1983: "Killing Time," music by Jule Styne

Some of the many neglected gems
1955: "(Let's Get to) The Main Event," lyrics and music with Bill Sawens and Harold L. Grant; mambo rhythm, courtship as boxing match
1956: "You Bring Out the Lover in Me," music by Philip Springer; suggestive swinger
1957: "(It's) Too Good to Talk About Now," music by Cy Coleman; playful charm song

1960: "Give a Little Whistle," music by Cy Coleman; funny, cheery good-bye song

1963: "Bad for Each Other," music by Harold Arlen; low-down, witty, ambiguous

1965: "Loved One," music by Jack Segal; tender, ambiguous waltz

1965: "Say No More," music by Lee Pockriss; sexy rhythm ballad

1967: "Where You Are," music by Elmer Bernstein; restless song of irresistible attraction

1967: "Touch and Go," music by Elmer Bernstein; realistically ambivalent rhythm song

1970: "Come Summer," music by Cy Coleman; love's aftermath—jaunty, angry, or sad?

circa 1970: "Myrtle's Parade," music by Lee Pockriss; affirmative, defiant march

circa 1970: "Wish Me," music by Lee Pockriss; challenging waltz of agonized midlife angst

circa 1972: "Walk on Air," music by Lee Pockriss; affirmative, soaring charm song

19

"NICE 'N' EASY" (1960)

Marilyn Keith Bergman (1928–2022), lyricist

Like Grace LeBoy in the 1910s and Joan Whitney in the 1940s, in the 1950s Marilyn Keith married her writing partner, Alan Bergman. Together, Marilyn and Alan helped to craft a new pop tradition. From the late 1960s into the mid-1990s, the Bergmans created songs that thrived on charting albums as well as the Easy Listening and Adult Contemporary charts. These smooth-flowing, often abstractly poetic songs created a much-needed oasis for ballad singers, some of whom had matured during the Tin Pan Alley era. Many of these numbers were movie theme songs, often title songs. Quintessential examples include their two most recorded songs: "The Windmills of Your Mind" from *The Thomas Crown Affair* (1968) and "The Way We Were" introduced by Barbra Streisand in her 1973 starring vehicle of the same name. The Bergmans and Streisand became as close as family, working together many times over several decades; and the singer proved to be the perfect "voice" for their lyrics.

Before that, throughout the 1950s and early 1960s, Marilyn Keith and Alan Bergman were busy scripting and producing as well as creating, amid their many songs, a scattering of hits of moderate proportions and a failed Broadway score in 1964. But it was not until 1967, when Marilyn was thirty-eight and Alan forty-two, that they truly hit their stride with a title song for an Oscar-winning movie, "In the Heat of the Night," a charting disc for Ray Charles. For the next three decades and more, they enjoyed the kind of success that Keith's female predecessors could only have dreamed of:

steady movie assignments; TV theme songs; a parade of Gold records, Platinum records, and double- and triple-Platinum records; and awards (among the many were three Oscars, four Emmys, and two Grammys)—plus, for Marilyn, being the first woman on ASCAP's board and, for fifteen years, its president, guiding ASCAP into the digital age.

Each in their own way, Sylvia Dee, Annie Ross, Fran Landesman, and the Bergmans worked to find and develop a post–Tin Pan Alley style, from which the influence of ragtime, early jazz, and Swing Era jazz weakened and often disappeared. (In that same era, their peers were doing similarly, such as Stephen Sondheim and the team of Hal David and Burt Bacharach.) Before that happened, however, Marilyn Bergman, as Marilyn Keith, contributed to the final glory years of the Great American Songbook with numbers for top singers like Peggy Lee and Frank Sinatra, especially "Nice 'n' Easy." Although Marilyn Keith's later career as Marilyn Bergman is

Figure 19.1   Marilyn Keith Bergman, as so often, in Washington, DC, the seat of the nation's power, with her colyricist (and husband) Alan Bergman, 2002. (John Mathew Smith and www.celebrity-photos.com, from Laurel, Maryland, USA, Creative commons BY-ShareAlike 2.0, https://creativecommons.org/licenses/by-sa/2.0, via Wikimedia Commons.)

thoroughly narrated through many profiles, interviews, and obituaries, little has been written about her early years on Tin Pan Alley.

BIOGRAPHY

At a New York City performing arts high school, Marilyn studied piano and, in the afternoons, went over to the home of Bob Russell ("Taboo") to play for him while he wrote lyrics. At an undetermined point, she changed her last name from Katz to the less Jewish-sounding Keith. While going to college, she slipped on wet stairs and broke both shoulders. She traveled across the nation to be taken care of by her parents; they had moved to Los Angeles—as had Bob Russell. During her recovery, Russell encouraged her to try writing lyrics by speaking them into a tape recorder (as in figure 7.1).

In January 1952, Bob Russell had copyrighted a song with composer Lew Spence; by the end of December 1952, so had Marilyn Keith. Her first copyright had the luck to be quickly recorded by Barbara Ruick, on the MGM label, and Peggy Lee at Capitol (although the label held back release for more than a year): "That's Him Over There." A top-flight lyric snugly fitted to a serviceable tune, this first Keith work established her ability, with economy and craft, to transport the listener into a dramatic scenario— unexpectedly encountering an ex-sweetheart: "I see a face in this room full of faces / I'm trying hard not to stare."

Four copyrights in 1953 followed, one with Helen Lawson, three with Spence. Of the latter, a country tune, "Restless Heart," was taken up by the venerable Shapiro, Bernstein firm. The disc by Slim Whitman was listed as "coming up in the trade" for an impressive ten weeks.

Keith had no copyrights in 1954—with no hint of why—but in 1955 she made two important connections. First, in August, she began register- ing her collaborations with choral leader and composer Norman Luboff. Together they wrote the television theme song for *The Adventures of Champion* (1956), which only ran for a season in the United States but for forty years was rerun uncounted times in England. There, the series name was changed to match the Keith-Luboff song, "Champion, the Wonder Horse," which had also received a rousing disk rendition by Frankie Laine.

Also in 1955, Keith connected up with Alan Bergman, a television pro- ducer who had turned his occasional songwriting (lyrics and, sometimes, melodies) into his main occupation on the advice of Johnny Mercer. By early December 1955, Keith, Bergman, and Lew Spence were registering copyrights as a collaborative trio. (In later life, the pair stated they met in

1956, but this copyright date indicates it was the autumn of 1955.) Decades later, Alan and Marilyn would recall that Spence was collaborating with Bergman in the mornings and Keith in the afternoons, and so the composer suggested the two lyricists work together. The pair also remembered first meeting at a party at Spence's house. The two lyricists had a lot in common: two nice Jewish "kids" (Frank Sinatra would always call them "the kids") from Brooklyn (they had been born in the same hospital) transplanted to Los Angeles, struggling in the pop song industry.

Keith, Bergman, and Spence—together, apart, and in various combinations—labored for years on piecework, typical of life in the music business. Marilyn and Alan adapted the novel *Hans Brinker* into a one-act musical for *Ice Capades of 1957*; they created special material for club acts; they wrote for the booming children's records market; and they gave English lyrics to tunes from around the world. They enjoyed some prominent plugs. Bergman and Spence won a disc by Fred Astaire of "That Face"—not a charting item but in the long run a respected semistandard.

Keith created a lyric to match the title of a best-selling novel *King of Paris*. Set to a sweeping waltz melody by its conductor Paul Weston, sung by his wife Jo Stafford, chorus led by Norman Luboff, "King of Paris" was a kind of family affair. Promotional copies of the novel and the record were sent out to disc jockeys around the nation; regionally it reached some of their top ten playlists, and its flip was also charted as a success.

In 1958, Marilyn and Alan married. Also, the Keith-Bergman-Spence trio landed a plug with Frank Sinatra, the flip of his hit "Mr. Success." To match the singer's style, they took Sinatra's closing phrase from his broadcasts, "Sleep Warm." Frank Sinatra then conducted the accompaniment for Dean Martin as the latter rendered it on his concept album of sleepy-time songs, *Sleep Warm* (1959).

"Yellow Bird," English lyrics to a Caribbean tune, landed on Norman Luboff's 1957 charting album, *Calypso Holiday*. In 1959, the Mills Brothers enjoyed a hit single of the piece, followed by ones in 1961 from the groups led by Arthur Lyman and Lawrence Welk. Also in 1961, "Yellow Bird" entered the sheet music best-seller lists for more than two months; despite the dominance of records, this was still a prize goal. Marilyn and Alan valued "Yellow Bird" as their first real hit song, after many years of slogging through the mills of Tin Pan Alley.

Although from 1958 onward, Keith wrote almost exclusively with Bergman, she continued to send in a few solo efforts for copyright through 1961. She started to call herself Marilyn Bergman on the registrations with their 1964 Broadway score, *Something More!* Her final copyright as Marilyn

Keith was in 1966. In 1967, with the establishment of the pair's glory years, she became consistent in using Marilyn Bergman as her professional name.

The Bergmans were happy to be interviewed about their professional life but kept quiet about their personal life. There are no *Billboard* notices about their marriage or the birth of their daughter (who grew up to be movie producer Julie Bergman Sender). To an extent, this applied to their creative life as well. Marilyn related that "our process is very private," even with a trusted composer: "We find that we whisper to each other, it's very strange. Usually we take the melody and go away." Though they could write lyrics first, or supply titles first, they would "always prefer the melody first."[1]

The spouses managed to work together, Marilyn said, "the way porcupines make love—carefully." The key elements were compromise ("we'll let it go for the moment, come back to it the next day and look for a third way to do it"), professionalism ("not to have fallen so in love with what you have written that you can't find a better way"), and "respect, trust—all of that," which, Marilyn claimed, "is necessary in a writing partnership or a business partnership or in a marriage." Further, "We're thinking separately when we're not together, so we'll bring something different into the room when we get together to work."

As with Dorothy Fields, Marilyn emphasized that "just sitting and getting the idea" was the central task, thereafter applying their "craft or skill." They always worked to serve the character—of the movie, play, or singer—and getting a successful independent song was just a byproduct. When without an assignment, Alan recalled, they would practice by taking stories from any source and create "songs based on the characters or situations." Once the idea was in place, Marilyn emphasized, "when we write, we *sing*." In the end, the exchange was so intimate they could never remember who wrote what.

"NICE 'N' EASY"

In 1960, a call went out for a tune for the upcoming Frank Sinatra album, planned as a collection of love ballads from his 1940s repertoire. With Nelson Riddle's fresh arrangements, strings sprinkled with jazz solos, the LP would be the perfect backdrop for courtship. Keith, Bergman, and Spence were among the many who submitted numbers. The trio realized that the musical approach of the album could also describe an approach to romance, "Nice 'n' Easy." Brilliant; but when Spence demonstrated the tune to Sinatra, the crooner picked it up "with the tips of his fingernails and let it fall to the ground like so much garbage." Luckily, Hank Sanicola (perhaps having learned his lesson after rejecting "Witchcraft") slyly kept playing the tune while Sinatra was around. Finally, the singer asked about "that cute little thing," and Sanicola let the forgetful singer assume that he had already approved it.[2] Not only was it chosen as the LP's title song, but it was issued as a single as well. This procedure was unprecedented in Sinatra's history of concept albums, although it became standard practice in the industry during the next ten years.

Lew Spence's melody has the form of AA´BA´´ plus an extension that is not quite a C-segment. Similarly to Jule Styne's "Just in Time," it focuses on chromatic half-steps; and subtle syncopations create an irresistible momentum. The tune moves gently yet sinuously, and Keith and Bergman match every slinky curve. As David Jenness and Don Velsey opine about the Bergmans, "in the songs with Spence, the writers are perfectly matched, as if they had found just the partners they needed."[3] "Nice 'n' Easy" combines the sexy implications of Carolyn Leigh's "Witchcraft" with the charm of Comden and Green's "Just in Time," and, like those numbers, this song also builds dramatically. Fittingly for a song about prolonging pleasure, the song climaxes twice: during the release, and then in the extension of the final A-section. With the upward thrusting penultimate line, the writers create an adrenaline surge with the words, "To rush would be a crime!" And then with great skill they gently put on the brakes to resolve the entire song with a relaxed, "'Cause nice 'n' easy does it, every time."

The lyric is explicit about the beginning of romance and falling in love, but it is also easy to interpret it as being about kissing and caressing or, indeed, having sex. As Jenness and Velsey state, the lyric is "amusingly suggestive . . . sexy and insinuating."[4] When recording the tune, Sinatra experimented with a spoken tag to end the track. In the issued take, he says, "Like the man said, one more time"; this could easily refer to the music, for the band and singer then repeat the final lyric. In the alternate take, however, Sinatra manifests more fully the sexual possibilities, concluding, "Isn't that better, baby?" This version was only issued many decades later, in a time of more sexual frankness—an era that "Nice 'n' Easy," as well as "Witchcraft," helped to anticipate.

The words and melody combine to create a picture of reassurance and confidence. Yet each singer and listener is left to decide the reasons for this urging to take things slowly, and shadings of anxiety or bossiness are an option. Seen most positively, the song expresses a happy philosophy: a wish to savor every moment of life, especially the beautiful experiences of falling in love and physical intimacy.

The *Nice 'n' Easy* album was among Sinatra's most successful, and the "Nice 'n' Easy" single being a hit was a bonus (although its sales were not record breaking). The tune also proved to have tremendous "legs": from the up-tempo "go-go" instrumental version by the Si Zentner Orchestra in 1962 to the slow and tender vocal by Barbra Streisand in 2011, various album tracks and singles of the song charted for many decades. Further, Frank Sinatra kept the song in his repertoire throughout the rest of his career. His daughter, Nancy Sinatra, also recorded it (as the flip of her hit single "Happy"). The family tradition continued when Michael Sinatra, the son of Frank Sinatra Jr., recorded his version of "Nice 'n' Easy" in the early twenty-first century.

Frank Sinatra can't be topped in his mixture of graininess and smoothness, swagger and vulnerability, swing and lyricism. His lightly swinging groove on "Nice 'n' Easy" set the mold for many others, internationally—for example, Michael Bublé's 2004 live recording, widely popular from Australia to the Netherlands. Peggy Lee quickly realized the song also suited her persona. Within the space of ten months, she did it twice on the *Ed Sullivan Show*: the first time, swing style (in a medley with Bernice Petkere's "Close Your Eyes," another song of comforting sensuality), the second time, with a Latin beat. Both Lee and Sinatra were under contract to the Capitol label; the company probably prevented her from recording her version and thereby cutting into his sales. Finally, in 1966, Lee was allowed to issue her Latin version on an album, spurring her to more live performances. She returned to "Nice 'n' Easy" yet again in 1992 concerts. In all her renditions, Lee demonstrates that a woman's cheerful confidence is as sexy as a man's.

In 1964, Charlie Rich recorded "Nice 'n' Easy" for the Groove label, with a single that was successful in his home area of Memphis and bubbled under the charts nationally. Rich skillfully blends blue-eyed soul with country twang; the accompaniment is pure Nashville sound. His medium tempo version gets pretty funky, with prominent percussion, blasts of brass, and a women's chorus blissfully interjecting "Ah" before singing in counterpoint to a men's chorus. Many aspects of Rich's conception and phrasing were imitated by Frankie Randall in his 1967 "Nice 'n' Easy" single that briefly passed through the Adult Contemporary chart. Rich himself then used much the same arrangement when he rerecorded "Nice 'n' Easy" for the Epic label in 1970, and this time he won the hit single, on the Country charts, that he deserved. The track simultaneously appeared on his signature charting album, *Boss Man*. Transferring to RCA-Victor, Rich again issued "Nice 'n' Easy," same arrangement, and it was on both a single and another best-selling LP. Compilation albums of Rich's signature songs were prominent on the Country charts in 1974, 1977, and 1978, all with the Keith-Bergman-Spence tune on it. Indeed, in the 1970s Charlie Rich pretty much owned "Nice 'n' Easy," another demonstration of the versatility of the Tin Pan Alley style.

Along with being ASCAP's president, Marilyn Bergman cofounded the Hollywood Political Women's Committee; wrote (with Alan) the opening for Clinton's inauguration festival; and, at the request of Vice President Al Gore, was appointed to be part of the US government's council for information infrastructure. Thereby, she became the only creative artist helping to set national policies at the start of the twenty-first century. Ironically, her influential political status was initially built on a foundation of modest, swingy songs like "Nice 'n' Easy." Thankfully, her early works endure and carry into the future the taste of that golden era.

Marilyn Keith Bergman and Alan Bergman's hits
* An asterisk indicates lyrics by Marilyn Keith alone.

Songs that made their mark with charting singles
1955: "Restless Heart," music by Lew Spence*
1957: "King of Paris," music by Paul Weston*
1957/1959: "Yellow Bird," traditional, adapted Michel Mauleart, further adapted Norman Luboff
1960: "Nice 'n' Easy," music by Lew Spence
1960: "Ol' MacDonald," traditional music adapted by Lew Spence
1961: "Sentimental Baby," music by Lew Spence
1967: "I Believed It All," music by Al Ham
1967: "In the Heat of the Night," music by Quincy Jones
1968: "The Windmills of Your Mind," music by Michel Legrand
1969: "What Are You Doing the Rest of Your Life?," music by Michel Legrand
1970: "Pieces of Dreams (Little Boy Lost)," music by Michel Legrand
1970: "Sweet Gingerbread Man," music by Michel Legrand
1971: "Theme from *Summer of '42* (The Summer Knows)," music by Michel Legrand
1972: "Brian's Song," music by Michel Legrand
1973: "The Way We Were," music by Marvin Hamlisch
1976: "I Believe in Love," music by Kenny Loggins
1977: "You Don't Bring Me Flowers," music by Neil Diamond
1982: "It Might Be You," music by Dave Grusin

1982: "How Do You Keep the Music Playing," music by Michel Legrand
1984: "The Way He Makes Me Feel," music by Michel Legrand
1984: "Papa, Can You Hear Me," music by Michel Legrand

Some songs that made their mark on charting albums
1967: "Make Me Rainbows," music by John Williams
1968: "So Many Stars," music by Sérgio Mendes
1968: "Like a Lover," original lyrics by Nelson Motta, music by Dori Caymmi
1968: "His Eyes, Her Eyes," music by Michel Legrand
1971: "I Was Born in Love with You," music by Michel Legrand
1972: "Summer Me, Winter Me," music by Michel Legrand
1974: "You Must Believe in Spring," French lyrics by Jacques Demy, music by Michel Legrand
1975: "Christmas Memories (Christmas Mem'ries)," music by Don Costa
1979: "The Promise (I'll Never Say Goodbye)," music by David Shire
1980: "What Matters Most," music by Dave Grusin
1981: "The Island," Portuguese lyrics by Vitor Martins, music by Ivan Lins
1982: "Someone in the Dark," music by Rod Temperton
1983: "A Piece of Sky," music by Michel Legrand
1984: "L.A. Is My Lady," music by Quincy Jones
1987: "Where Do You Start," music by Johnny Mandel
1988: "On My Way to You," music by Michel Legrand
1991: "A Christmas Love Song," music by Johnny Mandel
1994: "Ordinary Miracles," music by Marvin Hamlisch
1999: "Love Like Ours," music by Dave Grusin
2003: "More in Love with You," music by Andre Previn
2007: "I Knew I Loved You," music (from 1984) by Ennio Morricone
2018: "Walls," music by Walter Afanasieff

Other standards
1967: "Cinnamon and Clove," music by Johnny Mandel
1975: "I Have the Feeling I've Been Here Before," music by Roger Kellaway
1978: "Fifty Percent," music by Billy Goldenberg
1995: "Moonlight," music by John Williams

Some neglected early gems
1952: "That's Him Over There," music by Lew Spence; dramatic monologue of lost love*
1958: "Sleep Warm," music by Lew Spence; gentle, loving ballad

1961: "Live It Up!," music by Lew Spence; swinging song of cheerful philosophy

1964: "One Long Last Look," music by Sammy Fain; zestful goodbye song, poignant yet jaunty

1964: "No Questions," music by Sammy Fain; catchy charm song of besotted romance

1966: "Sure As You're Born," music by Johnny Mandel; groovy modern jazz song

20

WHAT HAPPENED NEXT?

Sadly, there seems to be a disconnection between women songwriters in pop music today and their foremothers who matured during the Tin Pan Alley era. For instance, Taylor Swift's big musical influences included Joni Mitchell. Joni Mitchell's big musical influences included Annie Ross and Billie Holiday. But has Taylor Swift been influenced by Annie Ross and Billie Holiday? If so, nobody is talking about it. To offer another example, Madonna was inspired by Patti Smith, who was inspired by Janis Joplin, who was inspired by Bessie Smith. But neither Madonna nor Patti Smith testify that Bessie Smith was among their chief musical influences. If even celebrity songwriters like Bessie Smith, Annie Ross, and Billie Holiday are no longer touchstones for young women, what chance have Anne Caldwell ("I Know That You Know"), Doris Tauber ("Them There Eyes"), Barbara Belle ("A Sunday Kind of Love"), Mayme Watts ("Alright, Okay, You Win"), and so many more? Pop culture amnesia is erasing these women songwriters.

WHAT HAPPENED NEXT TO TIN PAN ALLEY?

"Tin Pan Alley is gone. I put an end to it," Bob Dylan famously said.[1] He and his peers like Joni Mitchell fused the roles of performer and songwriter to an extent far greater than their predecessors. In doing so, they wiped the historical slate clean.

The singer-songwriter mode is partly a philosophic and aesthetic choice: how to best tap into life experiences in a way that is cathartic for the writer and also that listeners can relate to. It is partly a commercial imperative: to maximize your profit, find a way to benefit not just from the record but also from owning the copyright. It is also partly a marketing strategy: make sure the public knows the product is new and fresh. Combining performer and writer became a must. For example, in 1963, when African American Deanie Parker auditioned for Stax Records, she was told, "If we're going to cut a record, you've got to have your own song. A song you created."[2] So she went home and wrote "My Imaginary Guy," the start of her recording career. From one view, Parker was pushed into becoming a songwriter. From another, she was given the freedom to create, the opportunity to make a fuller statement as a musical artist.

Rock-and-roll shook up the status quo, further helping to open pop music up to new styles. Women tunesmiths wrote landmark rock-and-roll songs: Dorothy LaBostrie, "Tutti Frutti" (1955); Enotris Johnson, "Long Tall Sally" (1956); Mae Boren Axton, "Heartbreak Hotel" (1956); Felice Bryant, "Wake Up Little Susie" (1957); Janie Bradford, "Money (That's What I Want) (1959); and many others. These works contrast with the songs focused on in this book. The songs of Tin Pan Alley were designed for the family piano, to be heard live. The songs of later decades were designed for electric instruments, to be heard on the transistor radio (from 1957 on), boom box (from 1966 on), and earbud (from 1984, but really taking over in the 2000s). In this new era, the copyright owners were still called "publishers," but they were less concerned than previously with creating printed copies of songs. Admittedly, even before 1957 the trend was there; but after that, more than ever, the record companies *became* the publishers.

In terms of style, singer-songwriter Melissa Manchester ("Come In from the Rain," 1976) puts it well: the Tin Pan Alley model was "melody-driven," with "very long melody lines, which support long, developed lyrical ideas." By the time Manchester began to write her hits in the 1970s, pop music had changed to being "rhythm-driven." Harold Arlen ruefully reflected that his type of tunes were obsolete in "a percussive era."[3]

Meanwhile, more and more, the producer was the true creator of a recording. By and large, songs of the Tin Pan Alley period were written to be singable. By contrast, songs from about 1958 onward were written to be produceable. First, in the 1950s, Les Paul and Mitch Miller invented the idea of the arrangement and technology combining to fabricate a unique "sound" for each single. Then, in the 1960s, Phil Spector, Berry Gordy, Brian Wilson, Don Kirshner, and others asserted themselves as the controlling hands, fabricating an entire sonic landscape, often editing together layer after layer of sound. With such an approach, producers often took their place as cowriters of the hits, and performers were sometimes interchangeable. These producers were always men; in the 2020s, sadly, they usually still are (more than 97 percent, according to one report).

In the early 1960s, the Brill Building housed 165 music publishing offices, including not only such venerable ones as that of W. C. Handy but also many newer firms. The building lent its name to a whole genre of pop that flourished from 1957 to 1964—"the Brill Building sound." True, Joan Whitney, Sylvia Dee, Kay Twomey, and others of the earlier generation were occasionally able to write for this new era, bridging the generation gap. But the Brill Building style is typified by songs for youth, by youth. Carole King and Ellie Greenwich launched their songwriting careers at the age of seventeen. Even more impressively, Janis Ian was quite capable of crafting a landmark pop hit about interracial teen romance, "Society's Child (Baby, I've Been Thinking)," at age fifteen.

Even while Carolyn Leigh and Marilyn Keith Bergman were finding the chief market for their goods shifting from singles to albums, Ellie Greenwich ("Da Doo Ron Ron," 1963) was finding the early 1960s "the era of singles," which she and her peers greeted with wholehearted joy: "Talk about excitement!" Their core audience consisted of teenagers like themselves. For future historian Susan Douglas, growing up at this time, "music became the one area of popular culture in which adolescent female voices could be clearly heard." This was partly due to lyrics and melodies created by their peers, such as Georgia Dobbins ("Please, Mr. Postman," 1961) at Motown or Cynthia Weil ("You've Lost That Lovin' Feelin'," 1964) at the Brill Building.[4]

WHAT HAPPENED NEXT TO WOMEN IN THE POP MUSIC INDUSTRY?

It is hard to generalize about the place of women songwriters in the post–Tin Pan Alley world. New US centers of production grew, such as Motown in Detroit, Stax in Memphis, Laurel Canyon in Los Angeles, Music Row in Nashville, and many more. New genres proliferated, in what seems like a never-ending process of defining niche tastes. The global population explosion, the Jet Age, and the Digital Revolution combined to give recording artists a huge international audience. Music performers and writers could make a lot more money than before.

With rock-and-roll came a near erasure of the jazz eras—and the even greater erasure of the women of Tin Pan Alley. In the 1980s and 1990s, journalist Lucy O'Brien interviewed hundreds of women in the popular music industry and emerged with "a sense of the crucial importance of women as role models."[5] But very few would know about the possible female role models among songwriters of just a generation past.

From Lucy Fletcher to Marilyn Keith Bergman, the women in this book struggled to find a place in the popular song industry. If some of them finally achieved sustained success, it was due to all their efforts. As with so many advances, it is easy to ignore how much work it took. Take Franne Golde, who penned hits from "Gettin' Ready for Love" (for Diana Ross, 1977) to "Stickwitu" (the Pussycat Dolls, 2005). Golde soberly reflects on how she was limited in her career choices due to being a woman: "One of the few places where there is comfort and security is as a songwriter— there have always been women songwriters, it's somewhere to fit in. It's not like trying to run a record company."[6] It is true "there have always been women songwriters": music probably began with mothers improvising songs for the infant; and women writers were there at the start of Tin Pan Alley. But it is not true that women songwriters have "always" been allowed a place of "comfort and security" in the pop music scene. How melancholy that Golde had been taught so little about the struggles of those who paved her way.

As Golde indicates, despite the expansion of the popular music industry, women still struggled—still do struggle—to take an equal place within it. In a tally of the two hundred top songwriters on the *Billboard* charts from 1955 to 2000, only eleven are women, a measly 5.5 percent. The most familiar names are, of course, the star singers: Valerie Simpson ("Ain't No Mountain High Enough," 1967), Carole King ("You've Got a Friend," 1971), Madonna ("Like a Prayer," 1989), Janet Jackson ("That's the Way Love Goes," 1993), and Mariah Carey ("All I Want for Christmas Is You," 1994). Also on the list are self-effacing composer-lyricists like Diane Warren ("I Don't Want to Miss a Thing," for Aerosmith, 1998). Warren, from her first hit in 1983 deep into the twenty-first century, navigated the digital age with her favorite tools: an audio tape recorder, a pencil, and a pad of paper. She inherited the mantle of Queen of Hollywood Song from Marilyn Bergman, with over one hundred movie themes to her credit.

What accomplished women! But so few of them on the list! At least all of them achieved the kind of multidecade careers forged earlier by only a very, very few Tin Pan Alley heroines like Mabel Wayne and Dorothy Fields.

The twenty-first century has been almost as bleak for women in terms of market share, despite the celebratory tone of some 2020s Grammy Award ceremonies. According to the 2023 Annenberg study, women are still only 10 to 15 percent of charting songwriters—about the same as it was during the Tin Pan Alley era. Admittedly, many songs are now written by a long list of writers, with three to eight creators for each composition. Therefore 43 percent of hit songs have at least *one* woman songwriter involved—a higher proportion than before. But more often than not, each woman is a lone female in a long list of male names—still the "only woman in the room" (speaking figuratively, for with remote collaboration rarely are all songwriters in the room at one time). The woman with the most hits in the decade of 2012 to 2022 was Nicki Minaj ("Bang Bang," 2014), with twenty credits in the charts. But her accomplishments pale beside that of Drake (forty-nine credits) and seven other men who all outrank her.

Taylor Swift ("Shake It Off," 2014) is the woman with the second highest score for the 2012–2022 decade, with seventeen charting credits during that period. (She is also a rare woman at the top of the pop charts to frequently have sole authorship of her material.) She has benefited from the example of women like Dolly Parton ("I Will Always Love You," 1973) and Whitney Houston ("Queen of the Night," 1995) who kept control of themselves professionally, as performers and as songwriters. They lived careers as copyright holders that predecessors from Lovie Austin through to Carolyn Leigh strove for, but in the end could not hold on to.

WHAT HAPPENED NEXT TO THE TIN PAN ALLEY STYLE?

As for the Great American Songbook that grew out of jazz, Tin Pan Alley, Broadway, and Hollywood—the repertoire that Lovie Austin and Carolyn Leigh and hundreds of other women helped create—it became yet another niche market. True, new songs growing out of this tradition continued to be written and become widely known. In 1967, Carolyn Leigh produced "Step to the Rear," that continues "And let a winner lead the way." Not only did singles by Marilyn Maye and Bing Crosby carry it on to the adult charts, but the public took the anthem to its heart. During the 1968 elections, campaign rally rights for "Step to the Rear" were bought by candidates right, left, and center. But with each decade there were fewer and fewer songs stemming from this tradition to be so embraced by the masses.

Younger writers sometimes still imitate the Tin Pan Alley style. For example, among her many movie songs, Diane Warren wrote one with a big band arrangement for *The Shadow* (1994), set in the 1930s. Her compelling melody for "Some Kind of Mystery" hints at what she could do in this genre. Jeanine Tesori is the first woman composer to sustain a multidecade career on Broadway, with the long runs and awards to prove it. In *Thoroughly Modern Millie* (2002), set in the 1920s, she builds the melody of "Only in New York" into a showstopper, one that could almost be of the Tin Pan Alley period. Singer-instrumentalist Nellie McKay can write a cheery, easy-going "If I Ever Had a Dream" (2009) in tribute to Doris Day's persona, capturing something of the spirit of Day's legacy. Yet despite the millions of tracks sold and streamed, the market for both vintage Tin Pan Alley and neo–Tin Pan Alley songs remains a minor subcategory in the music business.

The contributions of women songwriters to that diminished market have been obscured. Admittedly, since the early twentieth century, there have been moments when women songwriters of Tin Pan Alley were spotlighted. A couple of radio broadcasts in the 1930s featured only songs by women. In 1976, Naura Hayden released an album entirely of such works, from Kay Swift to Carolyn Leigh. The event was so rare that the president of ASCAP, Stanley Adams, threw a party to celebrate. In 1977, the Songwriters Hall of Fame had a grand opening reception for their exhibit called (brace yourself) *Here's to the Ladies*. Among the distinguished attendees were Kay Swift, Doris Fisher, Bonnie Lake, Mary Rodgers, and many others of the Tin Pan Alley era.

In 1982, the veteran Broadway and supper club singer Sylvia Syms had a revelation: "I have been singing songs all my life without being aware they were written by women." At the Kool Jazz Festival she produced an entire concert in tribute to them, called (brace yourself again) *This Time for the Ladies*. Despite the soon-to-be-outdated term "ladies," Syms was working in the right direction. At least she refused her male colleague's suggestion to call it *The Playgirls*, insisting, "I never refer to these women as 'girls.' They're women."[7]

Over the next forty years, small record labels began to issue albums devoted to the women composers and lyricists from the worlds of Broadway and jazz, by Kaye Ballard, Barbara Lea, Peter Mintun, Judi Silvano, horn-player Mike Kaupa, and others. In 2009, jazz-and-blues singer (and jazz conservatory voice teacher) Pamela Rose produced her *Wild Women of Song* project, an album, book, and consciousness-raising concert devoted to female songwriters of the jazz eras. It proved a major success for her on college campuses, at jazz festivals, and in clubs internationally. All such tributes inspire some fleeting media attention to the women songsmiths of the Tin Pan Alley era; but a deeper and longer-lasting cultural impact has yet to be made.

If, in the 1960s, Bob Dylan "put an end" to Tin Pan Alley, the irony is that Dylan—and a slew of his contemporaries—eventually began to satisfy the market for tributes to the Great American Songbook. For Dylan, it was through his 2015 album *Shadows in the Night*, which is (typically) dedicated not to songwriters but to a singer—in this instance (again, typically) a male singer, Frank Sinatra. Among songs from this collection, Dylan particularly liked to feature in live performances Carolyn Leigh's anguished existential plea, "Stay with Me" (a 1963 hit for Sinatra). Alongside Dylan and many other men (Rod Stewart, Paul McCartney, James Taylor, and others), female singer-songwriters like Joni Mitchell, Carly Simon, and Melissa Manchester have also done well with such tribute albums. These women write their own songs to include alongside the jazz standards of past generations. Yet Mitchell, Simon, and Manchester do not include any songs by their female peers of those previous generations, oddly, sadly.

Or perhaps it is not so odd or sad. Perhaps a self-conscious emphasis on women songwriters implies an unnatural division between all who are simply *humans*, from *humus* (dirt, soil, earth), those who are of the Earth. Perhaps the partitioning of women, as in this book, does disservice to a vision of a gender-blind society. Yet even third wave feminists, who might argue that distinctions should not be drawn between genders, will admit that the society in which women of Tin Pan Alley struggled did not share that view. Those twentieth-century women had to grapple with the attitudes of their own time, not ours. This book is a tribute to how well they did it.

If there is still a place for visibility politics, may this book help to make visible—and audible—the women songwriters of the past. They certainly asserted their voices in a hostile environment. Despite the obstacles, they bequeathed to posterity many, many high-quality works. The forty songs featured in this book are their testimonials, conveying their messages of what music was about, what life was about, and what the United States was about. Through their songs, these women helped to create an American art.

NOTES

PREFACE

1. Kyle Denis, "Miley Cyrus Celebrates Her Grammy Nominations," *Billboard*, November 10, 2023.

2. Mesfin Fekadu, "Female Acts Win All Televised Awards at Grammys," *Hollywood Reporter*, February 4, 2024.

3. Katherine Spillar, ed., *50 Years of Ms.: The Best of the Pathfinding Magazine That Ignited a Revolution* (New York: Alfred A. Knopf, 2023), 74.

CHAPTER I

1. "Miriam Stern Leaves AGAC," *Billboard*, April 19, 1969, 6. During this early era, the SGA was called the Songwriters Protective Association.

2. Tom Macklin, "Women Songwriters," *Music Journal* 10, no. 3 (March 1952): 30–31, 74–79, at 76.

3. Rosalind Shaffer, "Women Taking Up Song Writing for the Talkies," *Chicago Daily Tribune*, February 16, 1930, G5.

4. J. Fred Coots, "Passport to Tin Pan Alley," *Variety*, March 1, 1950, 42.

5. Arleen Abrahams, "Mabel Wayne Returns to Tin Pan Alley with Ballads and Waltzes," *Burlington Times-News* (NC), September 5, 1968, 21, Associated Press; Helen Hover, "Out!—You Tin Pan Alley Sallys," *Billings Gazette* (MT), June 6, 1937, 36, King Features Syndicate; "Gifted Girls Who Write Songs," *Syracuse Herald* (NY), December 16, 1928, 65, NEA Magazine.

6. Hover, "Out!"

7. Phyllis Battelle, "All's Fine and Dandy in Song Writing," *Piqua Daily Call* (OH), August 2, 1976, 4; Hover, "Out!"

8. *The Girls in the Band: Female Jazz Musicians*, a documentary directed by Judy Chaikin (One Step Productions, 2013).

9. Abrahams, "Mabel Wayne."

CHAPTER 2

1. Anne Key Simpson, "Those Everlasting Blues: The Best of Clarence Williams," *Louisiana History* 40, no. 2 (Spring 1999): 179–95, at 193, citing Martin Williams, *Jazz Masters of New Orleans*, 107; "Sugar Shortage Inspiration for 'Sugar Blues,'" *Afro-American*, February 8, 1941, 13.

2. "Clarence Williams Scores Once More with 'Sugar Blues,'" *Pittsburgh Courier*, December 5, 1936, 22.

3. "Sugar Shortage."

4. "Clarence Williams Scores."

5. The website JazzStandards.com, in their ranking of "the thousand most-frequently recorded jazz standards," places "Sugar Blues" in position 791. All such notes that follow accessed May 24, 2024.

6. The little extra mark, as in A´, indicates that although the melody basically repeats, it does so with a small variation.

7. "News of City and Valley," *Calexico Chronicle*, October 10, 1922, 4; "Musical Song Hit Is Offered to Public," *Calexico Chronicle*, October 11, 1922, 4.

8. "Hiker Singing the Mexicali Rose Is Scoring Success," *Calexico Chronicle*, April 16, 1923, 1.

9. "Mexicali Rose Composer Honored—History of Composition Told," *Calexico Chronicle*, May 2, 1968, 1.

10. "Inside Stuff: Music," *Variety*, November 23, 1938, 33.

11. Sally Placksin, *American Women in Jazz, 1900 to the Present: Their Words, Lives, and Music* (n.p.: Wideview Books, PEI Books, 1982), 38.

12. "American Stage," *The Stage*, January 19, 1928, 22; "Dorothy Donnelly, Dramatist, Dies," *New York Times*, January 4, 1928, 19.

13. The JazzStandards.com ranking for "I Know That You Know" is 285.

14. Lynn Abbott and Doug Seroff, *Original Blues: The Emergence of the Blues in African American Vaudeville, 1899–1926* (Jackson: University of Mississippi Press, 2017), 172.

15. Abbott and Seroff, *Original Blues*, 166, 174–75; Gene Jones, "Bessie Smith," *Oxford African American Studies Center* (database), 2009, originally in *The Encyclopedia of African American History, 1896 to the Present*.

16. David Evans, "Bessie Smith's 'Back-Water Blues': The Story Behind the Song," *Popular Music* 26, no. 1 (2007): 97–116, at 99.

17. The JazzStandards.com ranking for "Back-Water Blues" is 982.

18. Hilary Mac Austin, "Armstrong, Lillian 'Lil' Hardin," *Oxford African American Studies Center*, 2005, originally in *Black Women in America*, second edition.

19. The JazzStandards.com ranking for "Struttin' with Some Barbecue" is 556.

20. "Glaser vs. Leeds on Source of 'Some Barbecue,'" *Variety*, February 12, 1958, 53.

CHAPTER 3

1. Vicki Ohl, *Fine and Dandy: The Life and Work of Kay Swift* (New Haven: Yale University Press, 2004), 6; the quote is from Swift's grandmother, herself a composer.

2. Josephine M. Bennett, "Feminine Frills" (column), "'Your Hands Play a Part, Too,' Says Enchanting Libby Holman," *Billboard*, August 17, 1929, 38.

3. Alec Wilder, *American Popular Song: The Great Innovators, 1900–1950* (London: Oxford University Press, 1972), 467, 469.

4. Ohl, *Fine*, 60.

5. The JazzStandards.com ranking for "Can't We Be Friends" is 632.

CHAPTER 4

1. Although *lyricist* Dorothy Fields exceeded Wayne in her success, productivity, and longevity, Wayne's track record was supreme as a woman *composer* of the Tin Pan Alley milieu.

2. "Mabel Wayne Only Girl Contract Writer—Feist's," *Variety*, May 8, 1929, 71; "Mabel Wayne, Songwriter," *Christian Science Monitor*, October 8, 1929, 13.

3. "Mabel Wayne, Songwriter."

4. "Mabel Wayne, Songwriter."

5. Walter Winchell, "Winchell on Broadway" (syndicated column), *Nevada State Journal*, November 10, 1954, 4.

6. "Mabel Wayne, Songwriter."

7. The JazzStandards.com ranking for "In a Little Spanish Town" is 667.

8. "Inside Stuff—Music," *Variety*, September 5, 1928, 56, 58.

9. "No Dames on Special," *Variety*, May 8, 1929, 35.

10. "Mabel Wayne East," *Variety*, August 28, 1929, 57.

11. Edward Eliscu, *With or Without a Song: A Memoir* (Lanham, MD: Scarecrow Press, 2001), 93–94; see also 123–24, 217–18.

CHAPTER 5

1. "Mabel Wayne, Songwriter."

2. The label of the Eugenie Baird 78 single, seen on the Internet Archive, specifies Al Stillman as the author of the additional lyrics.

3. "Margarita Lecuona," *EcuRed*, accessed February 11, 2022, https://www.ecured.cu/Margarita_Lecuona; Ramón Faiardo, "Margarita Lecuona," *Habana Radio*, accessed February 11, 2022, http://www.habanaradio.cu/articulos/margarita-lecuona/.

4. The JazzStandards.com ranking for "Taboo" is 850.

5. Joe Laurie Jr., "Lefty Harks Back to When 'Contact Men' Were Called Songpluggers," *Variety*, August 7, 1940, 35.

6. Wilder, *American Popular*, 470.

7. The JazzStandards.com ranking for "Them There Eyes" is 264.

8. Helen Hover, "Out!"

9. Arthur Kinney, *Dorothy Parker, Revised* (Chapel Hill: University of North Carolina, 1998), 11; Marion Meade, *Dorothy Parker: What Fresh Hell Is This?* (New York: Villard Books, 1988), 203, 208.

10. Meade, *Dorothy Parker*, 105; John Keats, *You Might as Well Live: The Life and Times of Dorothy Parker* (New York: Simon and Schuster, 1970), 90.

11. "Bing Crosby Argues with Jack Kapp," *YouTube*, accessed March 14, 2022, https://www.youtube.com/watch?v=iD3vb5-Ahns.

12. The JazzStandards.com ranking for "I Wished on the Moon" is 386.

13. Linda Dahl, *Morning Glory: A Biography of Mary Lou Williams* (New York: Pantheon, Random House, 1999), 29, 77.

14. Dahl, *Morning Glory*, 108.

15. Dahl, *Morning Glory*, 259–60.

16. Donald Clarke, *Wishing on the Moon: The Life and Times of Billie Holiday* (Penguin Books, Viking, 1994), 184.

17. Clarke, *Wishing*, 183–84; Stanley Dance, *The World of Earl Hines* (New York: Charles Scribner's Sons, 1977), 182.

18. Placksin, *American Women*, 111; Dance, *World*, 182.

19. Placksin, *American Women*, 109.

20. *Billie Holiday: The Last Interview—and Other Conversations* (Brooklyn, NY: Melville House, 2019), 54; "Blind Femme Composer Tune Bought by Marks," *Variety*, December 13, 1950, 62; Advertisement, *Cleveland Call and Post*, April 14, 1951, 5C.

21. The JazzStandards.com ranking for "Some Other Spring" is 631.

22. Dance, *World*, 182.

23. Peter Jennings, with Tom Sandler, *Until I Smile at You: How One Girl's Heartbreak Electrified Frank Sinatra's Fame* (Victoria, BC: Castle Carrington, 2020), 21–22, 27, 32–33, 42.

24. Jennings, *Until I Smile*, 33–34.

25. Jennings, *Until I Smile*, 39.

26. "A Tribute to Harold Cohen," *Billboard*, May 27, 1939; Jennings, *Until I Smile*, 40, 42.

27. Jennings, *Until I Smile*, 31; "A Tribute to Harold Cohen."

28. Jennings, *Until I Smile*, 41, 44–45.

29. Jennings, *Until I Smile*, 17, 12; Ed O'Brien and Scott P. Sayers Jr., *Sinatra: The Man and His Music* (Austin, TX: TSD Press, 1992), 10.

30. Allen Forte, *The American Popular Ballad of the Golden Era, 1924–1950* (Princeton: Princeton University Press, 1995), 326.

31. The JazzStandards.com ranking for "I'll Never Smile Again" is 428.

32. Jennings, *Until I Smile*, 52, 94, 97, 113, 128.

CHAPTER 6

1. Peter Mintun, interview with the author, December 30, 2021; Peter Mintun, "Introduction," in Dana Suesse, *Jazz Nocturne: And Other Piano Music with Selected Songs* (Mineola, NY: Dover Publications, 2013), 8. "Suesse" is pronounced "Sweese," rhyming with "peace."

2. Mintun, "Introduction," 5–6.

3. Mintun, "Introduction," 6.

4. Mintun, "Introduction," 6; Mintun, interview with the author.

5. Dana Suesse, interviewed by Harold Boxer, *The Voice of America* radio broadcast, December 12, 1974, accessed online May 17, 2022, https://soundcloud.com/peter-mintun/sets/dana-suesse-interview-1974.

6. Mintun, interview with the author.

7. Mintun, "Introduction," 6.

8. Dana Suesse, scripted interview with John Reed King, *Personally It's Off the Record* radio broadcast, 1942; Mintun, "Introduction," 9.

9. The JazzStandards.com ranking for "My Silent Love" is 746.

10. Suesse, interview with King, *Personally It's Off the Record*.

CHAPTER 7

1. The JazzStandards.com ranking for "Willow, Weep for Me" is 13.

2. Tighe E. Zimmers, *Tin Pan Alley Girl: A Biography of Ann Ronell* (Jefferson, NC: McFarland, 2009), 5.

3. Zimmers, *Tin Pan Alley Girl*, 12–13.

4. Zimmers, *Tin Pan Alley Girl*, 14.

5. Zimmers, *Tin Pan Alley Girl*, 23, 25, 122.

6. Zimmers, *Tin Pan Alley Girl*, 33.

7. Zimmers, *Tin Pan Alley Girl*, 19.

8. Gunther Schuller, *The Swing Era: The Development of Jazz, 1930–1945* (New York: Oxford University Press, 1989), 493.

9. Wilder, *American Popular*, 467.

10. Forte, *American Popular*, 321.

CHAPTER 8

1. Warren W. Vachè, *The Unsung Songwriters: America's Masters of Melody* (Lanham, MD: Scarecrow Press, 2000), 368. The name Petkere is pronounced "PET-care."

2. "Writing of Popular Songs Easy for Young Housewife," *Muncie Morning Star*, January 9, 1933, 12; "Inside Stuff—Music," *Variety*, January 3, 1933, 82; Peter Mintun, "Bernice Petkere—Biography," *Internet Movie Database*, https://www.imdb.com/name/nm0677675/bio?ref_=nm_ov_bio_sm, accessed July 14, 2022.

3. "Writing of Popular Songs Easy"; Mintun, "Bernice Petkere"; "Radio Chatter: East," *Variety*, August 23, 1932, 42.

4. "Vaudeville Personalities," *Vaudeville News*, October 23, 1925, 8.

5. "Disc Reviews," *Variety*, August 2, 1932, 53.

6. "Queen of Tin Pan Alley," *Urbana Daily Courier* [*The Evening Courier*], June 19, 1934, 8.

7. Mintun, "Bernice Petkere"; Russell, "Eviction Blues," *Los Angeles Times*, March 3, 1988, WS1; Ron Russell, "Good Samaritan Buys Condo for Widow," *Los Angeles Times*, March 13, 1988, WS5; Liz Smith, "Minnelli, on Tour, Planning a New Album," *Palm Beach Post*, August 19, 1993, 47. Petkere had also controlled the copyright for "Close Your Eyes" for a while in the early 1960s; advertisement for Bernice Petkere Music, Inc., *Billboard*, May 8, 1961, 12.

8. The JazzStandards.com ranking for "Close Your Eyes" is 298; for "Lullaby of the Leaves," it is 251.

9. Forte, *American Popular*, 315–18.

10. Fitzgerald also changes six words in the verse: to "Lullaby of the Leaves," four to extract the Southern references and one to make more immediate the statement "*Now* I find myself alone."

11. Wilder, *American Popular*, 482, also 111, 229–30, 231, 235, 314, 317, 418, 475, 479, 482, 487; Rivka Galchen, "The Melancholy Mystery of Lullabies," *New York Times*, October 14, 2015.

12. Mintun, "Bernice Petkere."

CHAPTER 9

1. "Maria Grever, 57, a Composer, Dies," *New York Times*, December 16, 1951, 90.

2. Grace Turner, "When Food Is an Event," *This Week* magazine section, September 6, 1936, 14.

3. Herbert Marks, "Herb Marks 'Renews' His Copyright with Sixty-Year Firm His Dad Founded," *Variety*, December 9, 1953, 51, 58.

4. "Maria Grever," *Wikipedia*, accessed March 31, 2020, citing Lee M. L. Rodriguez, *Maria Grever: Poeta y Compositora* (Potomac, MD: Scripta Humanistica, 1994).

5. Wilder, *American Popular*, 486.

6. The JazzStandards.com ranking for "What a Difference a Day Made" is 367.

CHAPTER 10

1. Kristin Stultz Pressley, *I Can't Give You Anything But Love, Baby: Dorothy Fields and Her Life in the American Musical Theater* (Guilford, CT: Applause Theater and Cinema Books, 2021), 2; Henry Kane, *How to Write a Song* (New York: Macmillan, 1961), 177.

2. Kane, *How to Write*, 171.

3. Charlotte Greenspan, *Pick Yourself Up: Dorothy Fields and the American Musical* (Oxford, UK: Oxford University Press, 2010), 41, 45; Kane, *How to Write*, 173–74.

4. Alyn Shipton, *I Feel a Song Comin' On: The Life of Jimmy McHugh* (Urbana: University of Illinois Press, 2009), 136; Greenspan, *Pick Yourself Up*, 87, 144.

5. Pressley, *I Can't Give*, 79, citing Irving Drutman, "Lew Fields Left Behind Him a Talented Family," *New York Herald Tribune*, December 14, 1941.

6. Pressley, *I Can't Give You*, 116–17; also Mary Rodgers and Jesse Green, *Shy: The Alarmingly Outspoken Memoirs of Mary Rodgers* (New York: Farrar, Straus and Giroux, 2022), 250–52.

7. Pressley, *I Can't Give You*, 126, quoting the recording of a 1972 presentation, *An Evening with Dorothy Fields*.

8. Greenspan, *Pick Yourself Up*, 100.

9. Greenspan, *Pick Yourself Up*, 101.

10. Mark Steyn, *Mark Steyn's American Songbook, vol. 1* (Woodsville, NY: Stockade Books, 2008), 22; Wilder, *American Popular*, 74; Greenspan, *Pick Yourself Up*, 106.

11. *Perspectives: The Great American Love Song with Nicky Campbell*, broadcast on ITV London, May 17, 2015.

12. Greenspan, *Pick Yourself Up*, 41.

13. *Perspectives . . . with Nicky Campbell*, interview with David Lahm.

14. The JazzStandards.com ranking for "The Way You Look Tonight" is 27.

15. Pressley, *I Can't Give You*, 117.

CHAPTER 11

1. Johnny Mercer, "The Obligation of the Writer," *Variety*, October 20, 1954, 44.

2. David Jenness and Don Velsey, *Classic American Popular Song: The Second Half-Century, 1950–2000* (New York: Routledge, 2006), 56.

3. Frank Sinatra, June 9, 1957, heard on *Frank Sinatra Live! Seattle Washington Concert*, Jazz Hour JH-3001.

4. Korey Rothman, "Somewhere There's Music: Nancy Hamilton, the Old Girls' Network, and the American Musical Theater of the 1930s and 1940s" (dissertation, the University of Maryland, 2005), 172.

5. Wilder, *America Popular*, 502–3.

6. The JazzStandards.com ranking for "How High the Moon" is 21; that for "Ornithology" is 462.

7. David Osser, interview with the author, December 1, 2022 (with a letter from Goetschius to Osser read aloud), and email correspondence, January 7–9, 2023.

8. David Osser interview; "Bert Parks to Be an Attraction at Miss Tennessee Pageant," *The Jackson Sun*, July 12, 1967, 1, 11.

9. "'Bambino' Song Is Inspiration of Happy Mom," *Courier-Journal* [Louisville, KY], December 12, 1954, Section 4, 9; David Osser interview.

10. David Osser interview.

11. "85% Network Programs Using and Killing Radio Theme Songs," *Variety*, January 19, 1932, 57. Thanks to Will Friedwald for supplying this citation.

12. Bonnie Lake's "I've Got Your Number" is a different song than the famous 1962 one with lyrics by Carolyn Leigh, mentioned in chapter 18.

13. Adela Rogers St. Johns, *No Goodbyes: My Search into Life Beyond Death* (New York: McGraw-Hill, Signet, New American Library, Times Mirror, 1981), 62, 66–67; Sam Irvin, *Kay Thompson: From Funny Face to Eloise* (New York: Simon and Schuster, 2010), 68, 79.

14. The title is also often given as "The Man with *a* Horn."

15. Ivan Hunter, email to the author, April 7, 2020.

16. Peter Richmond, *Fever: The Life and Music of Miss Peggy Lee* (New York: Henry Holt, 2006), 149.

17. Peggy Lee, *Miss Peggy Lee: An Autobiography* (New York: Donald I. Fine, 1989), 105–6.

18. Richmond, *Fever*, 149–50; Irving Berlin, "Song and Sorrow Are Playmates," in *The Irving Berlin Reader*, ed. Benjamin Sears (Oxford: Oxford University Press, 2012), 169–72.

19. Arnold Shaw, *Honkers and Shouters* (New York: Macmillan, 1978), 71.

20. Reportedly, this is the correct spelling of Claude Demetruis's last name, though one can find it spelled variously as Demetri, Demetrius, Demetrious; and sometimes the "M" in the middle is capitalized.

21. The JazzStandards.com ranking for "A Sunday Kind of Love" is 752.

22. The Belle-Rhodes "Early Autumn" (1947) is not the enduring standard "Early Autumn" (1952) with a Johnny Mercer lyric.

23. Greil Marcus, "Is This the Woman Who Invented Rock and Roll? The Deborah Chessler Story," *Rolling Stone*, June 24, 1993; quotations in the Deborah Chessler section are from this unless otherwise noted.

24. Stuart L. Goosman, *Group Harmony: The Black Urban Roots of Rhythm and Blues* (Philadelphia: University of Pennsylvania Press, 2005), 208.

25. Michael Allen Harrison and Alan Berg, *Soul Harmony*, CD liner notes (Harrison-Berg Presents, 2019).

26. "Inside Orchestras—Music," *Variety*, December 7, 1949, 47.
27. "Mills Tries to Keep 'Ribbons' Off Radio," *Billboard*, November 5, 1949, 18.
28. Wilder, *American Popular*, 518.
29. The Evelyn Danzig-Sylvia Dee "Teddy Bear" (1955) is not the 1957 Elvis Presley hit.

CHAPTER 12

1. Donald Clarke, *Wishing on the Moon: The Life and Times of Billie Holiday* (Penguin Books, Viking, 1994), 343.
2. Julia Blackburn, *With Billie* (New York: Pantheon Books, 2005), 94; Stuart Nicholson, *Billie Holiday* (Boston, MA: Northeastern University Press, 1995), 92.
3. *Billie Holiday: The Last Interview—and Other Conversations* (Brooklyn, NY: Melville House, 2019), 62.
4. There have been questions about how many songs Holiday wrote, which Keith A. Dames answers: "Homage to Eleanora: A Musical Journey Through the Billie Holiday Songbook" (master's thesis, City University of New York, 2022).
5. Kim La Vern Purnell, "I Sing, Therefore I Am: The (De)Construction of Identity Through the Autobiography, Personal Narrative, and Music Lyrics of Billie Holiday" (dissertation, University of Georgia, 2000), 107–8.
6. Clarke, *Wishing*, 191; Billie Holiday and William Dufty, *Lady Sings the Blues* (London: Penguin, 1956, 1984), 87.
7. Clarke, *Wishing*, 275.
8. "Detroit," *Boxoffice*, April 30, 1962, ME-4.
9. Ted Gioia, *The Jazz Standards: A Guide to Repertoire* (Oxford: Oxford University Press, 2012), 131.
10. The JazzStandards.com ranking for "God Bless' the Child" is 316.

CHAPTER 13

1. Quoted by David "Chet" Williamson Sneade, "Good Morning Heartache," *Worcester Writers of the Great American Songbook*, http://worcestersongs.blogspot.com, accessed April 27, 2023.
2. "*Born to Swing* Starts Crown Pro on Way to Broadway," *Billboard*, February 26, 1944, 17.
3. Bruce Bastin with Kip Lornell, *The Melody Man: Joe Davis and the New York Music Scene, 1916–1978* (Jackson: University Press of Mississippi, [1989,] 2012), 167.
4. The JazzStandards.com ranking for "Good Morning Heartache" is 316.
5. Gioia, *Jazz Standards*, 134; Marian McPartland (with Alicia Keys), *Piano Jazz*, NPR broadcast of April 13, 2004, at thirty minutes.
6. Higginbotham's "Mean and Evil Blues," recorded by Dinah Washington in the late 1940s (and later Dakota Staton, Nina Simone, and others), starting "I'm

mean and evil," is not the same as the "Mean and Evil Blues" that Washington recorded in the early 1950s, starting "Well, you're mean and you're evil."

7. Bastin, *Melody Man*, 133.

CHAPTER 14

1. "Tunesmiths Sing Blues in Royalties Plea," *Evening Star*, July 16, 1953, A-1, photo on A-3.

2. Charlie Cochran, email to the author, August 8, 2023.

3. Dennis McLennan, "Doris Fisher, 87," *Los Angeles Times*, January 25, 2003; John Kobal, *Rita Hayworth: The Time, the Place and the Woman* (New York: W. W. Norton, 1977), 207.

4. Erskine Johnson, "In Hollywood," *Sunday News-Democrat* (Tallahassee, FL), June 16, 1946, 5.

5. "Tunesmiths Whip Up Song in 30 Minutes," *Shreveport Times*, November 24, 1946, A15, United Press.

6. Erskine Johnson, "In Hollywood" (column), *Sunday News-Democrat* (Tallahassee, FL), June 16, 1946, 5, Newspaper Enterprise Association.

7. McLennan, "Doris Fisher, 87," *Los Angeles Times* obituary, quoting a 1947 interview.

8. Johnson, "In Hollywood"; "Millionaire Accuses Wife in Alimony Fight," *Detroit Free Press*, September 17, 14A.

9. Kobal, *Rita Hayworth*, 199.

10. Kobal, *Rita Hayworth*, 200.

CHAPTER 15

1. Doren Voeth, email to the author, November 24, 2020.

2. Doren Voeth, email, November 24, 2020.

3. "One World and Coo Coo," *Billboard*, April 20, 1946, 37; the article wrongly credits "Imagination" to lyricist Eddie DeLange.

4. Doren Voeth, email, November 24, 2020.

5. Philip Furia, *The Poets of Tin Pan Alley: A History of America's Great Lyricists* (New York: Oxford University Press, 1990), 44.

CHAPTER 16

1. "Popular Songs Composed by Talented Housewives," *Calgary Herald*, October 11, 1961, 35.

2. Jack O'Brian, "Duchin Out, May Abandon Band Career," *Minneapolis Morning Tribune*, December 9, 1945, 45.

3. Stephen M. Silverman, *Sondheim: His Life, His Shows, His Legacy* (New York: Black Dog and Leventhal, 2023), 179.

4. Michael Whorf, *American Popular Song Composers: Oral Histories, 1920s–1950s* (Jefferson, NC: McFarland, 2012), 200.

5. Henry W. Clum, "Seen and Heard: 'Chickery Chick,'" *Democrat and Chronicle* [Rochester, NY], December 8, 1945, 1.

6. Henry W. Clum, "Seen and Heard: Amateurs Must Learn," *Democrat and Chronicle*, August 30, 1947, 1; "Letters: Why Songsters Have Hard Sledding," *Democrat and Chronicle*, March 13, 1946, 12.

7. Cynthia Lowry, "Housewife Turns Out Hits Far from the Maddening Crowd," *Abilene Reporter News* [TX], August 12, 1951, 28, Associated Press.

8. "Women's Work," *Daily World* [Opelousas, LA], October 4, 1951, 4, United Press.

9. Virginia Safford, "Virginia Safford" (self-titled column), *Minneapolis Star*, August 1, 1951, 28.

10. Lowry, "Housewife."

11. *Annie Ross—No One But Me*, BBC documentary (directed by Brian Ross [no relation], 2012), at 56:56.

12. Jenness and Velsey, *Classic American*, 335.

13. *Annie Ross—No One But Me*, at 8:00.

14. *Annie Ross—No One But Me*, at 9:50.

15. "This Week's Best Buys," *Billboard*, February 7, 1953, 30; Joe Taysom, "The Song Joni Mitchell Called 'a Musical Epiphany,'" *Far Out*, July 8, 2023.

16. *Annie Ross—No One But Me*, at 21:25; Glenn O'Brien, ed., *The Cool School: Writing from America's Hip Underground* (New York: Literary Classics of the United States, Library of America, 2013), 109.

17. "Fran Landesman—Collaborator and Friend," *SimonWallace.org*, accessed December 15, 2023; Cosmo Landesman, *Starstruck: Fame, Failure, My Family and Me* (London: Pan Macmillan, 2008), 43; Craig Sams, "Fran Landesman—Obituary: Poet and Lyricist Whose Songs Became Standards," *Guardian*, August 10, 2011.

18. "Remembering Jazz Lyricist and Poet Fran Landesman," *Fresh Air*, NPR.org, July 29, 2011.

19. Cosmo Landesman, *Starstruck*, 26, 234, 235.

20. Interview of Fran Landesman by Jim Kirchher, "Fran Landesman—Living St. Louis," https://www.youtube.com/watch?v=C4GAPp7GyWw, accessed January 11, 2024.

21. Ann Charters, ed., *The Beats: Literary Bohemians in Postwar America, part 1: A–L* (Detroit, MI: Bruccoli Clark, Gale Research, Book Tower, 1983), 340.

22. Cosmo Landesman, *Starstruck*, 35.

23. The JazzStandards.com ranking for "Spring Can Really Hang You Up the Most" is 755.

CHAPTER 17

1. Al Kasha and Joel Hirschhorn, *Notes on Broadway: Conversations with the Great Songwriters* (Chicago: Contemporary Books, 1985), 114.

2. Andy Propst, *They Made Us Happy: Betty Comden and Adolph Green's Musicals and Movies* (New York: Oxford University Press, 2019), 30, quoting ASCAP advertisement, *Billboard*, February 19, 1999.

3. Humphrey Burton, *Leonard Bernstein* (New York: Doubleday, Anchor Books, 1994), 130.

4. "Jule Styne Salute—Ethel Merman, Sammy Davis, Comden and Green, Phyllis Newman," television special hosted by Merv Griffin, 1978, *YouTube*, posted by Alan Eichler, accessed October 30, 2023, at 46:00; Abel Green, "New Acts: Margaret Scott," *Variety*, April 18, 1945, 45; "Night Club Reviews—Blue Angel, New York," *Billboard*, September 15, 1945, 34.

5. Kasha and Hirschhorn, *Notes*, 112.

6. The rankings for songs from *On the Town* are from SecondHandSongs.com.

7. Kasha and Hirschhorn, *Notes*, 73, 67; Propst, *They Made*, 22, citing a Richard Morrison feature in the *Times* [London], March 14, 2005.

8. Kasha and Hirschhorn, *Notes*, 43; Betty Comden, *Off Stage* (New York: Simon and Schuster, 1995), 136, 138; Red Reed, "Laughs and Lyrics," *A Party with Betty Comden and Adolph Green*, CD booklet, 1977, DRG, CD-2-5177.

9. Betty Comden, *Off Stage* (New York: Simon and Schuster, 1995), 124, 216.

10. Miles Kreuger, "Becoming Comden and Green," in *Comden and Green's Broadway*, program booklet for the 22nd Annual S.T.A.G.E. benefit concert, Los Angeles, CA, March 10–12, 2006; Steyn, *Mark Steyn's American*, 53; Kasha and Hirschhorn, *Notes*, 69.

11. Propst, *They Made*, 187, quoting John Gruen, *Close-Up*; Kasha and Hirschhorn, *Notes*, 113, 115.

12. Theodore Taylor, *Jule: The Story of Jule Styne* (New York: Random House, 1979), 11; Ken Bloom, *The American Songbook: The Singers, the Songwriters, and the Songs* (New York: Black Dog and Leventhal, 2005), 201; Kasha and Hirschhorn, *Notes*, 114.

13. The JazzStandards.com ranking for "Just in Time" is 230.

14. Kasha and Hirschhorn, *Notes*, 73.

CHAPTER 18

1. Stephen Sondheim, *Look, I Made a Hat: Collected Lyrics (1981–2011) with Attendant Comments, Amplifications, Dogmas, Harangues, Digressions, Anecdotes and Miscellany* (New York: Alfred A. Knopf, 2011), 309.

2. Dickie Kleiner, "The Marquee" (column), *Glens Falls Times*, October 12, 1954, 15. I draw here and below on my telephone and Zoom interviews with June Silver, March 4–7, 2024.

3. Ron Dyke, "Lady Song Writer Can't Read Note of Music," *Metronome*, August 1957.

4. Dyke, "Lady Song Writer."

5. Bloom, *American Songbook*, 197.

6. Andy Propst, *You Fascinate Me So: The Life and Times of Cy Coleman* (New York: Applause, Hal Leonard, 2015), 142, citing Jerry Parker, "A Revival of Harmony," *Newsday*, February 14, 1982, B7.

7. Kasha and Hirschhorn, *Notes*, 53; Propst, *You Fascinate*, 142, quoting Coleman's ASCAP oral history interview of September 13, 2002; Steyn, *Mark Steyn's American*, 91.

8. Robert L. Daniels, "I've Got Your Number: Romance, the Rat Pack and Carolyn Leigh," *Variety*, May 31, 2008, quoting Winer, at the 92nd Street Y's *Lyrics and Lyricist* program; Dick Kleiner, "The Marquee" (column), *Glens Falls Times* (NY), October 12, 1954, 15, quoting Leigh.

9. Wilfrid Sheed's words for Coleman's sentiments, *The House That George Built, with a Little Help from Irving, Cole, and a Crew of About Fifty* (New York: Random House, 2007), 296; Propst, *You Fascinate*, 78.

10. Will Friedwald, *Sinatra! The Song Is You: A Singer's Art* (New York: Scribner, 1995), 250.

11. Bloom, *American Songbook*, 197.

12. The JazzStandards.com ranking for "Witchcraft" is 705.

CHAPTER 19

1. The quotations in this portion are from the following sources, all accessed online January 18, 2024: Michael A. Kerker, "Marrying the Image: Alan and Marilyn Bergman," *ASCAP*, April 1, 2007; "Marilyn Bergman, Half of an Oscar-Winning Songwriting Duo, Dies at 93," *New York Times*, January 10, 2022, A18; Duane Byrge and Mike Barnes, "Marilyn Bergman, Oscar-Winning Lyricist, Dies at 93," *Hollywood Reporter*, January 8, 2022; Adam Sweeting, "Marilyn Bergman Obituary," *The Guardian*, January 12, 2022; Raja Razek and Dakin Andone, "Marilyn Bergman, Award-Winning Lyricist, Has Died at 93," *CNN*, January 8, 2002; Elizabeth Blair, "Oscar-Winning Lyricist Marilyn Bergman Has Died at 93," *NPR*, January 8, 2022.

2. Friedwald, *Sinatra!*, 256. At least two online discographies claim the first recording of "Nice 'n' Easy" was in 1956, by jazz-cabaret singer-pianist Mel Fitch. In January 2024, however, his record label informed me by email that the correct recording date for Fitch's version is 1961.

3. Jenness and Velsey, *Classic American*, 248.

4. Jenness and Velsey, *Classic American*, 247.

CHAPTER 20

1. Peter Aspden, "One Man Killed the Pop Song," *Financial Times*, October 8, 2010.

2. Burkhard Bilger, "Soul Survivors," *New Yorker*, June 5, 2023, 49–59, at 49.

3. Greg Shapiro, "Saluting 'The Fellas' in Song," *WAG* (magazine), December 2017, 29; Max Wilk, *They're Playing Our Song* (New York: Atheneum, 1973), 48.

4. Lucy O'Brien, *She Bop: The Definitive History of Women in Rock, Pop and Soul* (New York: Penguin, 1995), 67; Susan J. Douglas, *Where the Girls Are: Growing Up Female with the Mass Media* (New York: Times Books, Random House, 1994), 87.

5. O'Brien, *She Bop*, 2.

6. O'Brien, *She Bop*, 404.

7. John S. Wilson, "Festival Celebrates Women of Jazz," *New York Times*, July 2, 1982, C1.

SELECTED SONG INDEX

GENERAL INDEX

A&R men, 156, 222

Adams, Lee, 260

Adams, Stanley, 129–30, 132, 133, 136, 137, 284

African Americans, 14, 15, 21–22, 23–24, 31–32, 35–36, 50, 64, 68, 71, 73, 81–82, 85–86, 124, 136, 156, 172, 176–77, 179, 185–86, 191, 195–96, 198, 202, 225, 237, 230, 238, 250, 258, 280

Alexander, Edna Belle, 73

Alexander, Van, 63, 68, 69

Anderson, John Murray, 54

Andrews Sisters, 21, 68, 69, 172

Annie Get Your Gun, 140, 151

Anthony, Ray, 166

Arden, Bee, 91

Arlen, Harold, xvii, xx, 44, 147, 153, 154, 191, 267, 280

Armstrong, Irene (Kitchings), 85–89, 94, 155, 187–88, 189, 196, 231

Armstrong, Lil Hardin, 34–37, 50, 155

Armstrong, Louis, 34–37, 44, 51, 74, 115, 165, 173, 196

Arnaz, Desi, 71, 176

Arnold, Polly, 182

ASCAP (American Society of Composers, Authors and Publishers), xvi, 3, 6, 39, 47, 64, 66, 69, 92, 120, 131, 134, 139, 156, 191, 195, 199, 202, 208, 221–22, 232, 233, 236, 247, 260, 270, 276, 299

ASCAP 1941 radio ban, 3, 69, 71, 92, 191, 222, 233

Astaire, Fred, 8, 64, 95, 145–46, 148–49, 272

Austin, Lovie, 21–24, 50, 81, 283

authorship, questions of, xvi, xvii, 7–8, 14–22, 36, 37, 55, 69, 71, 73–74, 79, 82–83, 109, 112, 166, 168, 169, 171–74, 186, 189–90, 192, 199, 202

Autry, Gene, 20, 21, 57, 58, 94

Axton, Mae Boren, 280

ABOUT THE AUTHOR

Michael G. Garber, PhD, is an interdisciplinary historian of American popular songs of the first half of the twentieth century and an award-winning college teacher.

Michael, called "the Singing Scholar," has a PhD in theater from the City University of New York, Graduate Center, and is trained in several fields: the history and analysis of theater and film; in modern dance with Barbara Mettler; and extensively in the use of music and the arts for well-being with John Diamond, MD. During the writing of this book, Michael was a visiting researcher at the University of Colorado, Boulder; the University of Kansas; and the University of Winchester.

He makes use of his eclectic background and deep connection with the songs of Tin Pan Alley in his first book, *My Melancholy Baby: The First Ballads of the Great American Songbook, 1902–1913* (University Press of Mississippi). It was rated "highly recommended" by *Choice* magazine and won a Certificate of Merit from the Association for Recorded Sound Collections. His scholarly articles and encyclopedia entries all focus on investigating underexamined corners in the history of jazz and Broadway repertoires.

Michael also presents widely, including at international conferences as well as for numerous community groups, on the history of popular music and the American musical. He also leads community music engagement programs with people from ages four to ninety-four. He lives with his wife in Westchester County, New York.

His unique background and training, thorough research, in-depth knowledge, and personal love of song make his writings equally appropriate for scholars, musicians, and all enthusiastic listeners of popular music.

Website: www.michaelggarber.com